THE RESPONSIBILITY OF POWER

Photo by Blackstone-Shelburne, New York

THE RESPONSIBILITY OF POWER

Historical Essays
in Honor of Hajo Holborn

Edited by
LEONARD KRIEGER and FRITZ STERN

Doubleday & Company, Inc., Garden City, New York

1967

The quoted passages from Friedrich Schiller in the Gordon Craig essay entitled "Friedrich Schiller and the Problems of Power" are by permission of the Frederick Ungar Publishing Company, Inc. from *Wallenstein*, translated by Charles E. Passage (1958).

Library of Congress Catalog Card Number 68–10559
Copyright © 1967 by Doubleday & Company, Inc.
All Rights Reserved
Printed in the United States of America
First Edition

CONTENTS

PART III. THE DILEMMA OF POWER IN THE DEMOCRATIC AGE

CONTRIBUTORS

ROLAND BAINTON, Emeritus Professor of Church History at Yale University, is the author of many works on Reformation history. His books include *Studies on the Reformation* (1963), *The Reformation of the Sixteenth Century* (1952), and a biography of Luther, *Here I Stand* (1950).

JOHN M. BLUM, Professor of History at Yale University, is author of several works on American history, among them *From the Morgenthau Diaries* (1959), *The Republican Roosevelt* (1954), and *Woodrow Wilson and the Politics of Morality* (1956).

GORDON A. CRAIG is Professor of History at Stanford University and Honorary Professor at the Free University of Berlin. Among his works on European history are *The Politics of the Prussian Army, 1640–1945* (1955), *From Bismarck to Adenauer: Aspects of German Statecraft* (1958), *The Battle of Königgrätz* (1964) and *War, Politics, and Diplomacy* (1966).

PETER GAY, William R. Shepherd Professor of History at Columbia University, is author of *The Enlightenment* (1966), *A Loss of Mastery* (1966), and *Voltaire's Politics* (1959).

DIETRICH GERHARD is Professor Emeritus of History at Washington University, St. Louis, Mo. and at the Max-Plank Institut für Geschichte. He is author of *Alte und Neue Welt in Vergleichender Geschichtsbetrachtung* (1962) and *England und der Aufstieg Russlands* (1933).

FELIX GILBERT is Professor in the School of Historical Studies at the Institute for Advanced Study in Princeton. Among his studies are *Johann Gustav Droysen und die Preussisch-Deutsche Frage* (1931), *To the Farewell Address: Ideas of Early Ameri-*

can Foreign Policy (1961), and *Machiavelli and Guicciardini* (1965).

HANNA H. GRAY, Associate Professor of History at the University of Chicago, has written on Renaissance intellectual history.

HANS RUDOLF GUGGISBERG, a graduate of the University of Basel, is author of *Sebastian Castellio im Urteil seiner Nachwelt* (1956) and *Das europäische Mittelalter im amerikanischen Geschichtsdenken des 19. und des frühen 20. Jahrhunderts* (1964). He is Professor of History at the Free University of Berlin.

THEODORE S. HAMEROW, Professor of History at the University of Wisconsin, is the author of *Restoration, Revolution, Reaction* (1958), and *Otto von Bismarck: A Historical Assessment* (1962).

RICHARD N. HUNT, Associate Professor at the University of Pittsburgh, has written *German Social Democracy 1918–1933* (1964).

WERNER KAEGI is Professor of History and Chairman of the Historisches Seminar, Basel University. He has published four volumes of *Jacob Burckhardt: Eine Biographie* (1947–67) and many other studies.

OTTO KIRCHHEIMER, late Professor of Public Law and Government at Columbia University, has written *Political Justice: The Use of Legal Procedure for Political Ends* (1961), *Politik und Verfassung* (1964) and, in collaboration with Georg Rusche, *Punishment and Social Structure,* as well as other works in comparative government.

LEONARD KRIEGER is University Professor of History at the University of Chicago. He has written *The German Idea of Freedom* (1957) and *Politics of Discretion* (1965).

ANDREW LOSSKY is Professor of History at UCLA. He is author of *Louis XIV, William III, and the Baltic Crisis of 1683* (1954).

HERBERT MARCUSE, former Professor of Politics and Philosophy at Brandeis University, is now Professor of Philosophy at the University of California at La Jolla. He is the author of *One Dimensional Man: Studies in the Ideology of Advanced Industrial Society* (1964), *Reason and Revolution: Hegel and the Rise of Social Theory* (1941), *Soviet Marxism, A Critical Analysis* (1958) and *Eros and Civilization: A Philosophical Inquiry into Freud* (1955).

ARNO J. MAYER, Professor of History at Princeton University, has written *Political Origins of the New Diplomacy* (1959) and *Politics and Diplomacy of Peacemaking* (1967) and is co-author of *The Historian and The Diplomat* (1967).

HENRY CORD MEYER, Professor of History at the University of California, Irvine, has written *Mitteleuropa in German Thought and Action, 1815–1945* (1955); "Das Zeitalter des Imperialismus" in *Propyläen Weltgeschichte,* Vol. IX (1960); and *Five Images of Germany* (1960, 1966).

JAMES H. NICHOLS, of the Princeton Theological Seminary, edited J. Burckhardt's *Force and Freedom* and has written *History of Christianity, 1650–1950: Secularization of the West* (1956) and *Romanticism in American Theology: Nevin and Schaff at Mercersburg* (1961), among other works.

OTTO PFLANZE, Professor of History at the University of Minnesota, is the author of *Bismarck and the Development of Germany: The Period of Unification, 1815–1871* (1963) and one of the editors of *Documents on German Foreign Policy, 1918–1945* (1949ff.).

HENRY L. ROBERTS, formerly James T. Shotwell Professor of History and Director of the Russian Institute at Columbia University and presently Professor of History at Dartmouth College, is the author of *Rumania: Political Problems of an Agrarian State* (1951), *Russia and America* (1956), and several other books and articles on European diplomacy and East European affairs.

CARL E. SCHORSKE, Professor of History at the University of California, Berkeley, has written *German Social Democracy 1905–1917* (1955) and essays on European political and cultural history.

WILLIAM E. SCOTT, Associate Professor of History at Duke University, is the author of *Alliance Against Hitler: The Origins of the Franco-Soviet Pact* (1962); *Le Pacte France-Soviétique* (1965).

WALTER M. SIMON, Professor of History at the University of Keele, in England, has written *European Positivism in the Nineteenth Century, an Essay in Intellectual History* (1963), *The Failure of the Prussian Reform Movement 1807–1819* (1955), and *Germany: A Brief History* (1966).

FRITZ STERN, Professor of History at Columbia University and permanent visiting professor at the University of Constance, is the editor of *Varieties of History* (1956) and the author of *The Politics of Cultural Despair* (1961).

EDITORS' INTRODUCTION

Two purposes have guided the design of this testimonial volume for Hajo Holborn. It is intended both as an expression of appreciation addressed to a great scholar and influential teacher by his academic debtors and as an illustration of his role in the history of history. Such has been the scope of Hajo Holborn's achievement that these two aspects of it—the range of his performance and the character of his effect—have been supplementary rather than coincident, and the frame of this book follows from the effort not simply to reflect but to integrate both.

The depiction of Hajo Holborn's influence and accomplishments in their full extent would require a broad canvas indeed. It would identify the friends and students who equally have learned from him, and it would not only specify the public figures as well as the professional historians who inhabit both categories but also include the European and American continents over which they are spread. He has, with equal facility, helped to mold colleagues, graduate trainees, and undergraduates. An analogous quality of comprehensiveness has marked his scholarship. As writer and teacher, his history has ranged the whole spectrum of space from Russia to America, of time from the ancient Greeks to contemporary international relations, and of field from the philosophy of history to diplomatic and military history. He has, moreover, worked these fields historiographically with the historical material and methods appropriate to each, and synoptically with an encompassing grasp of human culture ranging from theology to the social sciences. A faithful testimonial would, finally, have to illustrate both the grand humanistic tradition that exalts the inherent value of all knowledge about man and the practical genius that can elicit from this knowledge what men require for the improvement of their own lives, since both are comprised in the finely modulated Holborn approach.

But such a testimonial, indicative as it might be of the scale of Hajo Holborn's work, would nonetheless distort what is most profound in its impact. Powerful albeit unobtrusive, a mesh of meaning pervades the rich panorama of Holborn's history, composing its parts, organizing its variety, rationalizing its factual profusion. The compartmented fields which we may enumerate to show his versatility are actually breached in his writing by innumerable filaments of historical logic that convert formal juxtaposition into vital relationships. German national history is highlighted in the context of European culture and reassessed in the light of generic Western values. Contemporary American history is enriched by the European historical tradition. The history of European diplomacy is penetrated by its own internal economic and social development and put in its place vis-à-vis the extra-European world. Historiography is deepened by the dimension of the philosophy of history and serves, in its turn, as a running thread of intellectual history from the classical Greeks to the present. The religious history of the Reformation is penetrated by the intellectual history of the Renaissance and then conditioned, for its dissemination, by the political and social milieu that favored Protestant innovation and Catholic renewal alike. Bismarck, the arch-realist of politics, has his assumptions explicated by the intellectual history of his age, while Hitler, arch-verbalist and ideologist, is artfully reduced to his elemental psychic impulses. And so it goes, cable upon cable of interpretation across the separate ages and the diverse activities of man.

More than most historians, Hajo Holborn experienced the diversity of history as well; on two continents and amidst world-historical upheavals, he witnessed its intricate unfolding, often at exceptionally close quarters. As an active political being, he lived through and fought against the slow disintegration of the Weimar state. As an American in the Office of Strategic Services, he observed and participated in the marshaling of democratic power to overcome Nazi tyranny and to establish a society in postwar Germany that would at last prove compatible with democracy. Holborn saw the many contradictory influences that shape an epoch—from brute force to the intangible dominance of an idea and the mysterious power of a man. He has always been vitally interested in contemporary affairs and brought to them his understanding of the past, even as that understanding was sharpened by his insights into the actual historical process. The historian's mutually reinforcing comprehension of past and present has rarely been so clearly illuminated as in Holborn's thought. His simultaneous participation in politics and his dispassionate scholarship recall Mommsen's career and confession that at heart he had ever been an *animalum politicum.*

Holborn, the son of the scientific director of an imperial research institute in Berlin, has always been at home in an academic milieu. He knew, however, from early on that the vicissitudes of political power invade even the remotest corner of academic life. He was sixteen when the Hohenzollern empire collapsed and a democratic republic was established in order to give the defeated country a new and popular government. Shortly afterward, he entered Berlin University and began his studies under such renowned teachers as Friedrich Meinecke and Karl Holl; he discovered that after the disastrous events of 1918–19 a few historians at least felt compelled to reconsider their previously secure and nationalistic approach to the German past. In fact, Holborn's career has coincided with continuous agitation and revision in German historiography, both inside Germany and outside. His own *History of Modern Germany* represents the first thoroughly balanced and comprehensive reinterpretation after decades of turmoil.

Holborn's life as a student was short and distinguished. When he was twenty-two he published his first contribution in the *Historische Zeitschrift* and at twenty-six he became Privatdozent in Heidelberg, the youngest in Germany. His steady stream of publications manifested his early maturity and his remarkable independence from admired teachers who, as in Meinecke's case, had become close friends. His early writings ranged from Bismarck's diplomacy to various aspects of the origins of the postwar world; in all his works, he displayed an openness to foreign scholarship and new ideas that was far ahead of the insular and provincial guild he graced. It was perhaps symptomatic of his own interests that Holborn's first major biographical study should have been of Ulrich von Hutten in whom, as his beautifully empathetic portrait shows, literary and political aspiration were felicitously fused.

Holborn was at once recognized and befriended by Meinecke, whose own extraordinary connections with men of power and public life the younger scholar came to share. But the friendship of elders and his rapid successes could not inhibit Holborn's political commitment. He was one of the very few true, outspoken liberals and democrats of Weimar, not a hesitant *Vernunftsrepublikaner,* which was the most his teachers managed to achieve. As proof of his commitment, he accepted a position at the Berlin Hochschule für Politik, which he held simultaneously with his Heidelberg appointment. In the last, charged years before Hitler's rise to power, he was in the thick of academic battles against Nazi unreason, and for his efforts was widely known and intermittently attacked as a leftist, which in his case meant no more than that he had moved close to the Social-Democratic Party. In his final years in Germany, he took his place as a respected and immensely promising scholar who combined austere responsibility to his discipline with a strongly developed sense of civic obligation. He early achieved a characteristic unity of life and work, of sentiment and actions, which has been a quiet model for many on both sides of the Atlantic.

When Hitler came to power in 1933, Holborn realized at once that the new regime would leave no scope for either a moral civic life or independent scholarship. He emigrated early, though he knew the inevitable difficulties entailed in the search for a new intellectual home and a new audience in an unfamiliar milieu and with a foreign language. The choice to emigrate rather than to make compromises or keep silence was open to all; it was taken by few.

Those few, however, had a profound impact, especially in America. That small band of scholars embodied in their very presence in America the excellence and precariousness of European culture. They brought the essentials of their erudition, unencumbered now by trivial disputes or parochial concerns, to a generation of American students, which had been steeled by the depression, but remained spiritually unbroken, open and receptive. Holborn's career at Yale epitomizes the possibilities of this encounter, though even in his case difficulties of adjustment burdened the first few years. In his new home, he rethought some of the premises of historical scholarship, and to his old themes was now added an abiding interest in the philosophy of history, embodied in his probing essays on past masters and persistent problems.

After Pearl Harbor Holborn joined the O.S.S., where his scholarly talents were once again applied to immediate political issues. *Emigré* hatred of his native country was alien to Holborn —as indeed it was to most of his colleagues. After the war, he aided German colleagues individually and German academic life collectively, but he refused as a matter of course all entreaties and invitations to return there permanently. His home is America.

From an American perspective, he grasped the magnitude of Europe's eclipse. *The Political Collapse of Europe,* translated into most European languages, has become the standard treatise on the decline of the Great Powers in Europe, whose early dominance Ranke had authoritatively depicted. From an American perspective also, he wrote his magisterial German history. But Holborn's life and work demonstrate the ambiguity of national identifications. It is not accidental that he concluded his work on Hutten, the famed national hero of the Germans, with a veiled admonition to his erstwhile German colleagues: "Throughout the centuries with all their variations, the appeal to Ulrich von Hutten belongs only to those for whom the nation is a way of ascent to *Humanitas.*" Hajo Holborn's own career exemplifies the ever-present possibilities of this ascent, even in an age of nationalistic passions unimaginable in earlier times.

Because Hajo Holborn's impact upon twentieth-century historiography has been his demonstration of the coherence that runs through the widest reaches of historical experience, the only adequate testimony to his role must be an integral book rather than a set of essays illustrative either of his compass or of a favored field. We have chosen "the responsibility of power" as the theme of such a book not because we deem it *the* central thread of Hajo Holborn's historical concern—his respect for the spontaneity and multiformity of the human experience has been far too great for obsession with any single theme—but because it is *a* central thread with the comparative advantage of epitomizing more definitely than any other the fruitful reciprocity through which he brings the varied forms of historical experience to bear upon a fundamental human dilemma and brings the ubiquity of the dilemma to bear, as a persistent and unifying motif, upon the multifarious interests of men. Because the responsibility of power is a universal theme that crystallizes the problematic relations of actualities and ideals, as Hajo Holborn has taught us, it aligns acts and ideas, includes both the European and American experience, joins remote and modern history, and embeds the stream of history in the human condition.

This book is addressed, then, both to the continuity of a fundamental problem and to the variety of solutions (and evasions, which are a kind of solution) that men have found for it during the half-millenium of history that we call our own. In our presentation, then, the problem of power is single. It excludes, however interesting they may be in themselves, the separable problems relating to the acquisition of power or to the different standards that men apply before and after they acquire power, and it focuses only on the primary problem in the exercise of power. The problem is simply this: how have men settled the conflicting claims of the purpose for which power over men is supposed to exist and of the power without whose preservation the purpose supposedly cannot be realized? The solutions have varied with the kind of power and the nature of the purpose as well as with the relationship between power and purpose, and if the problem is a constant measure the permutations in the solution have sounded the changes in our history.

Because the contributors have recognized the unity amid diversity required both by the theme and by the standards of the historian who has inspired it, their essays may be regarded as chapters in a collaborative whole. In a formal sense, some of us are students and others of us friends of Hajo Holborn, but in this respect as in so many of the others that concern him the formal distinctions are permeated by more significant connections. Hajo Holborn's students have become his friends; his friends have all learned from him: they should be identified simply as participants in this testimonial to his achievement.

Leonard Krieger and Fritz Stern

PART I

THE FORMATION OF
SOVEREIGN POWER

Chapter 1

POWER AND RESPONSIBILITY:
THE HISTORICAL ASSUMPTIONS

Leonard Krieger

"Power," in its general usage, is an original faculty of individuals and a simple substance of societies. In both applications it defines rather than is defined; it is constituent rather than constituted. Its dictionary definition—the capacity to act upon a person or thing, or a person or thing with such a capacity—is at once so elemental and so indiscriminate as to underline the generic role of power as an ultimate and undifferentiated factor. Indeed, a recent political encyclopedia has accentuated both its finality and its ubiquity even further by making it coextensive with all existence as the power to be that preserves the identity of every existing being.[1]

Now, it is usual for dictionaries and encyclopedias to devitalize terms, but in this instance philosophers and theorists have endorsed the same formal vacuity. From the ancient Greek notion that "every man has power who does that which he wishes at the time when he wishes," through Hobbes' idea of it as a "present means, to obtain some future apparent Good," to Bertrand Russell's "production of intended effects," theorists have simply affirmed its irreducible neutrality as a universal concept and have developed its character in terms rather of its accretions from external relations and special contexts than of tendencies inherent in the primitive concept.[2] At the start of its career in the Western tradition the Roman jurists used the concept of power (*potestas*) without ever defining it, and now, too, according to a contemporary authority, power is neither observable nor explicable

---

[1] *Staatslexikon*, 6th ed., (Freiburg, 1960), V, 499.

[2] *Lesser Hippias*, in *Dialogues of Plato* (B. Jowett, tr., New York, 1937), II, 718; Hobbes' *Leviathan* (Oxford, 1909), p. 66; Bertrand Russell, *Power: A New Social Analysis* (New York, 1938), p. 35.

in itself but only in its external "manifestations and results." "We know, or we believe we know, what power does, but we are unable to define its substance and essence."[3]

The elemental attitude toward unqualified power that has been persistent in our culture, then, makes it a positive reality that is ontologically impenetrable and morally neutral. But equally persistent and equally stable have been two alternative sets of qualities that have been built into this elemental concept, each furnishing power with an identity and an ethical tendency. One set identifies power in relation to other elemental concepts and bears a positive ethical implication; the other identifies power as a function of the social circumstances in which it is most frequently exercised, and bears a negative ethical implication. Both refer equally to the fundamental concept of power and set up the real problem of power in our history, which has not been the simple conflict between power and ethics but the more intricate conflict between two fundamentally different ways of relating power to ethics.

The first set of qualities, which has been recognized as a consistent group in every period of our culture, consists in the marks that identify the peculiar character of power in contradistinction to such related concepts as "force" and "violence." All three share in a fundamental category of natural and human reality—the transmission of actual effects from a subject to an object—but power is distinguished by its possession, in addition, of three mutually compatible qualities: potentiality, reciprocity, and—surprisingly—spirituality.

1. It is obvious from the derivation and derivatives of the term itself—power, like the French *pouvoir,* stems from *potere,* to be able, and yields "potential" as well as "potent"—that power signifies not only, like force and violence, an act with effects, but also the capacity for such acts and effects. The identification of capability, or potentiality, as a quality of power has implied a positive notion of its relation to moral purpose. For potentiality implies a *telos.* It requires that the ends toward which a power is exercised be the primary determinants of whether that power exists or not. Thus purpose is built so integrally into the very

[3] Fritz Schulz, *Principles of Roman Law,* M. Wolff, tr. (Oxford, 1936), p. 45; Karl Loewenstein, *Political Power and the Governmental Process* (Chicago, 1965), pp. 3–5.

notion of power that power becomes unthinkable as a separable means to an extraneous end. In such an indissoluble structure of end and means, it becomes thinkable only in terms of the end it is realizing.

For the clearest grounding of this implication we must go back to Plato and Aristotle, because their explications have become our implications in the cases of all those common concepts—such as power—whose meaning we continue to assume. Plato not only endowed the inseparable union of power and purpose with a logical structure but clearly identified as a *moral* purpose the purpose that is a necessary ingredient of power. One has power, his argument ran, when one does what one wills; necessarily, one wills ends, not means—men do not "will that which they do," but "that further end for the sake of which they do a thing"; since men always do "indifferent"—that is, morally neutral or mixed—things "for the sake of the good," men will only the good—"we will . . . that which is our good, but that which is neither good nor evil, or simply evil, we do not will." This good, moreover, is not what the doer "thinks" is good but what is actually good, whether the doer thinks so or not. Since in this connection as in others Plato saw good as the juncture of real self-interest, knowledge, justice, and honor, "our good" is identical with the good as such. Since, finally, power is by general consensus "a good to the possessor," and since, as has been shown, his good is *the* good considered as the constant object of his will, power exists only in the realization of the good.[4]

Thus was born the influential notion that power must be revered as a necessary aspect of the good, but in Plato's original sense of this notion the reverence was due it only because power could be nothing but a necessary aspect of the good. His integral association of power and goodness rested upon an assumption that men of later ages were to drop when they adopted his conclusion. His conclusion that power is a good was predicated on the assumption that the primary ingredient of power is knowledge. The basis of this assumption was that the goodness and indeed the very existence of power is as utterly dependent upon realizing an ideal object as the act of knowledge is upon apprehending a real object. For "the realm of ideals is the real

[4] *Gorgias,* in *Dialogues of Plato,* I, 524–27.

world" and as such it can be apprehended only through the power of knowledge, "the most powerful of all" the faculties. The ideal must be so apprehended because "the power either to affect . . . or to be affected" that is the distinguishing "mark" of all "real things" is essentially the power to be known through these effects and is thus the obverse side of knowledge, which is "the power of knowing the real as it is."[5] Power is exercised essentially in acts of knowledge, then, and this conjunction of power and knowledge serves to guarantee the necessary relationship of power to the ideal object which they share. Because of this conjunction, acts of will must follow from acts of knowledge, and the power of the will is unthinkable apart from good ends already apprehended by the power of knowledge.[6]

Subsequently, men were to depart from Plato's assumption. They separated reality from ideality, will from reason, the existence from the morality of power, and from the new postulate they were to draw the new conclusion that power was itself a means with detachable ends, an instrumental reality whose value varied with the degree in which it moved the real toward the ideal. But the Platonic connotation of power was never wholly lost. The modern agony of power can be traced, at least in part, to the admixture of moral finality into the instrumental judgment upon power.

For the doctrine of potentiality, as for so many other doctrines, Aristotle's role was to make Platonic ideas susceptible to this kind of osmosis. Where Plato's contribution to the connotation of power was the ethical necessity of conceiving it in terms of an ideal end, Aristotle's was the natural necessity of conceiving it in terms of some end, whatever its kind. He thereby generalized the teleological dimension of power into a basic constituent of all reality, but in this very process introduced the problem that was henceforth to plague wielders and theorists of power alike. For

[5] *The Republic of Plato* (trans., with int. and notes by Francis Macdonald Cornford, Oxford, 1941), pp. 171, 180–81; *Sophist,* in Francis Macdonald Cornford, *Plato's Theory of Knowledge* (London, 1946), pp. 234, 237.

[6] *Lesser Hippias,* in H. N. Fowler, *Plato* (Cambridge, Mass., 1939), pp. 473–75. This early dialogue has not been definitely authenticated as Plato's, but this question is irrelevant here since its demonstration of the paradox that must follow from the assumption of a will power separate from knowledge of the good is part of the Platonic legacy.

if he indelibly identified power with potentiality and recognized it in this sense as one of "the principles common to all things," he also made this ubiquitous power move inexorably toward ends at once distinct from it and both necessary and superior to it.[7]

Thus on the one hand the very proposition that Aristotle affirmed as the primary definition of power—"a source of movement or change, which is in another thing than the thing moved or in the same thing *qua* other"—he deliberately used as the basis for his analysis of potentiality, stating explicitly that the sense of power as potentiality "is the reason of the inquiry in the course of which we have discussed these previous senses also."[8] But on the other hand as potentiality, power is necessarily implicated in a larger process which relates it continuously to ends and renders it subordinate to them. Power is, in this process, paired with "actuality" in a development through which things are pulled continuously by what they are potentially capable of becoming toward what they really are. Power is here related to actuality as matter is to form, effect to cause (in all but the material sense of cause), possibility to "complete reality."[9] Thus, power and actuality "are different," and the chief mark of their distinction is that an actuality pertains to an activity in which the end is present whereas a power pertains to a movement in which it is not. But by the same token power, as the principle of movement, is "relative to the end" present in the actuality that gives it direction: "actuality is the end, and it is for the sake of this that the potency is acquired."[10] Since, as an end, the actual is "prior"—that is, superior—to the potential in both substance and value—an end for Aristotle is not the stage "that is last . . . but only that which is best"—Aristotle confirmed to this extent the Platonic legacy which assigned the meaning of power to the end it served. But unlike Plato's seamless union of power and the good, Aristotle also bequeathed the notion that power refers to the original materials of reality and therefore is itself a principle qualitatively distinct from the end that gives it form and value. If, then, Aristotle's dominant legacy was a doctrine of potentiality

[7] *Metaphysics*, in Richard McKeon, ed., *The Basic Works of Aristotle* (New York, 1941), pp. 687, 874–76.

[8] *Ibid.*, pp. 765–66, 820–25.

[9] *Ibid.*, 822–24; *Physics*, in *ibid.*, pp. 236–38; G. R. G. Mure, *Aristotle* (New York, 1964), pp. 10–13.

[10] *Metaphysics*, in *Basic Works of Aristotle*, pp. 823, 826–29.

that reinforced the definition of power in terms of a single process of ends and means, he also initiated the rift between ends and means within this process and insinuated the tendency to assign the primary locus of power more to the material means than to the moral end, which thus exists outside it.

2. The second of the qualities that redounds to power from its due location among the concepts is its reciprocity, that is, the necessity of an exchange between the subject and object— or, in Aristotle's more appropriate terms, the agent and patient— of a power relation. It was Aristotle indeed who provided the philosophical foundation for the reciprocal quality of power when he argued that any exercise of power was a single act constituted both by the capacity of the agent to effect a change in the patient and by the capacity of the patient to change when so affected.[11] The modern socialized counterpart of this argument can be found in the general agreement, even among those commentators who come closest to equating power and force, that power is distinguished from force "by operating reciprocally between those who hold and exercise power . . . and those to whom it is directed."[12] It is "always a two-sided relationship."[13] The implication of this reciprocal quality in power is crucial to any consideration of it. The import is this: however undifferentiated the essence of power may be, relative to other concepts it gets articulated into a process with agents, patients, media, and stages; it is then not a nugget, not a currency to be simplistically either expended or—Midas-like—expanded, but a relational world unto itself, with its own tensions, its own values, its own structure, equipping it to negotiate on equal terms with other conceptual worlds.

3. Power, finally, takes its place among those concepts that are invisible and intangible not by abstraction but by direct reference to realities that are themselves metaphysical. In part

[11] *Ibid.*, p. 765; *Physics*, in *ibid.*, pp. 256–57; John Herman Randall, Jr., *Aristotle* (New York, 1960), p. 191.

[12] Loewenstein, *Political Power*, p. 6.

[13] Franz Neumann, *The Democratic and the Authoritarian State* (Glencoe, 1957), pp. 3–4. See also Bertrand de Jouvenel, *On Power: Its Nature and the History of its Growth* (Boston, 1962), p. 25; Russell, *Power*, pp. 16–18; Guglielmo Ferrero, *The Principles of Power* (New York, 1942), pp. 40–42.

this quality follows from the aforementioned mysterious essence of power; in part it follows from the aforementioned quality of a not-yet-existent potentiality, which transcends the temporal dimension of physical acts and effects; in part it follows from the usual focus upon power as a relation among men and hence upon its psychic aspect. But whatever its source, the consequence of this super-sensible quality is clear enough: it has led men to think of power, in comparison to the physical connotations of coercion and violence, as a more inclusive reality whose center of gravity lies in the spiritual, moral, and legal arenas. In the striking evocation of a recent commentator, the social agents of "the struggle for power . . . are not, like living creatures, visible and tangible; they bear a close resemblance to those beings, intermediary between gods and men, which the Romans called *Genii,* and which they imagined to be always present among men, . . . invisible and bodiless."[14]

The upshot of these three qualities—potentiality, reciprocity, spirituality—which have been imputed to power as a member of the community of concepts has been to make of power a cross section of total reality from a dynamic perspective, slicing through all levels from natural compulsion to moral precept and competing on an equal basis with the other fundamental organizing principles of life.

But equally characteristic of the whole span of our culture has been the other approach to power, addressed to a context far different from the original matrix of these three conceptual qualities and projecting a thrust quite contrary to their positive bent. When power has been considered solely within the field circumscribed by men's political and social circumstances, its generic definition and conceptual qualities have been retained, but in a selective form that stresses the instrumental, material, and pejorative connotations of power. In its political employment, then, power gets defined simply as "the control of other men"—that is, "the exercise of effective social control of the power holders over the power addressees."[15] If this formulation is compared with the generic definition of power as the capacity for effective action, it clearly entails more than merely the exclu-

[14] *Ibid.,* p. 17.
[15] Neumann, *Democratic and Authoritarian State,* p. 3; Loewenstein, *Political Power,* p. 6.

sive focus on other persons. What is involved, within the sphere
of interpersonal relations itself, is the shift in emphasis from the
capacity to the effect. Where the stress in the generic definition
is on the self-disciplined creativity of the agent of power, the
stress in the political definition is on the palpable subordination
of the patient of power. Where the qualities of generic power
separate power off from "force" and "violence," the qualities of
political power separate it off from "right," since the stress both
on external effects and on the manipulation of others, which
is in political power, tends to segregate it from the stress both
on capacity and on self-assertion that is in "right."

With this shift, the three qualities of the power concept take
on a correspondingly altered aspect. The connotation of potentiality which relates action to an end persists, but in the political
context the end is altered from a purpose to an effect, and the
vision of power as a process scaled down from the realization of
the good to the production of a faithful mechanism of response.
As a corollary, the finite tendency of potentiality, in its original
sense, to surpass every stage of itself toward its end becomes, in
the political context, the tendency of power, bereft of its purpose,
toward infinite expansion of itself. In the revealing language of a
contemporary: "the struggle to magnify itself is of Power's essence. . . . There ensues a growth of Power to which there is no
limit, a growth which is fostered by more and more altruistic ex-
ternals, though the motive-spring is still as always the wish to
dominate."[16]

It follows that in the political context the quality of reciprocity
in power is unbalanced, as the source of power overshadows the
object which is the locus of its effect. Thus, political power "in
its pure state consists . . . in command, a command which has
an independent existence," while "submission" is "always a relatively passive factor" that comes "later in time" than command.[17]
And again: "those who wield political power are compelled to
create emotional and rational responses in those whom they
rule."[18] The implication of reciprocity in this form is its multi-
plier effect, making for the intensification of power as force.
This quality which, in its generic form, signified the continuous

16 de Jouvenel, *On Power*, pp. 4, 119.
17 *Ibid.*, pp. 97–99.
18 Neumann, *Democratic and Authoritarian State*, p. 4.

interchange between a subject that can act and an object that can react now signifies a direct current of energy in which the object participates only as the pole serving to complete the circuit.

Even the intangible quality of power, finally, has been transfigured rather than denied in this materially and mechanically oriented political universe of discourse. The spirituality of power has turned, in this context, into the demonology of power, and we find, indeed, that one of the few serious histories of political power has as its primary theme the demoniacal element in the idea of power by which the will of modern man has been "possessed."[19] Despite all due professions of scientific neutrality, this implication of evil in segregated political power has mobilized a whole tradition, castigating the immoral consequences of amoral power and spanning our culture from Socrates' dour pronouncement that "the very bad men come from the class of those who have power" to Acton's notorious reiteration that since "power tends to corrupt and absolute power corrupts absolutely, . . . great men are almost always bad men."[20] Behind such an apparent paradox as this strain represents, with its imputation of moral evil to a quasi-physical political power ostensibly separated from moral ends, is clearly the judgment that, however material and mechanical in its operation, political power also possesses a spiritual relevance that makes it measurable on the scale of universal morality. Hence the preface which Acton affixed to his epigram on the corruptibility of power: "I cannot accept your canon that we are to judge Pope and King unlike other men. . . ."[21]

There have been, then, two constant and fundamental ideas of power in our culture—one positive by implication and asserting the necessity of a built-in end for the very concept of power, the other negative by implication, asserting the instrumental nature of power, and deducing its separability from ends that necessarily are external to it. These attitudes are, of course, distillations and are rarely to be found in their pure state for any actual situation, past or present. But since these attitudes com-

---

[19] Gerhard Ritter, *Die Dämonie der Macht* (6th ed., Munich, 1948), p. 15.

[20] *Gorgias*, in *Dialogues of Plato*, I, 586; Acton to Creighton, April 5, 1887, in John Emerich Edward Dalberg-Acton, *Essays in Freedom and Power* (Boston, 1949), p. 364.

[21] *Ibid.*

pose the very meaning of the term, they have nonetheless been ingredient in every situation, whether practical or theoretical, where men have been conscious that it is "power" they have been exercising or discussing. Since what we call explanation usually consists in analyzing an action into its ingredients and then rationalizing their recombination for that action, the explanation of any application of power must start from the identification of the two basic attitudes in their due proportions for that application.

In terms of this analysis, then, the familiar formulation of the primary problem that calls for explanation in most situations of power poses the wrong question. The problem is the responsibility of power, and the familiar formulation is whether the domination by some persons over other persons has been used as a means to a further end or as an end in itself. But this is a question that is put from the point of view of only one attitude—the attitude, prevalent in our own age, that we have called here the implicitly negative attitude—and consequently it can account for only one strain in the situation to which it is applied. This is a question that may suffice for force but not for power in the double meaning we have distilled from it—a double meaning in terms of which the men who use power are compelled to think by the very atmosphere of the culture they breathe.

Actually, the responsibility of power has two meanings, derivative from the two basic attitudes toward power, and these meanings are not only different but opposed. If in the familiar sense it means the responsibility that power owes, in an equally fundamental sense it also means the responsibility that power owns. In the first sense the assumption is that power is a mechanism with no ends of its own and the issue is whether men with power are responsible to ends that are no part of it; in the second sense the assumption is that power has built-in ends distinctively appropriate to it and the issue is whether men with all kinds of ends are responsible to the requirements of this power.

Thus the problem of power, both for the men who exercise it and for the men who judge its exercise, is something more than the simple question of whether the power is being used responsibly or irresponsibly. Since there are two categorical attitudes toward power and two corresponding criteria of its responsibility men must determine what kind of power is intended

and what it is intended for before a powerful act can be committed or judgment upon it rendered. This determination may
be a simple matter of choice: either power is considered a real
instrument and the responsibility for its use is measured by reference to a whole set of ends independent of it, or it is considered
the quality of a definite end which makes that end realizable,
and the responsibility of an act is measured by reference to the
establishment, preservation, and extension of the power for that
end. Once this choice is recognized, it can be ascertained whether
the appropriate judgment of any act of power is upon its responsibility or irresponsibility in view of an acknowledged end or
upon the fitness of a particular kind of responsible power to a
particular situation.

But typically the relationship among the different assumptions
about power and the different notions of responsibility is not so
clearly disjunctive. It tends rather toward inclusive compromises
than toward exclusive choices. For one thing, most men feel the
pull from both the main currents of power—they feel both that
it is an actual tool, at once neutral and dangerous, which can
be employed for all manner of purposes and that, as an integral
part of certain practical goals, it imposes obligations which must
be fulfilled before it can become a reality. Most men, consequently, have tried to find a place for both attitudes. The other
testimonial of the composite structure to be found in most uses
and theories of power is more compelling, for it expresses a
persistent objective connection between the two main meanings
of power. Both of these meanings have proved so unstable by
themselves that the protagonists of each have characteristically
borrowed attributes from the other when they have worked out
their policies and doctrines of power. Thus those who have started
from the instrumental nature of political power have tended to
import moral ends as the only stable bases for judging its exercise.
Those, on the other hand, who have started from the teleological
notion originally located in ethical power as the capacity to
realize the Good have tended to shift its locale to a segregated
political arena in the quest for a sure practical realization of at
least the external conditions of the Good, and they have tended
to single out effectiveness as the only stable basis for judging the
exercise of power.

It follows that two questions must be asked of each use of

power, if we are to explain it: first, in what proportions did the alternative aspects of power enter into any situation; and secondly, how were the alternatives related to each other in the person, idea, institution, or event that was authoritative for the situation. The manifestations of power in our culture have been and continue to be bewildering in their variety, and only our realization that men's consciousness of the responsibility *of* power has covered a responsibility *to* as well as a responsibility *by* power will permit their arrangement into a semblance of rational order.

History affords one mode of such an arrangement. Indeed, from the Greeks' Thucydides to our own Holborn, a distinguished line of historians has seen in power a feature of human society especially accessible to their discipline, and they have made it a central strand of their professional concerns. In part, to be sure, the persistent interest of historians in the facts and ideas of power reveals more about historians than it does about power: the kind of action most prominently associated with power has been political action, and the attraction that it has had in this guise for historians is a measure of the exclusive focus upon politics in the tradition of history and of the continuing special kinship with politics that historians feel even now that the focus is no longer exclusive. But the attraction is also predicated upon factors in the problem of power that seem especially susceptible to the historical approach:

First, the commonly attested mystery at the heart of power and the consequent dependence upon its manifestations for the understanding of it are qualities particularly appropriate to a discipline that, perhaps more than any other, deals in the simple alignment of manifestations rather than in the penetration to a substance or law behind them.

Secondly, power is a combination of idea and fact that transcends the usual distinction between theory and practice, and one of the characteristic endeavors of history is precisely to show the running connections between theory and practice. This characteristic of power, signalized by the historian's interest in it, is crucial to the understanding of power because it is so easily misunderstood. It is easy to think that, because there are ideas of power and facts of power, the ideas have been taken up into theories, the facts have been the ingredients of practice, and the essential division in the nature of power follows the usual division between theory and practice. But as our earlier considerations show and the historian's approach confirms, the actual relationships of power are precisely the reverse of this. Both ideas and facts enter into every act of power, for, as we have seen, over and above any duality about power and its ends, there is general agreement that power as such is an invisible, bilateral force with visible, unilateral effects: therefore, far from the ideas and facts bifurcating into theory and practice, theory and practice have each to deal with both the ideas and facts of power. Thus theories of power have been characteristically predicated on a political "realism" that tailors ideals of power to achievable factual results; rulers who are not theorists have characteristically measured the factual results of their commands by conformity to policies that were not facts. Hence the distinction between the theory and practice of power is not a fundamental distinction for the study of power. On the contrary, because they do have the same ingredients and are commensurable, the historian can use power as a central theme with which to tie together the theoretical and practical aspects of an era and as a unifying theme with which to connect the theoretical and practical aspects of successive eras.

What we can expect, then, from the historical approach to power is: first, the dramatic portrayal of the infinite variety of the combinations actually undertaken by men to escape the awful dilemma posed by the conflicting claims of the responsibility to power and the responsibility by power throughout the period of modern history, when the dilemma has been most urgent—this will be the function of the succeeding chapters; and secondly, an analysis of the common assumptions that cradled all these combinations and set up the initial framework of thought and action within which the varied solutions have taken their place and may be related to one another—this will be the function of the brief disquisition that follows.

By general consensus, the problem of power as we know it is coeval with the modern period of history.[22] Although this judgment is more tautological than informative—since it is precisely because familiar issues like that of power have their origins around 1500 that historians have marked the start of modern

---

[22] Friedrich Meinecke, *Die Idee der Staatsräson in der neueren Geschichte* (Munich, 1924). See also Ritter, *Dämonie der Macht,* pp. 29, 109.

history there—it does indicate that the problem of power then took a form qualitatively different from what it had been theretofore and structurally continuous with what it was to be thereafter. The turning point is usually located—and there is no reason to dispute it—in the impact of the invasion through which the territorial states of western and central Europe broke open the city-state system of the Italian peninsula, for it shocked Italian humanist-politicians like Machiavelli and Guicciardini into consciousness of the implications of Renaissance political practice and it spread the political standards and ideas that were most advanced among the Italians into the receptive monarchies of Europe. *That* the power syndrome then took the basic political form it was to retain through the following centuries is clear enough, but since the constituents of this syndrome, as we have seen, go back to the Greeks and since more recent elaborations upon it obscure our view of the original break, *what* this new form was, in comparison to earlier patterns, is more doubtful. But if we approach this question in terms of the two constant strains in the attitude of Western man toward power, then the nature of the change that created the problem of power in its modern form around the beginning of the sixteenth century may be formulated: whereas the ethical and political notions of power had remained on their different levels and had not directly engaged each other, the new focus upon the state now adduced political means as necessary to the first and political ends as necessary to the second. Thus the notion of political power as a means was for the first time brought into direct confrontation with the notion of it as an end, and the modern conflict of responsibility by and to power set up. From this turning point we can look back to the ancient origins and medieval development of the separate generic and political attitudes; and forward to their early modern convergence into a single unstable and ambiguous scheme of power.

The ancients initiated both attitudes, and the manner of their initiation indicates the separate orbits they were to travel for centuries. For the Greeks spawned the generic notion of power and the Romans the political—a circumstance that helps to explain why in subsequent ages utopians have tended to evoke the Greeks and realists the Romans. The Greeks, indeed, had no authentic notion of political power at all, for the simple reason that the notion of political authority is essential to the notion of political power and, as Hannah Arendt has pointed out, the egalitarian polis left the Greeks with no idea of political authority, forcing them to borrow surrogates from the non-political authority of fathers over families, reason over existence, soul over body.[23]

Plato, to be sure, did acknowledge "power" in the political sense, but his usage of it in this sense signified something categorically different from what he otherwise meant by power and indeed from what our whole tradition has characterized by the term. In its political context, "power" for Plato simply connoted force: it was a mere psychological fact without value in itself, an impulsive product of pugnacity and ambition, and a quality of the "spirited element" in the soul that was entirely distinct from and subordinate to the "rational element"; "political power" was correspondingly entirely distinct from and subordinate to the intellectual and moral power that was seated exclusively in the rational element and was the only authentic power. Political force—to call it by its proper name—was, moreover, unstable: either it was controlled by reason and became a function of intellectual and moral power, or it tended to degenerate into despotism and thereby to the self-negating servitude under the despotism of appetite that spells impotence.[24]

With his passion for the practical accommodation of principle Aristotle might be expected to stand in contrast to Plato and to represent the origins of an opposite tradition celebrating the moralization of political power, but in fact it is precisely because his determined accommodation of ethics to the political community stopped abruptly short of accommodation to political power that Aristotle furnishes a most impressive testimonial to the separate roots of moral and political power in our tradition. For when he wrote both that "the state is a creation of nature" and that by nature "some should rule and others be ruled," he was referring to different aspects of nature and did not intend the two judgments to be combined into the moral justification of a distinctively political power.[25] Aristotle did indeed mean to give moral justification to the state, for it filled the ethical role of "the

[23] Hannah Arendt, "What was Authority?" in *Nomos,* I (1958), pp. 84–97.
[24] Cornford, ed., *Republic of Plato,* pp. 61–62, 289–94, 300–2.
[25] *Politics,* in *Basic Works of Aristotle.* pp. 1129, 1132.

end" and "the best" in human nature—that is, it existed "for the sake of the good life."[26] But the natural power of men to rule others, on the contrary, was not political at all: it referred to a household and not to a state, "which is a government of freemen and equals"; and it pertained to human nature in the sense of the original needs and not of the moral ends of man.[27] In the state, power belonged not to men but to the law, and not by dint of any political constitution but by dint of the law's ethical capacity to "habituate" men to "become good." Only this ethical capacity of the law, as "a rule proceeding from a sort of practical wisdom and reason," sufficed to turn natural force into political "compulsive power," for "virtue, when furnished with means, has actually the greatest power of exercising force: and as superior power is only found where there is superior excellence of some kind, power seems to imply virtue."[28]

Aristotle undoubtedly contributed to later misconstructions through his ambiguous harnessing of physical force to moral power in the flexible notion of nature, but the fundamentals of his position tallied with the single Greek legacy to the tradition of power: what is distinctive to power is the ethical capacity to realize good ends; political power, properly so-called, does not exist; there is only a political application of a general ethical power employing as a means a political force, which, when divorced from this moral direction, becomes impotent and illegitimate. In Aristotle's terms, although a good citizen need not be a good man, "the good ruler is a good and wise man."[29]

The Romans, on the other hand, initiated the notion of a distinctive political power, valid in its own right. The form they gave it, moreover, emphasized its indifference to the ethical and teleological type of power, for they measured the validity and defined the nature of political power in terms of its origins rather than its ends. The Romans were alert, as the Greeks never were, to the possibility of choosing between political and non-political ways of life, although, like Cicero, they usually argued for the superior morality of the civic choice.[30] But the

---

[26] *Ibid.*, p. 1129.
[27] *Ibid.*, pp. 1128, 1135.
[28] *Nicomachean Ethics*, in *ibid.*, pp. 1109–10: *Politics*, in *ibid.*, p. 1133.
[29] *Ibid.*, p. 1180.
[30] Cicero, *On the Commonwealth* (New York, n.d.), Bk. I, XVIII–XX.

alternative was reflected within the Roman law in the clear differentiation of public from private law and the validation of political relations as an autonomous sector of human existence. Within this sector, power (*potestas*) became an accepted legal category referring to the rights and duties incumbent upon any public office from the sovereign to the lesser magistrate.[31] This Roman legal usage marked the start of the long history of power as an autonomous political concept, with the function of signifying the activity of legitimate public authority. But what defined an authority as a power in this sense was precisely its legitimacy—that is, its lawful origin. When Cicero maintained that "although the people have the power, the Senate has the authority,"[32] he was making the characteristic Roman reference to power as the rightful source of public control. Where the Greeks had initiated responsibility to ethical power, the Romans intiated responsibility to political power, but so long as the one was concerned with moral ends and the other with political origins there was no bar to peaceful coexistence.

The separate vintages and different characters of the two strands of power—the ethical and the political—in pre-modern history were confirmed and intensified during the Middle Ages, when they were brought into juxtaposition and found to function without mutual interference. They dovetailed in theory and traveled their own orbits side-by-side in practice. Medieval theorists took both the Roman notion of a political power defined by its source and the Greek notion of an ethical power defined by its end, and, by attaching the unifying scheme of the Christian dispensation to both termini, not only affirmed both notions but aligned them in a compatible system. On the one hand they buttressed the originative character of political power with St. Paul's doctrine that "there is no power but of God, and the powers that be are ordained of God"; on the other hand they affirmed the transcendent spiritual end of all power by defining it in terms of preparation for salvation. The theoretical history of the Middle Ages may be viewed, indeed, as a process that led from the unbalanced emphasis on a Christianized legitimate power through the synthesis of legitimate political with teleological ethical power to the unbalanced emphasis upon Christianized ethical power.

[31] Adolf Berger, *Encyclopedic Dictionary of Roman Law* (Philadelphia, 1953), p. 640.

[32] Latin quotation in Arendt, "What Is Authority?" in *Nomos*, I, 100.

St. Augustine sponsored the first stage, with his stress upon God as "the Creator . . . of all powers," who has "all power of giving or taking away sovereignty ascribed unto Himself alone" and who gives earthly kingdoms "both to good and bad as Himself likes."[33] Although St. Augustine prefigured the medieval syndrome in his direction of the earthly city to man's instruction for Judgment Day, the direction toward this end is God's power, not man's. As for earthly political power—that is, "man's subjection to man"—it is born of sin and aims simply at "earthly peace"—that is, "orderly rule and subjection."[34] Small wonder that the elaboration of Papalist theory and the canon law in the early Middle Ages, building on both the Roman and Augustinian heritage, developed the notion of a political power founded on divine appointment through Peter and associated integrally with legitimate authority. This power, divisible by devolution, therefore always referred to the authority behind and above it. Finally —and most strikingly—it was accompanied by the principle of "automatism," grounded in the power of the Keys, which automatically assured the realization of the end of the power in the very act of its exercise.[35] To be sure, insofar as the arena of this political power was the Christian church, it had, as for St. Augustine, a built-in purpose, but again this was a subordinate motif. The doctrines both of Papal sovereignty and of theocratic kingship asserted the plenitude of powers from divine appointment for their side and conceded the teleological use of the other sword for circumscribed purposes to the inferior opponent.[36]

The reception of Aristotle in the thirteenth century restored, along with nature, the dignity of the teleological and ethical notion of power that the Greeks had associated with it, but now in a context directly and compatibly related to the political concept of appointed power. As might be expected, the organization of the two contrary principles into a single architectonic system was highlighted in Aquinas. He made God the author of nature, and therefore of the state as a natural institution. The human inclination and reason that operated it were valid because they con-

[33] St. Augustine, *The City of God* (New York, 1945), I, 154, 157, 171.

[34] *Ibid.*, II, 253–54.

[35] Walter Ullmann, *Principles of Government and Politics in the Middle Ages* (London, 1961), pp. 34–36, 54.

[36] *Ibid.*, pp. 64, 130.

formed to His natural law by divine preordination—that is, they are "the divine light in us." But since "the nature of a thing is its end"—that is, since it is the nature of any thing, including the state, to move toward its end by the law of its own being—the same will of God that was the ultimate authority for power in the state also bound that power to the well-being of the community that was its end. Thus Aquinas argued that there was power of a political kind—that is, "lordship" over free men—before the Fall both because "God established man" in the "natural order" with the prescription that the just should rule and because "the social life of men"—which is equally natural—"would be impossible if someone should not preside to direct them to the common good."[37] But just as political power points back ultimately to appointment by God, just so it points forward ultimately to an end that is, also, not simply civic but moral and religious. For despite Aquinas' nominal attempt to assert the autonomy of the political status, the concept of political power could simply not yet support its own ends. ". . . The end of a multitude and the end of one man must be judged to be the same. . . . It seems that the ultimate end of an associated multitude is to live according to virtue. . . . But because man, in living according to virtue, is ordained to an ulterior end, which consists in the enjoyment of God, . . . the ultimate end of a congregated multitude is not, therefore, to live according to virtue, but through the virtuous life to attain to the enjoyment of God."[38] The virtuous life is the charge of "the king, to whom the height of rule in human things is committed," and the enjoyment of God is the charge of the priests, but since the virtuous life "is ordained, as to its end, to the blessed life in heaven" so all kings "ought to be subject" to the highest priest, who is "the successor of Peter."[39] Thus did Aquinas close his circle, unifying ordained political power and teleological moral power by reference to the creative and providential functions of the one God.

Aquinas' synthesis was the expression in theory of a conjunction between the two notions of power that featured the practice

[37] Aquinas, quoted in Ewart Lewis, *Medieval Political Ideas* (London, 1954), I, 174–75.
[38] *Ibid.,* I, 178.
[39] *Ibid.,* I, 179.

of the same period, albeit obviously in a looser form. The apogee of the feudal monarchy in the thirteenth century affords a concrete manifestation of the ideas of power which Aquinas was translating into abstractions. The feudal monarch combined in himself two kinds of power: first, a theocratic power that he claimed by grace of God and that conferred upon him supreme authority, including authority over the laws; and secondly, a feudal power that was his by virtue of contract and that subjected his authority to the law of the contracts.[40] Now, it is easy to recognize in the first the political power of origins, and if we remember both that the power derivative from a contract is conditional upon fulfillment of the contract and that the feudal contract was a mixture of public and private obligations, then we may recognize in practical dress the generic notion of power that associates it with the fulfillment of a non-political, natural end. However ill-assorted, the fact was that they did coexist in the same kings and together constituted the power of the medieval kings. Nor should we forget that even when the prince's—or Emperor's—theocratic power was interpreted teleologically by the Papal party as the temporal sword within the Christian community, the theory that the secular political function subserved a religious end expressed a practice that made cooperation with the national Church and the preservation of a religio-moral order real conditions of princely power.

Such different strains of power could coexist in practice and collaborate in theory so long as regalian powers were additive rather than collective, so long as the distinction between public authority and private rights was tenuous in them, and so long as the ruler's role was to enforce the mélange of existing law. But as new needs and new possibilities evoked definite policies through new legislation, and as sovereigns increasingly outlined an identifiable sphere of political power against the congeries of private and ecclesiastical right-holders, the theoretical concord and practical toleration between the powers dissolved. In theory, where the implications of the process can be traced most clearly, the first break came in the wonted arena of medieval political doctrine—the Papal-Imperial conflict. The novelties introduced into this struggle during the fourteenth century by William of

[40] Ullmann, *Principles,* pp. 117–53.

Occam and Marsiglio of Padua rejected the medieval answer to the problem of power in its own terms and set up the problem that would be tackled during the sixteenth century in the terms of the sovereign territorial state. The form that the problem of power thus took for early modern history may be gleaned from the main points of this late medieval theorizing upon it. First, the determination of political power by its source was undermined by the twin steps of denying that the power of the Church was political and that the political power of the state was divinely instituted. Secondly, in reference to the political power of the state, the emphasis upon the primacy of command over reason in establishing the validity of the law through which power in the state was exercised undermined the *a priori* authoritative character of the rational natural law for civil law, thereby rendering political power measurable only by the freely chosen ends of the human community. Thirdly, the power of the secular ruler derived from the original power of the community—i.e., the "corporation of citizens"—as its "efficient cause"—but the final cause of both the derived and the original political power is "the good life as its end."[41] Finally, the communal end, which thereby defines political power, was presumably to be understood only in a "temporal and earthly" rather than an "eternal or celestial" way, but this effort to specify a distinctively political end for political power retained the traditional reference to ultimate moral and religious purposes for its validity: "the good life" of the state requires correctives not only of the "suffering" but of the "corruption" of man. Consequently the priesthood must be a part of this state and "the teaching of the divine laws and doctrines virtually a necessity" to it, since "the tranquillity of the community" depends on "the goodness of human actions, both private and civil."[42]

Thus, when rulers and intellectuals began, from the early sixteenth century, to define what was the nature of the power that they had inherited along with the claim of each territorial sovereign to be "emperor in his own realm," they were confronted with a situation in which the conflict of authorities was rendering dubious the claim to political power by divine legitimation at the same

[41] Marsiglio of Padua, quoted in Lewis, *Medieval Political Ideas*, I, 185, 188–89.
[42] *Ibid.*, I, 185–87.

time as the definition of political power in terms of its collective ends continued to be dubious by virtue of the extrapolitical ground of those ends.

It was in response to this situation that the two fundamental attitudes of Western man to power developed into the opposed processes whose variable relations run through modern history. For it was now that the exercise and idea of political power developed an end appropriate to itself and that the defenders of spiritual ends faced up to the antithetical political character of the means required to realize them. Thus was responsibility *to* power aligned against responsibility *by* power as alternative processes, each equipped with its own system of ends and means and, maddeningly, both claiming to constitute the responsibility *of* power. Machiavelli set up the model for the first of these systems, the religious reformers exemplified the second.

As a model-maker, Machiavelli may be viewed here not in himself but for his contribution to the modern assumptions about power. Whatever he meant to say, he had two permanent effects: first, he created the notion of political power as an autonomous process, with means and ends tailored to each other as distinctively political factors, and categorically divorced both from any non-political legitimacy of origins and from any non-political ground of purpose; secondly, the impression he left of an implicit illegitimacy of origins and an implicit immorality of ends—an impression partially the result of misunderstanding his radical plea for the independence of the political relationship and partially the result of his own undeniable ambiguities on these scores—created the problem of political power as an autonomous process, that is, the problem of the real as well as moral necessity of its relationship to extrapolitical origins and ends.

On the first count, the external structure of his thought itself articulates the development of political power into a relational world of its own to which obedience is due. If the monarchism of *The Prince* and the republicanism of *The Discourses* are taken to signify rules for the foundation and maintenance of states, as successive stages in their lives—and Machiavelli implied that they might so be taken[43]—then the ingredients of political power get crystallized out: *The Prince* treats the qualities of a political

[43] Niccolò Machiavelli, *The Prince* and *The Discourses* (New York, 1950), pp. 138–39.

power *ex nihilo,* that must establish its own legitimacy; *The Discourses* treats the civil vitality that preserves states in a world of flux, and sets forth the teleological definition of political power that turns the standards of *The Prince* into means toward this end. The measurement of political power by domestic order and external independence that is common to both stages is a function of the common political framework that attunes means to ends. The difference between the emphasis upon the monolithic authority of the ruler and the competitive energy of the citizens as the prime constituents of this order and independence measures the distinction between means and ends within the common political framework.

But here was precisely where ambiguity entered, indicating the presence in Machiavelli himself of the problem that his successors were to meet in his pattern of power. For at the initial terminal Machiavelli could not resist grounding the origins of political power in the moral depravity of man, and at the final terminal he remained fundamentally ambivalent on whether the end of political power was ultimately defined by the production of the order and independence of the republic through the civic virtues of the people or by the production of good and virtuous men, on the Roman model, through the good citizenship inculcated by the laws of an orderly and independent republic.[44] Thus here, at the very beginning of the modern political ethic of power, both of the problems that have plagued its subsequent history took their rise: the relationship of politics to ethics as a relationship of ends to ends and the osmosis of ethical qualities into the parallel process of political power.

The familiar division of social thought into the basic categories of "utopian" and "realist" sponsors Thomas More vis-à-vis Machiavelli as the modernizer of the ethical strand in the tradition of power.[45] Both the secular ethic of solidarity and the compatible political means of an authoritarian and expansionist governing power that equally characterize More's *Utopia* do seem to support this way of organizing the tradition. But the difficulties men have had in determining the intent of the *Utopia,* deliberately suspended as it is in a hypothetical void between More's practical statesmanship and his religious piety, indicates

[44] For this problem, see *ibid.,* pp. 118–20, 382–83, 530.
[45] Ritter, *Dämonie der Macht, passim.*

rather that, from the point of view of the problem of power at
least, it represents a mixed form of the tradition. For the modern
problem of ethical power in its purest sixteenth-century form we
must turn rather to the religious reformers of all denominations,
who perpetuated the tradition of a spiritual, non-political morality
but who now felt compelled to associate it with a political power
that had become independent of it. This pattern of power is
visible in all the major reformers, but its implications and attendant problems are most obvious, if not most representative, in
the extreme case of Luther, the most non-political of them all.

Luther's whole career was an object lesson in the dissolution
of the medieval integration which had measured political power
by its realization of a religio-moral end, in the recognition that
had now to be accorded to both independently, and in the new
tensile relations that had to be established between them. Neither
in his religiosity, nor in his ethic, nor in his politics, was Luther a
modern, but only in his relating of them. During his early reforming years down through the Diet of Worms in 1520 he retained the three categories in their late medieval connections.[46]
Concerned primarily with the awakening of faith that was the
transcendent end of earthly life and focusing on the reform of
the church whose visible aspect created the external conditions
for the spiritual workings of its invisible aspect, he measured
power simply by the realization of these conditions as the temporal incorporation of spiritual ends. The whole body of Christians
become capable of power by virtue of this end, for by ordination
"all . . . have like power" in matters of church, and "the first
man who is able should, as a faithful member of the whole
body, do what he can. . . ."[47] "The temporal power," which
is specially "ordained by God to punish evil-doers and protect
them that do well," is simply, by virtue of this temporal ordination, the most appropriate Christian member, since he need only
augment this original political power by the teleological increment
of reforms in church organization and moral reforms in the Christian community at large.[48] In other words, in the mixed realm of

[46] Hajo Holborn, *A History of Modern Germany: the Reformation*
(New York, 1959), pp. 126–44.

[47] "An Open Letter to the German Nobility," in Martin Luther, *Three
Treatises* (Muehlenberg, 1960), pp. 14, 21–24.

[48] *Ibid.,* pp. 17, 24.

clerical and moral reform, which is at once "spiritual and bodily," the original power of the temporal authorities becomes a functional power of the Christian community; whether this additional power is acquired or not depends only on whether the reforms are in fact consummated "by the temporal authorities or by a general council."[49]

But the condemnation at Worms and the subsequent political persecutions of Lutherans undermined Luther's assumption of the automatic connection between the temporal power divinely instituted to punish the disorderly and its service of a reformation of church and morals. In 1523 he was asserting "the right and power" of any true Christian congregation to judge doctrine, reform itself, and choose its own preachers, and he was limiting the power of the temporal authorities to "body, property, and what is external on the earth."[50] But very soon the sectarian consequences of the congregational principle and the heretical doctrines of popular movements were forcing Luther back, however reluctantly, to reliance upon the established temporal powers for ecclesiastical functions. From the new relationship he was forced to accept between the spiritual goal, which remained primary, and the political power, which was his only means for its social realization, came the modern dilemma of moral power. For Luther came both to distrust the Christian vocation of the temporal authorities and to recognize their indispensable necessity for the organization of the true Christian church.[51]

Luther's dilemma became so fundamental for modern history because the circumstances merely brought to the surface countervailing tendencies that were constant within Luther and have been paradigmatic for crusading idealists ever since. The drive for spiritual purity that led Luther to emphasize the gulf between God's two realms—the realm of spirit whose principle was freedom and the realm of the world whose principles were order, compulsion, and power—was balanced by the equally urgent drive for spiritual universality that led him to bridge the two

[49] *Ibid.*, p. 45.

[50] *"Dass eine christliche Versammlung oder Gemeine Recht und Macht haben, alle Lehre zu beurteilen, etc.,"* in Martin Luther, *Ausgewaehlte Werke* (3rd ed., Munich, 1962), III, 94–100; *"Von weltlicher Obrigkeit, etc.,"* in *ibid.*, V, 25.

[51] Paul Althaus, *Die Ethik Martin Luthers* (Gütersloh, 1965), pp. 151–58.

realms in the striving for the widest possible diffusion of spirit.[52] But once spirit was put abroad in the world, its way had to be cleared through the world and its purity protected from the world by the worldly authority that alone had the power to perform these functions. Thus the church, which was the vehicle of the spirit in the world, became inevitably and ambiguously engaged with the temporal power, which was the vehicle of worldly compulsion upon the path of the spirit.

Luther could have resolved this encounter simply, as Calvinist and Catholic Monarchomachs were to do later, by asserting that the establishment and defense of the true church defined the possession and exercise of political power, and Luther did in fact vary somewhat the ecclesiastical powers of the prince in accordance with his religious orthodoxy. But what makes Luther so notable a representative of the modern dilemma of power was precisely his continued acknowledgment that the temporal power was as such independent of the spiritual end it was its primary duty to serve. However joined in function, temporal power and spiritual end originated in two different worlds and were qualitatively contrary. He sought to accommodate them by subtle distinctions. By having recourse to the exceptional powers permitted by emergencies, by deducing the disorderly civil consequences of heresy, and by distinguishing the duties of "love" freely assumed by the prince as the most honorable Christian in the community from the jurisdiction of his temporal office, he sought to justify the coercive power of the prince in matters of clerical organization, discipline, and doctrine.[53] But Luther's most telling testimonial to the new political context of spiritual power lay neither in his vacillations nor in his accommodations— it lay rather in his ultimate paralysis. He was profoundly torn between his commitment to a political power that could be a power only by saving his church and his commitment to a political power that could save his church only by retaining its earthly independence of it. So profound was his dilemma that he, who had denied the power of Papacy and Empire because he

[52] For a theological view of this relationship, see Heinrich Bornkamm, *Luthers Lehre von den zwei Reichen im Zusammenhang seiner Theologie* (Gütersloh, 1960), *passim*.

[53] *"Unterricht der Visitatoren an die Pfarrherrn im Kurfürstentum zu Sachsen,"* in Luther, *Ausgewaehlte Werke.* III. 101-4.

could do no other, relinquished to the discretion of the instrumental temporal power the choices that he could not make for himself. When the Saxon Elector's government broke through Luther's fine distinctions to establish the doctrine and organization of the Lutheran church under the authority of the temporal power, he bowed and accepted the result.[54] And when, on the other side of the relationship, the German Protestant estates prepared to resist the divinely appointed Emperor in the name of the Lutheran faith, Luther reluctantly accepted this as well.[55]

In this guise there appeared on the modern scene the concept of a political power that was inherently antithetical and therefore infinitely responsible to the ideal that gave it meaning.

From the two kinds of power symbolized by Machiavelli and Luther—from the political power that developed its own end with borrowed values and from the spiritual power that borrowed its own means from politics—but one step remained to produce the composite structure of power that has dominated our history for the past two momentous centuries. The consolidation of the sovereign states in practice and the crystallization of political science in theory during the seventeenth and eighteenth centuries merged the two types into an apparently single phenomenon, in which the former external relations have assumed the shape of internal qualities of power. But this unified idea of power exhibited the trace of its dual constitution in the iridescence that has let the sources, the ends, and the relations of the sources to the ends of power assume different hues according to the angle from which they are viewed. When the Machiavellian political categories of order and independence were expanded by the absorption of traditional religious, moral, and legal norms into the more faceted and ambiguous categories of the public interest and the general welfare, they could be and were alternatively seen as political ends morally justifying their inherently compatible political means, or as ethical ends socially determining their inherently antithetical political means. Again, when the divine source of traditional political power was merged into the sacred constituent force of consent, it could be and was seen alternatively as a political means indissolubly integrated with the

[54] Holborn, *History of Germany: Reformation*, pp. 186–87.
[55] Pierre Mesnard, *L'Essor de la philosophie politique au XVIᵉ siècle* (Paris, 1952), pp. 227–28.

political ends that were the objects of the consent or as an arbitrary product of free will infinitely separated from the ends it should serve. In practice as in theory, these two aspects of the merger were articulated into two successive stages.

In practice the welding of utilitarian and moral ends into extended political purpose was most exemplary in the achievement of the great French state-builders of the seventeenth century. The "state" that Richelieu and Louis XIV carved out as the exclusive arena for the sovereign's absolute power was more than a purely political unit. It extended the meaning of "political" from its earlier punitive and servicing connotation by adding the dimension of those powers that clerical and social corporations had exercised in the assertion and defense of their religious, ethical, and private rights. Thus the "reason" or "interest of state" that the French statesmen now set up as the end of their sovereign powers they took to include the happiness and perfection of their subjects. Correspondingly, the traditional norms of divine, natural, and fundamental law became not limitations upon but definitions of their power.

The second practical stage in the convergence of the two traditions of power set in toward the end of the seventeenth century, when disputes about the porous ends of the state raised challenges to the legitimacy of the political power that was deemed to have overpoliticized these ends. In their different ways, both constitutionalists on the British model and "enlightened despots" on the model of the Prussian Frederick the Great acted to merge the Machiavellian and religious strains of political origins. They postulated the idea of consent as the source of political power, in a form that would both relate it to the ends of the state as the objects of the consent and retain the element of arbitrary and prescriptive will as a source of power sufficiently independent of its ends to confer stability on the power and autonomy on the ends. Perhaps the most dramatic example of this process was the Prussian "philosopher-king," who, torn between his love of power and his respect for cultural freedom, recast the origins of political authority into a form appropriate to its delimited function.[56] He replaced divine right with the right of irrevocable consent as the basis of a political power that

[56] Hajo Holborn, *A History of Modern Germany: 1648–1840* (New York, 1964), pp. 240–42.

would be authorized to exercise absolute authority within a definite area of secular activity and would be restrained from areas of culture extraneous to popular consent.

But the most revealing examples of the two stages were the theories of Spinoza and Rousseau, the two philosophers most unafraid to carry the implications of their respective traditions to their logical conclusions. Spinoza is notorious for having done precisely that to Machiavelli. Since, he declared, in nature "her right is co-extensive with her power" and therefore "every individual has the sovereign right to do all that he can," in a democracy—which Spinoza thought the most natural and the best form of government—"each individual hands over the whole of his power to the body politic," which "will then possess sovereign natural right over all things; that is, it will have sole and unquestioned dominion."[57] In appearance, this is the most categorical approval of naked political power ever penned; in actuality it is simply the most faithful translation of as much of moral reason as can be squeezed into political terms. For this declaration of his *Theologico-Political Treatise* must be read against the background of his *Ethics,* where Spinoza integrates all existence in God: "all things are conditioned to exist and operate in a particular manner by the necessity of the divine nature."[58] When, therefore, Spinoza indicated that government dominated as far as its power extended, this was not merely a description of political mechanics but an application to politics of the *a priori* cosmic order governing all things. On the basis of this assumption it made sense when Spinoza exalted the state as the embodiment of reason, since the state connected men and reason recognized the connection of things, and when he demanded unconditional obedience, since the dictates of reason are the basis of virtue.[59] But what is crucial for our purpose is this: when Spinoza chose to put the ethical basis of the state in terms of its power, the moral quality he built into his political end determined the inherent limits of politics in the ethical life.

What Spinoza, starting from mechanism, did for the ends of political power, Rousseau, starting from the ethical end, did for

[57] *A Theologico-Political Treatise,* in *The Chief Works of Benedict de Spinoza* (New York, 1951), I, 200–6.
[58] *The Ethics,* in *ibid.,* II, 68.
[59] *Ibid.,* II, 204–5.

its origins. Starting from the ideal of man's harmony with himself through self-fulfillment, Rousseau condemned existing societies, with their accidental origins and arbitrary forms, and constructed a hypothetical scheme of nature and society in which he sought to demonstrate that the origin of political power was a moral necessity. Envisioned in a state of nature, man knows neither morality, nor association, nor power; he knows only immediate needs and instincts, and for the rest has only potentialities that are unrealizable in that state.[60] The power relationship among men is born with the act of political association and remains forever tied to it. This power is simple, inalienable, indivisible, and total, precisely because it is a product of the infinitely reciprocal relations subsisting inimitably among all the members of the original association, and it is this origin that makes it possible for the power of the general will to realize the moral and rational potentialities of man. Thus Rousseau attached the ethical connotation to the very source of political power thereby, and, in the effort to concoct an instrument of power that would be appropriate to its transcendent end, he opened the way for a transfer of loyalty from the end to the instrument itself.

The early modern convergence of the two traditional strands set the stage for the variety of attitudes toward power since the eighteenth century. The apparently simple fact of sovereignty to which men have reacted so passionately in such contradictory ways is actually a construct whose internal accommodations mask the duality of its constituents. Beginning from the indubitable fact of political power, men as different as Bismarck and Chamberlain could turn it into an end in itself because they saw it as a process with its own political ends to which the responsible statesman would subordinate outlying social and moral purposes. Beginning from the primacy of ethical and cultural values, men like Schiller and Burckhardt would see in the same fact of political power a neutral instrument whose moralization reversed the order of means and ends and spread corruption in its wake. But most characteristic of our times have been the dual personalities—the Germany forty-eighters, Ebert, Rathenau—who have split themselves asunder trimming their ideals to fulfill their responsibility to

[60] Robert Derathé, *Jean-Jacques Rousseau et la science politique de son temps* (Paris, 1950), pp. 131–51.

the very political power they were responsibly directing toward the fulfillment of these ideals.

And when the politicians and the intellectuals have finally made their decisions, they must then pass under the equally wall-eyed judgment of us, the observers, who call them opportunist when they shift from one mode of responsibility to the other upon different occasions, visionary when they despair of the power of the political mechanism to serve a transcendent goal we do not like, and unprincipled when they define power in terms of the attainable and so scale down a transcendent end that we do like. Given this overlay of simplistic observation upon a complex reality, the problem of power is a problem of knowledge before it is a problem of judgment. We must know the kind of power being exercised before we can judge whether it is exercised for good or for ill.

Chapter 2

MACHIAVELLI: THE ART OF POLITICS AND THE PARADOX OF POWER

Hanna H. Gray

Inquiry into Machiavelli's conception of the responsibility of power has focused sometimes on his considered ideas as to the accountability, obligation, and purpose of political strength and action, sometimes on the motives that inspired his writing and that underlay its prescriptions for statesmen and political institutions. Some have concentrated on Machiavelli's stated views as to the ends sought by politics, the politician, and the state; others on the implications or logical consequences that arise out of his approach and method. That Machiavelli neither expounded nor intended to provide a classically integrated system of political philosophy is clear enough. That the consequences of his thinking can be variously developed, and developed in ways he might never have foreseen or acknowledged, there can be no doubt. These truths only deepen the mysteries that remain. To what and for what was power responsible in Machiavelli's eyes? Is that query in fact susceptible to positive answers? Do power and responsibility exist in any necessary relation to one another for Machiavelli, or is it precisely his point that this question misleads, that it even contradicts his teaching? And why did Machiavelli's writing not give final and explicit resolution to these issues, so crucial to our own understanding of Machiavelli and of his historical influence?[1]

[1] All citations to *The Prince* and the *Discourses* are to Niccolò Machiavelli, *Il Principe e Discorsi sopra la prima deca di Tito Livio* (*Opere,* Vol. I), ed. Sergio Bertelli and with an introduction by Giuliano Procacci (Milan, Feltrinelli, 1960). The translations are mine. The literature on Machiavelli is large and often controversial. Two excellent and selective sources for it may be found in the critical bibliographical essay, "Machiavelli," by Felix Gilbert in his book *Machiavelli and Guicciardini. Politics and History in Sixteenth-Century Florence* (Princeton, 1965), pp. 316–30,

In its most particular sense, "responsibility" may be taken to mean the accountability of those in power, their answerability for a power or series of powers that they hold or exercise in trust. In a second limited connotation, it could refer to the immediate aim or duty to whose fulfillment power is to be directed; in this case, however extraordinary the power and overriding the responsibility, neither might be generalized or conceived as permanent. In a larger sense, "responsibility" might refer to the essential purpose or cause that power, or the man possessed of power, serves. In

and in the bibliographical notes contained in the Bertelli edition as well as in the subsequent volumes of the *Opere* published by Feltrinelli and which include the *Lettere* (Vol. VI), the *Arte della Guerra* (Vol. II), and the *Istorie Fiorentine* (Vol. VII). Eric W. Cochrane, "Machiavelli: 1940–1960" (*Journal of Modern History*, XXXIII, 1961, 113–36), gives a comprehensive survey of recent scholarship. The following works, all of which have in varying ways contributed to the present interpretation, are those which in my judgment have the greatest interest and the most stimulating significance for the discussion of the problem of power in Machiavelli: Rudolf von Albertini, *Das florentinische Staatsbewusstsein im Übergang von der Republik zum Prinzipat* (Bern, 1955); Giorgio Cadoni, "*Libertà, repubblica e governo misto in Machiavelli*" (*Rivista Internazionale di Filosofia del Diritto*, XXXIX, 1962, 462–84); Ernst Cassirer, *The Myth of the State* (New Haven, 1946), pp. 116–62; Federico Chabod, *Machiavelli and the Renaissance* (London, 1958), and especially pp. 126–48 on "Machiavelli's Method and Style"; Fredi Chiappelli, *Studi sul linguaggio del Machiavelli* (Florence, 1952); Francesco Ercole, *La politica di Machiavelli* (Rome, 1926); Felix Gilbert, *Machiavelli and Guicciardini*, together with the series of articles which have been translated and published as *Niccolò Machiavelli e la vita culturale del suo tempo* (Bologna, 1964); J. H. Hexter, "*Il Principe* and *lo stato*" (*Studies in the Renaissance*, IV, 1957, 113–38); Lauri Huovinen, *Das Bild vom Menschen im politischen Denken Niccolò Machiavellis* (Helsinki, 1951); Judith Janoska-Bendl, "Niccolò Machiavelli: Politik ohne Ideologie" (*Archiv für Kulturgeschichte*, XL, 1958, 315–45); E. W. Mayer, *Machiavellis Geschichtsauffassung und sein Begriff virtù* (Munich and Berlin, 1912); Friedrich Mehmel, "*Machiavelli und die Antike*" (*Antike und Abendland*, III, 1948, 152–86); Friedrich Meinecke, *Die Idee der Staatsräson in der neueren Geschichte*, ed. W. Hofer (Munich, 1960), pp. 29–56; Augustin Renaudet, *Machiavel* (Paris, 1952); V. Santangelo, "Il concetto di storia in Niccolò Machiavelli" (*Giornale Italiano di Filologia*, XV, 1962, 259–69); the following fundamental studies by Gennaro Sasso: *Niccolò Machiavelli. Storia del suo pensiero politico* (Naples, 1958), "Sul VII capitolo del *Principe*" (*Rivista Storica Italiana*, XLIV, 1952, 177–207), "*Machiavelli e la teoria dell' anacyclosis*" (*Rivista Storica Italiana*, LXX, 1958, 333–75), "*Polibio e Machiavelli: costituzione, potenza, conquista*" (*Giornale Critico della Filosofia Italiana*, XL, 1961, 51–86); J. H. Whitfield, *Machiavelli* (Oxford, 1947), "On Machiavelli's Use of *Ordini*" (*Italian Studies*, X, 1955, 19–39).

this instance, there might well exist a plurality of ends or results for which he is held responsible and by which his individual actions or total performance would be measured. In a still more general sense, the question of the "responsibility of power" goes to the issue of the end, the purpose, the ultimate obligation that are to be served by and that finally define the legitimacy or essence of organized society or of the state.

Insofar as "power" connotes compulsion or the capacity to compel, force and its exploitation, "responsibility" suggests a control, whether moral or legal, that rationalizes and regulates what might otherwise be irrational or non-rational, immoral or amoral, by specifying the conditions under which and the goals for which power may be rightfully employed. Further, such goals are held to lie outside the individuals or institutions in which power is embodied, having to do with the good or benefit or claims of some larger whole or group or ideal. Necessarily, then, the question of the responsibility of power includes those of the relation between might and right, politics and ethics, of the role of political power in the sphere of public morality and of its relation to other realms—the private, the cultural; possibly the natural and perhaps the transcendent.

Machiavelli, in his major political works, scarcely confronted any of this range of questions in a central or direct form. Yet the questions he did ask, and the solutions he proposed to them, made the problem of the responsibility of power singularly acute, not only as one to be argued by his successors, but also as one to be treated in the interpretation of Machiavelli's thought as such. Machiavelli did, of course, touch on a number of the relevant issues, and others he brought at least clearly into the open. His failure to pose certain questions need not imply that he was always indifferent to them or that he lacked answers. But some process of inference and deduction must always mediate. To paraphrase Machiavelli will not reveal what he thought, or even what he did not think, about the responsibility of power. To arrange together those passages from his works that might appear to bear on the problem is frequently to misread a theorist who insisted that all general statements made sense only in conjunction with the concrete analysis and example that lent them force and validation.

The results that Machiavelli's interpreters have reached owe
their variety in part to their different starting points, in part to
quite different understandings of what is implied by the "responsibility of power." Differing judgments of the relationship
The Prince and the *Discourses* bear to one another create another
difficulty, for any conclusion may well depend on the weight
assigned to each, the degree to which the one is used in explicating
the other, and the dominant themes that are then stressed in
Machiavelli's view of political power and its uses.

We have, then, Machiavelli the Machiavellian, Machiavelli the
absolutist, Machiavelli the teacher of tyranny and the satirical
enemy of despotism, Machiavelli the idealistic or popular or
constitutional republican, Machiavelli the Italian or Florentine
patriot, Machiavelli the impassioned reformer and the detached
scientist, Machiavelli the typical Renaissance thinker and the
post-Renaissance man, Machiavelli the moralist, the amoralist, and
the immoralist, Machiavelli the first theorist of *raison d'état,*
Machiavelli the technician of personal power, Machiavelli the pessimist, and Machiavelli the optimist. The most interesting Machiavelli we have is no one of these things but a complex figure
placed against the background of his time, culture, and experience,
primarily an interpreter of and preacher to his age and situation,
part innovator and part traditionalist, part humanist and part anti-
humanist. Together, all these Machiavellis represent the first distinctively modern political thinker. All raised—and for some,
they gave unequivocal answers to—the fundamental questions of
the responsibility of power as these came to be argued by his
successors to our day. Separately, these Machiavellis hold conflicting theories as to the nature and the responsibilities of power.

Machiavelli's political and historical writings describe a world
that is wholly political. This of course includes, indeed em-
phasizes, the military. As history, in its written representation,
consisted for Machiavelli in the analytic narrative of politics and
warfare, so history was composed in actuality of politics and
warfare, indissolubly linked. The struggle for power, and the
conditions that shaped it, was not a single aspect of reality, but
its essence. The "real" truth that Machiavelli sought to expose
and to make the basis for effective action in the historical world
had its origin in no external frame of reference. It was neither

sustained nor limited by any independent criterion of value internal to his world.

The conquest and maintenance of power, whether by an individual like the prince or by a collective individual like the *respublica romana:* such was the organizing theme of Machiavelli's writings. Its acquisition, preservation, and extension in a world where politics was all appeared to need no justification. The question of responsibility as accountability seemed not to require asking or answering. In a particular sense, that was not entirely so; within the constitution, for example, of the Roman Republic a magistrate who held certain powers was answerable for the functions he performed. Machiavelli of course took note of that fact, but his account of the Republic was not directed toward seeing in such forms of responsibility the lessons of power. It can be argued, too, that Machiavelli's intention in *The Prince* was to achieve a particular purpose at a time of extraordinary crisis and that the power of the new prince, freed from so many traditional sanctions, was to be exercised in the immediate interest of a higher good or necessity, whether that be interpreted as the regeneration of a decadent people, the expulsion of the foreigner from Italian soil, or the creation of a new and viable state on the Italian peninsula. But it cannot be argued that the *motive* as such identifies the considered end or responsibility of power for Machiavelli more generally. The policies to be adopted by his new prince, while sometimes indicated to be especially well suited to critical times and corrupt societies, are in no way restricted to a given time or place, and it is princely power, not the obligations of one prince, whose possibilities Machiavelli is exploring.

The successful achievement and retention of power by the prince appear self-sufficient activities in Machiavelli, despite his final plea to employ that power in the causes of victory against the invader and of triumph over oppression and decay. The imperial and domestic power of the Roman Republic at its height, enduring beyond the span of other commonwealths, shining in health as the reverse image of diseased societies, immortalized by an exemplary greatness, demanded no judgment that lay outside its own accomplishment of an extensive and durable power. It was irrelevant to demonstrate, as others might, that this power had been used in the service of some higher value—

for example, to create or disseminate a kind of civilization, to bring peace and justice, to make possible the flowering of reason or the potentialities of man, to realize the precepts of natural law and right, to bring about the common good. Nor did Machiavelli invoke the power of Rome as basis for an exclusive commitment to republicanism as the single form of political organization in which alone there existed the capacity for attending to and realizing the values for whose sake society existed. In the Rome of Machiavelli's analysis, power had been shared among contending classes through the mixed constitution, at times delivered up to a single legislator, fixed and enlarged through conquest. Power had been embodied in both laws and men. It had not merely compelled obedience or held men in thrall or been exploited for special interests; it had also created, stimulated, and enforced the growth of certain energies and qualities, considered desirable, in the citizens of Rome and in the body politic. But none of these facts can define the responsibility of power for the men who possessed it, the institutions that embodied it, or the empire that maintained it. These powers, and their effects, served the power of Rome. Similarly, *The Prince* is neither an argument for monarchy nor a statement about the "legitimate" uses of royal power. Machiavelli's preference for republics was clear, but he applied the same standards both to princely power in its diverse forms and to those forms of power that had existed and could be conceived to exist under republican regimes.

We cannot, then, assert that Machiavelli was primarily interested in the responsibility of power in its particular senses. To identify his immediate hopes with his ultimate conception of the ends of power is to see that he cared passionately about the reformation and salvation of the Italian political system and that he believed its rescue an aim that power might still effect; it does not tell us what forms of accountability power ordinarily conveys for him. That Machiavelli conceived Rome's rule as having satisfied a common good does not make this the measure of the exercise of her power, and consequently of power in general. That the benefits of security accrue to the citizens of his good principality and his ideal republic alike may suggest that power was to be judged by that intent, but Machiavelli never stated this as his principal concern. On the contrary, he tended to say that security fortifies the power that protects it and must be modified according to its needs; the security of power itself, in time and in importance, preceded all else.

If it is the responsibility of those who rule to use their power so as to maintain the health and grandeur of the political community or to secure their own continued strength and capacity for action, then it might appear either that power is a responsible agent in realizing the interests of the state or that it is essentially irresponsible. In the first instance, we may ask whether there is some superior or rational standard that regulates the interest and defines the purpose of the state and thus the conduct of power; in the latter, whether the power that looks only to itself claims justification by success and might alone.

For Machiavelli, the "interests of the state" and the "interests of those who hold political power" are not simply separate or separable. The term *"stato,"* which he used so frequently, has many different senses, the most common of which convey the connotations of "the effective apparatus of political power," "the organized political community," and "government."[2] Machiavelli could, of course, have had the conception, without defining the term, of "the State" in its full range of modern meanings, but the objectified and abstracted being with an existence apart from the individuals who are attached to it and from the institutions that carry out its political functions never makes its full appearance in Machiavelli. Nor is there in Machiavelli's thought an entire division between person and office. In *The Prince,* for obvious reasons, he tends naturally to equate personal power with that of the "State." In the *Discourses,* with their emphasis on law and political participation, that tendency remains, however modified, not only because power needs frequently to be reinvested in the reformer-legislator, but also because the Roman "state" represents a collective individual and a collective power. Power cannot, then, be something simply attributed and subordinated to the State. But insofar as the political community and its institutions retain historical vitality and survive to maintain a life beyond that of the individuals who have ruled them, an im-

[2] For discussion of the meaning attached to the word *"stato"* in Machiavelli, see Ercole, *La Politica,* Chiappelli, *Studi,* pp. 59 *sqq.,* Hexter, *"Il Principe* and *lo stato",* and in particular, Chabod, *Machiavelli and the Renaissance,* pp. 116–17, Whitfield, *Machiavelli,* p. 93, and Gilbert, *Machiavelli and Guicciardini,* pp. 177–78, 328–30.

portant distinction emerges between prince and the organized principality and still more between the leaders of the republic and the *respublica romana*.

If we accept these modifications of Machiavelli's understanding of the State and adopt that term in his own more usual senses and in the contexts of their use, we can go on to ask whether the ends of the state, the interests of the state, or the reason of state can define the responsibility of power in Machiavelli's view.

The legitimacy of the state and hence of the power it wields lay outside Machiavelli's concern. He did not proceed from an investigation or hypothesis of the origin of society in order to decide its rightful ends. He did not make an original purpose or justification the measure of existing societies, nor did he declare the conditions under which the social bonds might be presumed to be dissolved. Machiavelli did not raise the problems, so much discussed in his own day, of the right of resistance, of the mutual rights and duties of subjects and rulers, of the hierarchy of claims attached to different groups and institutions in a society, of the validity of law, of the relation between positive law and the normative commands of conscience or of natural law. He discussed instead the growth and adaptability of existing states, the nature and effects of conspiracy and revolution, the relation of ruler to ruled, the struggle of interest and faction represented by contending political classes, the capacity of law to exact obedience, to direct citizens, and to project power, the evolution of laws to fit the changing requirements of specified types of political society.

In short, Machiavelli took organized society to be a given fact of human history. States indeed had "founders" who gave them their fundamental shape and enabled them to survive, and the principles of such founders had often to be reasserted and extended later. These founders, in Machiavelli's analysis, were intensely rational men with a clarity of vision and design, with political ability and constructive intelligence. But their immediate purposes and provisions might differ widely. They could come to power by means that were superficially "legal" or "illegal," and the states they founded were not "legitimized" by providence, natural right, or pre-existent ideals of public welfare.

In the *Discourses* Machiavelli did speak twice about the earliest

beginnings of social life and government.[3] The first passage explains that *"città,"* or city states, may be founded either by
natives or by foreigners, and that in the first instance, the *città*
comes into being as people find themselves unable, when dispersed, to live securely and so come together (sometimes of
their own accord, sometimes by the authority of some one man)
to a single place where they can live more conveniently and
defend themselves more easily. The second passage occurs in
the course of Machiavelli's consideration of the initial step in
the cycle of governments and constitutions. It represents a fairly
free adaptation and condensation of Polybius, who is Machiavelli's
major source for the whole of the larger discussion. What it
omits from Polybius' account is as revealing as what it includes.
Machiavelli writes as follows:

> Chance has given birth to these different kinds of government
> amongst men; for at the beginning of the world the inhabitants
> were in number, and lived for a time dispersed, like beasts. As
> the human race increased, and in order to be able better to defend
> themselves, they began to respect among themselves the man who
> was strongest and of greatest courage, and they made him, so to
> speak, their head and obeyed him. From this arose the knowledge
> of the good and the honest as distinct from the bad and the
> vicious; for seeing a man injure his benefactor aroused at once
> two sentiments, that of hatred and that of compassion, among
> men. They blamed the ingrate and honored those who showed
> themselves grateful, and thinking that they in turn might suffer
> the same wrongs, to prevent similar evils, they set to work to make
> laws and to ordain punishments for those who contravened them.
> From this came the knowledge of justice.

In Polybius' account, the men who lived like "beasts" were
like them, too, in their instinctive herding together and in their
subjection to a despotic rule of the strongest rather than to a rule
of reason. But men were distinguished from beasts by the
faculty of reason. From the state of nature they could proceed
to form family ties and then to social relation among themselves.
Next there arose the idea of kingship and the notions of duty,
morality, and justice. Genuine kingship, and by implication, genuine society, were made possible by substituting reason for vio-

---

[3] The first passage is in *Discorsi,* I, i; the second in I, ii.

lence and justice for fear. Royal power rested on men's reasoned conviction of its utility.[4]

In Machiavelli's narrative government brings about the recognition of "good" and "bad" and of justice. Both spring from the needs of self-defense, as does the initial act of forming society. This picture of the origins of government does not make it rest on a fundamental act of consent or contract; the coming together is almost instinctive or is stimulated by a strong leader. The agreement to live together creates no binding obligation, implies no lasting commitment on the part of the rulers, and assumes no fixed limitations on the power they may exercise. There is no model of family to precede and suggest a metaphor for the duties of the political community, no norm of "reason" to define the basis on which power over others ought to rest. It is not the moral order that gives birth to society and for whose sake power exists. Men in society come to know or to believe in a moral order, and while this may be good, it is not stated to be *the* good of society, nor is power limited to its expression and confined within its precepts. Justice, the product of mutual need, of vicarious fear and sympathy, is rendered through law. Law is in turn the product of power, and the administration of justice, not the realization of inherent rights or of pre-existent Justice, one of its results.

When Machiavelli goes on to describe how kingship deteriorates into tyranny and the consequent fall of tyranny, he does not argue that tyranny no longer has a right to power or that it has failed to serve the purposes of reason and the higher good. Tyranny collapses because it makes enemies, arouses contempt and terror, forces the occasion for conspiracy. Inevitably it will be overthrown by aristocracy. Machiavelli did not on the whole regard the tyrant, especially the unsuccessful one, as an attractive figure; he did not approve very highly of tyranny. But the tyrant's power has an equal claim to exist and to prevail. The tyrant may be condemned; he is not on that account sentenced, as though he had failed his trust, to deposition.

It would be easy to conclude that Machiavelli believed that power served only its own interests and those of the "state" or that he was in fact presenting in fundamental outline the doctrine

[4] Polybius, *Histories*, VI, 5–6.

of reason of state. For power produces results conceived as beneficial without their "good" prescribing the nature or responsibility of power. Hence the "good" must rest within the world of power itself. Further, Machiavelli discarded all those traditional sanctions through which the means employed by power could be judged by their ethical content as well as by their fulfillment of a superior end. In consequence, two possibilities may be argued: the first, that Machiavelli was making an absolute division between politics and morality, restricting the teaching of the former to the lessons of power itself; the second, that he was preaching a new political gospel in which the ultimately "moral" end consisted in the right of the state, the properly "moral" means in the necessity of state. If it be objected that it is scarcely possible to define "reason of state" apart from a fully "modern" understanding of the state, the question can be rephrased and so modified in terms of Machiavelli's notions of the possession of power, the government and apparatus of power in political society, or the historical Roman *respublica*. Any one of these, the first most clearly in *The Prince,* the last in the *Discourses,* the second in the context of either work, might be taken to be in Machiavelli's universe the version of what the state represents in ours.

In *The Prince* and in the *Discourses* Machiavelli set out to dispute and to extinguish what he thought were the common and fixed clichés of political thinking and their fatally misleading consequences for political action. The actual, the effective truth, the truth taught and confirmed by history and experience—the two were identical—had lain obscured in ignorance, disdained at the cost of ruin and impotence. True knowledge and programs of effective action required the exploration and acknowledgment of politics in the world as it actually was, not as it ought or might be imagined to be. History, the sphere of politics as it had been and would continue to be in reality, became the major source for theory, for policy, and for successful political action; and history, too, had not been read or approached in the right way, nor had its lessons been understood for what they were.

When Machiavelli spoke of the folly of those who had tried to teach rulers their craft by setting before them perfect images of republics and principalities that had never been seen or known to exist in reality, his protest was not against the method of creating ideal types which could stand as concrete models for

assimilation and imitation, but against their lack of relevance to
or derivation from "reality" as he conceived it.[5] When he speaks
of the failure of his contemporaries to study ancient history and
to draw from it an art of politics, his words strike us, on their
surface, oddly, for surely many humanists had believed they were
doing just that. But Machiavelli's point was that they had not
done so in fact, for in addition to lacking system, they had
simply not understood what history, and thus reality, were in essence about.[6] Machiavelli himself constructed ideal models: in
The Prince, of types of princely power and action and of the
figure of the Prince; in the *Discourses,* of the mixed republic, its
power and its heroes. That Machiavelli may have "idealized"
the new prince by rewriting the career of Cesare Borgia and
endowing him with capacities of foresight and calculation he may
never have possessed, or that he "idealized" Rome and her great
men to an even greater degree, makes him no less an anti-
idealist in the sense that he meant when he dismissed illusory
utopias and ethical codes in favor of the *verità effettuale.* His
hopes for political salvation or regeneration in his own time
show only that anti-idealists need not always be very realistic.

The real truth, according to Machiavelli, is that traditional
ethics afford no guide to the acquisition, use, or maintenance
of power; the political art that seeks to control and to exploit
power must seek its precepts elsewhere. This is so because men
in general are, or at the very least must always be assumed to
be, vicious, dominated by selfish interest. It is so also because
the means to the effective exercise and securing of power must
be constantly adapted, and as economically as possible, to those
ends; such means are often inconsistent with morality in its
common vocabulary, often incapable of achieving such ends if
confined to the limits of this morality, and sometimes even more
"moral" in their consequences. It is so because history has
proved it to be so beyond any doubt; the exemplary achievements
of the past are its sufficient demonstration.

But if traditional morality offers no absolute standard, neither
does its opposite; Machiavelli pointed out that "immoral" means
might be equally self-defeating, sometimes by virtue of their
very immorality. Political judgment consisted in the choice of

[5] See especially *Principe,* Chapter XV.
[6] See especially *Discorsi,* I, Proemio.

those means most appropriate to the realization of a given political purpose in the light of all the forces, circumstances, and possibilities that obtained, the conflicting interests that might be at work, the consequences and new situations that might result, the capacities at one's disposal, the characters of those involved, and the ultimate effects to be expected for one's own position of power. One must, clearly, avoid ruin and any diminution of power; one must try to make that power more secure by using it well. None of this is possible without insight into the fundamental character and needs of the political world and its inhabitants.

The political world is one of conflict that, however changing its superficial forms, can never be quieted. It is a world in which competing interests try continually to grasp its privileges and riches and in which the struggle for power is dominant. Machiavelli organized the competition of interest around two classes, which he believed were found in all societies as two major political interest blocs, the nobles and the people. Uncontained, their strife became a destructive warfare between factions laying claim to full possession of the state. In healthy societies, their strife could be kept within bounds and channeled so that the tensions and energies released vigor into their life and institutions. Rome stood as the prime example of this second possibility. Her mixed constitution was the visible expression of the constructive triumph the political struggle might produce. Under no conditions, however, could these conflicts be brought to static resolution. To control them or to find some equilibrium was simply to harness their potentially dangerous effects, and the effort to do so had to be unremitting.

For Machiavelli, the constant tension of interests within the state had its parallel in the relations among states. Princes and republics naturally acted toward the outside world in such a way as to serve their own interest. Their interest had to do not only with extending territory, gaining rule over others, and defending themselves from attack or the threat of attack, but also with their internal situations of power. Rome's expansion came out of internal needs as well as external ambitions, and her expansion in turn created new possibilities and problems for her internal life. So, too, Machiavelli teaches the prince to see and to act on the interconnection that exists between his maintenance of power at home and his conquest of power abroad, between good laws and good arms.

The identification of self-interest with that of the larger whole is never complete, although it is sometimes close, as in Machiavelli's picture of the early Roman Republic. There is no final aggregation of competing interests whose sum is that of the princely government or of the *respublica*. Individuals and groups may be bent to the will of power; the law may educate or constrain them to serve some more general purpose. But interest remains just that. The interest of power lies in self-perpetuation. The interests of power remain particular ones, subject to redefinition in the light of changing circumstances.

Machiavelli conceived of politics as art in several senses. His radical separation of power from ethics seemed to give politics a sphere of its own with laws of its own. That politics was to be derived from, and its proper activities expressed through, history, through reality as it was, made it an art or technique for the attainment and preservation of power. As the art of rhetoric sought to persuade and not necessarily to specify the ends of persuasion, that of medicine to heal and not to judge the significance of human life, so the art of politics was directed toward power without needing to justify that goal further. Machiavelli's idea of an art of politics conformed to an important classical meaning of "art": he set out to discover and to codify the principles that underlay actual practice, not to theorize about practice from abstract premises. His "ideal" state represented an analytic model of a state that had in fact existed. As the ancient rhetorician claimed only to be generalizing from the practice of effective oratory to a series of precepts and thus to a system of the modes of persuasion, so Machiavelli asserted that his method lay in generalizing from the actual practice of effective statecraft to the truths and modes of power. His categories and precepts represented not the "absolute" but the most highly probable truths that could be so formulated; they needed always to be tested and shaped in the changing light of circumstance and situation. Machiavelli's conception of *"virtù"* in its non-moral use implies that art has its own virtues, those qualities by virtue of which its techniques are applied and its products conceived and molded. It implies also the idea of a "virtuoso," the practitioner excelling in the art who combines the capacity to

realize the ends of his art with their successful realization and
who so defines his "virtue" by his "art." The virtuoso of power,
whether prince or legislator, can be judged by the work of art
he produces. It is good or bad according to its effectiveness, and
what renders it noteworthy and successful may be ascribed to the
qualities, actions, and policies he has brought into play.

In Machiavelli's teaching, power must take cognizance of traditional morality. The existence of the latter is another of the facts
of the political world. If men are not what they ought to be, it
is nonetheless true that they wish to maintain the convictions
and appearances of ethical life. Appearance is itself a crucial
foundation and support of life and of power. "Men in general,"
said Machiavelli, "are as much affected by what things seem to
be as by what they are; often, indeed, they are moved more by
the appearances than by the reality of things."[7] Men of political
virtuosity, who comprehend what lies beneath the surface and
who demand the substance rather than the shadow of power,
learn to convert those appearances to their own uses. They learn
to know the importance and the skill of "seeming" good, of playing a public role. Morality in its common acceptance may thus
serve the purposes of power; real power rests on something else
again. It may depend equally on the use of deception and the
appearance of honesty; both contribute to the ultimate authority
that the possessor of power exerts. His art is in part an art of
persuasion; by image and by action he must convince those
whom he rules or seeks to rule that he is what he appears to be,
that things are really what they seem. The persuasive effect of such
power in turn increases its authority, its ability to produce its
desired results. Hence the emphasis, constant throughout Machiavelli's writings, on "reputation." Reputation represents the composite of substantive force and capacity that adhere in the ruler
or ruling institution with the compelling belief in their authority
and efficacy; reputation inspires obedience, veneration, fear, and
submission in the ruled and in the rulers' opponents.

Machiavelli's conception of politics as art and of art as con-
taining its own end, his idea of forms of political virtue distinct
from moral virtue, and his conviction that politics was a "good"
art—these all lead to the conclusion that the acquisition of
power was therefore in some important sense a good. They also

---

[7] *Discorsi,* I, xxv.

lead to the questions: Did Machiavelli substitute one morality for another? Did he make the state and its power the dominant ethical value that overrode all others and embodied the highest prescriptive standard of right?

The *Discourses* in particular might appear to provide the material for such an interpretation. There, still more explicitly than in *The Prince,* Machiavelli celebrated the greatness of the founders and heroes of states, praised and deplored the passing of the self-sacrificing devotion of citizens and the grandeur of power that had animated Rome. There he stated firmly that all means were proper that were needed to protect the *patria* from defeat and collapse and that extreme measures were requisite and justified when invoked in the cause of establishing and securing the state and its power.[8] If these aims reflect the "good" of society, then they can become "moral" ends. Power may thus be legitimized, its necessary means may become the "virtues" of the new morality, and the "state" may personify its conscious and constant norms.

However, these elements of a doctrine of "reason of state" take on a somewhat different complexion in the context of Machiavelli's own personalization of power and his insistence on its historical basis. For Machiavelli it is men, not institutions or abstractions, who carry out the struggle for power, win its victories, and lose its battles. Fundamental law, healthy institutions, a respected and invigorating religion, sound military systems, if possible, a certain antiquity and tradition surrounding solidly rooted foundations strong enough to continue the growth and adaptation of the political society that builds on them—these things are of the greatest importance, and all build power. But behind them lie always the directive genius of men and the decisive action of men. The power of institutions rests ultimately upon the men who legislate and guide and use them. If they protect power, they cannot sustain it of themselves; if they incorporate power, they in effect continue that of the men whose activities have produced it; if they contain "reason," it is the rational planning and the rational consequence of human action. Without the regenerating and reforming force of great men, the institutions, however good, will decline and fail. When crisis

[8] See especially *Discorsi,* I, ix and III, xli.

comes, good institutions may delay, but they cannot of themselves
prevent, destruction. The emergency measures that must then
be taken flow out of the reasoned plans of men in power. Power
aims to perpetuate itself; its reason is that of the men who control it. Their success in doing so brings them glory, reputation in
and beyond their own lifetimes. Some of that they lend to those
who live under them or by their side; some to the institutions
that survive them. Thereby they help perpetuate the principality
or the republic. Their service is not to an abstract right but to the
reasons of their own situation. Nor do their reasons become
the source for the single meaningful morality of their society,
although they try to instigate in the citizens ethical capacities
useful to the body politic. Traditional morality is still not destroyed, for there remain whole areas of private, social, and spiritual life, which power does not seek to rule. "Moral" virtue
continued to exist as something separate from, even when it was
exploited in the service of, political purposes and interests.

Still, there can be no doubt that for Machiavelli the political
art *was* a "good" art, and not merely in aesthetic terms. If the
idea of "art" implies a system directed toward an end internal
to itself, it does not necessarily imply the *self-sufficiency* of art
or the doctrine of *ars gratia artis*. Nor does it imply that the
consequences of the art may not be good, even though the art
does not define itself through or depend on its exterior results.

In dealing with power and its effective exercise, Machiavelli
frequently coupled their success with the terms of security, stability, durability, greatness, glory. They are at once self-justifying
and indicative of larger assumptions about the role of power in
the historical world. Politics is art for Machiavelli, and therein
lies the paradox of power. True power implies no responsibility,
whether legal or moral. But without it, the very conception of
human responsibility has no meaning. The world of politics is an
autonomous realm, existing by laws that cannot be legislated
from without. It can be ruled, at least on occasion, by the power
developed and established through an art that makes the capacity
for ruling and for sustaining power its end. And yet the "state"
is not an end in itself. Power is its own reward, but not its only
one. Art is not *gratia artis*.

For all their important differences of emphasis, perspective,
speculative interest, and immediate intent, Machiavelli's *Prince*

and *Discourses* maintain a consistent position on the nature and responsibility of power. That teaching finds its clearest and most coherent expression in *The Prince;* the treatise is a sustained argument on that central theme. Machiavelli's preoccupation here with the "new" prince had much to do, of course, with his belief that time and place demanded a leader who could construct a wholly new power in Italy. But more significant is what the figure of the new prince symbolizes. He typifies power in its purest form. This power is stripped not only of moral but of institutional sanctions. Behind it lie no territorial traditions or dynastic prestige or customary loyalties and rituals. The new prince is the personification of power in isolation from its usual forms. It becomes effective power in the political world through the prince's art and action. Its responsibility is to allow human will and purpose to achieve the modest but heroic victories of control and stability, which are all that intervene between chaos and order, between total subjection to contingency and necessity and the freedom, however limited, that political rule based on real power can realize, at least for those who maintain it.

The world that power confronts and tries to master is wholly political. In it the state of nature stands dominant at worst and at best lies only partially submerged. The conditions of this world are those of struggle and of flux. Its life is one of constant movement, change, and insecurity. It is bent by necessity and propelled by an irrational fortune. It possesses neither reason nor design. Its inhabitants are victims of chaos, slaves to need and circumstance, oppressed by their enemies of time and nature.

In Machiavelli's political drama, power alone can conquer such a world. The conquest requires *virtù; virtù* requires power. Without it, men can exert no control over the historical world but can only be ruled by it. If the order they create is transitory, it is still order, and it is a construction of human will and intelligence. There is never total victory over the opposing forces of chaos; strife and change are always in the world, but they can be to some extent contained and harnessed. Time remains, and the yearning for harmony and timelessness can never be satisfied. But the constructions of power possess some durability and stability, have gained some victory over time, and the glory of the political artist wins him a kind of immortality.

The possession of power and its effective exercise make pos-

sible a kind of freedom. It is a partial freedom from enslavement
to nature and chance, which rests at the same time on the acceptance of the world as it is. One can rule Machiavelli's world;
one cannot change it. Flexibility is necessary, for one can withstand but not annihilate the movement of time. One can win
the game of politics, but one cannot expect the game to yield
and one can neither invent nor change its rules. The limitations
of human nature, and therefore of power, the conditions of the
world, and therefore of the exercise of power, cannot be altered.

Human power can relate only to the actual conditions of this
world, and it must therefore be political power. Human responsibility, the capacity to act rationally and creatively rather than be
acted upon, must find its expression in politics. The fullest possibilities of human freedom, of will and reason, are realized
through the designs by which the "matter" of the political world
is given form and order, through the decisive acts by which the
course of events is shaped, through the active assaults and calculated defenses made against potentially destructive forces which
might otherwise inundate men, through the conversion of these
forces to the purposes of human will.

Political power makes possible this kind of freedom. It trans-
forms the illusion of human responsibility into reality. As Machiavelli's new prince typifies power, so he personifies the conception of human responsibility that Machiavelli attaches to its
effects. It is not the obligation of the ruler to provide the same
freedom for all; in the fullest sense, freedom belongs only to
those to whom power belongs, although the ruled will naturally
benefit in security and order. The ruler's power, when it is strongest, depends ultimately on himself and his own *virtù*. He typifies
the possibilities of human achievement, and at the same time he
points to the exceptional and personal character of greatness.
Machiavelli's conviction that the virtue and authority vested in
institutions emanated from the *virtù* of founders, leaders, and
legislators leads to the same personification of power and responsibility.

Machiavelli assigned the role of power to the world of history
as he conceived it in its determining reality. He permitted to
power the exercise of a political domination unhampered by
external standard and obligation. He continued to make individual capacity and art its center. Yet Machiavelli was not

preaching the need or the right of absolute power, nor the absolute claims of force. On the reverse side of the image of a political power that might seek its own will and glory and that in fact is answerable to nothing was the picture of human responsibility. Their existences were linked. Politics was art, and power its agent; power created the conditions of such freedom as men might have in the historical world and might express in its art. Power and responsibility were both illusions until they received concrete historical shape. They, too, were subject to change; their existences were only less mortal than were the men who exercised them. In the complex details of power, in its individual acts and strategies, in the intermittent accomplishment of responsibility were revealed at once the necessary acceptance of limitation, the partial victory over time and its disorder.

Chapter 3

THE RESPONSIBILITIES OF POWER
ACCORDING TO ERASMUS OF ROTTERDAM

Roland H. Bainton

This series of essays in honor of Hajo Holborn is devoted to the theme of the responsibilities of power as viewed by men and movements from the Renaissance to our own time. No figure more appropriately belongs here than Erasmus of Rotterdam because, since the 1930s, every work referring to him is replete with recurrent references to the name Holborn, by virtue of the unsurpassed edition of the *Ausgewählten Schriften* by Hajo and Annemarie Holborn (München, 1933).

If Erasmus had been asked what he thought about the responsibilities of power he would undoubtedly have answered, scholastic *au fond* that he was, by calling for distinctions. There are different kinds of power. There is political power wielded by rulers within and without their domains. There is spiritual power, which is the particular province of churchmen, and would that they used no other. And there is literary power, for of a truth the pen is mightier than the sword.

In discussing political power Erasmus, like Machiavelli, focused attention upon the person of the prince. This was not because Erasmus identified the state with the prince. There can be no prince without a state. There can be a state without a prince.[1] But the person of the prince could not have been disregarded in the two most distinctively political tracts of Erasmus because they were addressed to princes. The first was the *Panegyric of Philip of Burgundy*[2] and the second the *Institute of the*

---

[1] IV, 601. References where not otherwise indicated are to the Louvain edition of the *Opera*. This reference is to the *Institutio Principis Christiani* which is translated into English by Lester K. Born, "The Education of a Christian Prince," *Records of Civilization* XXVII, 1936.

[2] IV, 507–54.

Christian Prince, addressed to Charles, later to be the emperor.[3]
These two works appear at first to be little more than a catena of
maxims drawn from the wisdom of antiquity, but there are differences and there are contemporary applications. Whatever Erasmus
appropriated from the classical world was passed through the
Christian alembic. With Plato and Cicero Erasmus affirmed that
only he is fit to be a ruler who has no desire to rule.[4] But this view
of kingship as an onerous responsibility is brought by Erasmus
under the rubric of the *Imitatio Christi.* Rulership is a form of
cross-bearing, since the ruler must forego pleasure, assume cares,
labor long, curtail sleep in order that his subjects may rest securely.
He must be ready to endure ingratitude and reviling, and, if he
cannot rule without injustice, must be ready to resign.[5] The prince
is subject to grave temptations. Peter denied his Lord when he
was in the courtyard of the high priest, and the courts of pontiffs
and princes are the very places where Christ is most readily denied.[6]

Nevertheless the Christian must run the risks and assume the
responsibilities. Nor should the Christian prince neglect his proper
tasks in order to engage in pious exercises. Let him not spend so
many hours rattling off prayers that he leaves undone that for want
of which the state may gravely suffer. Compare the prince, if you
will, to Martha and the priest to Mary. Grant that to pray, medi-
tate, and sacrifice is more perfect than to care for the state, still,
this is the prince's task. Grant that the work of the priest is of a
higher order than if the prince by his vigilance should avert war.
Nevertheless, under the circumstances, this is a greater good because of all the other evils thereby obviated. Nor has one the right
to say that the prince does not pray. He may plead with God more
effectually in a very few words. If he stills the tempests of war, de-
fends the liberty of the people, staves off famine, appoints incor-
ruptible magistrates, he pleases God better than by saying six
whole years of prayers. Not that I disapprove of prayers. But they
are not the prince's job.[7] What Erasmus here says sounds very
much like Luther's doctrine of the calling.

[3] *Ibid.,* 559–615.
[4] Born, *op. cit.,* p. 160, note 59.
[5] IV, 568A–B and 571D.
[6] VII, 265E.
[7] IX, 623 and VII, 494.

But not only must the prince be devoted to his vocation. He must also be noble, generous, compassionate, magnanimous, and, above all, wise—in a word, Plato's philosopher king.[8] But how is he to be obtained? One would suppose that Erasmus would have favored popular election, since he repeatedly averred that government rests upon the consent of the governed,[9] but he was deterred from recommending this expedient because in the early Church the election of bishops was marred by riots and bloodshed. In any case, in the age of Erasmus popular election was *ohne politische Bedeutung,* as Hajo Holborn would say, since the hereditary principle prevailed. It has this advantage: one knew from the outset who was to become a prince, and his training could begin in infancy. Great care should be exercised in the choice of his tutor, on whom the responsibility of power rested more heavily perhaps than on the prince himself.[10] The tutor must be no flatterer. In fact, the ideal tutor would be a horse because it does not know the difference between a prince and a pauper.[11] The program of education for the prince recommended by Erasmus does not follow the model of Castiglione's *Cortegiano.* The prince is not to be taught how to dance, dice, and dine.[12]

When we come to the specific tasks of the prince we find that Erasmus would have him devote maximum attention to domestic and minimum to foreign affairs. Although an internationalist, Erasmus was in many respects a political isolationist. He did not wish to see the restoration of the ancient Roman Empire, or even of its shadow, the Holy Roman Empire. When invited by the imperialists of the court of Charles to edit Dante's *De Monarchia,* Erasmus politely evaded the assignment.[13] The difficulty with universal monarchy is that the prince cannot be personally acquainted with all parts of his domains. If his capital should be at Constantinople, how could he tell what was going on in Ethiopia or on the Ganges, and, if he knew, what could he do about it? Besides, the discovery of new lands not yet explored makes it appear that the earth is of immense vastness.[14] The prince should be intimately acquainted

---

[8] IV, 565F–566A, and *Erasmi Epistolae,* ed. Allen, abbreviated as EE VI, No. 1555.
[9] IV, 577B and IX, 1209D.
[10] IV, 562E.
[11] IV, 585C.
[12] IV, 566B.
[13] EE VI, No. 1790A, p. 470.
[14] EE II, No. 586, pp. 584–85.

with his own domain and should travel very little in any other. Woe to the land whose prince is always on leave of absence.[15] Princes should eschew foreign alliances and above all marriages beyond their borders. What sense is there in an arrangement whereby a marriage suddenly turns an Irishman into a ruler of the Indies, or makes a Syrian into the king of Italy?[16] Actually royal marriages do not insure the peace. England made a matrimonial alliance with Scotland, but James of Scotland nevertheless invaded England.[17] Even treaties are to be avoided, for they do not cement friendship, but serve rather as pretexts for accusations of bad faith.[18] But if there is not a universal state, how, then, is peace to be preserved? Not as Dante supposed, through a world monarchy. Great states, as a matter of fact, have never been brought into being save by great slaughter.[19] Peace is to be achieved by concord among small independent political units. This concord is the more fitting and should be the more attainable in a society whose unity is cemented by the Christian bond, where the universal monarch is Christ Himself.[20]

Within his own realm the prince is the *pater patriae*. He is, of course, to use the sword to repress the bad and protect the good, as Paul said in Romans 13. But the coercive power is to be used with the utmost restraint. The death penalty should be exacted only as an ultimate recourse. The prince should rule not by intimidation but by persuasion and consent. He is to look after the economic needs of the land, to regulate weights and measures, suppress monopolies, build dykes to keep out the sea (Erasmus is, of course, here thinking of his native Netherlands). He is to restrain luxury by sumptuary legislation, abolish public mendicacy by making the able work and caring for the infirm.[21] There is scarcely a social reform advocated in More's Utopia for which a parallel is not to be found in the works of Erasmus.[22]

One of the most imperative duties of the prince is to keep his

---

[15] IV, 591A.
[16] IV, 637B.
[17] IV, 604E.
[18] IV, 603–4.
[19] II, 956C Adage 4101, *Dulce Bellum*, translated by Margaret Mann Phillips, *The Adages of Erasmus,* Cambridge, England, 1964, p. 320.
[20] EE II, No. 586, p. 585.
[21] In addition to the *Institutio* see the letter to Zasius EE V, No. 1352, p. 261.
[22] This is abundantly evidenced in the admirable notes by Edward Surtz in his edition of the Utopia in the Yale edition, 1965.

land in peace. War violates the very nature of man who is endowed with reason that he may compose his differences reasonably. He is gifted with speech to communicate his wishes. He alone is able to laugh and to weep that a wrangle may be dissipated by a jest and a quarrel dissolved in tears. War is carnal, war is brutal, war is irrational, war is costly. As the Emperor Augustus said, it is like fishing with a golden hook more valuable than any fish and likely to be lost in the fishing.[23] War is the sum of all villainies. It scorches the land, abrogates the laws, wrecks all Christian fraternity. Thus classical and Christian themes are blended, while prudential and ideal motives are interwoven.[24]

Some have wondered whether Erasmus was sincere in his pleas, since his most important tract, the *Querela Pacis,* was written at the instance of the Chancellor Jean Sauvage,[25] at a moment when the imperial policy favored peace. But let it be borne in mind that the essential themes of the *Querela* were already to be found in an essay that Erasmus wrote while still in the monastery,[26] and again in the adage *Dulce Bellum,* for which there was no political prompting. The suggestion has also been made that Erasmus advocated peace because he was born in Holland, a little land that depended for its security upon peace between the great powers.[27] To this it may be said that Erasmus' earliest protest was not directed against wars between the great powers but between two feudal families in the Netherlands, the Hoeks and the Kabeljauws.

One may inquire whether his propaganda for peace contained anything novel. For the most part indeed he drew from classical and Christian antiquity. But there are some points that go beyond

[23] Suetonius, *Augustus* XXV, Loeb ed. I, p. 159.

[24] These themes are so recurrent in Erasmus that to list all of his statements would be to enumerate all of his works. The chief tract on the subject is the *Querela Pacis* available in more than one English translation, the adage *Dulce bellum inexpertis* referred to above, the chapter in the *Institutio,* the preface to the Paraphrase of John's Gospel addressed to Francis I, the colloquies *A Fish Diet* and *Charon,* for which see the notes by Craig Thompson, *The Colloquies of Erasmus,* Chicago, 1965, pp. 388–90. The secondary literature is extensive. See in particular Robert F. Adams, *The Better Part of Valor,* Seattle, 1962, and my article "The Complaint of Peace of Erasmus, Classical and Christian Sources," reprinted in *Collected Essays* I, Boston, 1962.

[25] EE I, p. 19.

[26] *Oratio de Pace et Discordia* VIII, 546–52.

[27] Gerhard Ritter, *Machtstaat und Utopie,* 1940, revised and translated. *The Corrupting Influence of Power,* 1952.

earlier pronouncements. Erasmus punctured the theory of the just war. It had been built up first in classical times by stages, culminating in the formulation of Cicero. A war to be just, he said, must have as its object the vindication of justice and the restoration of peace. It may be waged only under the auspices of the state. The code requires a formal declaration, respect for treaties, the sparing of the innocent, and the humane treatment of hostages and prisoners. Augustine christened the code by adding that the motive must be love and that justice can be on one side only because a just war requires an unjust war. The entire theory rests on the analogy between war and the administration of justice within the civil state, and this is precisely the point Erasmus punctures. The civil state, he reminds us, has juridical machinery whereby impartial judges can appraise a dispute and determine where justice lies. In wars between states there is no such juridical body. Each side adjudges its own cause to be just. But, as a matter of fact, in disputes over territory justice is impossible. What strip of territory is there that has not been held at divers times now by one state and now by another? On the ground of one-time ownership the Romans might expect to hold Spain or Africa, and Padua might try to recover the site of ancient Troy because, according to Virgil, the founder of Padua was a Trojan. A dispute as to who should own a piece of land cannot be resolved by an appeal to previous possession. It can be resolved only by mutual accommodation.[28] Nothing so penetrating as this had previously been said, and nothing wiser has since been said.

The proper way to settle disputes, according to Erasmus, is the way of arbitration, and the preferred arbitrators in his mind were churchmen. "Are there not bishops?" demands Erasmus, "Are there not abbots and scholars, are there not irreproachable magistrates?"[29] In suggesting arbitration Erasmus was in no sense an innovator. The Greek city states had practiced arbitration extensively, though never sufficiently to prevent devouring one another. Close to the time of Erasmus widespread examples are available from over the whole of Europe, from the Baltic to the Balkans, from Scandinavia to Spain. Such instances were rare in the twelfth century, increased in the thirteenth, abounded in the fourteenth and the first half of the fifteenth, and then suddenly dropped off, pre-

[28] II, 964E–965C from the *Dulce Bellum,* tr. Phillips, *op. cit.,* pp. 340–41.
[29] IV, 609B.

sumably because of the rise of the nations with their inordinate ambitions. Erasmus was harking back to the late Middle Ages, but in his preference for churchmen as arbitrators he was looking rather to the time of an Innocent III. In the cases cited above the arbitrators were normally laymen: a monarch, a nobleman, or perhaps a board set up by the contestants. There were, to be sure, some examples of churchmen, especially in Italy, but on the whole there was an indisposition to look to the Church, because she might inject claims of her own. Erasmus was anachronistic in supposing that the Church could reassume the role of arbitrator when she was herself so heavily involved in disputes. But he was not altogether lacking in realism. Pope Leo, he said, should not try to mediate, for assuredly the kings would not listen.[30]

There is a power that resides in the hands of the ruler. There is a power that resides in the hands of the ruled. This power, according to Erasmus, should not be exercised by way of rebellion, because such violence creates more havoc than the abuse it seeks to correct—witness the Peasants' War in Germany. Rather the power is to be exercised by non-cooperation. What is to be done, inquires Erasmus, if a tyrant requires something contrary to the will of God? The answer is not insurrection, but emigration, and if this is not feasible, then martyrdom.[31]

Now we turn to the Church. Erasmus insists that her power is spiritual and should be that and that only. The making of treaties by the pope with kings is monstrous. As the father of all he should make a pact with none and should promote concord equally with all.[32] War-making on the part of the pope is unspeakable. Against no pope did Erasmus so rail as against that pope in armor, Julius II. Here again Erasmus has been charged with insincerity because, when he was in Italy, Cardinal Riario, the nephew of this pope, asked him for an essay setting forth the pros and the cons of the war of Julius against Venice. Erasmus complied and marshaled the arguments for and against in the usual rhetorical form of the *suasoria* and the *dissuasoria*. He made the dissuasive much more cogent than the persuasive, but to his chagrin the cardinal made use only of the arguments in favor of the war. This document has

[30] EE IX, No. 2599. On medieval arbitration Roland H. Bainton, *Christian Attitudes to War and Peace,* New York, 1960, paperback 1965, pp. 116–17.
[31] V, 1023.
[32] EE V, 1417.

been lost,[33] but later in life Erasmus outlined the dissuasive. The gist of it was this: that the clemency of the Supreme Pontiff, whose weapons are prayers and tears, ill comports with plunging the Christian world into tumult, carnage, and bloodshed for the sake of a piece of mundane territory.[34]

Neither should churchmen call upon the state to place the sword at their disposal for the repression of heresy. The only penalty to be inflicted by the Church is excommunication, exclusion from the sacraments of the Church with an eye, not to the destruction, but rather to the reclamation of the offender. There should be no civil control over ecclesiastical penalties. Moreover, churchmen should realize that their anathemas will not be automatically endorsed by God. The keys were given to Peter because of his profession of faith rather than because of his character or his office. The keys belong to the entire Christian congregation when and only when inspired by the spirit of God. The power of the Church lies in the power of the Gospel, to be made manifest in works of mercy and to be proclaimed to the people by every channel of communication.[35]

This brings us to the power of the word. It may be exercised by churchmen. It may be exercised by scholars. Frequently scholars were churchmen, though not invariably. It might be exercised by princes. No matter by whom spoken, the word is the power of God. Christ Himself was called the Word. This is His most distinctive title. Men also are called lights of the world, sometimes angels, and even gods, but men are never called the Word of God. The best term with which to express this title in Latin is not *verbum,* as in the Vulgate translation, but rather *sermo.* Both words have been used to render the Greek word *logos,* which had a double meaning. It is the reason immanent in the world and in man. In this sense it may be translated by *ratio.* But it is also this reason finding expression in speech, not just names for things, *verba,* but meaningful discourse, *sermones,* sermons if you will. Christ was

[33] EE 1, p. 37.
[34] V, 898C–D.
[35] These views of Erasmus are set forth in many of his writings. I have dealt with his position as to religious liberty in "Castellio Concerning Heretics," *Records of Civilization* XXII, 1935, reprint 1965. Attention may be called to Erasmus' treatment of these themes in his *Paraphrase of the Gospel of Matthew,* Chapters 13, 16, and 18 in Volume VII of the Louvain edition.

the sermon of God. The same cannot be said of men, but in their
sermons they are to proclaim Christ the "sermon of God,"[36] "the
eloquence of God" (vi, 3356).

This is Christian eloquence. The importance of eloquence for
the humanists has been splendidly set forth by Hanna Holborn
Gray.[37] Erasmus took over the whole humanist program for reforming the mind of Christendom by the power of the word, the
word of man rendered persuasive by the art of the rhetorician,
the word of God which is powerful in weakness, and compelling
even in halting speech, but which should not disdain the aids of
artistry if they be not obstrusive and meretricious. Eloquence without sincerity is vain.[38] Let the preacher then be trained in all of
the techniques of persuasion, whether of dialectic or of rhetoric.
If it is possible to train elephants to dance, lions to play, and leop-
ards to hunt, it should be possible to teach preachers to preach.[39]

The power inherent in the word lays upon the writer, the
scholar, the preacher, the obligation to make use of it in order to
reach the people. Erasmus in his political thinking has been considered an aristocrat. He certainly did not have an exalted opinion
of the masses. But he did say that government rests upon the consent of the governed and consent must be won by persuasion.
The ruler himself by the use of the word can incite his subjects to
war, and again by the use of the word can allay their dissensions.[40]
The people at large are the audience to be addressed by those
skilled in the employment of the word. Theologians have no right
to make of their discipline an esoteric amusement for the discussion of abstruse questions which do not minister to piety or
Christian deportment. Poets have no right to divert themselves with
erotic banalities. Preachers have no right to make a game of their
ability to play upon the emotions of the crowd. Erasmus tells the
story of a preacher who bragged of his ability to provoke tears.
"Yes," scoffed his vicar, "from boys and silly women." "You sit
in the front of my congregation tomorrow," retorted the preacher,
"and I'll make you weep." The wager was accepted. The preacher
began with a magnificent picture of the mercies of God, then re-

[36] V, 771.
[37] "Renaissance Humanism: the Pursuit of Eloquence," *Journal of the
History of Ideas* XXIV, 1963, pp. 497–514.
[38] V, 783B.
[39] V, 813.
[40] V, 836D.

proached the ingratitude of man and turning to the vicar demanded, "And are you so base as to deny God even a tear?" The
vicar wept. The preacher said, "I win," and sat down. That evening at the table when the preacher boasted of his victory, the
vicar commented, "I did not weep because of what you said, but to
think that you would so prostitute your gift."[41]

The scholar, the writer, the poet, the preacher, and the ruler
are all obligated to reach the people. Therefore the Scriptures,
which communicate the word of God, should be made available in
all vernaculars. "And I would like to see my paraphrases of the
Scriptures," said Erasmus, "in the hands of the farmer, the car-
penter, the mason, yes and of harlots, pimps and Turks."[42] He
was speaking to those who feared that the Scriptures in the vulgar
tongues would find their way into such vulgar hands. The reply
was that Jesus consorted with tax gatherers and women of the
streets, for whom also those in power have a responsibility.

[41] V, 982A–B.
[42] VII, preface to Matthew, p. 1 and V, 823A.

Chapter 4

SEBASTIAN CASTELLIO ON THE POWER
OF THE CHRISTIAN PRINCE

Hans Rudolf Guggisberg

Modern students of the Reformation remember Sebastian Castellio mainly as the antagonist of Calvin, as the passionate critic who, after the execution of Servetus, raised his voice in an ardent plea for religious toleration. To a very large extent the story of Castellio's life is indeed the story of this plea and of the ensuing conflict with the reformers of Geneva. It was an uneven struggle. On the one side stood the solitary humanist scholar, Calvin's former collaborator who had left Geneva when theological and personal differences made it impossible for him to stay there any longer. He was not disposed to accept any kind of doctrinal authority that seemed to be incompatible with the text of the Holy Scriptures. Religion to him was basically a matter of the individual conscience. He held that nobody had a right to "force the conscience" of his fellow man, let alone to persecute or kill him for reasons of religious disagreement. On the other side stood the iron-willed leader of the Reformation of Geneva who clearly recognized the necessity to enforce the discipline within his newly established church and to eliminate everything that might threaten its doctrinal unity. Compromise with dissidents was absolutely impossible for him if he were to fulfill his great task, a task for which he firmly believed he had been chosen by God.

Outwardly, the struggle ended with Castellio's defeat. Although he had never suffered outright persecution, his life was full of hardship and tribulation. He never had a strong following. He was held in high esteem by a small circle of friends and sympathizers, but the majority of his contemporaries failed to grasp the significance of his ideas. When he died in Basel on December 29,

1563, the Reformed leaders of Geneva and Zurich openly rejoiced, and those of Basel were, to say the least, not altogether
unhappy.

Nevertheless, Castellio's thought, especially his conception of
religious toleration, was to live on. It was to influence various
theological and philosophical thinkers of later generations. It
stands at the beginning of an intellectual tradition at whose end
we find the catalogue of the Rights of Man. The significance of
Castellio's contribution to the intellectual development of the
sixteenth century and the importance of some of his works for
subsequent periods of European intellectual history are no longer
questioned by modern scholarship. As to the motivation and the
general context behind his doctrine of toleration, however, there
are still some open questions. The character of his political
ideas illuminates both.

In many passages of his writings on religious liberty, Castellio
stated his views on the responsibilities and duties of the Christian
magistrate. To him, toleration as a problem of human coexistence
was also a political problem. This was only natural, for his
was an age in which the belief in the divine office of the magistrate was still widespread and predominant, although there were
disagreements as to the exact relationship between the civil and
the ecclesiastical authorities within the Christian state. The notions of the Savoyard humanist were much less radical than
those of some other representatives of the so-called "left wing
of the Reformation," but like his views of God, man, and salvation they contained elements that made them appear basically
different from the ideas of his foremost adversaries, Calvin and
Beza.

It is interesting to note that some of Castellio's most revealing
statements on the tasks of the civil magistrate in a Christian
state appear in writings dedicated to princes. Although he never
explicitly stated his personal preference for either the monarchical or the republican form of government, he seems to have
felt a respect for the office of the Christian prince that he did
not feel for that of a republican magistrate. Four times in the
course of his life he dedicated important works to princes: The
first edition of his Latin translation of the Bible appeared in 1551
with an *epistola nuncupatoria* addressed to the youthful King of

England, Edward VI.[1] Four years later he dedicated the French
translation of the Bible to Henry II of France.[2] His most famous
work, the tract *De haereticis an sint persequendi,* had been
published in March 1554, nine months before the French Bible.
The first and perhaps most important part of this anthology of
pronouncements against the killing of heretics is the lengthy
epistle to Duke Christopher of Württemberg, which Castellio wrote
under the pseudonym of Martin Bellius.[3] When he published the
De haereticis in French translation some weeks after the Latin
original, he added a letter of dedication to Count William of Hesse,
which preceded the one addressed to Duke Christopher.[4]

We propose to use these four writings as a documentary basis
for our brief study because they are highly representative of
Castellio's views concerning the responsibilities of the Christian
magistrate in general and the Christian prince in particular. Most
of the ideas expounded here can also be found in Castellio's
other writings, but nowhere else are they so clearly and systematically set forth. The four prefaces also contain all the
characteristic elements of Castellio's plea for religious liberty.
Considering the eminence of the persons to whom they are
addressed, this is certainly not coincidence.

I

Within the general development of Castellio's philosophical and
theological thought, the preface to his Latin translation of the

[1] *"Sebastianus Castalio Eduardo Sexto Angliae Regi clariss"* in *Biblia,
interprete Sebastiano Castalione, una cum eiusdem annotationibus* (Basel:
Johannes Oporinus, 1551), foll. α 2ro–α 5ro.

[2] *"A trespreux e tresuictorieux prince Henri de Valois, second de ce
nom . . ."* in *La Biblia nouvellement translatée avec la suite de l'histoire
depuis les tems d'Estras jusqu'aux Macabées, e depuis les Maccabées
jusqu'à Christ: item avec des Annotations sur les pages difficiles.* Par
Sebastian Chateillon (Basel: J. Herwagen, 1555), fol. *2 ro/vo.

[3] "Martinus Bellius Christophoro Duci Virtembergensi S." in *De haereticis, an sint persequendi, et omnino quomodo dit cum eis agendum,
Luteri et Brentii, aliorumque multorum tum verterum tum recentiorum
sententiae* (Magdeburgi, per Georgium Rausch [=Basel: J. Oporinus],
Anno Domini 1554, Mense Martio, pp. 3–28.

[4] "Le traducteur à Très Illustre Seigneur et Prince, Monseigneur Gul-
laume, Comte de Hesse, Salut" in *Traicté des hérétiques, A savoir, si on les
doit persecuter, Et comment on se doit conduire avec eux, selon l'advis,
opinion, et sentence de plusieurs autheurs, tant anciens, que modernes*
(Rouen, par Pierre Freneau . . . [=Basel/Lyon?], 1554), pp. 3–10.

Bible occupies a place of particular interest. It is the earliest of his writings in which the plea for religious toleration in the Christian state is set forth. The fact that it was written and published in the first months of the year 1551 shows very clearly that this plea was not precipitated by the execution of Servetus —which took place on October 27, 1553—but that it had begun to take shape in Castellio's mind several years earlier. And it is quite possible that this preface has propagated Castellio's ideas more widely than the *De haereticis* and the later pamphlets against Calvin and Beza, because the Latin Bible was republished much more often than these works during the sixteenth, seventeenth, and eighteenth centuries.[5] The 1551 preface does not bear the marks of the struggle that were to characterize many of Castellio's later writings; it lacks both their passionate tone and their rhetorical power. Castellio is not yet speaking as an accuser; he avoids direct allusions to persons and events. Only here and there does the reader perceive traces of the author's personal experience, i.e., of the intolerance the former principal of the Collège de Rive had had to endure from the pastors of Geneva, which finally caused him to leave the city in 1544.[6]

But in spite of its dispassionate tone and somewhat theoretical method of argumentation, the dedicatory epistle to King Edward VI reveals the characteristic elements of Castellio's thought with surprising amplitude. And for the specific subject of this essay it is a source of fundamental significance. Before we examine its statements concerning the responsibilities of the Christian prince, however, we must briefly summarize its general contents.

At the outset Castellio explains the motive behind his Latin translation of the Holy Scriptures: He undertook the arduous task in order to help spread the Word of God among men of all nations. He wants to lay it before the reader in the clearest, most perspicuous, and most elegant of languages: the language of Cicero. But Castellio has no illusions. Learned translations alone will not bring the Word of God toward its fulfillment. In spite of a general interest in arts and letters the world lives in a state of darkest ignorance concerning many religious matters. This ignorance becomes obvious again and again in the innumerable conflicts that arise between Christians who do not agree over the

[5] Ferdinand Buisson, *Sébastien Castellion, sa vie et son oeuvre* (Paris, 1892), Vol. 2, pp. 355–61 (Bibliography).
[6] *Ibid.,* Vol. 1, p. 181ff.

meaning of certain passages of the Bible. The reason for the many misunderstandings, Castellio asserts, is not indifference toward God's commandments but rather a general lack of real Christian piety and charity. Only when these virtues are in full and salutary practice again will the fatal ignorance be lifted from the world, and only then will there begin the *aureum saeculum* of which the prophet speaks when he predicts the coming of an age of peace in which the peoples "shall beat their swords into plowshares and their spears into pruning hooks." This age is still far away, and the signs of its coming are scarce.[7]

After reading these sentences one recalls that the humanist scholar who wrote them not only translated the Bible into Latin and French but was also to translate and re-edit the *Theologia Germanica* and the *Imitatio Christi*.[8] The ethical basis and the spiritualistic tendency that seem to have characterized his theological ideas even before the outbreak of the famous conflict with Calvin and Beza, are also discernible in the following paragraph of the preface to Edward VI. Here Castellio comes back to an analysis of the basic evil of his time. It is not at all surprising that he was later to include this passage in the documentary collection of the *De haereticis,* for it leads straight to the center of his plea for toleration. He points out again that many Christians who do not agree with each other on how to fulfill certain commandments of God resort to violence and go so far as to kill each other. They do not try to imitate the many examples of human and divine clemency that are set before them in the Holy Scriptures. And when they persecute and kill others who hold different opinions in religious matters, they pretend to act in the name of God. They disregard the parable of the tares, and they repeatedly forget that Christ admonished his followers: "Judge not that you be not judged." The use of terrestrial arms in conflicts over spiritual matters is absurd. Here Castellio introduces a metaphor that recurs often in his later writings. He asserts that religious conflicts ought to be settled in the same way that diseases are healed: by remedies that have a contrary effect.

---

[7] "Sebastianus Castalio Eduardo Sexto . . .", fol. α2vo; Mic. 4, 3.

[8] The first editions appeared in Basel (J. Oporinus) in 1557 and 1563 respectively.

Christianorum hostes sunt vitia, contra quae virtutibus certandum
est, et contrariis remediis contraria mala curanda, ut doctrina
ignorantiam pellet, iniuriam vincat patientia, superbiae modestia
resistat, pigritiae opponatur diligentia, contra crudelitatem pugnet
clementia, simulationem prosternat sincera et se Deo probans
religiosa mens, animusque purus, et qui uni Deo placere studeat.[9]

These are the true aims of the Christian religion; only they will
lead to peace and understanding and to the victory of truth.

It is quite logical that at this point for the first time Castellio
defines the authority—or rather the limits of the authority—of
the civil magistrate: it is strictly limited to the punishment of
those who commit crimes like murder, adultery, theft, false witness, and the like, "which God has commanded to be punished."
The civil magistrate—*a Deo ad bonos defendendos constitutus*—
has to preserve peace and order.[10] He has no right to interfere
with the religious affairs of the subjects. Over these only God
has the power to judge; his children must wait in all humility
until his judgment is given. Those who try to anticipate it and
permit themselves to attack or kill others because of religious
disagreement do not act in His name. On the contrary, they commit the worst of sins against His commandment.

Here we have Castellio's view of the duties of the civil magistrate set forth in apodictic conciseness. Taken in this form and
used as the basis of a general appreciation of Castellio's political
thought, it might, however, lead to oversimplified conclusions
that would place him too far to the left within the so-called
"left wing of the Reformation." As even the relatively limited
documentary basis of this study will show, although his fundamental tenet never changed, Castellio was able to see the problem in a more general context and to characterize it with greater
differentiation.

This applies to the preface of 1551 if we turn to those
passages in which Castellio addresses the young English King di-

[9] "The enemies of the Christians are the vices which must be cured by
virtues, just as diseases must be healed by remedies with a contrary effect.
Thus, learning must drive out ignorance, patience overcome injury; modesty
must resist pride, diligence oppose laziness; clemency has to fight cruelty,
and insincerity must be laid low by a mind transparent, pious, pure, and
devoted to God." *De haereticis*, pp. 121–22.

[10] "Sebastianus Castalio Eduardo Sexto . . . ," fol. α 4vo; *De haereticis*,
p. 122.

rectly and thereby reveals his conception of the moral qualifications a Christian prince must have. He does so twice, once at the
very beginning and a second time in the last part of the epistle.
In the first few sentences he explains why he has dedicated his
work to the youthful monarch. There are three reasons. The first
is the fact that under this ruler England has become a haven of
peace for all who are persecuted on account of their faith in
other countries. The second is the King's obvious wish to support
the propagation of the Word of God in his realm: Castellio knows
that two scholars have been commissioned by the royal government to prepare a Latin translation of the Bible. Because of the
sudden death of one of them the work has remained unfinished,
and now he wants to fill the gap by presenting to the King his
own version. The third reason for the dedication is the King's
alleged inclination toward the study of the classical languages in
which he was guided by a *magister eruditus*.[11] In other words,
the King shows the laudable characteristics of a protector of
humanistic studies, and therefore the humanist from Basel honors
him by dedicating to him his "magnum opus."

In the concluding paragraphs of his preface, Castellio turns
to the future and states the expectations he has placed on the
young ruler of England. He knows, of course, that Edward is
still a child.[12] But the few things he has heard about him seem
to justify great hopes for a glorious future. Here Castellio puts
down some remarks of a more general character concerning
Christian kingship: The king holds a divine office. God has put
the lives of men into the hands of kings. Therefore one must
not cease to hope and pray that they execute their duties according to His commandments.[13] In order to clarify the meaning
of his words, Castellio supplements them with two lengthy quotations from Deuteronomy 17 and Proverbs 16. It becomes evident that if his plea for religious toleration is based on the Holy
Scriptures, the same is true of his conception of the Christian
prince.

Very eloquently Castellio expresses his hope that Edward VI

11 Ibid., fol. α 2ro.

12 In 1551, Edward VI was 14 years old.

13 "Itaque Deum oramus, vobis ut eam mentem iniiciat, ut vos de
vestris animis (qui in Dei manu sunt) tanto magis sitis solliciti, quam ii
sunt de suis corporibus, qui vident suam vitam vobis in manu esse
positam: quanto animi interitus gravior est quam corporis" (fol. α 5ro).

will become a ruler of men according to the laws of God and the admonitions of Solomon. The study of the Bible will help him understand and execute his task. And he ends his dedicatory address with the most appropriate wishes that can be imparted to a Christian prince: *Opto tibi Mosis clementiam, Davidis pietatem et Solomonis sapientiam.*[14]

It cannot be doubted that motives of a more directly personal nature also inspired Castellio's dedication, and they may help us to understand the arguments of his preface more clearly and to see them in relation to their historical background. I have tried elsewhere to describe this background in detail, so a brief summary may suffice here.[15]

In the first sentence of his epistle, Castellio states that some friends persuaded him to dedicate the Latin Bible to the English King. These *"amici"* must be sought among his learned colleagues in the printing firm of Johannes Oporinus and among a wider circle of scholars who had their works published there. It is not without interest to note that from 1548 to 1553 there appeared in Basel a considerable number of learned books that were in some form or other addressed to Edward VI or to influential members of his government. Thus Castellio did not stand alone with his dedication. Like many centers of the Reformation on the Continent, the city of Basel took a great and hopeful interest in English affairs during those years.[16]

When Castellio praised England as a haven of peace for foreign refugees, he knew what he was talking about. He had come to Basel as an emigrant himself in 1545, and now six years later, his situation was still difficult. Although he was not molested for his religious views and had even found employment with Oporinus, he was still extremely poor, and his future seemed anything but secure. (The appointment to the chair of Greek at the University came in 1553, but it was not to be the end of

[14] *Ibid.* The last part of Castellio's epistle reminds one of some passages of Erasmus' *Institutio principis Christiani.* Cf. *Desiderii Erasmi Roterodami Opera omnia,* t.3 (Leiden, 1703), coll. 567F, 569B–C, 571C–D. To support his argument, Erasmus had quoted the same passage from Deut. 17: 18–20.

[15] Cf. H. R. Guggisberg, "Sebastian Castellio und die englische Reformation," *Festgabe Hans von Greyerz* (Bern, 1967), pp. 319–38.

[16] Manfred E. Welti, *Der Basler Buchdruck und Britannien* (Basel, 1964), pp. 175–85.

his worries.)[17] It is quite possible, therefore, that when in February 1551 he wrote his epistle to the English King, Castellio was already contemplating the possibility of moving to England himself. He knew about other scholars who had done this. Some of them had evidently been successful: not only had they found a friendly welcome, they had also been appointed to university posts and received honorable commissions from the royal government. In his allusion to the Latin translation of the Bible that had been undertaken at the King's order but then left unfinished, Castellio obviously referred to the work commissioned to Martin Bucer and Paul Fagius and to the latter's death which had occurred on November 23, 1549.[18]

Like all the other learned authors who, during the years of Edward's reign, dedicated their volumes to the young monarch, Castellio was undoubtedly aware that in addressing himself to the King he really spoke to those powerful men of his entourage who governed the country, led the Church, and protected the scholars in his name. If he wanted to make his work known in England, he had to bring it to the attention of these eminent gentlemen. With his compliment to the King's *magister eruditus* he recommended himself in a discreet way to Sir John Cheke. This great English humanist was highly admired by some Basel scholars, notably by Castellio's friend Celio Secondo Curione.[19]

We know that Cheke was full of praise for Castellio's work. He intended to persuade the King to remunerate the translator generously for his dedication. But nothing came of it. The young English Josiah, for whose benefit Castellio had drawn the picture of the ideal Christian prince, died of a terrible illness at the age of sixteen. All the hopes and expectations expressed so eloquently in the preface to the Latin Bible lay shattered.[20]

[17] Buisson, *op. cit.*, Vol. 1, pp. 230–61.

[18] Constantin Hopf, *Martin Bucer and the English Reformation* (Oxford, 1946), p. 14. Richard Raubenheimer, *Paul Fagius aus Rheinzabern, sein Leben und Werken als Reformator und Gelehrter* (Grünstadt/Pfalz, 1957), p. 113. Cf. also H. C. Porter, *Reformation and Reaction in Tudor Cambridge* (Cambridge, 1958), p. 51ff., and V. H. H. Green, *Religion at Oxford and Cambridge* (London, 1964), p. 93.

[19] Cf. Welti, *op. cit.*, pp. 175, 181f.

[20] Cheke's reaction to Castellio's Latin translation of the Bible is described in two letters which the English theologian Christopher Carlile sent to Castellio on March 19, 1554 and on April 29, 1562. Basel, University

Castellio never received a recompense of his labors, and he never went to England himself.[21] After Mary Tudor's accession to the throne, Cheke came to the Continent, now a refugee himself. He lived in Strassburg for some time and in 1554 visited Curione in Basel. On this occasion he may also have met Castellio. But the once-eminent Englishman was no longer in a position to fulfill the secret hopes of his Savoyard colleague. Castellio's dedicatory epistle to Edward VI could not have missed its original purpose more completely.[22]

II

The preface to the French translation of the Bible, which Castellio addressed to King Henry II of France, has never become as well-known as his epistle to Edward VI. It is considerably shorter, more concise in its content, and less revealing as a biographical source. The main reason for its relative obscurity is the fact that the French Bible (which was to be a popular version and not one for scholars) was published only once, in January 1555.[23] It seems, however, that the preface was written at an earlier date and circulated in manuscript form in the

---

Library, ms. Ki.Ar. 18b, foll. 308–9, 323–24. The two letters are reproduced, but incompletely and not without a number of mistakes, by Buisson, *op. cit.,* Vol. 2, pp. 414f., 458f.

[21] Cf. Castellio's letter to Queen Elizabeth, January 7, 1559. Here the humanist reminded the Queen of England of the recompense which had been promised to him. He praised her for having opened her realm to foreign exiles again. He also admonished her to remain tolerant in religious matters. As far as we know, the letter had no consequences. Its autograph (draft copy) is preserved in the City Library of Rotterdam (Collection of the Remonstrant Church, ms. 505). It is printed in Buisson, *op. cit.,* Vol. 2, pp. 444–46.

[22] On Cheke's life cf. Walther L. Nathan, *Sir John Cheke und der englische Humanismus* (Bonn, 1928). On his visit to Basel: M. Sieber, *"Die Universität Basel und ihre englischen Besucher,"* Basler Zeitschrift für Geschichte und Altertumskunde, 55 (1956), p. 88.

[23] Because if its popularizing style, its frequent use of "patois" words or words not generally current, Castellio's French translation of the Bible was severely criticized by Calvinists as well as by Catholic scholars. Cf. H. R. Guggisberg, *Sebastian Castellio im Urteil seiner Nachwelt vom Stäthumanismus bis zur Aufklärung* (Basel and Stuttgart, 1956), pp. 23ff., 128. H. E. Keller, *"Castellios Uebertragung der Bible ins Französische,"* Romanische Forschungen, 71 (1959), pp. 383–403.

summer of 1553.[24] Its main theme is again that of religious toleration. Like the preface to the Latin Bible, it shows that Castellio's irenic ideas were conceived well before the execution of Servetus.

As a ruler of a Christian kingdom, Henry II certainly did not measure up to Castellio's ideals. He was known as a cruel persecutor of religious dissenters. Although he gave assistance to the German Protestant princes in their struggle against the emperor, he was unrelenting in his attempts to extirpate the *"Luthéristes"* in his own country. During the short time of its existence (1547–50), his *Chambre ardente* condemned to death more than five hundred adherents of the Reformation.[25]

We have no reason to assume that Castellio, who maintained personal contacts with many French Protestants, did not know about these things.[26] Why then did he dedicate his second Bible translation to this King? At the end of the address he provides one answer himself: since the Latin version had been dedicated to the late King of England who was a zealous student of that language, he thought it appropriate to dedicate the French version to the ruler of the French people. Again Castellio states that the idea had been suggested to him by his friends.[27]

Another indication as to the motives of the dedication can be found in the title of the preface: *A trespreux e tresuictorieux prince Henri de Valois, second de ce nom, par la grace de Dieu Roi de France, trêchrêtien, Sebastian Châteillon son suiet, Salut.* It was certainly not without premeditation that Castellio referred to the fact that he was a subject of the King of France here where it could not be overlooked by anyone who opened the heavy volume.[28] The reference seems to show three things: First, Castellio wanted to demonstrate that he felt himself to be under a particular obligation to his addressee, who was the *Roi de France trêchrêtien* even if he persecuted the Protestants. Sec-

---

[24] *Calvini Opera*, 14, p. 586. Cf. the "Introduction" of S. van der Woude to the facsimile edition of the *De haereticis* (Geneva, 1954), p. vii; Roland H. Bainton, "Sebastian Castellio, Champion of Religious Liberty," *Studies on the Reformation* (London, 1963), p. 152, n. 10.

[25] John Viénot, *Histoire de la Réforme français des origines à l'Edit de Nantes* (Paris, 1926), pp. 212–53.

[26] Buisson, *op. cit.*, col. 2, p. 243ff.

[27] Fol. *2vo.

[28] He was absolutely entitled to call himself a subject of the French King. The Duchy of Savoy stood under French authority from 1536 to 1559.

ond, he obviously also wanted to express his loyalty to the people of the French-speaking nation for whom he had, after all, undertaken his second translation of the Bible. And finally, the reference seems to indicate that Castellio, after having lived in the city-republic of Basel for almost ten years, still considered himself a foreigner.[29]

The address to Henry II contains neither flattery nor outright accusation. It is delivered in a tone of quiet persuasiveness. Like the epistle to Edward VI it lacks the passionate force of the later works. The King is not criticized as a person, there are no direct attacks against the manner in which he rules over his subjects. There are no allusions to particular events or persons, at least as far as we can see. The central idea is familiar to the reader who knows the preface to the Latin Bible. Castellio points out that the prince, although he holds his office by the grace of God, may not anticipate God's judgment by putting to death those subjects who seem to be possessed by false religious tenets. He must wait until God speaks. Castellio introduces his argument with an allegory taken from military life that he may have thought appropriate to convince the King:

> *Quand en bataille la nuit survient, on cesse de combattre jusqu'-*
> *au jour, de peur que d'aventure en frappant a l'aventure, au lieu*
> *des ennemis on ne tue ses amis, comme ainsi soit qu'il vaille*
> *beaucoup mieux épargner ses ennemis, que de tuer quant-et-quant*
> *ses amis. Autant en fait-on de jour: c'est que apres qu'on est*
> *venu aux mains, et est on mêlé les uns parmi les autres, l'artil-*
> *lerie cesse, de peur de l'inconvenient que dit est.*

A little later the allegory is taken up again:

> *Croyez moi, sire, le monde n'est aujourd'hui ne meilleur, ne plus*
> *sage, ne mieux voyant qu'alors. Parquoi ce seroit le meilleur,*
> *tandis que les choses sont tant douteuses, ou tant brouillées,*
> *d'attendre de décocher, jusqu'a tant que le jour leve, ou que les*
> *affaires soyent mieux demêlés, de peur que parmi ces tenebres et*
> *brouillis on ne face chose, de laquelle il faille puis apres dire,*
> *Je ne le pensoi pas.*[30]

[29] Castellio never sought to acquire citizenship in Basel.

[30] "As soon as the night falls over the battlefield, the fighting parties interrupt the battle until the next day, because they fear that friends may be killed instead of enemies. It is certainly wiser to spare one's enemies instead of killing some of one's friends. The same is done also in the day-

It may surprise us to hear Castellio speak like an expert tactician. But the allegory illustrates his argument very well, and it can be combined in a convincing manner with the parable of the tares.[31]

Taken as a whole, the preface to the French Bible impresses the reader as a simple and straightforward defense of religious toleration in the Christian state, but also—and perhaps even more—as a document of Castellio's unwavering respect for the high office of the Christian prince. He does not go into controversial details here. As in the epistle to Edward VI, he neither discusses nor uses the term "heretic." His views concerning the responsibilities of the Christian magistrate were to become more differentiated, once he started to reflect on the question of what a heretic really was. Even if we did not know that the address to Henry II was in circulation as early as 1553, we would, on the basis of the simplicity of its argument, have to assume that it was written before the *De haereticis*.

III

When he read the *De haereticis* for the first time in late March 1554, Theodore Beza at once recognized in the preface by Martin Bellius the same spirit that was in the dedicatory epistle of Castellio's Latin Bible. This led him to the assumption that "Martinus Bellius" was only a pseudonym of Castellio and that the Savoyard who had once been Calvin's trusted collaborator was the real author of the introductory address to Duke Christopher of Württemberg. Beza also realized very soon that the *Farrago Bellii* (as he usually called the book) had been printed in Basel and that Castellio had been one of its editors, if not the

---

time: as soon as the hand-to-hand fighting begins and the two parties are mingled into each other, the artillery stops shooting for the same reason.

"Believe me, my lord, the world today is neither better nor wiser nor more enlightened than in the past. In view of so many doubtful and confused issues, it would be better, therefore, to refrain from shooting and wait until daybreak or until things are better disentangled, so that in the darkness and confusion we avoid doing something of which we would have to say afterward: 'I did not mean to do it.' " "*A trespreux . . . prince Henri de Valois . . .*" fol. *2ro.

[31] *Ibid.*

chief editor and compilator.[32] The identity of Bellius and Castellio having since been established more than once, we need not dwell on this point any longer.[33]

That the preface by Martin Bellius should have reminded Beza of Castellio's epistle to Edward VI is not at all surprising. It contains all the arguments of the earlier work. There are also some new themes such as the definition and a lengthy discussion of the term "heretic" and the Erasmian distinction between fundamentals and non-essentials for the realization of a Christian life.[34] This essay reveals for the first time the whole range of theological presuppositions that stand behind Castellio's plea for religious liberty. In many paragraphs the reader encounters reflections that were to be further developed in later writings such as the *Contra libellum Calvini*[35] and the *Conseil à la France désolée*.[36] There are even some anticipatory traces of the rationalistic keynote that was to characterize Castellio's last work *De arte dubitandi*.[37]

In 1554, Duke Christopher of Württemberg, to whom the epistle is addressed, was in the fourth year of his reign. After the conclusion of the treaty of Passau in 1552 he was fully engaged in bringing about the so-called "Second Reformation" in his country. One of his foremost problems was the question of how to handle the Anabaptist and Schwenckfeldian minorities who could, of

[32] Letters of Theodore Beza to Henrich Bullinger, March 29, May 7, and June 14, 1554. *Correspondance de Théodore de Bèze, publiée par F. Aubert et H. Meylan,* Vol. 1 (Geneva, 1960), pp. 123f., 127f., 129ff.

[33] For a discussion of this problem cf. S. van der Woude, *op. cit.,* pp. iv–xv.

[34] Cf. Bainton, "Sebastion Castellio, Champion of Religious Liberty," p. 162f.

[35] The *Contra libellum Calvini* was not printed in Castellio's lifetime. Its first edition dates from 1612 and was published in Holland. Cf. Guggisberg, *op. cit.,* p. 79f.

[36] *Conseil à la France désolée auquel est montrée la cause de la guerre présente et le remède qui y pourroit estre mis, et principalement est avisé si on doit forcer les consciences.* L'an 1562 (s.l.). Critical edition by Marius F. Valkhoff (Geneva, 1967).

[37] With the exception of the chapter "De justificatione" (first published as an appendix to the edition of the *Dialogi IV,* Gouda, 1613), the *De arte dubitandi* remained unpublished until 1937. In that year appeared Elisabeth Feist's edition in the *Studi e documenti* of the Reale Accademia d'Italia, Vol. 7: *Per la storia degli eretici italiani del secolo XVI in Europa, testi raccolti de D. Cantimori e E. Feist* (Rome, 1937), pp. 277–430.

course, not be integrated into the new *Landeskirche*.[38] Here
Castellio had some reason to hope for a peaceful settlement because Duke Christopher's religious adviser was John Brenz. The
irenic views of this moderate reformer had become known much
earlier. As early as 1528 Brenz had published a pamphlet in
which he had stated that heresy, being a spiritual offense, cannot
be touched by the sword of the civil magistrate.[39] It is not surprising that this tract came to occupy a prominent place among
the texts of the *De haereticis*.[40]

According to his own words, Castellio dedicated the book to
Duke Christopher because he believed that this prince was full
of good intentions and would use the information contained
therein to rule his people justly and well. But Castellio was not
concerned with the state of affairs in Württemberg alone. He indicates a second reason for his dedication which links the *Farrago*
somewhat surprisingly with the French Bible on the one hand and
with the *Conseil à la France désolée* on the other:

> *Deinde quod, cum sis potens et authoritatis praecipue, expedit
> in primis hanc rem esse tibi notam, ut et ipse tuis iuste et sine
> ulla iniquitate imperes: et aliis vicinis principibus, praesertim
> Galliae regi, idem ut faciant persuadeas, quo possit Christianae
> republicae status (qui tot iam annis tam misere laceratur) in
> tranquilliorem statum redigi, et populi ad vitae correctionem
> vocari, si forte Deus iram suam (qua in genus hominum inflam-
> matus est) avertere velit, et nos sui vultus lumine illuminare.*[41]

---

[38] Heinrich Hermelink, *Geschichte der evangelischen Kirche in Württemberg von der Reformation bis zur Gegenwart* (Stuttgart and Tübingen,
1949), pp. 17ff., 87ff.

[39] On Brenz cf. the "Introduction" to Roland H. Bainton (ed.), *Concerning Heretics, Whether they are to be persecuted ... An anonymous
work attributed to Sebastian Castellio* ... (New York, 1935), pp. 50–58.
See also: F. W. Katzenbach, "Der Beitrag des Johannes Brenz zur
Toleranzidee," *Theol. Zeitschrift*, 21 (1965), pp. 38–64.

[40] *De haereticis*, pp. 46–74.

[41] "Another reason was that in your high position of authority it is very
necessary that you be well informed about this matter, so that you may rule
your people justly and well, and that you may be able to persuade neighboring princes to do the same, especially the King of France, if it be at
all possible to restore tranquillity to that Christian nation which has been
so long and so miserably harassed, that the people may be called to correct
their lives, if God is willing at all to avert His wrath which He has conceived against the race of men, and if He is willing to enlighten us by
the light of His countenance." *Ibid.*, p. 17. After this passage there follows

Here we see very clearly that Castellio was anxious to avoid giving the impression that the *De haereticis* had been written, compiled, and published merely as an answer to the execution of Servetus. The aim of the book was obviously more general. It was to defend not a man but a principle.[42] Moreover, the passage again shows that the troubles of France were a matter of constant concern to Castellio long before he wrote his famous *Conseil*. The feeling of allegiance to the French-speaking nation seems never to have left him.

For our study the most important part of the preface by Martin Bellius is the beginning. Nowhere else in Castellio's writings do we find more convincing evidence of the fact that he never doubted the divine character of the princely office.

In the famous parable of the white robe with which he opens his address, Castellio compares the relationship between the prince and his subjects to that of Christ and His followers. Just as the subjects must obey the prince's orders and not speculate on his motives or dispute among themselves concerning his person, the followers of Christ should do the same in awaiting His coming. He commanded them to prepare white robes for His return, that is to say, that they should live together in a Christian manner and love each other. They should not dispute as to the state and the office of Christ, where He is, how He is seated at the right hand of the Father, how He is one with the Father, etc. and thereby forget what He ordered them to do. This curiosity, Castellio asserts, creates worse evils:

> *Haec enim vel scientia, vel scientiae opinione falsa inflati homines, alios prae se superbe despiciunt: quam superbiam sequitur deinde saevitia et persecutio, ut iam nemo fere alium, ulla in re a se discrepante ferre possit.*[43]

This is how, in Castellio's opinion, religious conflicts and in-

---

a *laudatio* on Brenz. Castellio could not know that both Duke Christopher and his adviser were soon turning back to a policy of religious persecution. *Concerning Heretics,* Introduction, p. 58.

[42] Servetus is not mentioned in the *De haereticis*. His case is discussed extensively, however, in the *Contra libellum Calvini.*

[43] "Men are puffed up with knowledge or with a false conception of knowledge and look down upon others with contempt. Pride is followed by cruelty and persecution, so that now hardly anyone is able to endure another who differs from him in the slightest thing." *De haereticis,* p. 6.

tolerance have always come into the world. The followers of Christ have failed again and again to distinguish between the fundamentals and the non-essentials in the teachings of the Bible. Here he turns again to the prince. What would you do, he asks him, if a man were brought before you for having said that he believed you were his prince but that he did not agree with the majority of the people concerning the clothes you will wear when you return to your capital city, and concerning the meaning of some of your orders? Would you condemn such a citizen? Castellio gives the answer himself:

> *Non arbitror; et si tu adesses, laudares magis hominis simplicitatem et obedientiam, quam damnares ignorantiam: et si alii hominen interficerent, profecto tu in eos animadverteres.*[44]

In other words: Castellio expects the Christian prince to be not only a just and humane ruler but also one who is able to distinguish between the fundamentals and the non-essentials. If he is able to do this, he becomes a model to his subjects. They will learn from him how to follow Christ. As a holder of a divine office he is comparable to God in his relationship to the common man. As a Christian ruler he leads his subjects toward a Christian life.

IV

Count William IV of Hesse was the son of Philip of Hesse and the son-in-law of Duke Christopher of Württemberg. In 1554, when Castellio dedicated the French edition of the *De haereticis* to him, he was not a reigning prince. He did not succeed his father until 1567 when the territory was divided and he received Hesse-Cassel. He had, however, carried the major responsibility for the administration of the whole of Hesse during his father's captivity from 1547 to 1552. A staunch ally of Maurice of Saxony and a successful economic reformer of his country,[45] William was also an outspoken liberal in religious

---

[44] "I do not think so. If you were there, you would rather praise the man's simplicity and obedience than condemn his ignorance. And if others came and killed him, you would surely punish them." *Ibid.,* p. 9.

[45] B. Gebhardt, *Handbuch der deutschen Geschichte,* 8th edition, Vol. 2 (Stuttgart, 1955), pp. 101, 378.

matters. Like his father, he was unwilling to inflict the death penalty on the Anabaptists. He was reluctant even to punish them with banishment or imprisonment or to put any constraint upon them concerning the baptism of their children. During his whole life he showed sympathy and understanding to oppressed religious minorities.[46]

One can understand, therefore, that Castellio should have deemed it appropriate to honor this German prince also with a dedicatory address. In its assertions concerning the office of the Christian prince, the preface to the *Traicté des hérétiques* appears as a summary of the three earlier epistles, but at the same time (and like the address to Christopher of Württemberg) it points to some of Castellio's later writings. Particularly at the beginning, the reader is reminded of the epistle to Edward VI of England. After having complimented Count William on his knowledge of the French language, Castellio admonishes him to take to heart the teachings of the Old Testament concerning the holy office of the prince. Again we are confronted with the now familiar ideal of the prince as the model servant of the Lord who provides for his people the great example of a godly life. There is also a lengthy reaffirmation of what Castellio considers to be the fundamentals of true religion, perhaps even more clearly stated than in the epistle to Duke Christopher and once more revealing the influence of Erasmus.

The most interesting part of this preface is, however, the paragraph in which Castellio again discusses the limitations of the authority of princes and magistrates. His statements are considerably clearer and more differentiated here than in the preface to the Latin Bible of 1551. They are also of interest because they denote the limits of Castellio's conception of religious toleration.

At first he asserts that sins of the heart (*péchés du coeur*), such as infidelity, envy, hate, and also heresy are to be punished by the sword of the Spirit (*au glaive de l'Esprit*) which is the Word of God. Here the civil magistrate has no authority to interfere. But this does not imply that he is wholly without power in churchly affairs. On the contrary: it is his right and duty to interfere in the Church if he can do anything to prevent the

[46] Unlike Christopher of Württemberg, he never reverted to religious persecution. He died in 1592. *Concerning Heretics,* Introduction, p. 91ff.

evil-minded from injuring the good, in either their property or their persons. For this principle which is based on Romans 13, Castellio has a number of examples:

> *Que si quelqu'un trouble la République en battant, ou frappant aucun sous couleur de religion, le bon Magistrat le peut punir, comme celui qui fait mal au corps et biens, comme les autres malfaicteurs, mais non pour sa religion. Que s'il advient que quelqu'un se gouverne mal en l'Eglise, tant en la vie, qu'en la doctrine, l'Eglise doit user du glaive spirituel, qui est de l'excommunier, s'il ne veut recevoir l'admonition. Puis estant excommunié, s'il persévère en sa mauvaise entreprise jusques à faire commotion et troubler tout, le bon Magistrat Chrestien le peut avertir, qu'il ait à ne plus troubler l'Église en enseignant ses hérésies et blasphèmes qui sont apertement contraires à la parole de Dieu, comme est la doctrine de ceux qui nient la création du monde, l'immortalité des ames, la Résurrection, et aussi ceux qui disent que l'on n'a que faire de Magistrat, à fin qu'ils puissent mieux troubler toutes les Républiques à leur fantaisie, sans être reprins, et punis de leur mauvaise et effrénée nature, laquelle ne vit qu'en trouble et noise, à laquelle l'Esprit de Dieu est du tout contraire. Que s'ils persévèrent après de désobéir aux Princes et aux Magistrats, alors ils les pourront punir et châtier; mais non jusques à les faire mourir. . . . Mais le bon Magistrat se contentera de les punir par quelque amende d'argent, et telles autres semblables punitions; puis en la fin s'ils persévèrent, de les bannir de leur pays, qui sera leur dernière punition. Que si d'aventure ils retournaient, ils les pourraient garder en quelque lieu, s'ils ne s'amendent.*[47]

[47] "If someone disturbs the commonwealth by an assault under color of religion, the good magistrate may punish him because he has done damage to bodies and goods like any other criminal, but not because of his religion. If someone conducts himself badly in the Church, both in his life and in his doctrine, the Church must use the spiritual sword, which is excommunication, if he does not accept admonition. If, after being excommunicated, he perseveres in his evil conduct to the point of disturbing the peace, the good Christian magistrate may see to it that he no longer troubles the Church with his heresies and blasphemies which are clearly contrary to the Word of God. Such is the doctrine of those who deny the creation of the World, the immortality of the souls, and the resurrection, as well as of those who repudiate the office of the magistrate, so that they may better disturb all the states to their satisfaction, without reprimand and without being punished for their bad and uninhibited nature, which only lives on trouble and noise. To such behavior the Spirit of God is utterly alien. If they persevere in disobeying princes and magistrates, they may be punished and

Here we have the whole catalogue of the punishments that, according to Castellio, the Christian prince and magistrate can and must inflict on heretics. The only punishment that is utterly rejected is the death penalty.[48] Thus, in the last of his four dedicatory addresses to Christian princes, Castellio has stated the range of their spiritual authority and the character of their office with unique clarity.

He was to restate his opinion several times in later writings against Calvin and Beza, notably in the *Contra libellum Calvini* and in the *De haereticis a civili magistratu non puniendis*.[49] The Savoyard humanist wholeheartedly agreed with his adversaries on the divine nature of the office of the Christian prince and magistrate. He also agreed that heretics must be punished; but he never wavered in his conviction that they must not be put to death.[50]

V

Unquestionably Castellio's ideal of the office and authority of the Christian prince was a conservative one. It was firmly grounded in the Holy Scriptures and strongly tied to his conception of religious toleration. Although he believed that there

---

chastised, but not put to death. . . . The good magistrate will content himself with punishing them by a fine of money or some similar penalties. Then if they still continue, he may banish them from their country. This will be their last punishment. If, by any chance, they should return, they may be imprisoned if they do not amend." *Traicte des heretics*, p. 4f.

[48] Cf. Joseph Lecler, S. J. *Toleration and the Reformation* (New York/London, 1960), Vol. 1, p. 342.

[49] The *Contra libellum Calvini* was written as an answer to Calvin's *Defensio orthodoxae fidei* (1554). The *De haereticis a civili magistratu non puniendis* (written in 1554–55) was to refute Beza's tract *De haereticis a civili magistratu puniendis,* better known as *Anti-Bellius.* But Castellio could never publish this refutation. It is still in manuscript (Rotterdam, City Library, Coll. of the Remonstrant Church, ms. 508). An edition by Professor B. Becker of Amsterdam is in preparation. As to the contents of the tract, we have to be satisfied up to now with Professor Becker's summary in his article *"Un manuscrit inédit de Castellion," Castellioniana, quatre études sur Sébastien Castellion et l'idée de la tolérance* (Leiden, 1951), pp. 101–11. Its most important part is the one describing the limits of Castellio's conception of tolerance.

[50] Cf. Lecler, *op. cit.,* Vol. 1, p. 355f.; Johannes Kühn, *Toleranz und Offenbarung* (Leipzig, 1929), p. 337ff.

was a limit to the authority of the civil magistrate in religious matters, he never advocated the separation of Church and State. On the contrary, he was convinced that the State carried a great spiritual responsibility as the protector of the fundamentals of the true Christian religion: faith in God, obedience to His Word, peace, brotherly love and mutual understanding among the subjects. Castellio believed that the men who govern Christian states must make it possible for every one of their subjects to follow Christ and to live *sancte, juste et pie*.

This was his notion of the "responsibility of power." It is only natural that he tried to explain it with particular clarity whenever he addressed himself to a Christian prince. He expected more from princes than from other officeholders and magistrates. That none of his expectations was fulfilled is part of the tragedy of Castellio's life.

Chapter 5

RICHELIEU*

Dietrich Gerhard

Richelieu's life and thought were purposeful and disciplined to a degree that is difficult to comprehend. His practical judgments, however tentative, were always composed with a definite aim in mind, though his arguments were often presented in dialectical statements. An appraisal of his political thought can therefore be based primarily on his actions and his own justification as presented in letters and memoranda. Corresponding statements ascribed to him may be used as a supplementary source as long as they are in line with his thinking.[1]

* My Richelieu seminar at Washington University, St. Louis, Missouri, in fall 1965, as well as discussions with Dr. Ernst Hinrichs and Mr. J. Wollengerg at Goettingen have helped me to clarify the complex Richelieu problems.

[1] The abundant material originating mostly from Richelieu's dictation —not fully published—can be roughly classified into three groups. By far the larger part of them are memoranda, instructions and letters written for a specific purpose, many of which were published in d'Avenel's edition of the *Lettres, instructions diplomatiques et papiers d'état* (8 vols., 1853–77).

A second category comprises works of a wider scope: the theological treatises, which have drawn relatively little attention though they have all the appearance of authenticity, and the so-called political writings, the *Mémoires* and the *Testament Politique*. They were very likely the work of some of his secretaries who after his death used and reworked the material —to be sure, for a purpose by no means alien to the mind of their master— and who incorporated many pieces of an authentic nature.

The most recent edition of the *Mémoires*, reaching until 1629, ed. Lavollée, by the Société de l'Histoire de France (10 vols., 1907–31), was discontinued, on account of the criticism of the edition (cf. especially P. Bertrand in *Revue Historique*, Vol. 140 [1923]). For the period 1629 to 1638—the year with which the *Mémoires* end—the older edition in the collection of Michaud-Poujoulat has still to be used. The *Rapports et notices sur l'édition des Mémoires de Richelieu* (3 vols., 1905–22) contain important articles also on Richelieu's secretaries and collaborators. Already Ranke (*Französische Geschichte*, Vol. 5, p. 137ff., especially 173ff.) regarded the title *Mémoires* as a misnomer but stated that this *Histoire* contained in the midst of various incongruent pieces also authentic material.

For the *Testament Politique*, last edited by L. André (1947, 7th ed., 1957), cf. E. Esmonin, *"Sur l'authenticité du Testament Politique de*

A full evaluation of both his thought and his action, however, presupposes knowledge of the situation in which he had to consolidate the power of his king and to establish his own position. Therefore a brief sketch of the condition of France in 1624 when Richelieu took office seems appropriate.[2]

Richelieu," in *Etudes sur la France des 17e et 18e siècles* (1964), p. 219ff.; R. Pithon in *Schweizerische Zeitschrift für Geschichte*, Vol. 6 (1956); J. Engel in *Festschrift G. Kallen* (1957), who proves convincingly that the preface to the *Testament* is composed of two pieces relating to two different writings. The first of these, the *"Succincte Narration,"* in its main part seems to be the most authentic piece of the "political writings," rightly called by P. Bertrand *les vrais Mémoires*.

All that can be said of these two works at this time is that the best-known and most recent editions are based on manuscripts that have been proven to be of a secondary, derived nature. Even if we had the most original version at our disposal Richelieu scholars would still be faced by the problem to what extent the cardinal's own formulation was contained in the original manuscript. Furthermore, Richelieu was an intensive and penetrating reader. The catalogues of his library as well as excerpts of a manifold nature which are scattered through his left papers give evidence of this. For this reason a new edition would have to fulfill the most urgent requirement of Richelieu research: by way of textual criticism to show the models and borrowings in order to throw some light on the affiliation of his thought to the humanistic Neostoic and the Neoscholastic tradition which can be traced right into his formulations (cf. Erich Hassinger, "Das politische Testament Richelieus," in *Historische Zeitschrift,* Vol. 173 [1952], p. 501ff.).

Finally, we have a third type of source which stands rather by itself. Excerpts, examples from history—French, European, Ancient History—reflections, deliberations comprise the contents of a notebook which eighty years ago Hanotaux published under the rather misleading title *Maximes d'État et Fragments Politiques* (*Collection des documents inédits, Mélanges historiques*, Vol. 3), Paris, 1880. The full authenticity even of this volume of a more intimate nature has recently been questioned by Esmonin (p. 224ff.): whether the notebook really stems from the pen of the cardinal, or rather from that of one of his secretaries.

[2] The best recent treatment of France in the early seventeenth century is in Roland Mousnier's masterful *"L'assassinat d'Henri IV"* (1964); it supersedes the earlier analysis in the first volume of G. Hanotaux' *Histoire du Cardinal de Richelieu* (6 vols. since 1893, completed by the Duc de la Force). Alongside the older treatments of Richelieu by d'Avenel, *Richelieu et la monarchie absolue* (4 vols., 1884–90), and by Ranke, Hanotaux, Mariéjol (in Lavisse's *Histoire de France*) and Fagniez, *Le Père Joseph et Richelieu* (2 vols., 1894), the books by Louis Batiffol, one of the most penetrating Richelieu scholars, as well as George Pagès' *Naissance du grand siècle* (1948) and V. L. Tapié's *La France de Louis XII et de Richelieu* (1952) should be mentioned. Carl J. Burckhardt's biography (3 vols., Vol. 1 also in English translation) is full of psychological insight, in parts fascinating, but uneven. An attempt to relate Richelieu to the Baroque age is in Carl Joachim Friedrich's *The Age of Baroque* (1952). A very useful bibliography of recent Richelieu literature by William F. Church is in *Journal of Modern History*, Vol. 31 (December 1965).

I

Though the memory of Henry IV was carefully nurtured, his integrating power did not last beyond his death. Anarchy and impoverishment had not been conquered. The violence of the religious wars had abated, but the temper of the country had not basically changed for the better. A turbulent and impoverished nobility, still bent on rallying around the "Grands," presented as much of a problem as the strongly organized minority of the Huguenots in their fortified places, customarily referred to by historians as a "state within a state." Furthermore, whoever were to inherit the weak regime of the Queen Mother, Maria Medici, and later of the King's favorite, Luynes, had to cope with two strongly entrenched groups: the *noblesse de robe,* which by the Paulette had become hereditary holders of high offices, and the financiers—the "partisans"—to whom long-term contracts of tax farming had been granted since the time of Henry IV. From the 1630s on a long-lasting depression disastrously diminished the livelihood of large segments of the population[3] and even prior to that date popular unrest was endemic.

The great movement of Catholic Reform, which is inseparable from Richelieu and from his work, was only beginning to lay the foundation upon which a regenerated French Catholicism was to arise and to reform society. Yet the leaders of the Reform Movement—described by their opponents and by later historians as the *parti dévot*—were looking toward Spain for cooperation.

And indeed, in the early 1620s the combined Hapsburg power seemed to be as formidable as in the great days of Philip II. We must not be misled by hindsight of Spain's beginning decline. The fight for the Netherlands had never been abandoned. From Upper Italy to the Middle Rhine the Spanish position had been consolidated, leading eventually, after 1620, to the occupation of strongholds in the Palatinate, while simultaneously Hapsburg Imperial troops and, in their wake, the Counter Reformation pene-

[3] J. Meuvret in *Annales,* Vol. 8 (1953), pp. 215–19, and especially for France the excellent study of Pierre Goubert, *Beauvais et le Beauvaisis de 1600 à 1730* (1960) and his article on the French peasantry of the seventeenth century in Trevor Aston, ed., *Crisis in Europe 1560–1660* (1965).

trated into Northwest Germany. Who could have forgotten that
a Spanish garrison left Paris when Henry IV in 1594 entered
the city? The Spaniards by their geographical position could
threaten the French Crown with financial and military support of
the rebels. Again and again malcontents had turned to Spain for
support. In this situation Richelieu in 1624 promised the king,
as his retrospective statement goes, "with utmost zeal and with
all the authority entrusted to me to destroy the Huguenot party,
to curb the pride of the great nobles, to bring His subjects back
to their duty and to raise His name amongst foreign nations to
its proper position."[4]

Threatened from without and from within, the unity of France
depended solely on the crown. Significantly, contemporary jurists
regarded two laws as "fundamental" to the French political
order: the laws pertaining to succession to the throne and to the
inalienability of the Royal Demesne. Richelieu's policy as well
as his political thought was founded on these two premises—
the authority of the crown and the integrity of France. An analysis
of his thought and action would fall short without our briefly
acquainting ourselves with the bearer of the crown.

Louis XIII, born in September 1601, was sixteen years
younger than Richelieu. He had but one thing in common with
his father: the unshakable belief in his royal dignity. In Henry
IV this conviction was in harmony with a valiant, rich, and self-
assured personality. Louis, by contrast, was uncertain of himself,
beset by inhibitions, suspicious and melancholy, weak in health
and with limited intellectual ability, unimpressive in appearance.
Next to religion, it was royal self-confidence that sustained him
and, under the right guidance, could express itself in strong political action and in valiant military deeds.

Louis' position as head of the royal family was not secure
either. Until the dauphin, the later Louis XIV, was finally born
in September 1639, the king's brother Gaston, the heir presumptive
to the throne, a weak and vacillating young man, was the
natural center of intrigues against the King and his minister.
The Queen Mother, to whom Richelieu owed his rise to power,
was an ever-present menace: afraid of losing her hold on her
son, she challenged the Cardinal and his policy; in the famous
journée des dupes in November 1630 she lost out and finally

4 *"Succincts Narration,"* in *Testament Politique,* ed. André, p. 95.

fled to Brussels to become, under Spanish protection for more than a decade, another center of opposition.

From now on, more than ever before, Richelieu's whole position hinged on the confidence of the king. The relationship between these two men was the cornerstone on which the edifice of Richelieu's policy was to be built.

II

The core of Richelieu's political thinking was a concept that had come into its own in the later sixteenth century: *l'état*. It may be said that both crown and country were practically if not completely subsumed in it. King and state are sometimes put side by side in Richelieu's terminology; but very rarely—and then only on account of a special addressee—is the state included in the service of the king. Generally service of the state is the all-absorbing task to which everything else should be subordinated, and the king himself is asked to subordinate his sentiments to the interest of the state. Reason of state—a term popular with contemporary political writers—appears less frequently in Richelieu's writings than one would expect. More often demands for the sake of the existence of the state are made out of *nécessité*. "The salvation of man," he says in his great *avis au roi* early in 1629, "lies in the other world: but states do not exist beyond this world, their salvation can only be immediate or none."[5]

Service of the state is all-commanding and all-absorbing. Richelieu, though deeply concerned with restoring the traditional virtues and military functions of the nobility, did not hesitate in view of a suspected plot to ask officers to serve as his informants. When de Thou did not reveal the plot of his friend Cinq-Mars it was sufficient cause to have him executed.[6]

In order to keep the King in line Richelieu mixed frankness with fatherly and priestly persuasion, forever admonishing him to heed his royal duty. The more both were welded together in the constant fight against internal and external enemies, the more

---

[5] d'Avenel, Vol. 3, p. 195.
[6] Cf. the discussion of the case of Colonel Gassion by d'Avenel, Vol. 7, p. 846f.

any move against the minister became equivalent to treason against state and King. In the formulation of one of Richelieu's publicists, the great actions of the royal master and the zeal of his most loyal servant formed a more perfect union than the mind and tool of an artist could accomplish in his work of art.[7] Only a few months before his death the Cardinal insisted upon the removal of all Cinq-Mars' friends from the King's entourage with the argument: "Unless the whole of Christendom be persuaded that the King will not tolerate those who are not in agreement with the cardinal the state of France cannot be considered strong and secure."[8]

Did personal feelings of hatred or resentment enter into Richelieu's decisions? If they did, he knew how to rationalize and objectify them.

Richelieu's fabulous rise to power recurrently tempted jealous nobles to line up with political malcontents and even to make contact with the foreign enemy. A member of an old family from Poitou which had only recently been drawn to the court, he now became a *grandseigneur,* on a par with the high aristocracy with which his family intermarried. A true representative of the Baroque Age, as intent upon formal representation and splendor as on power, he became the owner of one of the largest fortunes in France, holder of innumerable benefices as well as remunerative fiefs, the protector of art and scholarship, one of the greatest collectors of his age, the builder of his own palaces and of a town named after him. His position—of his own making, to be sure—was so exposed that he had constantly to be on guard, under conditions reminiscent of the Italian Renaissance. Recurrently endangered by conspiracies—real or potential—threatening his life, he surrounded himself with guards of his own.

The physical circumstances of his life must not be forgotten. From his early years he was beset by recurrent illness and was constantly aware of the limitations of his physical strength. His physicians had to accompany him everywhere and more than once barely succeeded in saving him from death. By sheer will power, and with the help of an elaborately organized secretariate, which worked day and night, he was able to wrest the utmost

[7] Hay du Châtelet in the preface of his *Recueil* of 1635 quoted by Hanotaux in *Histoire du Cardinal de Richelieu,* Vol. 4, p. 231.

[8] d'Avenel, Vol. 7, p. 165.

from his frail body. In his later years he often had to be carried from place to place; when he was no longer able to use his right arm he had to resort exclusively to dictation.

The responsibility he had coveted and the circumstances under which he had to make decisions made him feel, in his own words, near death.[9] Yet he had chosen this way of life and it was commensurate with his personality. In general he regarded the *homme de bien* as the norm to follow, but in other notes which may be authentic he pointed out that the great man under the pressure of necessity is permitted to make decisions that normally are not legitimate.[10]

The new concept of sovereignty, though infrequently used by Richelieu, was a basic supposition of his thought and action. Royal sovereignty had to be established in the face of an attitude that made one of Gaston's followers feel surprised to be charged with high treason for his participation in an uprising. Every method was pursued, from imprisonment by royal order, from exile—enforced or "voluntary"—to formal trial, by the intendants or by courts, which sometimes were especially selected to insure compliance with the cardinal's interpretation of the case.[11] Richelieu summarized the intended effect when a few weeks before his death he stated in a memorandum for the King: "The withdrawal of many of the Grands from the court and from France—enforced or voluntary—has made this state safe."[12]

According to the contemporary thinking of Neostoic humanists both the king and his council should be guided by reason and moderation. The position of the council was inferior only to that of the king. In the characteristically theological formulation of the *Testament Politique* it was stated that the king had to work through his council as God works through secondary

[9] d'Avenel, Vol. 3, p. 208.

[10] Several statements in the *Maximes d'État,* ed. Hanotaux, center around the *grands esprits.*

[11] The trial of the Maréchal de Marillac is a case in point. Since some of the indictments related to Marillac's alleged mismanagement at Verdun, the case was taken from the uncooperative Parlement of Paris and handled by a special commission of the Parlement of Dijon. Even then Hay du Châtelet (cf. above n. 7) was temporarily sent to the Bastille when as member of the commission he did not conform with the Cardinal's opinion; cf. Hanotaux, Vol. 4, p. 239f.

[12] Oct. 27, 1642 (d'Avenel, Vol. 7, p. 166).

causes.[13] Those who interpreted Richelieu to the public—prefer-
ably without directly naming him—could claim that as councilor
he was a model of caution and prudence. Indeed, his outlook
was always pragmatic, each action was dominated by his *vision
relatée*,[14] which also included experience gained from history.
Even in his expression, passion is always fully controlled and
guided exclusively by reason.

And yet reason, he would point out to the king, required the
most severe punishment of any action contrary to the King's
command; only by this method could the state be made secure.
The anarchic condition in which he found France required capital
punishment to be inflicted on officers and troops as much as on
individual nobles whose customary dueling bordered on murder.[15]
In one of his admonitions to the king Richelieu contrasted the
King of Spain, who could easily be tempted to go beyond the
legitimate limits of his power and thus to sin by commission,
with the situation of the King of France who, due to the French
inclination toward levity and indulgence, could sin only by omis-
sion.[16] Doubtless he felt that such royal severity did not conflict
with justice and religion, which his master, *Louis le Juste,* regarded as the bases of his kingdom.

The right decision must be taken at the right moment; the
statesman is obliged to weigh all the circumstances and then act
with determination. Human affairs, like the human body, are
subject to growth and decline, and whether in action by attack or
by preservation the right phase has to be made use of. The
traditional metaphors of captain and physician as similes for king
and statesman have a very precise meaning in Richelieu's language.

Human life and human affairs, however, to whose transitory,
fleeting nature the state gives direction, are under God, as the
sovereign king is sovereign under God. We have to ask in what
wider context Richelieu conceived the state; we have to understand his notion of the world in which his state was embedded.

---

[13] André (ed.), p. 289.

[14] An expression of M. Deloche, *Autour de la Plume du Cardinal de
Richelieu* (1920), p. 11.

[15] The execution of Bouteville, a member of the Montmorency family,
in 1627 for killing another noble in a duel, contrary to the King's recent
decree, was meant to set an example but did so only to a limited extent,
cf. d'Avenel, *La noblesse française sous Richelieu* (2nd ed., 1914), p. 266ff.

[16] "Avis au Roi," January 13, 1629, d'Avenel, Vol. 3, p. 194.

This world for him comprised the relations of the state to the church, to other states, and to the society controlled by the state, and it was based on the religious and legal concepts underlying these relations.

III

Richelieu was a churchman as well as a statesman. His political activity certainly overshadowed all other functions, and he coveted some of his ecclesiastical dignities, particularly the cardinalate, for political and social reasons. Nevertheless, it would be wrong to underestimate either his ties with the French Church and the Catholic Reform movement, which was to reshape French thought and action, or the influence of theological thought on the formation of his mind.

In 1623, one year before he entered the King's council, Richelieu resigned as Bishop of Luçon. The experience in a mixed diocese, in which the reconversion of the Protestants had been one of his main concerns had, however, an effect upon his whole life. The man who in 1614 had been one of the spokesmen of the clergy in the Estates General retained a special affinity to the estate of the clergy. Not only were some of the most prominent members of the French hierarchy, from high aristocratic families, his most trusted advisers—among them such military leaders as Cardinal de La Valette, Archbishop of Toulouse, who acted as general, or Sourdis, the militant Archbishop of Bordeaux, a great admiral in the Mediterranean and in the Bay of Biscay—but the periodic assembly of the clergy, which by its grant of additional levies on Church income became, not without manipulation, one of his financial mainstays, was supported by him in its fight against transgressions by secular courts.[17]

Undeniably the institutional strength of the episcopate and the social provenance of its members served Richelieu's policy well, just as the income from the numerous benefices he held were the most substantial part of his fortune. Nevertheless a genuine and deep concern with the independence and functioning of ecclesi-

[17] Pierre Blet, "Le Clergé de France et la Monarchie, Étude sur les assemblées générales du Clergé 1615–1666" 2 vols. (*Analecta Gregorians*, Vol. 106/107, Rome, 1959).

astical jurisdiction accompanied him throughout life, to find its later expression in the *Testament Politique;* and his control of many abbeys, including such a prominent one as Cluny, was by no means an affair of mere sinecures. On the contrary, he was occupied to his final hours with carrying the "strict observants" —the movement of reform within the Benedictines and its related orders—to full victory.[18] The founding of the order of La Trappe among the Cistercians, more than twenty years after his death, can be related to Richelieu's constant endeavors for reform. The ecclesiastical reforms he envisaged and partly carried out were closely in line with the decrees of the Council of Trent and the great movement of Catholic reform. His fundamental concept of order and discipline can be said to have grown out of a spirit akin to the reform movement. For years he had provided, in one of the poorest and most vulnerable dioceses, the example of a resident bishop supervising parish work and deeply concerned with the dignity of the priesthood.

The judgment of posterity has been far too much influenced by his political conflict with some of the leaders of the reform who, as *parti dévot,* were willing to make political concessions to Spain for the sake of a united Catholic front. In Richelieu's opinion any such endeavors had to be defeated as contrary to the interest of the state. Nevertheless in his view, too, the state had to act within the wider context of a Christian world. When, according to our modern terminology, Richelieu means Europe he speaks of *Chrétienté,* basically an undivided Catholic Christendom.

At least four lengthy theological treatises stemmed from Richelieu's pen, two of them from this episcopal period, two published posthumously—one of them incomplete—from the period of open war with Spain.[19] According to the preface of the editor Jacques

[18] Paul Denis, *Le Cardinal de Richelieu et la Réforme des Monastères Bénédictines* (1913).

[19] *Les principaux points de la foi catholique défendus contre l'escrit addressé au roy par les quatre ministres de Charenton* (Poitiers, 1618). *Instruction du Chrestien* (Poitiers, 1622). *Traité de la perfection du chrestien* (Paris, 1647). *Traité qui contient la methode la plus facile et la plus assuréepour convertir ceux qui sont séparés de l'Eglise* (Paris, 1651). About Richelieu's possible authorship of other treatises in his Luçon period cf. Deloche, *Plume,* pp. 25ff. An attempt to relate Richelieu's political thinking to his religious and theological concepts in E. Hassinger's article, *Historische Zeitschrift,* Vol. 173.

Lescot, Bishop of Chartres and Richelieu's former confessor, Richelieu was still occupied with the last polemical treatise in the last months of his life. All his treatises, whether of a didactic or of a controversial nature, show the same absence of emotion and the complete prevalence of rational deduction. Two themes accompanied him throughout life: the central significance of the Church for the life of the Christian, and the reconversion of the Protestants. It would be vain to look in these treatises for an understanding of the fundamental concept of Protestantism, of justification by faith. The visible Church of Christ is the beginning and the end of his argument; his main concern is to prove that the *Église prétendue réformée* is no church, and that its members have to find their way back to the Church. The innate goodness of man which can be awakened and led in the right direction by the dispensations of the Church is implied, in the tradition of the Council of Trent and of Catholic humanism.

No wonder that Richelieu, certain of support by the Gallican Church, by no means encouraged an offensive attitude toward the Papacy[20]; no wonder that he cooperated with the Jesuits whose learning he valued highly and that he accepted them as royal confessors provided they did not mingle in politics.

In view of his close cooperation with ardent protagonists of the Church, not least with his friend and most loyal cooperator, Père Joseph, it would be contrary to all historical evidence not to take seriously the endeavors of Richelieu and of his associates, after the defeat of the Huguenots and after the demolition of other rebels' castles, to use the confiscated property for churches and convents. To be sure, no coercion of the Protestants was envisaged or enacted; by persuasion and mild pressure, including financial pensions to former ministers, they were to be led in the right direction.

IV

How are we to reconcile with this deep concern for the Catholic Church the foreign policy to which most of Richelieu's energies were devoted and whose attainments ranked higher than any of his other achievements? Was its most outstanding feature not the

[20] Cf. Blet, I 445, II p. 70f.

financial support of and even alliance with heretic powers, especially the Dutch and the savior of German Protestantism, Gustavus Adolphus? Was not the change in 1635 to open war against Spain after seven years of indirect warfare caused mainly by the necessity to keep these heretic allies in the war against the common enemy?

Richelieu never tired of pointing out that Spain exploited the Catholic cause for her own benefit—an argument that had its effect on the Pope, Urban VIII, who regarded Spain as a constant threat to the independence of the Italian states. After his first great success, the capture of La Rochelle in 1628, achieved in open fight against the English allies of the Huguenots and in the face of the ambiguous attitude of Spain toward the King's Protestant rebels, he had attained his goal of making France once more, as in the times of Henry IV, the counterforce that assured the liberty of Christendom.[21]

Yet was it permissible for the sake of the liberty of Christendom to strengthen the position of heretic states? To hand back control of that crucial strategic life line of the Spaniards, the Catholic Valtellin, to the Protestant Grisons might be justified on the basis of natural law since the Grisons had the sovereign power. In the cases of direct alliance with Protestant powers a variety of explanations was marshaled by Richelieu's publicists: reason, prudence, or the succinct statement that "the laws of the state differ from those of the canonists, and the principles of the school have nothing in common with political rules."[22] In contrast to such extreme statements Richelieu himself may have operated with a highly casuistic exposition[23]: that according to St.

[21] For the effect of the campaign against La Rochelle in Italy: Béthune in 1627 (Blet, I 374), and Richelieu's "Memorandum for Marillac 1630" (d'Avenel, Vol. 3, p. 709). His program against Spain in July 1624: *L'union des États de la maison d'Autriche séparés ôte le contre poids de la puissance de France qui donne la liberté de la chrétienté.* (*Mémoires,* Vol. 4, p. 220).

[22] Jérémie Ferrier in *"Catholique d'Estat."* I owe this reference to Mr. Jörg Wollenberg. Joseph Lecler in *Études, Revue fondée par les pères de la Compagnie de Jésus,* Vol. 214 (1933), p. 698 convincingly rejects the assumption of Louis Dedouvres, the champion of Père Joseph among recent historians, that Père Joseph or Richelieu were themselves involved in the *"Catholique d'Estat."* Lecler's articles in the *Études* are the best treatment of the religious aspects of Richelieu's foreign policy.

[23] Memorandum by an unknown author on the Dutch alliance (*Mémoires,* Vol. 5, appendix, pp. 283–308; cf. on the casuistic treatment of this question, also by Père Joseph, Lecler, p. 690ff.

Thomas one is permitted to make use of another's sin without sinning, just as one can make use of an infidel's oath in order to reveal an essential truth, or, in case of need, of a usurer's loan. Similarly, even if the sovereignty of the Netherlands were contestable and they could be regarded as rebels against their king, France could still sustain their revolt if this was the only way to defend herself against the Spanish danger. Such devices in the interest of the state, however, in the words of Père Joseph, "can only be made use of like poison of which a little serves as counterpoison but too much kills."[24]

Starting from the marriage contract of Henriette Maria with Charles I of England, Richelieu used every opportunity to insert in his treaties stipulations to safeguard the rights of Catholics. His constant endeavors were directed toward lining up Catholic powers, such as Bavaria, in the fight against the Hapsburgs. In vain he sought to prevent conflict between his Protestant and Catholic allies. His attempt to eliminate the religious elements from the struggle in Germany proved unsuccessful. Gustavus Adolphus, though financed by him, pursued his own aims; if it were not for his premature death, he might eventually have opposed Richelieu.

Undoubtedly his support of Catholic princes stood him politically in good stead, just as his program of monastic reform had its political side. In pushing the reform which had originated in Lorraine and in furthering a tie between the Lorraine and the French monastic houses he could strengthen French military control of Lorraine, one of his main goals. And in supporting the militant Archbishop of Trier, Philipp von Soetern, against Spain, he established French strongholds—though not permanently—in Philippsburg and Ehrenbreitstein, two key positions on the right bank of the Rhine. The capture and imprisonment of the Archbishop by the Hapsburg powers, moreover, provided him with an ideal opportunity to declare war on Spain in 1635 and to demand increased financial support from the French clergy. All these steps were moves of power politics against Spanish encroachments. When we consider the Hapsburg position in 1629, and again in 1634, after the battle of Noerdlingen, when the Cardinal Infante brought his victorious army to Brussels at the end of its long

[24] Lecler, p. 560.

advance from Italy, the danger of Spanish predominance was real enough.

The fight against Spain was not meant to lead merely to the coexistence of autonomous powers within a European system of states. It would be wrong to underestimate the strength and the persistence of the concept of Christendom. On his deathbed Père Joseph may have foreseen a very secular success, the capture of Breisach, which once and for all interrupted the Spanish control of the Rhine as the connecting link between Italy and the Netherlands. Yet Père Joseph lived and died with the plan of a common crusade against the Turks, which to him meant more than any of his actual exploits. And when in 1637 Father Caussin, the King's confessor, admonished him—only to be exiled by Richelieu for having meddled in politics—not to continue a war that brought ever-increasing harm to Catholic lands and into which Richelieu's policy was suspected to draw the Turk, Louis burst out: "I wish the Turk were in Madrid, then Spain would be forced to conclude peace and we could join hands to wage war on the Sultan."[25]

In Richelieu's thought and action neither religion nor law was separated from politics. His endeavors to justify his political moves from the religious angle are paralleled by legal considerations. Recently Richelieu's first drafts, which form the basis of the instructions for the French negotiators at the peace of Westphalia, concluded several years after his death, have been published.[26] The rediscoverer and editor of these drafts, Fritz Dickmann, after tracing Richelieu's constant effort to bring political necessities in line with the rules of law, summarizes his findings: "For Richelieu the great political decisions were also decisions of conscience; much more than we might expect he evaluates questions of power politics by way of legal concepts."[27] The medieval scholastic doctrine of the just war underlay his considerations. Every one of his moves in power politics was circumspect and every implication and possible consequence was envisaged; yet he was anxiously concerned not to take a step that

[25] Memorandum of December 1637 (d'Avenel, Vol. 5, p. 812).

[26] *Acta Pacis Westphalicae,* Serie I. Instruktionen, Vol. I, (Muenster, 1962).

[27] *Ibid.,* p. 4; cf. also F. Dickmann, *"Rechtsgedanke und Machtpolitik bei Richelieu"* in *Historische Zeitschrift,* Vol. 196 (1963).

could not be vindicated as being based on law. Against the encroachments of the Hapsburgs, it was necessary, with the consent of the respective authorities—often granted under pressure—to establish military strongholds, at least temporarily, that would permit France to aid princes of neighboring countries in their fight for autonomy or independence. Support of uprisings against a ruler was justified when, according to legal theory, the sovereign was bound by special contract, which he had violated, as the King of Spain was limited in relation to Catalonia and Portugal, or the Emperor in his relations to the German princes. On the other hand, the inalienability of the royal demesne remained the supreme law for French policy, not to be subordinated to considerations of power politics.

Once more it can be said that the fleeting and transitory human affairs to which political decisions relate are seen within a wider and more constant world determined by religious and legal norms.

V

One more task remains: to investigate the aims of Richelieu's internal policy and his accomplishments in this area.

Prior to his ministry Richelieu had remarked: "No civil war can exist without support from foreign powers, and they will never embark on assisting rebels against their king once his reputation abroad has been assured."[28] This meant that matters of internal reform were of only secondary significance, compared to the urgency of action abroad and the need for the crown to acquire the monopoly of power at home.

Subjects, he had stated at the time of his first ministry, who raise troops and levy taxes are acting contrary to what they owe to their King.[29] When he finally and permanently assumed the direction of affairs his greatest accomplishment was the concentration of power exclusively in the hands of the crown. In his words of 1627, "in well-organized and well-regulated states no individual, whoever he may be, can be permitted to have control

[28] Advice given by the Queen Mother to the King in 1623 at the suggestion of Richelieu (in *Mémoires,* Vol. 3, p. 317); cf. Hanotaux, Vol. 4, p. 299.
[29] Feb. 18, 1617 (d'Avenel, Vol. 1, p. 313).

over a large number of armed forces."[30] While fortifications in the border provinces were maintained and entrusted to loyal officers, elsewhere any occasion of revolt was seized upon to raze castles. Such occasions and demolitions did occur in regions of the Center, the South, and the Southwest. When during the revolt of the Fronde, after Richelieu's death, apart from the rising in Paris and the Spanish invasion of the northern border regions a lengthy military campaign had to be conducted only in Guienne, this limited war contrasted sharply with the extended and diffused campaigns of previous uprisings.

The crisis of autumn 1630 which culminated in the *journée des dupes*—*le grand orage* in the terminology of French historians—may be regarded as decisive for the course of Richelieu's internal policy. Marillac, *garde des sceaux* and hitherto Richelieu's closest cooperator, headed the opponents. He was imprisoned, his brother tried and executed, the Queen Mother eventually forced to flee. The last effort to oust the cardinal from the King's favor had failed. This personal struggle, however, had political consequences of a far-reaching nature. Contrary to the policy of Marillac's *parti dévot* whose aim had been reconciliation with Spain, French troops became permanently entrenched beyond the Alps. Once and for all the primacy of foreign policy—to put it in modern terms—was established.

From now on the *soulagement du peuple*—the alleviation of popular distress—which Richelieu's opponents claimed as their immediate concern[31]—and any fundamental reform of the kingdom were postponed to a far distant future, to the time of peace. Richelieu's regime became one of war, although open war with Spain was postponed until 1635, and all of its measures were subordinated to the necessities of warfare and diplomacy. His internal policy has to be seen against this background as against the background of recurrent rebellion and conspiracies.

The government, which, according to Richelieu's original plan, had meant to concentrate on both order and reform, became almost exclusively a government of order. Of the program to make the reign of *Louis le Juste* resemble the government of his ancestor, St. Louis,[32] very little materialized. Officials were not

[30] End of February 1627 (d'Avenel, Vol. 2, p. 393).
[31] Cf. G. Pagès, "*Autour du grand orage. Richelieu et Marillac. Deux Politiques,*" in *Revue Historique,* Vol. 179 (1937), pp. 63–97.
[32] The Règlement of 1625 (d'Avenel, Vol. 2, p. 169f.).

made easily accessible to the public; offices and courts were not thoroughly supervised; nor were councillors from the different orders included in the council as outlined in one of Richelieu's early drafts. On the contrary, the more the pressure of military and financial commitments increased, the more the government came to depend on the financiers, the *traitants* whom Richelieu deeply suspected and disliked; their loans were essential and their compensation consisted of long-term contracts, which placed large segments of the tax system under their control. The Cardinal's associates worked hand in glove with them. For lack of control, in spite of admonitions, they could not be prevented from providing liberally for themselves.[33]

Richelieu's efforts to strengthen commerce and shipping and to develop colonies have been rightly interpreted as an indication of mercantilistic thinking; the results, however, were meager. The country was bled white by ever-increasing taxation at the very time when a severe economic depression affected Western Europe. Recently historians have made systematic investigations of the frequent uprisings brought about by oppressive taxation and of the resistance of the privileged orders to new financial impositions.[34] The reduction of unnecessary expenses such as pensions and attempts at reforms in financial administration did not reach the root of the evil.

The longer Richelieu was in office and the more he was absorbed by immediate problems, the more his attitude became

[33] O. A. Ranum, *Richelieu and the Councillors of Louis XIII: A Study of the Secretaries of State and Superintendents of Finance in the Ministry of Richelieu, 1635–1642* (Oxford, 1963). In addition, Lababut on Bullion in *Le Dix-Septième Siecle*, No. 60 (1963). Richelieu's letter to Bullion of January 1639 (d'Avenel, Vol. 6, p. 27f.) was a last attempt, a year before Bullion's death to exert pressure on him, not, as Ranke (Vol. II, p. 405) assumed, a statement when Bullion became superintendent of finance. By 1639 Bullion had already had seven years of efficient, if corrupt, management of affairs.

[34] Cf. the book of the Russian historian, Boris Prochnev, also in German and French translations, *Les soulèvements populaires en France de 1623 à 1648* (1963), Mousnier's *Lettres et mémoires adressés au Chancelier Séguier* (2 vols., 1964) and his article in the *Revue d'histoire moderne et contemporaine*, Vol. 5 (1958). For Mousnier's thesis (against Porchnev) that the privileged orders were the main instigators of the revolt, R. Pillorget's article in *Le Dix-Septième Siecle*, No. 64 (1964) on the revolt in Aix gives further convincing evidence; for the plight of the nobles by fiscal pressure cf. Pierre Deyon, *"Rapports entre la noblesse française et la monarchie absolue"* in *Revue Historique*, Vol. 231 (1964), pp. 341–56.

pragmatic. His early plan to abolish both the venality and the heredity of offices was abandoned in view of the strongly entrenched position of the *noblesse de robe* and the other officeholders and in deference to the need for the sale of new offices as a source of new income for the crown. The *Testament Politique* states with regard to the venality of offices: "In an old monarchy the imperfections have become habitual, and the disorder has become, not without advantage, part of the order of the state."[35] These remarks have the ring of authenticity.

Basically the task of government was to maintain the different orders in their respective spheres[36] and functions and to revive their old virtues, which had been lost. The reforms of the clergy were meant to restore it to its old dignity, in both its priestly and its educational functions. The domestication of the nobility was to redevelop its old chivalric and military virtues and to incorporate the nobles into the King's army. The Third Estate was to serve the state in its different functions, as officeholders and as merchants. The few pages of the *Testament Politique* on the people,[37] scant and cruel as they may appear to the modern observer, are certainly in line with Richelieu's thinking: the people are regarded merely as objects, comparable to mules, to be kept working and subservient, but not to be overtaxed.

Regional authorities—the office of the governor in particular—were decisively weakened not by institutional reforms, as originally envisaged, but by changes of personnel. Richelieu filled these key positions with loyal members of the high nobility, among them members of his own family. The intendants took first rank among his most trusted and ruthless helpers. They were temporarily dispatched to the provinces to provide for the armed forces or to quell revolts and banditry and were given far-reaching discretionary powers while acting alongside the authorities. Whether stemming from the *noblesse de robe* or from the old *noblesse d'épée,* they proved themselves his most efficient tools, often

[35] André (ed.), p. 234.

[36] William F. Church, "Cardinal Richelieu and the Social Estates of the Realm," *Album Helen Maud Cam,* Vol. 2 (*Études présentés à la Commission Internationale pour l'Histoire des Assemblées d'États,* Vol. 24, 1961). For the relationship between power and order also Rudolf von Albertini, *Das politische Denken in Frankreich zur Zeit Richelieus* (Marburg, 1951). For the "Grands," O. A. Ranum in *French Historical Studies,* Vol. 3 (1963/1964).

[37] André (ed.), pp. 253–55.

belonging to the clientele of Councillors or even of a governor.[38]
They had to deal with the armies as much as with the provinces.
Progress in discipline and organization of the armed forces was in
large part attributable to them. In turn, the success of the army
was instrumental in winning over the nobility to the service of the
crown.

Institutional changes were not necessary; it sufficed to emascu-
late the intermediate powers below the crown and to override
their opposition. Revolts—actual and intended—and conspiracies of which Richelieu kept track through an extended network
of trusted informers, offered plenty of opportunity to deprive
enemies, if not of their life at least of their liberty, and to force
suspects into exile.

Even in his relations with the Parlement of Paris Richelieu
recurrently overcame its remonstrances in crucial issues by way of
a *lit de justice* or by *lettres de cachet* against individual judges.
Finally in 1641, the King issued a declaration to the effect that
matters of state and administration were of no concern to Parlement and that it was not permitted to intrude in them.

In this way the corporate order was sustained, but none of its
members could endanger the state. The supreme task was to
make the state secure by defeating the Spanish enemy and by
permanently eliminating his chance of cooperating with rebels
against the crown.

For this purpose minds, too, constantly had to be brought in
line. The *Mercure français* was an annual publication which assembled pieces of an explanatory nature to justify the governmental policy, and in 1631 it was supplemented by the *Gazette de
France*. Every week Richelieu's management of affairs was explained here while the tight censorship insured that the statements
of his opponents could reach France only secretly from abroad.

Finally it should be emphasized that even the tradition of
clientele, closely connected with corporate order as it had become,
was adapted to Richelieu's system. Since the sixteenth century a
new word, of ecclesiastical origin, had become frequent: *créature*.
"Society"—if we can use this modern term—was shot through
with clientele relations. Richelieu by no means thought of elimi-

[38] Cf. Mousnier in his introduction to *Chancelier Séguier* I, p. 32f., and
for the position of the intendant, his *État et Commissaire* in *Festgabe
Fritz Hartung, Forschungen zu Staat und Verfassung* (1958).

nating them if they could only be made harmless. Even Gaston's *créatures* were carefully nurtured. Richelieu's *créatures* occupied key positions in government. Their dependence on him was not only a factual one, it penetrated their whole being. Saint-Preuil, governor of the newly conquered Arras, when tried for indiscipline and sentenced to death, ended his last letter to Richelieu: "I carry with me the satisfaction that I have been, as I am until death, without reservation and without end, Monseigneur, your humble, most obedient and most obliged servant and creature Saint-Preuil."[39]

VI

Richelieu stands at the threshold of what became known as the classical age of French literature. In thought, action, and personality he foreshadows this great period of French national development. By founding the *Académie* he even initiates the new phase. In one of the early sessions of the Academy, the cardinal's spokesman expressed his master's opinion when he referred to French as a language especially suited for calm and unagitated reasoning.[40] With his disciplined passion Richelieu is akin to the heroic ideal and to the concept of the *honnête homme* as it had crystallized by the middle of the century.

Everything Richelieu did was subordinated to the service of the state. For a long time, later interpreters have either hailed him as the great liberator of the state and as a proponent of secularism, or they have indicted him as a despot or as the destroyer of Christian unity. On the latter it may be sufficient to refer to Montesquieu's judgment and to the evaluation by Hilaire Belloc. Characteristic of the positive, "revolutionary" appraisal is Augustin Thierry's statement that the cardinal was *"homme de révolution par qui ont été préparées les voies de la société nouvelle."*[41] Such an interpretation, overly influenced by the evolutionary approach, antedates the development in the customary manner of the nineteenth century. Twentieth-century historians, such as

[39] November 8, 1641 (Hanotaux, Vol. 6, p. 107f.; cf. also Vol. 4, p. 164ff.).

[40] J. Barin de la Galissonnière (Hanotaux, Vol. 6, p. 307).

[41] Augustin Thierry, *"Essai sur l'histoire de la formation et des progres du Tiers État"*, Ch. 8, p. 228.

Louis Batiffol and George Pagès, have instead shown the limits of the changes envisaged and brought about by Richelieu. In emphasizing his moderation they have contributed to the reinterpretation of absolutism, which is one of the characteristics of present-day historiography. Finally, the research of Joseph Lecler and Fritz Dickmann has shown how deeply Richelieu was tied to the tradition of religion and law; the latter has even emphasized that Richelieu's vision of the eventual peace embraced a system of collective obligations to secure the peaceful coexistence of all European powers.[42]

Are we then to deny that he paved the way to the autonomy of the modern state and to the preponderance of France in Europe? Not at all. It is necessary, however, to state that he did not aim at such a full emancipation of the state, that he saw the state embedded in a larger universe controlled by traditional legal concepts and by religion. In fighting for his own state and in securing for the French crown its sphere he did not see an unbridgeable chasm between the world of religion and morals on the one side and the world of politics on the other. Necessity and the interest of state were to secure a leading role for the French state in an existing world, which he did not intend to undermine, just as the monopoly of power in the hands of the crown was not meant to change the existing social order. Seen over a long period of time the results of his policy can, however, be said to have differed from his intentions.

By his identification of state, King, and himself Richelieu poses a problem. In his *French History* Ranke, referring to testimony from the direct entourage of Père Joseph, states: "In order to remain in power in France, Richelieu had to conclude the alliance with Sweden; in order to keep hostile influences from the melancholy temper of the king, in view of the continuous threat to his position, he declared open war on Spain."[43] A remark like this from the most cautious and most tactful of historians makes one ponder.

Richelieu himself never doubted his right to identify his own survival with the survival of the state. It is reported by an often

[42] Cf. Dickmann's article *Historische Zietschrift*, Vol. 196, and with regard to the implications of Richelieu's foreign policy the critical appraisal of Dickmann and von Albertini in Kurt von Raumer's articles in *Historische Zeitschrift*, Vol. 195 (1962) and Vol. 174 (1952).

[43] Ranke, Vol. 2, p. 339; cf. also p. 343.

quoted source that when he was asked on his deathbed to forgive his enemies he replied that he had no enemies but those of the state. According to another source—apparently an eyewitness—when confronted by the Holy Sacrament, prior to Extreme Unction, he said: "My Lord, you are the judge who is soon going to judge me. I ask you with all my heart to condemn me if I have had anything in mind but the good of religion and of the state."[44]

He was convinced that religious and moral motives could and should converge with reason. When he advised the Archbishop of Rouen to refrain from a controversial statement about Papal authority he wrote him: "Not only your conscience will oblige you to act in this way; prudence must lead you to the same conclusion."[45] Ambitious and power-hungry, without doubt, Richelieu believed in the harmony of conscience and prudence. Unless we accept this belief we miss one of the keys to an understanding of his enigmatic personality.

[44] L. Lalanne, *"Un récit inédit de la mort du Cardinal Richelieu"* in *Revue Historique*, Vol. 55 (1894) p. 305.
[45] End of 1633 (d'Avenel, Vol. 4, p. 511).

Chapter 6

THE NATURE OF POLITICAL POWER
ACCORDING TO LOUIS XIV

Andrew Lossky

Most people have carried away from their school days the impression that the political philosophy of Louis XIV is summed up in the simple formula *l'état—c'est moi*. We will not join in the endless and futile debate over whether Louis XIV ever uttered these words, or whether he was their real author if he did. Even if it is true that the seventeen-year-old King, wearing a hunter's outfit, entered the Parlement of Paris and used such an expression in his discourse before this assembly, its meaning would be different from what is usually imputed. The purpose of the royal visit was to warn the officers of the law that the conduct of policy, both internal and external, was vested in the King, not in the Parlement of Paris. A statement to the effect that the conduct of policy is not the province of the Supreme Court of the United States would hardly raise a single eyebrow today. Yet this would be a correct translation of the pithy dictum attributed to Louis XIV into the cumbersome language of modern constitutional law. The actions, pronouncements, and writings of Louis XIV clearly show that he never lost sight of the distinction between the body politic and the person of the prince who was called upon to direct it. Louis' concept of his responsibilities will become apparent if we examine the relationship between the king and the state as he understood it.

Our main source for this examination will be that body of confidential personal papers known as the *Mémoires* of Louis XIV, most of which date from the late 1660s and early 1670s, that is, from the early part of the reign.[1] To deduce from this

[1] We shall take it for granted that the *Mémoires* of Louis XIV are authentic. Though most of them were not actually penned by Louis himself, he supervised their preparation closely and made many changes in the

source all of the beliefs of Louis XIV for the entire reign, as is
sometimes done, would be a dubious procedure, for Louis' beliefs underwent many profound changes in the course of the
fifty-four years of his personal rule.[2] These changes affected
such issues as the role of Divine Providence in human affairs,
the nature of privilege, of property, and of fundamental law,
the degree of administrative centralization desirable in the state,
and the uses of history. Yet, amid all these changes, the King's
belief in the nature of royal sovereignty remained virtually
constant. This becomes apparent from a comparison between
Louis' *Mémoires* and another set of confidential papers, dating
from the end of the reign: Louis' letters written in 1701–15
to his grandson, Philip V of Spain, whom he was trying to
teach how to be a king.[3]

Louis' doctrine of political power was based on his concept of
human nature which he held with remarkable tenacity throughout his reign. It would be an exaggeration to say that Louis
thought all men to be hopelessly depraved, but he certainly did
not believe in man's innate goodness; in this point he differed
from the standard doctrine of his Jesuit friends and mentors.
The chief source of human imperfection is every man's par-

---

various drafts. For a discussion of this problem see Paul Sonnino, "The dating and authorship of Louis XIV's *Mémoires*," *French Historical Studies*,
III, No. 3 (Spring 1964), pp. 303–37. The references to Louis' *Mémoires*
in this article will be to J. Longnon (ed.), *Mémoires de Louis XIV*, Paris,
1927, which will be cited as "Longnon." Longnon's edition gives a readable
and reliable version of this work; it is more usable than the "critical"
edition of Charles Dreyss (*Mémoires de Louis XIV pour l'instruction du
Dauphin*, 2 vols., Paris, 1860), which is not quite as "critical" as its massive
scholarly apparatus makes it appear. The Longnon edition is also more
accurate than the editions by Grouvelle and by de Gain-Montagnac, both
of which appeared in 1806.

[2] On changes in Louis' beliefs see my article, "Some of the problems
of tracing the intellectual development of Louis XIV" in *Louis XIV and
the Craft of Kingship*, John C. Rule, ed., Ohio University Press, 1967.
Between 1661 and 1715 it is possible to discern at least nine distinct
periods in the intellectual life of Louis XIV.

[3] A. Baudrillart has identified 538 letters of Louis XIV to Philip V.
Most of them (401) are at present in the Archivo Historico Nacional in
Madrid. The Archives of the Ministry of Foreign Affairs in Paris also contain many of the drafts and copies (514). This important source has received surprisingly little attention. See A. Baudrillart, *Philippe V et la Cour
de France*, Vol. I (Paris, 1890), pp. 11–15, and his *Rapport sur une Mission
en Espagne aux Archives d'Alcala de Hénarès et de Simancas* (Paris,
1889), pp. 25, 49–70.

tiality toward his private interest and advantage. If given free play, man's egoism produces chaos and many tyrannies of the strong over the weak. To escape this condition men give up to the prince their "natural right" to enforce their personal justice. But such is the unreasonable nature of man that he will avail himself of every opportunity to regain this right, if only in part. It takes "heroic virtue," of which an ordinary person is not capable, to withstand such temptation.[4] Since human society is not made up of heroic saints, but of men of flesh and blood, the question arises how it should be organized so as to conform to the "natural order of things."

The concept of "natural order" belongs to a higher plane of reality than that of everyday life; it can generally be defined as the ideal order of the universe as it is conceived by God. Though Louis does not make use of the term "natural law" in the sense in which we find it in Grotius, it is clear that the norms of such a natural law are the ones that prevail in the "natural order." Unfortunately, owing to the corrupt nature of man, they are not self-enforcing, and it becomes the chief purpose and responsibility of power in the state to reduce all "to legitimate and natural order."[5] A formidable difficulty arises at this point, for those who wield power in the state, including the prince himself, are themselves but men, and therefore prone to corruption. How to resolve this difficulty was the chief preoccupation of Louis XIV in so far as he ruminated about the nature of things political, which he did more frequently than is usually imagined; this becomes apparent not only from the King's *Mémoires,* but also from the extensive correspondence on which he left his personal imprint.

No government can carry out its mission unless the supreme power in the state is absolute, that is, not limited by any human institution or persons in the exercise of its functions. Human nature being what it is, it is inevitable that the persons who could limit the supreme power would seek to use their influence to promote their private interests at the expense of the public. This leads to disorder, amid which the more powerful members of society usurp more and more authority and the people suffer under "thousands and thousands of petty tyrants."[6] Inevitably

[4] Longnon, p. 132.
[5] *Ibid.,* pp. 41, 134.
[6] *Ibid.,* p. 45.

it is the *bas peuple* who must foot the bill for the license of their social betters. Thus the republican form of government, whether it be aristocratic or democratic, is only a disguise for private interests, for the *magnum latrocinium* of St. Augustine. A limited monarchy, such as that established in England, or a council of regency is no better. True enough, Louis XIV was not entirely doctrinaire on this point. In olden, almost mythical times, political virtue had not been unknown among the ancient Romans, as well as among the inhabitants of France, who could be trusted to vote freely the appropriate "gratuitous donations" in their provincial estates. He admitted that in modern times, too, the air of Venice, for instance, was apt to foster political virtue and wisdom among the ruling citizens. Elsewhere, a great man like Cromwell, De Witt, or William III might rise above private interests to an understanding of the public good, and impart an element of grandeur to his state. But unless his action is accompanied by a thorough reform of the political structure, as in the case of Caesar and of other founders of empires, this greatness is transitory and only serves to emphasize the basic corruption of government by many heads.

The unlimited sovereign has many duties both to God and to "the public." As God's lieutenants on earth, entrusted by Him with the care "of the peoples and of the states," kings are accountable to God alone. They must recognize the over-all sovereignty of God, of which the kingly power is but a small part. God gives kingship to his lieutenants directly, not through the intermediary of the Church; the anointment or coronation merely serves to proclaim kingship before men and to render it more august in their eyes. God entrusts a good king not only with a part of His power but also with some of His knowledge.[7] The king must seek to please God by showing his gratitude for every favor received from heaven; "kings show their gratitude for [God's] favors by enforcing the observance of His laws."[8] Appropriate actions on the part of the king may include suppression of blasphemy, of dueling, of schism or heresy, fighting

[7] *Ibid.*, pp. 12, 35, 52, 57–63, 149, 225, 228–29, 255.
[8] Louis XIV to Philip V, June 8, 1704: *"Les Roys marquent la reconnoissance qu'ils ont des ses* [God's] *bienfaits en faisant observer ses loix,"* Paris, Ministry of Foreign Affairs, Correspondance Politique, Espagne, Vol. 143, fol. 282.

the infidel, or giving alms. Public tokens of respect to the Deity "may rightly be called the first and the most important part of our policy"; but, to be effective, these acts must not be hypocritical, nor must they be based on calculations of immediate interest.[9]

There are several ways in which God bestows His favors on kings. It is God who secures the obedience of the subjects to their lawful sovereigns; and, indeed, Louis notes that since the coming of Christ revolutions have become less frequent than they had been before.[10] God may even occasionally intervene directly to grant a victory (an "option of heaven") or some other success to the king. But such miraculous interventions of the Deity are rare, for God, who has Himself "established the natural order of things, will not easily violate it . . . either to your prejudice or to your advantage. [The supreme power of God] can reassure us in the hour of peril, fortify us in our labors, and enlighten us in the midst of our doubts, but it does not perform our work without us; for when it wishes to make a king fortunate, powerful, clothed with authority, and respected, its most usual way is to render him wise, clear-sighted, just, vigilant, and hard-working."[11] Let us note that at the time of the composition of the *Mémoires* Louis thought himself abundantly endowed with all these qualities. Later on, under the weight of misfortunes that beset him in his old age, Louis modified his view: direct interventions of God in human affairs became more common and awe-inspiring; one of the principal functions of the king was to bear them without murmur, "to adore the judgments of God," and by this conduct to seek to return into His favor.[12]

Apart from their duty to God, "kings owe, so to say, a public account for all their actions to the entire world and to all ages,"[13] especially to the future generations. This follows from their position in the state: "we are the head of the body whose members they [our subjects] are. It is only for their advantage that we must give them laws, and we must not use the power that we have over them except to work more effectively to

[9] Longnon, pp. 57–63.
[10] *Ibid.*, p. 255.
[11] *Ibid.*, pp. 118–19.
[12] This is one of the constant themes in Louis' letters to Philip V.
[13] Longnon, p. 13.

further their happiness."[14] All the different conditions of men "are held together [in society] only by a reciprocal exchange of duties. The marks of obedience and respect that we receive from our subjects are not gratuitous gifts, but are given in consideration of justice and protection which they claim to receive from us"; this is what holds the prince and the people "in an agreeable and honorable company."[15] Hence the interests of the prince and of the people "are but one," for, properly speaking, only the sovereign has no other real interest than that of the state and of all his subjects, who are his "true riches." "When [the king works] for the state, he works for himself: the good of the one makes for the glory of the other."[16]

The first duty of the commonwealth is self-preservation; "reason of state" is therefore paramount to all other laws, except, of course, the divine law. Utility should thus be the guiding principle of royal conduct: heaven has made the king the depositary of "public interest" or "public good," for which alone he is born, and at whose altar he must sacrifice everything, including what we would call his "personality."[17] Pursuing this line of reasoning, Louis wrote in 1679: "the interest of the state must come first."[18] We find this formula constantly repeated, like an incantation, by the men of his entourage; the King must have used it in the *Conseil d'en-haut* whenever he thought that his ministers were bringing extraneous matters into their deliberations.

There are many ways of serving the interests of the community, and Louis qualifies more than one royal function as "principal" or "first." The kings must, of course, reduce all elements in the realm to "the natural and legitimate order."[19] In this respect the King of France enjoys an inestimable advantage over his less-fortunate fellow monarchs: French society is so constituted that, though it is easy to disturb its natural order, it is even easier to restore it—in fact, this natural order restores itself, if given a chance to do so; hence arises that *"facilité"* of the monarchy,

14 *Ibid.*, p. 73.
15 *Ibid.*, pp. 67, 121.
16 *Ibid.*, pp. 42, 67–68, 197–98, 281.
17 *Ibid.*, pp. 31, 41, 43, 46, 149, 159, 180, and *passim*.
18 *Ibid.*, p. 280.
19 *Ibid.*, pp. 41, 134, and *passim*.

which is peculiar to France and which is one of her glories.[20]

To discharge his primary duty to the community, the king must uphold the laws in all their rigor; failure to do this is tantamount to "divesting oneself of royal dignity." The king must be the sole determinant of the law and of the jurisdictions within his realm, and he cannot delegate this part of his sovereignty to anybody else, so closely is it bound to the crown.[21] Kings are "born to possess and to command all"; as "absolute lords," they enjoy the "full and free disposition of all the goods, both secular and ecclesiastical," which they must use for the good of their states.[22] This is as extreme a claim to absolute sovereignty as we shall find in Louis XIV. We must add, however, that Louis' views on the nature of the laws, especially of the "fundamental laws" of the realm, underwent several changes. In the second half of his reign he no longer considered himself to be the source of all law, and toward the end of the reign he came to entertain grave doubts about his right to impose new taxes. The "fundamental laws" came to occupy a place closer to the divine law, that is, they were now beyond royal power. But with the waning of his role as the lawgiver, Louis XIV did not abandon his insistence on retaining in his own hands the royal function of decision-making in shaping the policy of the realm.

Since the king cannot properly discharge his duties unless his power is absolute, his first preoccupation must always be to preserve his authority and his glory; the latter is the mainstay of his power. The theme of "glory" is one of the constant elements in Louis' idiosyncrasy and he is never tired of talking about it. Much has been made of this preoccupation with his glory, but it is usually overlooked that the notion of glory is a complex one and goes far beyond the mere amassing of military victories.[23] A simple enumeration of some of the meanings in which "glory"

[20] *Ibid.*, p. 122.

[21] *Ibid.*, pp. 38–39, 138.

[22] *Ibid.*, pp. 197–98, 224.

[23] See, for example, G. Zeller, *"Politique extérieure et diplomatie sous Louis XIV," Revue d'Histoire Moderne,* VI (1931), pp. 124–43. To the best of my knowledge, R. M. Hatton has been the first to notice the complexity of "glory": see her essay "Louis XIV and his Fellow-Monarchs," in *Louis XIV and the Craft of Kingship,* John C. Rule, ed., Ohio University Press, 1967.

is clothed in Louis' *Mémoires* will suffice to demonstrate this point. True enough, glory acquired by arms seems to be attended by more *"éclat"* than that sought by other means. Yet, though valor is very important, it is not the only sterling quality in an ideal prince, for in glory, as in virtue, there must be variety. There is glory in great enterprises, foreign and domestic: in putting a French prince on the Polish throne, and in building the Languedoc Canal. There is glory in overcoming difficulties that cannot be avoided, but not in creating such difficulties, nor in rash action. There is glory in work toward the improvement of society and in spending money for public needs. There is glory in keeping one's word at the expense of one's immediate interest. And there is glory in moderation, in maintaining one's dignity, in curbing one's pride, in overcoming one's resentment, and in that mastery of oneself that ensures the conquest of one's natural inclinations by reason. Indeed, it is reason that guides us on the path of true glory.[24]

The concomitant of glory is high reputation—a fragile thing—which the princes must constantly seek and to which they must "subject themselves"; such reputation is one of the secrets of their success and advances their designs more than the sword. This search for public applause and high reputation, this all-consuming passion for glory, helps the prince to overcome some of his other passions and thus renders him more fit to rule his state in accordance with reason and with his true interests.[25] But, like all passions, the passion for glory carries some dangers with it: it may lead to excessive clemency,[26] or, worse still, to a confusion between the prince's "personal glory" and the glory of his state or "nation." The king must not put the former ahead of the latter, or ahead of the welfare and tranquillity of his subjects. He is above all a "depositary" of the glory of his predecessors and

[24] Longnon, pp. 18, 114, 143, 144, 148, 149, 179, 181, 208, 219, 238, 241, 252, 258.

[25] *Ibid.,* pp. 31, 40, 224.

[26] *Ibid.,* pp. 137–38. It should be noted, however, that while speaking of the abuses of clemency, Louis calls clemency "the most royal of all the virtues . . . the greatest thing that can be revered in us, for it is, so to say, one degree above our power and our justice" (*ibid.*). Toward the end of his reign Louis came to stress this royal virtue even more: see his letters to Philip V, July 2 and 1, August 1714, quoted in Baudrillart, *Philippe V et la Cour de France,* I, 652–53. In these letters Louis interceded with his grandson for the citizens of Barcelona whom he himself believed to be guilty of armed rebellion against their lawful sovereign.

of the interest of his successors. This treasure he must pass on, undiminished, to those who come after him.[27]

If the king can increase the treasure entrusted to his care, so much the better. In fact, he should "strive to bring all [conditions of men] to that degree of perfection which is appropriate to them." Though the difference between the rich and the poor will never be effaced, it should be possible to establish a social order where "no person, however indigent, would not be assured of his subsistence, either by his work or by a regular and well-ordered aid."[28] To bring this about, the king must not favor any class or any profession above the others: "I refused to support the interest of the *rentiers* against that of all France."[29] Every profession contributes to the maintenance of society in its own way, and the king must make sure that they can all carry out their functions, and not go astray, as they do from time to time. But, of course, the king must be mindful of the fact that he is only human, dealing with other humans, and that consequently it is not within his power to attain to that perfection that he sets before his eyes and toward which he must strive; nor can he hope to reform the age at one stroke.[30]

It is obvious that the prince cannot be a past master in all fields, but in the art of governing, at least, he should make himself unsurpassed by his subjects. This he can achieve only through hard work: "it is by this [work] that one reigns, and for this [work] that one reigns."[31] The steady application of Louis XIV to work is well known and need not be dwelt upon here. This work consisted mainly in gathering information, in "keeping one's eyes open on all the earth," and since Louis' curiosity was insatiable and his memory remained prodigious to the very end, he delighted in his work. He sat in council virtually every day of his reign, sometimes two or three times a day, when the pressure of business was great. No physical inconvenience or infirmity was allowed to interfere with this royal schedule. It is recorded that in the entire fifty-four years of his personal rule, Louis XIV fell asleep only twice during the de-

[27] Longnon, pp. 77, 88, 180, 277.

[28] *Ibid.*, pp. 97, 216–17.

[29] *Ibid.*, p. 98. The rich, according to Louis, should be made to pay, and the clergy should also bear their share of the material burden of maintaining the state (*ibid.*, pp. 72, 199).

[30] *Ibid.*, pp. 18, 130.

[31] *Ibid.*, pp. 21–23, 124, and *passim.*

liberations of his council, being overcome by fatigue after several sleepless nights.

Once the information is gathered in, one must reflect upon it in order to determine the most reasonable course of action to take. At this point the royal decision is usually dictated by plain common sense, which the king should cultivate within himself: "the principal function of kings is to let common sense work, and it always works naturally and without strain."[32] But what seemed to be a fairly simple task to the man of thirty, appeared in a different light to him by the time he was forty:

> *Souvent il y a des endroits qui font peine; il y en a de délicats qui sont difficiles à démêler; on a des idées confuses. . . . Le métier de roi est grand, noble et délicieux, quand on se sent digne de bien s'acquitter de toutes les choses auxquelles il engage; mais il n'est pas exempt de peines, de fatigues, d'inquiétudes. L'incertitude désespère quelquefois . . .*[33]

Here we witness one of the changes in Louis' understanding of the *bon sens:* as the king was becoming less naïve, the crystal-clear precepts of Cartesian reason no longer emerged easily and naturally from the accumulated information. Moreover, later on, the very principles underlying these precepts became less simple, as Louis began to take both the "fundamental laws" and history more seriously than he had done in the early part of his reign.

Nevertheless, whatever meaning Louis gave to "reason," he always insisted that it must be the sovereign guiding principle of every action. For the sake of "the perfect economy of reason" the king must at all times remain calm, unruffled by passions. To bring everything under the sway of reason, he must first make himself the embodiment of it; he must transform his own nature by reason, suppressing all personal inclinations that may be contrary to it. Only then will he be able to take on whatever character the circumstances might dictate, and to make use of these circumstances to procure his state every possible advantage.[34] Louis shares with the Cartesian classicists the belief that man can mold his character, or at least control its manifestations by the exertion of his will.

In shaping their character as rulers, kings must be mindful of

---

[32] *Ibid.*, p. 22.

[33] *"Réflexions sur le Métier de Roi,"* written in 1679, Longnon, pp. 280–82.

[34] Longnon, pp. 113–14, 117–18, 157, 229, 241, 280–81.

the defects to which their regal status may predispose them: personal pride (as distinct from the pride "of the place which we occupy"), vanity, taking flattery for truth, wishful thinking, as well as all those passions, which, however noble they may be in themselves, always "produce some smoke that obfuscates our reason."[35] And yet, it is a passion—the passion for his "interest, grandeur, and glory"—that helps the king to transform his character: in "a true king" this dominant passion consumes all other passions, and makes him "a little less human" than other men.[36] Let us remember, however, that "glory" implies the exercise of a great variety of virtues. Thus, by summoning self-interest and one of the passions to his aid, Louis seems to solve the difficulty created by entrusting the "public good" to the care of one selfish person. It is the king's own self-interest that drives him to further the public interest to the best of his ability; his interest, if rightly understood, is identical with the public interest, for the king's personal well-being can be assured only by the welfare of the entire community. A hundred years later, Frederick the Great advanced a similar argument in favor of his brand of "enlightened despotism."

What is true of a king would not be true of a minister or of a favorite: since he is only human, it is virtually certain that he will misuse his power to promote his private interest. Louis hoped that the very name of prime minister "would be forever abolished in France." True enough, there are certain situations when it is necessary to have all power concentrated in the hands of one minister—for instance, when the king is too young to govern by himself. Such a first minister must not only be capable, but must also be of sufficiently low birth not to aspire to some still higher dignity. But apart from the "monstrous elevation" of prime ministers and open favorites, there are other deformities, which, though they may not be immediately apparent, are yet equally dangerous. For instance, an unwary prince may imperceptibly fall into the hands of a clique of persons supporting one another's views and interests and able to put whatever they please into the sovereign's mind, to conceal the truth from him, and to let no men approach him but those who agree with them. Such cabinet government is as pernicious as the rule of a prime

[35] *Ibid.*, pp. 87–88, 123–24, 228–30.
[36] *Ibid.*, p. 40.

minister. It is also good for the king to be above the temptations of sex. However, if they prove to be irresistible, "in giving up our heart we should remain masters of our mind; we must keep separate the caresses of the lover and the resolutions of the sovereign." The royal mistress must never be allowed to speak to him about the affairs of state or about his advisers. Furthermore, there is another kind of dependence the prince must avoid: if he lets any one passion (apart from the passion "for the good in general") rule him and dictate all his decisions, then this passion will, in effect, play the role of a favorite who is allowed an undue share in the government of the realm.[37] Thus only a king who is free of prime ministers, favorites, cabinets, mistresses, and passions will be able to maintain reason in the saddle. The ideal king is dehumanized, and one hesitates to call him a person.

To apply the precepts of reason and to control other men the king must know human nature. We have already mentioned Louis' low opinion of mankind: all humans are egoists pursuing their private advantage. Exceptions to this rule are so rare that for all practical purposes they should be discounted. Differences between men are explained chiefly by differences between the private interests and passions that color their outlook. Fear and hope are the two mainsprings of human action; ambition, greed, and vanity are the three most common forms of hope. It remains to determine which stimulus to apply in each particular case to obtain the desired response from a person or from a group of people.[38]

Of all the functions of his government, the one that the prince must most jealously supervise in person is the control of the treasury. No other sphere of the administration offers such irresistible temptations to private appetites. Moreover, state finance is so complicated that a clever man will find many opportunities to enrich himself at public expense without being caught. Louis speaks with indignation of the "excessive and monstrous wealth of the financiers, drawn from the sweat, tears, and blood of the poor." If several financiers are such an evil, then what happens

[37] *Ibid.*, pp. 25, 114, 245–48, 258–59.

[38] *Ibid.*, pp. 83, 157–59, 167–68, 229, and *passim*. Louis' view of human nature is more fully discussed in my article " 'Maxims of State' in Louis XIV's Foreign Policy in the 1680's," in *William III and Louis XIV: Essays by and for Mark Thomson*, J. S. Bromley and R. M. Hatton, eds., Liverpool University Press, 1966.

if the control of all the monies of the state is vested in one superintendent of finances, that is, in one private individual? There is "a natural difference between the interest of the prince and that of his superintendents." A superintendent like Fouquet will always seek to introduce confusion into his department, so that he and his friends may peculate with that much more ease. There is only one escape from this danger: the prince must himself take over the toilsome job of the superintendent, no matter how boring its details may appear to him. The king cannot undertake anything, great or small, that does not involve expense; unless he is at all times fully aware of the state of his finances, he will be unable to make a move without the cooperation of his superintendent, with whom he will have to share all his secret thoughts, and who will be in a position to check any of the king's designs whenever he pleases. The superintendent of finances will thus become a prime minister *de facto*.[39]

In practice, though Louis acquired a certain general understanding of the finances, which he retained to the end of his reign, he found it impossible to live up to all his injunctions in this matter. The task was not only boring, but time-consuming, and Louis was a very busy man, especially since he seldom grasped the distinction between affairs of great and of little consequence. He was the first to admit that he was "often succoured in this work by Colbert, whom I charged with looking into the things that required too much [minute] examination."[40] It was not long before Louis got into the habit of simply telling Colbert to exercise his usual ingenuity in finding funds for the enterprises that interested him. The situation became even more serious when, during the crisis on the eve of the War of the Spanish Succession, Chamillart was made secretary of state for war apparently for no better reason than that he was a resourceful financial administrator. We should note, however, that Louis' controllers-general of finance were not only competent, but loyal and devoted to the King and to his service; in fact, the same can be said of nearly all of Louis' intimate advisers, no matter what Louis thought about human nature. Some of his best ministers, like Torcy, were deeply hurt by Louis' cynical view of their character, but continued to serve him faithfully.

[39] Longnon, pp. 66–73, 92–95.
[40] *Ibid.*, p. 69.

Even in the early part of his reign Louis realized that it is impossible for one man to know and to do everything. A great realm will never lack men suitable for all kinds of employment, and a great king will know how to combine and put to work the various talents of his best subjects. "The chief function of the monarch is to put each individual in a post where he can be useful to the public," and the art of doing so "is perhaps the first and the greatest talent of the princes."[41] To begin with, the ruler must consider those whom he appoints to the highest posts in the state, that is, his own immediate advisers. An enlightened, but inexperienced, monarch would do well to limit the number of his advisers to a few men; but one who is accustomed to transact great affairs, and who has complete control over himself, should not shrink from free intercourse with as many people as possible. In such conversations he will come to know personally *les plus honnêtes gens* of his realm and will learn a great many things that will give him that much better control over his regular ministers, who will find it difficult to deceive him.[42]

An enlightened and prudent ruler will always listen to counsel. Only fools will consider this to be a sign of weakness on his part. It is as dangerous not to take counsel as to be governed, and a prince who is guilty of such rashness hardly ever accomplishes what he sets out to do. Since the purpose of consultation is to enable the prince to arrive at the best possible decision, taking into account all the contingencies and difficulties that may arise, a council consisting of yes-men is not only useless, but dangerous: it is apt to precipitate the prince's ruin by confirming him in a false opinion or by pandering to some of his passions. Hence the king must especially cherish "those men who would know how to contradict us."[43]

However, the royal habit of consultation should not be allowed to degenerate into cabinet government. Having listened to advice, the king must maintain his independence of decision. To guard this independence, he must divide his confidence between several men of different views and different interests. He must also avoid bringing into his regular inner council men who might conceivably have some pretension to sit there by right of birth rather than

[41] *Ibid.*, pp. 25, 114, 271.
[42] *Ibid.*, pp. 246, 269–70.
[43] *Ibid.*, pp. 33–34, 166–67, 229–30.

by the sole will of the sovereign. Thus Louis often consulted with Turenne, Condé, or Vendôme on matters in which they were competent to give advice, but they never sat as regular members of the *Conseil d'en-haut*. In the later part of the reign, the Dauphin, and then the Duke of Burgundy, were brought into the Council; but they were future kings of France, and were invited mainly for training purposes. In addition to the precautions just noted, the king must keep well informed of his affairs, work hard, and know well the character of his counselors. The counselors will, of course, give interested advice. But if the king knows how to detect the hidden reasons that move them and how to distinguish between the solid arguments advanced in agreement with the reason of state and those prompted by private interest, he need not fear even the most corrupt adviser whom he must occasionally suffer because of his special professional competence. A minister closely watched by his master will find it difficult to deviate from the straight and narrow path, and will, in fact, feel himself more secure in his post.[44]

The precepts just summarized boil down to one: the king must study human nature and closely observe his advisers, both before and after their appointment. To discharge this, the most difficult and delicate part of his task, the monarch must relish the kind of work that it involves. He should take into account the general reputation of the prospective appointee, for "the public has no [special private] interest to serve, and it is difficult to deceive it for long." However, one should be wary of the opinions advanced by the candidate's friends and enemies, except in so far as the former try to excuse his shortcomings and the latter are forced to praise him. But, in spite of every precaution, chance will play a greater role than wisdom and foresight in matters of appointment; and, in wisdom, it is the part that may be called "sixth sense" (*génie*) that counts for more than counsel.[45] For, in filling high places, the king cannot rely on the advice of his closest counselors: their own personal interests are too much involved in such appointments.[46] "There are certain functions," says Louis, "where, holding, so to say, the place of God, we seem to participate in His knowledge as well as in His

[44] *Ibid.,* pp. 25, 30–31, 36, 167–68, 174–75, 245–48, 251, 275.
[45] *Ibid.,* pp. 26–27.
[46] *Ibid.,* p. 271.

authority: for example, in matters relating to the discernment of character, the assignment of employments, and the distribution of favors we make better decisions by following our own choice rather than the advice of our counselors, because, being placed in a higher sphere, we are farther removed than they from petty interests which could bring us to commit an injustice."[47]

In the appointment of bishops, a well-intentioned monarch, who scrupulously takes every possible precaution, will receive direct aid from God.[48] He cannot count on such supernatural aid in his other appointments, in which he is left to his own lights. In the fall of 1679, tormented by doubt as to whether he should dismiss Pomponne, his foreign minister whom he liked and respected, and unable to have recourse to his other counselors in this predicament, the king sat down to write a memorandum to himself, in which he tried to clarify his thoughts. This is the origin of that famous fragment that, in the following century, received the title of *"Réflexions sur le Métier de Roi,"* and that is one of the best examples of the "royal style" of Louis XIV.[49] The main argument on which Louis based the decision to dismiss Pomponne was that the king's first duty was to his state, in whose service he must immolate himself and overcome the promptings of his own nature. At least in striving to subordinate everything to reason, Louis XIV did not make an exception for his own person.

It may be objected that we have drawn an idealized picture of Louis XIV, that in reality he was human and had many failings. This is undoubtedly true; however, the purpose of this paper has not been to portray the person of the Sun King, but to bring out some of his ideas on the nature of power. If the King did not always follow his own precepts, in this he was not very different from other men. Yet few men have tried to live up to their ideals more conscientiously than did Louis XIV.

[47] *Ibid.*, pp. 228–29.
[48] *Ibid.*, pp. 127–28.
[49] The standard text of the *"Métier de Roi"* as it is usually published appears in Longnon, pp. 280–82 (cf. Che. Dreyss's version in his *Mémoires de Louis XIV*, II, 518–21). The original draft, in the King's hand, is in the Bibliothèque Nationale, Ms. Fr. 10,331, fols. 125–30. The first draft differs from the final version mainly in that it names Pomponne explicitly, speaks in the present tense of the necessity to dismiss him, and lays more faults at his door. It remains a mystery what caused Louis, apparently many years later, to seek out this paper and to alter it in a trembling hand.

PART II

THE LIBERAL CRITIQUE OF POWER

Chapter 7

FRIEDRICH SCHILLER
AND THE PROBLEMS OF POWER

Gordon A. Craig

No German literary figure of major stature has as strong a claim to inclusion in a volume of this kind as Friedrich Schiller, for power was the central theme of most of his dramatic work. If, as Hajo Holborn has written, Schiller always clung to the idea that the artist had a public responsibility and if "his didactic aim [was] to educate a future generation of free men,"[1] he chose to do this, for the most part, by teaching them about power, its legitimate and illegitimate forms, its uses and limitations, its ability to corrupt, the evil consequences of lusting after it on the one hand and refusing to take the responsibility for using it on the other, the moral ambiguities in which it involved those who tried to use it responsibly, and the relationship between all this and individual and collective freedom. For the age in which he lived, this was an appropriate, indeed almost inescapable, theme, as the poet pointed out in the prologue to his finest drama:[2]

> *Und jetzt an des Jahrhunderts ernstem Ende,*
> *Wo selbst die Wirklichkeit zur Dichtung wird,*
> *Wo wir den Kampf gewaltiger Naturen*
> *Um ein bedeutend Ziel vor Augen sehn,*
> *Und um der Menschheit grosse Gegenstände,*
> *Um Herrschaft und um Freiheit wird gerungen,*
> *Jetzt darf die Kunst auf ihrer Schattenbühne*
> *Auch höhern Flug versuchen, ja, sie muss,*
> *Soll nicht des Lebens Bühne sie beschämen.*

[1] Hajo Holborn, *A History of Modern Germany, 1648–1840* (New York, 1964), pp. 332–33.
[2] *Wallensteins Lager*, Prolog, lines 61–69. Author's translation.

[Now, at this century's forbidding end,
When actuality itself is changed
To art, when the struggle of imperious natures
For lofty goals is waged before our eyes,
And nations vie for mankind's mighty objects,
For dominance, for freedom—now art may
Try a more daring flight upon her stage.
Indeed, she must, if she will not be shamed
By what transpires upon the stage of life.]

These words speak as directly to our own generation as they
did to Schiller's, and his reflections on power are just as relevant
today as they were a century ago.

I

With the exception of *Semele,* his first work, and, perhaps, *Die
Braut von Messina* as well, all of the plays that Schiller completed and most of those that he left incomplete or in outline
deal with power in one of its various forms.[3] In most cases the
dramatic action is set in motion by someone who possesses or
seeks to possess power, transgresses the limits imposed by custom
or morality or prudence upon its exercise, and suffers the consequences. This protagonist is usually (we must make exceptions
for Franz Moor in *Die Räuber,* who is a monster, as well as for
the bureaucratic empire-builder Walter in *Kabale und Liebe* and
the sadistic provincial governor Gessler in *Wilhelm Tell*) a
person of more than ordinary gifts, possessed of the quality that
Schiller called *Grösse* and that we might call charisma, and of
nobility of character and deportment. His passion for power
nevertheless gradually deprives him of the freedom to give expression to his best qualities and forces him to act ignobly or
criminally before it finally destroys him.

The central figure in Schiller's third play, for instance, Fiesko,

---

[3] Thus, paternal authority is either the main or the subsidiary theme in
Die Räuber, Kabale und Liebe, and *Don Carlos,* royal power, either secular
or divine, in *Don Carlos, Maria Stuart, Die Jungfrau von Orleans,* and
the unfinished *Agrippina* and *Demetrius,* and institutional power in *Kabale
und Liebe* and *Wilhelm Tell* (the state service), *Wallenstein* and the unfinished *Die Malteser* (military establishments), the drafts for *Die Polizei*
and *Narbonne* (the police), *Don Carlos* (the Inquisition), and the long
story *Der Geisterseher* (secret societies).

Count of Lavagna, is described as being a "young, slender, brilliantly handsome man of twenty-three years, proud but within proper limits, friendly but in a kingly manner, with the flexibility of the courtier, and also the deceitfulness."[4] In Genoa he is universally liked and admired, and, when the excesses of the ruling duke's nephew cause disaffection with the House of Doria, both the nobility of the city and the common people turn naturally to him and ask him to lead them in the protection of their liberties. He refuses at first to commit himself and, even after he has joined a group of republican conspirators and become its dominant member, he continues to play a lone hand, using criminal elements (the Moor Muley Hassan and his agents) and connections with foreign powers to lay the basis for an insurrection, which he alone will control. When his preparations are made, Fiesko forces himself to examine his motives and to decide whether he wishes to establish a republic or to make himself a dictator. In a midnight soliloquy, he broods: "Here is the yawning gulf that marks the boundary of virtue; here is the line between heaven and hell. At this point many a hero has stumbled and fallen, and the world has covered his name with curses. At this point many a one has had doubts and stood firm and become a demigod." After an intense inner struggle he resolves to resist the siren call of ambition, crying out to the night sky: "To conquer a diadem is great! To reject it is divine! Avaunt, tyrant! Be free, Genoa—and I your happiest citizen!"[5]

Unfortunately, this resolution does not survive the dawn. Looking out over the sea and the city as the first rays of the sun touch them, Fiesko resumes the debate with his conscience and now loses himself in a dream of power. "The exalted mind has other temptations than the common one. Should it have to share its virtue with lesser ones? Should the armor that confines the puny body of the pygmy be forced to fit the frame of a giant? . . . Even if the betrayer's cleverness does not make the act of betrayal noble, yet can the prize ennoble the betrayer. It is shameful to empty a purse—it is daring to swindle a million—but it is unspeakably great to steal a crown! The shame abates with the grandeur of the sin! . . . A moment as prince swallows up the limitations of a whole existence. It is not the strife in life's

---

[4] *Die Verschwörung des Fiesko zu Genua,* Personen des Stücks.
[5] *Ibid.,* Act II, scene 19.

arena that makes it worthwhile, but its emoluments. Separate the thunder into its simple syllables and you can sing children to sleep with it; compress them into one sudden peal, and that majestic sound will move the eternal heavens!—I am decided!"[6]

After this, Fiesko moves implacably—deaf to the entreaties of his wife and unresponsive to a noble gesture of appeasement from the aged Andreas Doria—toward the betrayal of his fellow conspirators and the establishment of his own tyranny. But, as elsewhere in Schiller, his crimes bring their own punishment. He attains his goal over the corpse of his wife, whom he kills by mistake at the height of the street-fighting, and when this tragedy has no power to divert him ("Hear me, men of Genoa! Providence, if I understand her, has given me this wound only to test my heart for the greatness that is near!")[7] he is drowned by the dedicated republican Verrina.

The ability of power to corrupt, so masterfully described in *Fiesko,* is touched upon also in Schiller's other early plays. One senses that President Walter, in *Kabale und Liebe,* was a vain and rigid man, but not a bad one, until his position at court was threatened. Confronted with the possible loss of his authority, however, he does not hesitate to use illegal arrest, blackmail, and the most shameless calumniation of the girl his son loves in order to secure himself. And surely Gerhard Storz is correct in suggesting that even that impassioned advocate of liberty, the Marquis of Posa in *Don Carlos,* is not immune to power's malevolent influence, for, in the pursuit of his political aims, he has no scruple about betraying his friends, and in his advice to the king there is what seems to modern ears to be a suggestion of totalitarian behavior, for he is clearly just as willing to be ruthless in the choice of means to achieve his ends as the Grand Inquisitor is in his determination to defeat them.[8]

It is, however, in the later dramas, and particularly in *Wallenstein, Maria Stuart,* and *Demetrius,* that this theme finds its fullest and most sophisticated expression. Of the Emperor's *Feldherr,* of Mary's royal antagonist, the Queen of England, and of the false pretender to the Russian throne, it can be said with equal justice

[6] *Ibid.,* Act III, scene 2.
[7] *Ibid.,* Act V, scene 13.
[8] Gerhard Storz, *Der Dichter Friedrich Schiller* (3rd ed., Stuttgart, 1963), pp. 143, 146.

> It was their power that misled their hearts,[9]

but the nature of the seduction is in each case more complicated, the moral conflict more intense, and the motivation more ambiguous than in *Fiesko*.

At the beginning of the swiftly moving trilogy that bears his name, we find Wallenstein

> *den Schöpfer kühner Heere,*
> *Des Lagers Abgott und der Länder Geissel,*
> *Die Stütze und den Schrecken seines Kaisers,*
> *Des Glückes abenteuerlichen Sohn*

> [the creator of bold armies,
> The idol of the camp and scourge of countries,
> The prop and yet the terror of his Emperor,
> Dame Fortune's fabulous adopted son][10]

at the height of his power, but with its very basis threatened. The same jealous influences in Vienna which once before drove him into retirement are now threatening to transfer the bulk of his army to an Archduke who will be more responsive to orders from the capital and less forbearing in his treatment of the enemy. Wallenstein, who hopes to restore peace to the whole empire, fears that such a transfer of authority will prolong the war indefinitely, since Vienna does not in his opinion desire a cessation of hostilities. Quite apart from this, he cannot tolerate the prospect of losing his command. As his admirer Max Piccolomini says, he is a man born for power, whose inborn authority must find expression.

> *Max. Geworden ist ihm eine Herrscherseele,*
> *Und ist gestellt auf einen Herrscherplatz.*
> . . . .
> *Questenberg. Wer spricht ihm ab, dass er die Menschen kenne,*
> *Sie zu gebrauchen wisse! Überm Herrscher*
> *Vergisst er nur den Diener ganz und gar,*
> *Als wär' mit seiner Würd' er schon geboren.*
> *Max. Ist er's denn nicht? Mit jeder Kraft dazu*
> *Ist er's, und mit der Kraft noch obendrein,*
> *Buchstäblich zu vollstrecken die Natur,*
> *Dem Herrschtalent den Herrschplatz zu erobern.*

[9] *"Denn seine Macht ist's, die sein Herz verführt;/Sein Lager nur erkläret sein Verbrechen." Wallensteins Lager*, Prolog, lines 117–18.

[10] *Wallensteins Lager*, Prolog, lines 94–97. The translation is that of Charles E. Passage, *Wallenstein* (New York, 1958).

[Max. In him a ruler's soul has its existence
   And it is posted in a ruler's place.
. . . .
Questenberg. Who will deny that he knows men, and knows
   Moreover how to use them? But, in being
   The ruler, he forgets his stewardship
   Completely as though he were born to office.
Max. Well, wasn't he? By every talent for it
   He was, and with the further talent of
   The literal executive of Nature
   Who conquers ruler's rank for ruler's talent.][11]

Wallenstein is more powerfully influenced by the desire to extend his power than by the hope of achieving peace, although
he refuses to admit this to himself. Even before the threat of
replacement became actual, he was toying with the idea of leading his forces into the enemy camp and winning the Kingdom of
Bohemia for himself in consequence. He has deluded himself
into believing that it is a mere game that he has been playing,
a purely aesthetic contemplation of what he *might* do if he wished.

> *Der Kaiser, es ist wahr,*
> *Hat übel mich behandelt!—Wenn ich wollte,*
> *Ich konnt' ihm recht viel Böses dafür tun.*
> *Es macht mir Freude, meine Macht zu kennen.*
> *Ob ich sie wirklich brauchen werden, davon, denk' ich,*
> *Weisst du nicht mehr zu sagen als ein andrer.*

> [The Emperor, it is true,
> Has shamefully misused me.—If I wished,
> I could return him no small bit of mischief.
> It pleases me to realize my power.
> But whether I shall actually make use of it,
> Of *that* you know no more than any other.][12]

But the game has gradually begun to dominate him. Not only
has he sent messengers to the Swedes, to sound them out about
terms for an alliance, but he has begun to subvert his officers'
loyalty to the Emperor, hoping to persuade them to transfer their
oath of allegiance to his own person. In pursuit of this, he has
no respect for truth, morality, or the laws of friendship. To
arouse the formidable dragoon commander Buttler's resentment

---

[11] *Die Piccolomini,* Act 1, scene 4, lines 412–13, 437–41. Passage
translation.
[12] *Ibid.,* Act II, scene 6, lines 865–70. Passage translation.

against the imperial court and to tie him to his own cause, he has secretly frustrated that officer's ambition to secure a patent of nobility, while pretending to support it; to secure Max Piccolomini's loyalty, he exploits the young officer's love for his own daughter Thekla, although he has no intention of allowing it to be consummated.

The process of corruption is, in fact, already far advanced before Wallenstein's agents are apprehended with his dispatches to the Swedes in their possession. But it is only when that happens that he becomes aware of it himself and finds that he has been imprisoned by his fantasy.

> *Wie? Sollt' ich's nun im Ernst erfüllen müssen,*
> *Weil ich zu frei gescherzt mit dem Gedanken?*
>
> [What? Must I now fulfill my plan in earnest
> Because I toyed too freely with the thought?][13]
>
> *Wär's möglich? Könnt' ich nicht mehr, wie ich wollte?*
> *Nicht mehr zurück, wie mir's beliebt? Ich müsste*
> *Die Tat vollbringen, weil ich sie gedacht?*
>
> [Can it be possible? Can I no longer
> Act as I wish? No more retreat, if I
> So choose? Must I act out the deed because
> I thought of it . . . ?][14]

He discovers now that the freedom he dreamed of winning by transgression of duty has been irrevocably lost; he has no choice but to go ahead with an act of treason that will leave him in bondage. As Goethe wrote: "The enemy with whom he must now ally himself will be a far sterner master than was his legitimate one in the days before he lost his confidence"[15]; and this becomes clear to Wallenstein himself in that tense scene with the Swedish colonel Wrangel which Thomas Mann has described as one of the most masterful demonstrations of Schiller's extraordinary insight into the world of politics and diplomacy.[16] Now too, the extent of his disloyalty to his Emperor, to his own subordinates, and to his friends and his family is

[13] *Wallensteins Tod*, Act I, scene 3, lines 112–13. Passage translation.
[14] *Ibid.*, Act I, scene 4, lines 139–40. Passage translation.
[15] *Goethes Sämtliche Werke. Jubiläumsausgabe, herausgegeben von Eduard von der Hellen* (Stuttgart, 1902–7), XXXVI, 180.
[16] Thomas Mann, *"Versuch über Schiller,"* Gesammelte Werke (Oldenburg, 1960), IX, 912.

ruthlessly exposed by the loyal general Octavio Piccolomini; and as a result his troops refuse to follow him, and he is abandoned by Max, whom now, with clearer vision, he recognizes as a friend whose loss is insupportable.

> *Doch fühl' ich's wohl, was ich in ihm verlor.*
> *Die Blume ist hinweg aus meinem Leben,*
> *Und kalt und farblos seh' ich's vor mir liegen.*
> *Denn er stand neben mir, wie meine Jugend . . .*

> [And yet I sense what I have lost in him.
> The flower now has vanished from my life,
> And cold and drab I see it lie before me.
> For he stood next to me like my own youth . . .][17]

Even so, he persists, like Fiesko, in his course, until the grim and resentful Buttler, fearing that he may still be successful, strikes him down in his sleep.

The case of Elizabeth in *Maria Stuart* possesses more ambiguity than that of Wallenstein, for the Queen's authority is threatened by the existence of a rival with as strong a claim to the throne as her own, she is under public pressure to resolve the problem, and her councilors spend more time debating with each other than they do in giving her advice that she can follow.[18] Admitting this, she is nevertheless corrupted by the power to which she clings, and by her actions she confirms the grave warning addressed to her by her rival when, in the famous confrontation at Fotheringay, Elizabeth taunts her with her youthful crimes and infidelities. Mary answers:

> *Ich habe menschlich, jugendlich gefehlt,*
> *Die Macht verführte mich, ich hab' es nicht*
> *Verheimlicht und verborgen, falschen Schein*
> *Hab' ich verschmäht mit königlichem Freimut.*
> *Das Ärgste weiss die Welt von mir, und ich*
> *Kann sagen, ich bin besser als mein Ruf.*
> *Weh Euch, wenn sie von Euern Taten einst*
> *Den Ehrenmantel zieht, womit Ihr gleissend*
> *Die wilde Glut verstohlner Lüste deckt.*

> [I erred, but in a human, youthful way.
> I was seduced by power. I did not

[17] *Wallensteins Tod*, Act V, scene 3, lines 3442–445. Passage translation.

[18] Benno von Wiese, *Friedrich Schiller* (3rd ed., Stuttgart, 1963), p. 718.

Conceal or make a secret of it. With
A royal candor I disdained false seeming.
The world has known the worst of me, and I
Can say that I am better than my name.
But woe to you if from your deeds they once
Rip off the cloak of honor which you use
To hide the wild heat of your secret lusts.][19]

The Queen in the end makes her power secure, but only by means that deprive her of the services of her most faithful minister, while causing her favorite to abandon her in disgust.

In the fragment *Demetrius* the moral transformation that can be effected by the desire for power is presented with even greater dramatic force than in the two dramas already discussed. The hero, *eine hohe Natur,* handsome, spirited, noble in demeanor, but of obscure origins, grows up in a monastery in Russia, an existence that is repellent to him and which he finally escapes by fleeing to Poland, where he is given protection by the Woiwod of Sendomir. His proud nature soon involves him in trouble, for, insulted by a nobleman, he kills him, and as a commoner is sentenced to death. At the last moment, he is freed because a cross that he wears around his neck arouses the curiosity of his captors and indicates, not only that he is of noble birth, but that he is the rightful claimant to the throne of Russia, which has been usurped by Boris Godunow. This disclosure inflames his ambition, and he conceives it to be his duty to free Russia from tyranny and to bring *Glück* to its people. Yet from the very beginning his enthusiastic idealism has a sinister undertone that is to grow more dominant later on. In the first sketch of the play, Schiller has Demetrius speak the chilling words:

> *Schon fühl' ich da des Ruhmes Glanz mich lockt,*
> *Von keinen Wünschen sonst mich festgehalten.*
> *Macht braucht kein Herz; der Wille nur allein*
> *Spricht in den Handlungen das Leben aus.*

> [The glow of fame already leads me on,
> For I am not restrained by lesser passions.
> Power needs no heart; the will, and it alone,
> Expresses life in action.][20]

---

[19] *Maria Stuart,* Act III, scene 4, lines 2421–23, 2426–29. Translation by Charles E. Passage, *Mary Stuart. The Maid of Orleans* (New York, 1961).
[20] Benno von Wiese, *Schiller,* p. 793. Author's translation.

Urged on by the self-seeking daughter of his protector and supported by the majority of the Polish magnates, Demetrius sets out to regain the crown that he believes is rightfully his, and sweeps all before him. The Russian army defects to his cause; Tsar Boris commits suicide; the succession is open. But, at the high tide of Demetrius's triumphal advance toward Moscow, a man comes to him, reveals himself as the murderer of the true heir, and tells him that it was he who, in revenge for Boris Godunow's failure to reward him for his crime, found a boy who resembled the murdered prince, gave him the cross and others of his possessions, and placed him in the monastery. This sudden revelation that he is in fact an impostor has a shattering effect upon the pretender. Schiller's notes for the unfinished play read: "During this account a frightful change takes place in Demetrius. His silence is dreadful. At the moment of his greatest rage and despair, the murderer drives him beyond himself by defiantly and insolently demanding his reward. He strikes him down."[21]

Now a murderer himself, Demetrius presses on to the capital. The mother of the true Demetrius comes joyfully to meet him and senses, with terror, that he is not her son. He admits this, but challenges her to pretend that he is and to enjoy the privileges of regained status. "If I am not your son, yet I am the Tsar. I have the power! Fortune is with me!" (*"Ich habe die Macht! Ich habe das Glück!"*) He shows the weeping woman to the crowd, and convinces them that her tears are tears of joy.

His usurpation is now complete, but it is already doomed to failure. His reign is bereft of the idealism of his youthful projects. "A fearful element sustains him, but he does not control it; he is urged on by strange passions." He is suspicious and without friends; he gives preference to Polish councilors; he violates the usages of the country; he persecutes the monks in revenge for his unhappy youth. "Nor is he free from despotic caprices in moments of offended pride." A conspiracy forms and wins popular backing; the capital rises in revolution, and the conspirators press into the throne room. Demetrius seeks to appease them by promising to hand his Polish ministers over to their tender mercies (a final ignoble gesture), but they are unmoved. They

---

[21] *Demetrius, Abriss der weiteren Handlung.*

demand that the Dowager Empress swear on the cross that Demetrius is her true son, and, as she turns silently away, they cry, "Then die, impostor!" and stab him to death.[22]

II

Living as we do in an age in which many intellectuals have an instinctive revulsion against power, we are tempted to regard these great tragedies as expressions of something of the same kind of feeling. It would be a mistake to yield to this view. Like his friend Wilhelm von Humboldt, Schiller had a more realistic view of politics than he sometimes pretended to have, and he possessed a greater willingness to admit the requirements of state-craft than, let us say, Fiesko's wife Leonore, with her lament about the gulf between *Herrschsucht* and *Liebe* (an early example of the "Make love, not war" syndrome),[23] or Max Piccolomini, with his anguished cry

> *O! diese Staatskunst, wie verwünsch' ich sie!*

> [O this diplomacy, how I abhor it!][24]

He knew that power was one of the components of effective policy, and, while admitting its ability to corrupt its users and providing masterful studies of the ways in which it did so, he never argued that it could be disregarded.

Wallenstein's crime was not that he was a practitioner of power but rather that he sought to extend and employ it in an illegitimate and arbitrary way. If Schiller himself speaks out in the trilogy, surely it is through the lips of Octavio Piccolomini, Wallenstein's trusted friend, comrade in arms, and ultimate destroyer, when he says:

> *Mein Sohn! Lass uns die alten, engen Ordnungen*
> *Gering nicht achten! Köstlich unschätzbare*
> *Gewichte sind's, die der bedrängte Mensch*
> *An seiner Dränger raschen Willen band;*
> *Denn immer war die Willkür fürchterlich.*

---

[22] *Ibid.*

[23] *Die Verschwörung des Fiesko*, Act IV, scene 14. "*Liebe hat Tränen und kann Tränen verstehen; Herrschsucht hat eherne Augen, worin ewig nie die Empfindung perlt*," and so forth.

[24] *Die Piccolomini*, Act V, scene 3, line 2632. Passage translation.

[My son, those ancient and confining ordinances
Must not be scorned. They are inestimable
Counterbalances which oppressed men
Attached to the wild will of their oppressors;
For arbitrary will was ever dreadful.][25]

Wallenstein is contemplating the destruction of the very bond of custom and law that holds the Empire together, and the most likely result of this, Octavio knows, will be anarchy. Wallenstein himself has some sense of this, and one feels that he is almost appalled at times by the enormity of the action which he is contemplating. In the great soliloquy in which he recognizes that he no longer has the freedom to turn back, he ruminates:

Und was ist dein Beginnen? Hast du dir's
Auch redlich selbst bekannt? Du willst die Macht,
Die ruhig, sicher thronende, erschüttern,
Die in verjährt geheiligtem Besitz,
In der Gewohnheit festgegründet ruht,
Die and der Völker frommen Kinderglauben
Mit tausend zähen Wurzeln sich befestigt.

[What is this thing that you would venture? Have you
Acknowledged it before yourself with fairness?
You seek to overturn the tranquil power
Throned in possession hallowed by the years
And resting on the solid base of custom,
Attached to pious childhood faith of nations
By virtue of a thousand rugged roots.][26]

A few minutes later, the hard-headed Swedish colonel says, without mincing his words:

Solch eine Flucht und Felonie, Herr Fürst,
Ist ohne Beispiel in der Welt Geschichten.

[Such criminal defection, my Lord Duke,
Is without parallel in history.][27]

[25] *Ibid.*, Act I, scene 4, lines 463–67. Passage translation. See, on this point, the excellent article by Dolf Sternberger, *"Macht und Herz oder der politische Held bei Schiller,"* in *Schiller: Reden im Gedenkjahr 1959*, Bernhard Zeller, ed., (Stuttgart, 1961), pp. 326–29.

[26] *Wallensteins Tod*, Act I, scene 4, lines 192–98. Passage translation.

[27] *Ibid.*, Act I, scene 5, lines 325–26. Passage translation.

The crime of Demetrius is also one of failure to honor or even recognize the limitations imposed on power by law and custom; and indications of this are perceptible even before his discovery that he is an impostor. For his campaign to gain the Russian crown in the interest of legitimacy is inaugurated by a brazen attempt to bribe the Polish Sejm into declaring war on his own country.

> *Moskau ist reich an Gütern; unermesslich*
> *An Gold und edeln Steinen ist der Schatz*
> *Des Zars; ich kann die Freunde königlich*
> *Belohnen, und ich will's. Wenn ich als Zar*
> *Aufzieke auf dem Kremel, denn, ich schwör's,*
> *Soll sich der Ärmste unter euch, der mir*
> *Dahin gefolgt, in Samt und Zobel kleiden,*
> *Mit reichen Perlen sein Geschirr bedecken,*
> *Und Silber sei das schlechteste Metall,*
> *Um seine Pferde Hufe zu beschlagen.*

> [Moscow is rich in plunder; measureless
> In gold and gems, the treasures of the Czar;
> I can give royal guerdons to my friends,
> And I will give them, too. When I, as Czar,
> Set foot within the Kremlin, then, I swear,
> The poorest of you all, that follows me,
> Shall robe himself in velvet and in sables;
> With costly pearls his housings shall he deck,
> And silver be the metal of least worth,
> That he shall shoe his horses' hoofs withal.][28]

This attempt to debauch the Sejm is frustrated only by the courage, and the veto, of one man, Leo Sapieha, who speaks presumably once more for Schiller as he argues for law, justice, and the sanctity of treaties.

> *Bezogen hat er mit dreitausend Pferden*
> *Den Reichstag und ganz Krakau überschwemmt*
> *Mit seinen Lehensleuten. Eben jetzt*
> *Erfüllen sie die Hallen dieses Hauses.*
> *Man will die Freiheit unsrer Stimmen zwingen.*
> *Doch keine Furcht bewegt mein tapfres Herz;*
> *Solang noch Blut in meinen Adern rinnt,*

---

[28] *Demetrius,* Act I, lines 367–76. Translator unknown. Schiller, *Historical Dramas* (Illustrated Sterling Edition, Boston, n.d.).

Will ich die Freiheit meines Worts behaupten.
Wer wohl gesinnt ist, tritt zu mir herüber.
Solang ich Leben habe, soll kein Schluss
Durchgehn, der wider Recht ist und Vernunft.
Ich hab' mit Moskau Frieden abgeschlossen,
Und ich bin Mann dafür, dass man ihn halte.

[He's girt the Diet with three thousand horses,
And all Cracow is swarming like a hive
With his sworn feudal vassals. Even now
They throng the halls and chambers where we sit,
To hold our liberty of speech in awe.
Yet stirs no fear in my undaunted heart;
And while the blood keeps current in my veins,
I will maintain the freedom of my voice!
Let those who think like men come stand by me!
Whilst I have life shall no resolve be passed
That is at war with justice and with reason.
'Twas I that ratified the pact with Moscow,
And I will hazard life to see it kept.][29]

To resist the arbitrary use of power or to wield it within its
proper limitations in the interest of the community it serves
requires a sense of responsibility and a willingness to assume
risks and make sacrifices. Sapieha almost loses his life when he
defies the rabid majority of the Sejm; Stauffacher and his colleagues at the Rütli are placing their own lives and those of their
families at stake when they take the oath to resist the violation of
their traditional liberties by the arbitrary edicts of Gessler and the
imperial government.[30] And Octavio Piccolomini is placed in a
more cruel dilemma than either Sapieha or the Rütli conspirators.
In his defense of duty and law and imperial authority, he is
forced to violate all the rules of private morality, to betray his
oldest friend, whose life he saved at Lützen and who has trusted
him implicitly ever since, and to do so by means that alienate

---

[29] *Ibid.*, lines 439–51. Same translation.

[30] It is indicative of Schiller's awareness of the ambiguities of resistance
that he has the hero Tell remain aloof from this political movement. Tell
kills Gessler because he is convinced that the governor has violated the
moral law by forcing him to run the risk of killing his own son. There is
no trace of political argument in the soliloquy that precedes the assassination. See *Wilhelm Tell*, Act IV, scene 3.

the son he loves. For even when he is finally convinced of Wallenstein's guilt, Max's unworldly, idealistic heart is more moved by the *Feldherr's* proud fatalism

> *So lass uns das Notwendige mit Würde,*
> *Mit festem Schritte tun!*
>
> [So let us with firm step and dignity
> Perform the inevitable!][31]

than by his father's precepts of *Staatsräson:*

> *Es ist nicht immer möglich*
> *Im Leben sich so kinderrein zu halten,*
> *Wie's uns die Stimme lehrt im Innersten.*
> *In steter Notwehr gegen arge List*
> *Bleibt auch das redliche Gemüt nicht wahr—*
> *Das eben ist der Fluch der bösen Tat,*
> *Dass sie fortzeugend immer Böses muss gebären.*
> *Ich klügle nicht, ich tue meine Pflicht;*
> *Der Kaiser schreibt mir mein Betragen vor.*
> *Wohl wär' es besser, überall dem Herzen*
> *Zu folgen, doch darüber würde man*
> *Sich manchen guten Zweck versagen müssen.*
> *Hier gilt's, mein Sohn, dem Kaiser wohl zu dienen,*
> *Das Herz mag dazu sprechen, was es will.*
>
> [It is not always possible
> In life to keep such childlike purity
> As promptings of the inner voice would bid us.
> On constant guard against sly treachery,
> Not even honest spirits can remain
> Quite frank.—This is the curse of evil deeds:
> That they spawn further deeds and always evil ones.
> I split no hairs, I only do my duty.
> The Emperor has prescribed my conduct for me.
> It would be better possibly to follow
> The heart in every case; but in so doing,
> Many worthy ends would be rejected.
> The need here is, my son, to serve the Emperor.
> To that the heart may say what it may say.][32]

It is Octavio's tragedy that he cannot convince his son that the situation in Wallenstein's camp and the desperate threat to the

---

[31] *Wallensteins Tod*, Act II, scene 2, lines 834–35. Passage translation.
[32] *Die Piccolomini*, Act V, scene 1, lines 2447–60. Passage translation.

legitimate order justify the crooked ways that he travels. His sense of responsibility precipitates the crisis that leads to his son's death, and, although he succeeds in saving the Empire, he suffers the additional blow of being rewarded for his loyalty with a princely title that throws doubt upon his motives.[33]

Schiller had dealt with this problem of power and responsibility twelve years earlier in *Don Carlos,* although he had at that time somewhat less sympathy for the father-figure than he had when he created Octavio Piccolomini. It is difficult, nevertheless, to reread the dialogue between King Philip and his son at the beginning of the second act of *Don Carlos* without concluding that the King was wholly justified in his suspicions of his son's reliability and in his refusal to entrust an army to his care. The poet's heart was doubtless on the side of Carlos and his friend Posa, and yet the King outweighs them both. Bernt Heiseler has written: "It is indeed possible that this royal portrait issued from a level of Schiller's intuition of the nature of things that had not yet fully emerged into consciousness. . . . The poet *sees,* and makes us see, what it means to have to rule and at the same time to be a man, and that freedom alone cannot build a state."[34]

The lonely burden of royal power has never been more movingly described than in Philip's soliloquy:

> *Jetzt gib mir einen Menschen, gute Vorsicht—*
> *Du hast mir viel gegeben. Schenke mir*
> *Jetzt einen Menschen . . .*
> *Ich brauche Wahrheit.—Ihre stille Quelle*
> *Im dunkeln Schutt des Irrtums aufzugraben*
> *Ist nicht das Los der Könige. Gib mir*
> *Den seltnen Mann mit reinem, offnem Herzen,*
> *Mit hellem Geist und unbefangnen Augen,*
> *Der mir sie finden helfen kann.*

> [Now give me, gracious Providence! a man.
> Thou'st given me much already. Now vouchsafe me
> A man! . . .

[33] *Wallensteins Tod,* Act V, scene 12, lines 3867–68.

[34] Bernt von Heiseler, *Schiller,* translated and annotated by John Bednall, (London, 1962), p. 95. This is true also of Schiller's not entirely consistent portrait of the king in his *Geschichte des Abfalls der Niederlande,* Erstes Buch. On this, see also Benno von Wiese, *Schiller,* pp. 365–66.

I thirst for truth.—To reach its tranquil spring,
Through the dark heaps of thick surrounding error,
Is not the lot of kings. Give me the man,
So rarely found, of pure and open heart,
Of judgment clear, and eye unprejudiced,
To aid me in the search.][35]

Yet the human need is not allowed to interfere with the exercise of the royal office, and Philip is able to master his heart when his duty to the state makes this necessary. Nor can he be accused of failing to accept full responsibility for the decisions that reason of state requires. No Shrewsbury can silently reproach him for thrusting the blame for his own actions upon the shoulders of underlings, as is true in the case of Philip's counterpart in *Maria Stuart*.[36]

III

In March 1948, to his friend the Göttingen historian Siegfried Kaehler, Friedrich Meinecke wrote: "It always seems to me now that Schiller's *Demetrius* is a symbol of our destiny. Pure and noble when he started out: a criminal when he finished! Puzzling—but in any case very tragic. I cannot get over thinking about it."[37]

The remark was prompted by reflections upon the effects of what Fritz Fischer has called Germany's "grab for world power" and doubtless also by Meinecke's private feeling that the German people would have been happier if it had remained a *Kulturvolk* and never striven for national power at all. This was a theme that had once occupied Schiller, too, in the unfinished poem *Deutsche Grösse*, in which he expressed the idea that a nation's true strength lies in its moral worth. It is doubtful, however, that the poet ever believed that the German people should remain indefinitely in the fragmented and relatively power-

[35] *Don Carlos*, Act III, scene 5, lines 2809–11, 2820–25. Translation by R. D. Boylan, *The Dramas of Frederick Schiller* (London, 1912).
[36] *Maria Stuart*, Act V, scenes 14, 15.
[37] Friedrich Meinecke, *Ausgewählter Briefwechsel*, edited by Ludwig Dehio and Peter Classen (Stuttgart, 1962), p. 521.

less condition in which it existed in his time.[38] He had, as has
already been pointed out, too great a respect for power in its
legitimate and responsible forms for that.

If one must select a Schiller play as a symbol of what happened to Germany, perhaps a more appropriate one than *Demetrius* would be the one not yet discussed in these pages: the
first drama to make the poet's name known in his country, *Die
Räuber*. The complications of its plot and the chain of illogic
upon which they are strung make a detailed description of the
action inadvisable. In brief, it is the story of a young man, Karl
Moor, who is destined to wield political power, since he is the
eldest son of a count who is both old and infirm. Instead of
preparing himself for the job he has to do, by educating himself
in those subjects that will be helpful to him, he spends his time
at the university in boozing and brawling and cursing the century
in which he lives for its lack of challenge, opportunity, and
heroism. Worse still, he stays too long away from home and
apparently does not take the trouble to keep himself informed
about what is going on in his absence. Thanks to this failure,
his position is usurped by his younger brother. Instead of seeking
to correct this situation, he acquiesces in his exclusion from
power by becoming the leader of a band of robbers composed of
people like himself who are fleeing responsibility, and makes his
name a byword for crime and sensuality throughout Germany.
He eventually sickens of this and goes on a sentimental journey
to his home, where his arrival, with his faithful band on his
heels, makes a bad situation worse and, eventually, leads to a
holocaust in which the whole Moor family is wiped out.

It is not difficult for a twentieth-century reader to see in Karl
Moor the kind of true philistinism and shirking of responsibility[39]
that hampered Germany's political development and made possible the great abuses of power committed in its name in the
150 years that followed Schiller's death. The successors of this
muddled romantic, perpetually drunk with rhetoric and self-satis-
faction ("Put me at the head of an army of real men like myself,
and we will make Germany a republic compared to which Rome

[38] Meinecke seems to have agreed with this. See his remarks about
Deutsche Grösse in *Weltbürgertum und Nationalstaat* (7th rev. ed., Munich,
1928), pp. 57ff., 60.

[39] The coupling of the concepts is Thomas Mann's. See his essay on
Schopenhauer in *Essays* (New York, 1957), p. 288.

and Sparta will look like ladies' seminaries!")[40] were those "heroes of the word" of whom Gervinus wrote in 1849, who, taking no responsible share in the political life of their country, tended "to flee from real life into the ideal, to sacrifice the sound beat of instinct to excessive intellectual acrobatics, to weaken their ability to recognize the real by absorption in chimerical fantasies," and, when galvanized into action, to prove themselves capable of forms of behavior that no one "thinking of the state of our cultural development and domestic virtues" would have thought possible.[41]

There is no doubt that in 1780, when he finished *Die Räuber,* Schiller regarded Robber Moor as a heroic figure who—as Hajo Holborn has written[42]—fled into the untrammeled freedom of nature because he was disgusted with a degrading civilization. But in the twenty-five further work-crowded years that were granted to him, the poet's views changed and matured, and he began to say explicitly and with purpose what he had said inadvertently, perhaps unconsciously, in his youthful drama: namely, that one does not improve the quality of a civilization by running away from its problems and that the freedom that is gained by flight from the realities of human existence is illusory and self-defeating.

Moreover, living in the age of the revolution and of Napoleon, Schiller came to know something that his fellow countrymen in the second half of the nineteenth century and the first thirty years of the twentieth forgot or understood imperfectly—that the most inescapable of realities is power, simply because it is always there, to be used for good or evil, for the protection or the destruction of freedom. Because evil men lust after it and are unscrupulous in the ways they use it, men of good will must have the courage to seek it too and to learn its uses. Because it has the ability to corrupt, they must take the responsibility for defining the limits of its use and for seeing that they are respected. Because the problems of power are rarely simple, they must resist the temptation to take refuge from hard choices in

[40] *Die Räuber,* Act I, scene 2. *"Stelle mich vor ein Heer Kerls wie ich, und aus Deutschland soll eine Republik werden, gegen die Rom und Sparta Nonnenklöster sein sollen."*

[41] Georg Gottfried Gervinus, *Shakespeare* (Leipzig, 1849), quoted in Walter Muschg, *"Deutschland ist Hamlet," Die Zeit,* May 1, 1964.

[42] Holborn, *Modern Germany, 1648–1840,* p. 331.

sentimentality and moral posturing and be willing to accept the ambiguities of responsibility.

If a nation is to win or maintain its freedom, it must, in short, have a good many Sapiehas and Stauffachers[43] among its leaders, and it will on occasion have to depend upon its Octavio Piccolominis. Even if it is fortunate in possessing such leaders, it will not be certain of success; in his last years Schiller became increasingly aware of the variety of threats to which freedom is exposed and at times seemed skeptical about its chances of survival anywhere.[44] But, whatever may befall it, its future will at least be not as predictably catastrophic as it would if it were to rely on the wordy nobility of its Karl Moors.

[43] It is Stauffacher's eloquence that raises the mood of the conspirators on the Rütli to a pitch of patriotic determination. See *Wilhelm Tell*, Act II, scene 2, lines 1274ff., one of Schiller's most famous speeches: *"Nein, eine Grenze hat Tyrannenmacht./Wenn der Gedrückte nirgends Recht kann finden, . . ./Zum letzten Mittel, wenn kein andres mehr/Verfangen will, ist ihm das Schwert gegeben."*

[44] See Walter Muschg, *"Schiller—Die Tragödie der Freiheit,"* in *Schiller: Reden im Gedenkjahr 1959,* especially pp. 234–35.

Chapter 8

1848

Theodore S. Hamerow

The Revolution of 1848 remains one of the enigmas of German history. What other uprising succeeded at first so swiftly and bloodlessly? What other uprising failed in the end so dismally and utterly? In the exultation of the "springtime of peoples" the Baden liberal Karl Mathy wrote to his wife from Frankfurt am Main: "I live here not among men but among angels, and I sleep in a fairy temple." A year later he stood amid the ruins of that temple, contemplating the disintegration of the revolutionary movement. The gulf between the promise and the accomplishment seemed so vast that only some fundamental flaw, some congenital and irremediable weakness could account for it. The usual categories of historical explanation appeared too ordinary to make intelligible the enormity of the disaster. There had to be a unique and compelling reason for a defeat of such magnitude. For more than a hundred years scholars have been looking for that fatal defect which doomed the liberal uprising in Central Europe. And while unanimity regarding its nature is no closer today than it was a century ago, there is at least widespread agreement that the answer lies in a basic deficiency of either the political leadership or the social class or the entire nation involved in the revolution.

The most popular explanation of the failure of 1848 has been that the men who directed the revolutionary movement lacked the practicality to transform theory into reality. Toward the end of his life Carl Schurz, looking back at the insurrection he had defended in his youth, concluded that the Frankfurt Parliament "suffered from an excess of intellect, erudition, and virtue, and from a lack of that political experience and insight which recognize that the better is often the enemy of the good, and that

the true statesman will beware of forfeiting the favorable moment by endangering the achievement of the essential through an
obstinate insistence on the less essential." This is the familiar
thesis of the visionariness of German parliamentarians immortalized in a thousand textbooks.

A more subtle interpretation of 1848, favored by historians
on the left, maintains that the middle class, after gaining control
of the revolution, betrayed it to the reaction rather than accept
the emancipation of the proletariat. Jürgen Kuczynski restated
this classic Marxian position on the occasion of the centenary of
the March days:

> We know that the bourgeoisie failed in its struggle to win political
> power. It failed because it fought on two fronts, against the feudal
> nobility and against the working class. It fought against the work-
> ing class, because it was afraid that it would have to share with it
> a part of the political power to be won. And it fought against the
> nobility in order to win in the first place the power which it did
> not want to share with the working class. But because in the past
> it had been accustomed to becoming a millionaire without politi-
> cal self-determination, its leadership in the course of the revolu-
> tion inclined more and more toward a war on one front against
> the working class and in alliance with the feudal nobility.

Finally, in the years since 1933 the horrors of National Socialism encouraged the view that the failure of the revolution was
the result of an innate deficiency of the German national character. Especially in countries that had fought against the Third
Reich there was a feeling that Auschwitz and Buchenwald be-
tokened a depravity whose roots extended deep into the history
of Central Europe. Thus Edmond Vermeil wrote that "if one
investigates the reasons for the dramatic and disastrous climax
to the events of 1848 and 1849 within the German Confederation,
one discovers that they lie not so much in external causes as in
the mentality of the German people." There were even some
Germans who reached a similar conclusion regarding the civic
incapacity of their nation. For example, Theodor Heuss, soon to
become the first president of the German Federal Republic, conceded that the revolution revealed "the narrowness of the German
character, which we may praise or revile, but which we must
accept as something given." In this thesis the specific weaknesses

of liberal leaders and bourgeois Philistines are subsumed under the generic weaknesses of a people's mentality.[1]

Yet the attempt to explain 1848 through ideas and policies pursued in Germany ignores the fact that the revolutionary movement was not confined to Germany. It was a European phenomenon affecting the entire Continent from the English Channel to the Black Sea. Its course, moreover, proved everywhere the same. First there was a popular uprising which forced the old order to capitulate almost without a struggle. Then came a period of jubilation at the triumph of liberty, jubilation tempered by the awareness that the victors were divided over the use to be made of their victory. As these divisions became more pronounced, the defeated conservatives, recovering from their confusion, began to take the offensive. The last stage was the successful assault of the counterrevolution and the re-establishment of the political and social status quo. This was the basic pattern of development not only in Germany, but in France, Italy, Austria, and Hungary as well. It implies that everywhere in Europe the same cause produced the same effect, in other words, that the factors leading to the uprising transcended state boundaries.

Almost half a century after the outbreak of the revolution Friedrich Engels in his introduction to Marx's *The Class Struggles in France* explained that "what [Marx] had earlier deduced, half *a priori,* from defective material, was made absolutely clear to him by the facts themselves, namely, that the world trade crisis of 1847 had been the true mother of the February and March Revolutions and that the industrial prosperity which had been returning gradually since the middle of 1848, and which attained full bloom in 1849 and 1850, was the revivifying force of the newly strengthened European reaction." To be sure, there is little in Marx's writings or activities in 1848 to suggest that he realized the effect economic recovery was bound to have on the course of the uprising. Even two years later, when he wrote the articles

---

[1] Gustav Freytag, *Karl Mathy: Geschichte seines Lebens,* 2nd ed. (Leipzig, 1872), p. 263; Carl Schurz, *Lebenserinnerungen* (3 vols., Berlin, 1906–12), I, 168; Jürgen Kuczynski, *Die wirtschaftlichen und sozialen Voraussetzungen der Revolution von 1848–1849* (Berlin, 1948), p. 20; Edmond Vermeil, "An Historical Paradox: The Revolution of 1848 in Germany," in *The Opening of an Era: 1848,* François Fejtö, ed. (London, 1948), p. 223; Theodor Heuss, *1848: Werk und Erbe* (Stuttgart, 1948), p. 166.

comprising *The Class Struggles in France,* he was more interested in proving the inevitability of a new insurrection than in
analyzing the failure of the old. "A new revolution is only possible in consequence of a new crisis," he expounded. "It is, however, also just as certain as this." He even predicted the time of
the next depression: "If the new cycle of industrial development
which began in 1848 follows the same course as that of 1843–47,
the crisis will break out in the year 1852." But to Engels in
1895 the perspective of almost fifty years clearly revealed what
he and Marx had only vaguely surmised in the heat of battle,
namely, that the revival of the European economy had deprived
the revolution of the urgency and militancy essential for its success.[2]

There is ample statistical evidence that the food shortage which
helped produce the international wave of insurrection had already passed its crisis when the victorious revolutionaries prepared to consolidate their initial successes. In Germany the index of wholesale prices for agricultural products (1913 = 100) fell
from 88 in 1847 to 58 in 1848 and 48 in 1849, while for
cereal foodstuffs alone the figures were 122, 68, and 54. In
Prussia the cost of a scheffel of wheat, 50 liters, declined during those 3 years from 11.03 marks to 6.30 and 6.17. Rye went
from 8.62 to 3.82 and 3.18, and potatoes from 3.00 to 1.72 and
1.37. A pound of butter for which the consumer paid 68 pfennigs
in 1847 could be bought for 62 in 1848 and 55 in 1849. The
price of a pound of beef fell from 32 pfennigs to 31 and 21,
and of a pound of pork from 44 to 43 and 36. In other words,
the cost of living which had risen rapidly in the middle years of
the decade, reaching its apex in 1847, began to drop with equal
rapidity just as the revolution broke out.[3]

The business depression ended later than the famine, but it
was never as intense. The per capita value of foreign trade in
the Zollverein declined from 39.40 marks in 1847 to 36.60 in

[2] Karl Marx, *The Class Struggles in France (1848–1850)* (New York,
1964), pp. 10–11, 135; *Neue Rheinische Zeitung: Politische-ökonomische
Revue* (Berlin, 1955), p. 312.

[3] Alfred Jacobs and Hans Richter, *Die Grosshandelspreise in Deutschland
von 1792 bis 1934* (Hamburg, 1934), p. 82; "*Durchschnittspreise der
wichtigsten Lebensmittel für Menschen und Thiere in den bedeutensten
Marktorten der preussischen Monarchie,*" *Zeitschrift des königlich preussischen Statistischen Bureaus,* XI (1871), 243.

1848 and 35.60 in 1849. The output of the anthracite mines of Prussia diminished from 19,145,000 tons in 1847 to 17,572,000 in 1848, but then increased again to 18,197,000 in 1849. The Zollverein index of production for iron manufacture (1860 = 100) fell rapidly from 50 in 1847 to 40 in 1848 and then to 37 in 1849. The average for the entire decade, however, was only 36. The volume of capital investment in the Prussian railroads dropped from 109,989,000 marks in 1847 to 42,938,000 in 1848 and 52,111,000 in 1849. Yet revenues continued to climb from 22,500,000 marks in 1847, to 26,665,000 in 1848, and 32,349,000 in 1849. The nominal earnings of industrial labor, moreover, were generally unaffected by the hard times. Indeed, the index of average gross real wages in Germany (1900 = 100) rose from 57 in 1847 to 79 in 1848 and 86 in 1849, a reflection of the decline in the price of food.[4]

In any case, for a country that was still largely agricultural the increase in farm output proved more important than the stagnation of business. The pattern of demographic change reflected the ups and downs of the cost of living with remarkable fidelity. For Germany as a whole the number of marriages per 1000 inhabitants was 7.2 in 1847, 7.7 in 1848, and 8.2 in 1849. The figures varied from state to state, but they were almost without exception on the rise: 7.8, 8.3, and 9.2 in Prussia; 6.3, 6.6, and 6.7 in Bavaria; 7.7, 8.0, and 8.5 in Saxony; and 6.5, 6.6, and 6.8 in Württemberg. Only in Baden was there a slight decline from 6.7 to 6.6 and 6.5. The over-all birth rate increased from 34.6 in 1847 to 34.7 in 1848 and 39.7 in 1849, while the death rate first rose from 29.7 to 30.5, and then dropped sharply to 28.6. Emigration statistics, however, are the most sensitive measure of the economic recovery which coincided with the coming of the revolution. The outflow of population has been estimated at 78,800 in 1847, 59,000 in 1848, and 61,700 in 1849. The destination of the vast majority of the emigrants was the New World, for the number of Germans entering the

[4] Gerhard Bondi, *Deutschlands Aussenhandel, 1815–1870* (Berlin, 1958), p. 145; Jürgen Kuczynski, *A Short History of Labour Conditions under Industrial Capitalism: Germany, 1800 to the Present Day* (London, 1945), pp. 29, 32, 58, 84; *Jahrbuch für die amtliche Statistik des preussischen Staats,* I (1863), 513; *Statistisches Handbuch für den preussichen Staat,* II (1893), 304.

United States during these years was reported at 74,300, 58,500, and 60,200 respectively. In Prussia there were 14,900 authorized departures between October 1, 1846, and September 30, 1847; during the next twelve months the figure was 8300; and during the succeeding twelve it was 8800. The net increase in the population of the kingdom, representing the cumulative effect of changes in the birth, death, and emigration rates, was 44,200 in 1847, 8300 in 1848, and 165,800 in 1849.[5]

The Revolution of 1848 thus differs from the two classic revolutions of the modern period, the French and the Russian, in that it did not originate in a financial or military crisis that the old order could not resolve. It was rather a belated reaction against hard times, a protest against material privations that were already diminishing as a result of economic recovery. Nor was the ruling caste, which it temporarily displaced, a decorative court aristocracy enjoying exalted status without a corresponding civic function. The nobility of Central Europe, particularly in Prussia, was still a robust social class occupying a strategic position in the army, the bureaucracy, and agriculture. Its defeat during the March days had been the result of a failure of nerve, not the penalty for ineptitude. The sudden collapse of established authority on the Continent had surprised and demoralized the Junker landowners of the east. In Frederick William IV, moreover, they had a ruler incapable of withstanding misfortune. Alarmed by peasant unrest and discouraged by the pusillanimity of their King, they reluctantly acquiesced in the establishment of a new order that promised to save them from anarchy through constitutionalism. Even an uncompromising conservative like Bismarck admitted: "The estate owners, like all other reasonable men, tell themselves that it would be senseless and impossible to want to arrest or dam up the current of the time."

But the recovery of the economy during the spring months

5 Paul Mombert, *Studien zur Bevölkerungsbewegung in Deutschland in den letzten Jahrzehnten mit besonderer Berücksichtigung der ehelichen Fruchtbarkeit* (Karlsruhe, 1907), pp. 48, 105; Marcus L. Hansen, "The Revolutions of 1848 and German Emigration," *Journal of Economic and Business History*, II (1930), 635, n. 8; *Statistisches Jahrbuch für das Deutsche Reich*, I (1880), 19; T. Bödiker, "Die Auswanderung und die Einwanderung des preussischen Staates," *Zeitschrift des königlich preussischen Statistischen Bureaus*, XIII (1873), 2–3; *Statistisches Handbuch für den preussischen Staat*, II (1893), 96.

revived the courage of the landed aristocrats. It created the opportunity for restoring royal authority and noble prerogative through an alliance of the upper with the lower classes. An intensification of the famine and depression would have forced the revolution farther to the left. It would have produced an irreparable breach between the old order and the new by encouraging both to adopt desperate expedients. The liberals would have become more radical, the conservatives more reactionary. A compromise would have proved impossible. The alleviation of hard times, on the other hand, had the effect of moderating political passion. It suggested to the court the strategy of appeasing the bourgeoisie with political reform, while conciliating the proletariat with economic reform. The idea of rallying the masses to the support of the crown appealed especially to the opponents of the revolution. As early as the March days Joseph von Radowitz was assuring Frederick William IV that "the proletariat as such is by no means republican. This is a common error. Any form of government that would boldly and wisely take its interests in hand, that would devote itself to the system of progressive taxation, the entire problem of poor relief, and the regulation of the inequality between capital and labor, would have the 'common man' on its side and thereby an enormous force. To be sure, this is a dangerous course, but what is not dangerous now?"

The conservative policy of moderation gained support as the return of economic stability vitiated the justification for political radicalism. The program the rightist members of the Prussian national assembly published in June was reasonableness itself. "We want to develop political and religious freedom in keeping with the promises made to the people," it proclaimed. "We assert that in accordance with the concept of a constitutional form of government the rights of sovereignty are exercised jointly by the King and the people." Most important, "we seek in the realm of material interests the welfare of the people and especially of the working class, a fair criterion of the obligation to pay taxes based on the ability to pay taxes, the abolition of the feudal system with all its consequences, the elimination of manorial and domanial authority. Liberation of landed property from all servile obligations to which it is subject, the right of the proprietor to dispose of his land with complete freedom, and the limitation of the regalia." Who could take exception to such conciliatory proposals? A month later a correspondent for Marx's *Neue Rheinische Zeitung* reported from Stettin that a "part of our landowners is intelligent enough to consider the elimination of the privileges they have had until now a necessary condition for the acquisition by large landed property of the political influence that they need for the advancement of their interests." And in August, at the "General Assembly for the Protection of the Interests of Landowners and for the Advancement of the Welfare of All Classes of the Population," which the Junkers convoked in Berlin, Ernst von Bülow-Cummerow advocated a conservatism based on economic interest rather than ideological orthodoxy: "If this honorable assembly shares my views, we will refrain from all political debates. We will thereby avoid conflicts leading to disunion. Material interests have a significance outweighing all others. By pursuing them we will always be on firm ground. Let us exert all our energies to advance them, and if we are successful, we can count on the approval of the great mass of the people and of all propertied groups." This became the strategy of the successful counteroffensive the old order launched in the fall of 1848.[6]

The economic recovery that made the conservatives less conservative made the revolutionaries less revolutionary. It strengthened the hand of the middle-of-the-roaders to whom liberalism meant essentially the establishment of a social system dominated by individual talent rather than hereditary privilege. To them, free private property was the basis of civic progress, and any attempt to regulate its ownership would conflict with the underlying laws of economics. A government that tried to tamper with the natural interplay of material interests invited disaster. "The unequal distribution of goods is not artificial," expounded Konrad von Rappard before the Frankfurt Parliament. "It is established deep in the cumulative nature of landed property and capital that in a populous state they will always remain in the hands of only a small part of the nation. Legislation can change nothing in this regard. It should only remove the barriers that exclude individuals or entire classes from property." According to the moderates the social purpose of the revolution was to win freedom of opportunity for the gifted and the energetic, to create a new aristocracy of ability in place of the old aristocracy of birth. That is what Joseph Schneider meant when he argued in the national assembly for the abolition of titles of nobility: "I am certainly well aware that we will have an aristocracy of wealth and we will have an aristocracy of intellect, human nature unfortunately being what it is. But those, gentlemen, are natural aristocracies for which everyone is qualified and to which everyone can ascend. But an aristocracy of birth is never natural nor is it necessary."

Belief in a basic inequality in society led logically to belief in a basic inequality in politics. The liberal bourgeoisie that came to power during the spring uprising opposed the egalitarian demands of the proletariat as resolutely as the hierarchical prejudices of the aristocracy. For how could the ignorant and the propertyless be expected to resist the blandishments of rabble-rousers? "No civic order," maintained the constitutional committee of the Frankfurt Parliament, "of whatever sort it may be, monarchical or republican, will endure or achieve any kind of stability, if the right of decision in all political questions is placed in the hands of the great mass, which only too often lets itself be led without a will of its own, and which capriciously follows one leader today and another one tomorrow." Participation in public affairs had to be restricted to those who could demonstrate their intelligence and ability through the accumulation of property. Heinrich von Gagern, prime minister in the national government, was convinced that "the tendency of our time is to secure for the middle classes the preponderant influence in the state. While we have granted the individual all personal freedoms, the right of association, freedom of the press, fullest freedom of conscience, and whatever the individual might require to assert himself and establish the conditions for the exercise of political rights, we must provide for a wise exercise of political rights through such authoritative measures that the property owner is secure in his property, and . . . the state is not threatened by a mass influence which is not suited to our conditions."[7]

The end of the depression intensified the reluctance of the bourgeoisie to abandon its cozy theories of timocratic politics and laissez-faire economics. A firm alliance between the middle and lower classes might have saved the revolution despite the return of prosperity. Such an alliance, however, would have required a fundamental change in the economic relationships and institutions of Central Europe. A vigorous program of agrarian reform, for example, could have won for liberalism the support of the peasantry, the most numerous class of the population, but only at the expense of established property rights. And that was a price bourgeois parliamentarians, heartened by the upturn of business conditions, refused to pay. Marx, on the other hand, advocated the total destruction of the system of manorial obligations precisely because he recognized that it would create an irreparable breach with the past and make impossible any compromise between the new order and the old:

> [Consider] the most striking evidence that the German Revolution of 1848 is only the parody of the French Revolution of 1789. On August 4, 1789, three weeks after the attack on the Bastille, the French people in one day disposed of the feudal burdens. On July 11, 1848, four months after March barricades, the feudal burdens are disposing of the German people. . . . The French bourgeoisie of 1789 did not for one moment desert its allies, the peasants. It knew that the basis of its power was the destruction of feudalism in the countryside, the creation of a free, landowning peasant class. The German bourgeoisie of 1848 betrays without any scruple these peasants who are its most natural allies, flesh of its flesh, and without whom it is powerless against the nobility.

Yet the comparison was not altogether valid. The French people did not dispose of the feudal burdens in one day, and the creation of a free, landowning peasant class was a gradual process which became possible only as the revolution moved farther to the left under the pressure of financial and military exigency. It was the National Convention that liquidated the last remnants of

---

[7] *Stenographischer Bericht über die Verhandlungen der deutschen constituirenden Nationalversammlung zu Frankfurt am Main,* Franz Wigard, ed. (9 vols., Frankfurt am Main, 1848–49), VII, 5303. Cf. *ibid.,* II, 1313, VII, 2222, 5296.

feudalism in France. The men who guided the revolution in Germany, however, were no Jacobins. They were cautious middle-class liberals who refused to adopt desperate expedients in the absence of desperate needs. Their purpose was not to save freedom from reaction, but to defend it against attacks from the left as well as the right. And that meant defending the principle of private ownership, the basis of freedom. The economic committee of the national assembly maintained that "every private property, whether it consists of land or dues, is equally sacred and inviolable, and must be safeguarded by civil society, whatever political form of state the latter may assume. By destroying the protection of right and property it would destroy its foundations and vital elements, and so destroy itself." To acquiesce in the expropriation of the nobility might ultimately lead to the expropriation of the bourgeoisie. For was there any logical distinction between estates and factories, between rural and urban wealth? That was the danger against which Paul Pfizer warned the Württemberg legislature:

> Every demand to abolish the still existing feudal dues and to destroy completely rights which have until now been recognized by the state and protected by the courts because of the injustice, the severity, and oppressiveness which may partly be connected with them, every such demand . . . to end right and wrong by a stroke of the pen had to be rejected, for we know that from the destruction of land registers and stock ledgers it is only a step to the destruction of mortgage records and promissory notes, and from the destruction of promissory notes it is again only a step to the division of property or a general community of goods.

Most of the liberals of 1848 wanted to maintain the existing structure of society in Central Europe. They believed that the object of the revolution was not to abolish established rights of ownership, but to adapt them to the demands of a free capitalistic economy. This required first of all the transformation of manorial dues into money rents extinguishable by lump payment, and secondly, the removal of class restrictions on the acquisition of land. In other words, the same underlying principles that governed property relationships in industry would now be applied to agriculture. Economic obligations were to be based on written contract rather than common custom, while the prohibition of entailment was to make ability the only condition of rural proprietorship. The distinction in the forms of possession between manufacture and farming would disappear to make way for the untrammeled rule of laissez faire. The free interaction of private interests in pursuit of material gain was to solve the agrarian problem by ensuring the survival of the fittest. Wilhelm Löwe of Kalbe attacked entailed estates in language that anticipated Herbert Spencer: "I personally do not in the least wish that this property should always remain immovably in one hand, and when I consider the development of the people and the development of humanity, I want no one to have any longer this security which is born on the bed of ease. . . . Everyone should strive and toil; this struggle should not cease; everyone should also wage this struggle every moment in his small circle. In this way character will be steeled, self-confidence will be strengthened, in a word, the moral personality will be raised to a higher level." To such men rugged individualism was the best cure for the ills of the peasantry.[8]

The leaders of the revolution applied the same austere dogmas of laissez-faire liberalism to problems facing the urban working class. The latter consisted largely of skilled artisans whose livelihood was being threatened by the advance of industrialization. The economist Bruno Hildebrand pointed out to the members of the Frankfurt Parliament that "the German proletariat is not a factory but a handicraft proletariat. In the middle-sized and smaller towns there are the many small master tradesmen who have sunk, who are starving, and who must at present be considered proletarians. There are especially the numerous unfortunate master tradesmen who are engaged in homecrafts and compete with the machines. . . . The greater part of the master tradesmen is unfortunately made up of nothing more than proletarians who live from hand to mouth just like the day laborers." The artisan masses which had marched in demonstrations and fought on the barricades during the March days might have become the *sans-culottes* of the revolution in Central Europe. Hungry and embittered, they were the victims of the mechanization of production which had been growing steadily since the end of the Napoleonic

---

[8] *Neue Rheinische Zeitung*, July 30, 1848; *Verhandlungen der National-versammlung*, F. Wigard, ed., IV, 2403, 2549; *Verhandlungen der würt-tembergischen Kammer der Abgeordneten auf dem Landtage von 1848* (Stuttgart, 1848), pp. 229–30.

wars. What they wanted above all was a corporative regulation of manufacture, which would enable them to withstand the competition of the factory system. "It was found," proclaimed an assembly of journeymen, "that through the introduction of [industrial freedom] the rich became richer and richer, the poor poorer and poorer; that the middle class was ruined and the working class reduced to begging; [and] that the freedom which had been sought was no true freedom but only a caricature." Any political movement that undertook to protect the independent handicraftsman against industrialism could have won his backing.

This was a bargain, however, that the middle-of-the-road liberals were unwilling to make. It would have meant imposing new burdens on the business community, which was just beginning to recover from a serious depression. It would have meant tampering with the eternal laws of economics. They were determined to avoid experiments in mass welfare like those that had led to civil war in France during the June Days. Their credo could be found in the reports the economic committee submitted to the national assembly: "It is a demand of natural law that everyone be allowed to employ his individual skill profitably for his own advantage as much as he can, and to choose his occupation in accordance with his own inclination. If conditions make the choice of another form of employment necessary or desirable, the change to another form of livelihood should not be rendered difficult. . . . In competition lies an irresistible force of progress. Whoever does not accept it will be left behind." Not even the realization that the revolution was losing support could shake their rigid adherence to principle. It was better to risk a restoration of the old order than to shackle the economic energies of the nation. For what was the good of political liberty won by the sacrifice of economic freedom?[9]

The same logic made it impossible for the leaders of the revolution to establish an effective alliance with the industrial working class. Whether such an alliance could in any case have saved the new order is an open question. The factory proletariat

[9] *Verhandlungen der Nationalversammlung*, F. Wigard, ed., VII, 5285; W. Ed. Biermann, *Karl Georg Winkelblech (Karl Marlo): Sein Leben und sein Wirken* (2 vols., Leipzig, 1909), II, 451–52; *Verhandlungen der deutschen verfassunggebenden Reichs-Versammlung zu Frankfurt am Main*, K. D. Hassler, ed. (6 vols., Frankfurt am Main, 1848–49), II, 899, IV, 146.

was numerically weak and politically indifferent. Made up in large part of uprooted peasants driven from their villages by overpopulation, it lacked a sense of community and purpose. Nor had it yet developed an effective form of organization such as the guild system had once provided for the artisan masses. Most important of all, the factory proletariat was still without a collective feeling of social grievance. Employed in an expanding sector of the economy, it had not suffered the material and psychological hardships to which the independent skilled handicraftsman was exposed. Its earnings had generally remained stable during the years of the depression, and with the return of good times its economic position was improving. That is what Hermann Kriege, a former disciple of Marx, meant when he reported that "we cannot rely on the proletariat; the ideal proletariat does not exist." Even under the most favorable circumstances the liberal statesmen of 1848 may not have succeeded in transforming the labor force of the factories into an instrument of their policy. And such an attempt was certainly bound to fail without an extensive program of social reform, which they were unwilling to contemplate.

The Frankfurt Parliament rejected out of hand proposals for the establishment of minimum wage rates: "Aside from the fact that legal determination of the proceeds of labor presupposes a police state such as has not yet existed anywhere, a minimum wage would necessarily pull with it all prices of goods and even extend to the produce of the soil. . . . A fixed wage rate would furthermore deprive of their bread the workers who are less energetic, less able, who are weak from old age, but who now find work because a lower wage makes up for their inferior ability." A state guarantee of work for all citizens was worse still: "Such a guarantee would be the paralysis of diligence, a sanction of laziness, a paralysis of the energy which above all should animate and elevate this populace, if it is to overcome the harshness of its lot. . . . It is our duty to steel the trust in their strength of these classes on which the Providence of God has imposed labor as a necessity of life, . . . and to steel their moral courage by directing their trust to Providence." The only way to enable the worker to get ahead in economics as in politics was by establishing freedom of opportunity, the open-sesame of laissez-faire liberalism: "Germany should also consider labor sacred, but she should honor it by opening for the industrious worker the avenue to every position, even the highest in the fatherland. He must never be excluded, but he must also never be enfranchised if he has not demonstrated by what he accomplishes that he meets the criterion of capacity for a wise exercise of the political vocation." The rigorous ethic of the *juste-milieu* had only one answer for all problems of state and society.[10]

The revolution, to be sure, also had its democratic adherents. Some of them sat in the legislative assemblies of 1848, waiting patiently for an unexpected turn of events to thrust power into their hands. Others, afraid that legalistic scruples would only strengthen the predominance of the moderates, preached sedition and organized hopeless putsches. All of them, however, believed in popular sovereignty and manhood suffrage. Their ideal was not a constitutional monarchy of property and education, but the Jacobin republic of virtue. The faction of the *Donnersberg* in the Frankfurt Parliament proclaimed "liberty, equality, and fraternity as the principles whose realization is its task," while the militants congregating in the *Deutscher Hof* dreamed of a radical democracy in Central Europe:

> The party of the left . . . wants a popular representation arising out of the free choice of all Germans who are of age. . . . It wants the right of the individual German states to determine their constitutions, whether in the form of the democratic monarchy or in the form of the democratic free state. . . . It wants humanity. It accordingly wants in particular a system of education which has been completely altered, penal legislation based on humanity, and a military system built on a popular militia. It wants the elimination of all immoral state revenues, and a method of taxation in keeping with the ability to pay. It wants in general a thoroughgoing improvement in the social conditions of the people.

Nor did these radicals hesitate to subordinate the abstractions of classical economics to the vital needs of the community. Bernhard Eisenstuck, for example, advocated a system of social insurance: "You must create institutions that will impose on every employer, in proportion to the labor force that he uses,

[10] Veit Valentin, *Geschichte der deutschen Revolution von 1848–49* (2 vols., Berlin, 1930–31), II, 256; *Verhandlungen der Nationalversammlung*, F. Wigard, ed., VII, 5102, 5114, 5246.

the obligation of paying during the use of the labor force, that is, during the actual continuance of the contract, a tax solely for the benefit of the workers. This tax must flow into the state treasury and be publicly administered. And the use of this tax should be nothing other than the compensation of the labor force after it has been expended, that is, for the material support of invalid workers, the establishment of retirement homes, etc." Ludwig Simon on the far left was even ready to defend the appropriation of public funds for the relief of unemployment and want: "I for my part at least deplore far less the money that was spent in France for the 200,000 workers in the national workshops, or that was spent in Berlin by the state and municipal treasury for some 6000 workers in the time of anarchy, than the Silesians and Irishmen who died of hunger in a condition of law and order." Here was an incipient awareness of the social problems engendered in industrialization, an awareness that, if translated into government policy, might have won for the new order the lower-class support essential for its survival.[11]

Yet the radicals never came to power, because the times were not propitious for political or economic experiments. What the revolution needed was a great galvanizing crisis capable of evoking the hidden energies and resources of society. Under the pressure of national disaster a small faction of dogmatists and visionaries created the Jacobin republic and the Bolshevik dictatorship, successfully defying the world. The men of 1848, on the other hand, never matched these achievements, because they never grappled with the same elemental urgencies. How could they effect the transition from Mirabeau to Robespierre, from Kerensky to Lenin? Among them might have been found "some Cromwell guiltless of his country's blood," guiltless for lack of opportunity. Yet only the desperation born of military defeat or economic collapse could have produced a widespread resolve to break once and for all with the beliefs and loyalties of the past. The nineteenth century, the golden age of the European bourgeoisie, was too prosperous, too optimistic for great uprisings. It could produce theories, ideals, enthusiasms, and slogans, but it lacked that mass despair that is indispensable for a violent,

[11] *Parteiprogramme*, F. Salomon, ed., pp. 29–31; *Verhandlungen der Nationalversammlung*, F. Wigard, ed., VII, 5119, 5135.

fundamental alteration in the structure of society. The revolution failed not because of the weakness of the national character, not because of the treason of the middle class, not even because of the timidity of the leaders, but because of an unshaken faith that the basic civic and material needs of Germany could be met within the framework of established ideas and institutions.

Chapter 9

JURIDICAL AND POLITICAL RESPONSIBILITY IN NINETEENTH-CENTURY GERMANY

Otto Pflanze

Since 1945 German scholarship has been deeply concerned with the problem of the responsibility of power. No one can question the moral earnestness of this inquiry; German historians of both the older and younger generation are shocked by the moral depravity of the Nazi regime. Yet the issue has a practical as well as a moral side. Hitler and his cohorts are regarded as irresponsible because they vastly overestimated Germany's military capacity and their ambitions recklessly exceeded, at least after 1938, what Europe and the world could tolerate. One courageous scholar has aroused a bitter controversy by suggesting that this judgment should be extended to the First as well as the Second World War.[1] His critics wish to emphasize the gulf that lies between the monarchical regime which guided Germany's destiny in the first conflict and the revolutionary dictatorship which brought her to catastrophe in the second. They stress the discontinuity rather than the continuity of German political development. To this end they have analyzed afresh the careers and political outlook of Frederick the Great and Bismarck. In both of these statesmen German historians discern an ethic of power that is in stark contrast to the amorality of the Nazi regime and that provides contemporary Germans with a precedent upon which to build.[2]

---

[1] Fritz Fischer, *Griff nach der Weltmacht* (Düsseldorf, 1961).

[2] The most significant of these works are Leonhard von Muralt, *Bismarcks Verantwortlichkeit* (Göttingen, 1955), Hans Rothfels, *Bismarck und der Staat* (Stuttgart, 1953), Otto Vossler, "Bismarcks Ethos," *Historische Zeitschrift*, Vol. 171 (1951), pp. 263–92, Gustav A. Rein, *Die Revolution in der Politik Bismarcks* (Göttingen, 1957), pp. 307–54, Wilhelm Schüssler, *Um das Geschictsbild* (Gladbeck, 1953), and several

Bismarck is the favored model. He is less remote in time and he lived in a society far closer in its social composition and its problems to contemporary Germany than that of Frederick the Great. While Frederick ruled in an age of absolutism and "cabinet diplomacy," when monarchs and ministers were unrestricted by popular pressures in their conduct of affairs of state, Bismarck governed in a period of rapid industrialization and spreading literacy when mass movements and popular ideals had to be included in the calculations of statesmen. Bismarck stood on the threshold of our own age, Frederick was still outside the door. In contrast to Bismarck, moreover, Frederick was in some respects an anomaly in German historical development. As a deist and rationalist he was far closer to the French than to the German Enlightenment; he had little comprehension of and no sympathy for the philosophy of German idealism which during his reign began to dominate German intellectual life. Bismarck, on the other hand, was a master of *Realpolitik* in an age of realism and his religious faith was in close harmony with the Lutheran tradition. His career belongs more clearly than that of Frederick to the mainstream of German development since the Reformation.

About the sincerity of Bismarck's religious conviction there can be little doubt. The frequency with which religious sentiments appear in his speech and writing, both public and private, in the decades after his conversion in 1847 is ample evidence of the depth of his religious feeling. While he had no interest in dogma, it is true that his religious thought was cast in the Lutheran mold. Like Luther, he did not believe that man has the power to change the world. The statesman who is often credited with altering the direction of German and European history did not feel that he had the capacity to do anything but float and steer upon the "stream of time." In the Lutheran tradition he regarded the church as subject to the state; nor is there any sign that he gave to it any other function in society than the propagation of faith. There is no positive evidence that Bismarck followed Luther in conceiving the state as divinely instituted to

---

studies by Gerhard Ritter, *Friedrich der Grosse* (2nd ed., Munich, 1942), *Europa und die deutsche Frage* (Munich, 1948), and *Staatskunst und Kriegshandwerk,* Vols. I and II (Munich, 1954).

preserve the small band of true Christians from annihilation by a selfish and ruthless majority. Yet the influence of this conception is apparent in his political attitudes. He frequently justified the powers of the Hohenzollern monarchy in terms of divine right and he denied that Christian ethics had any direct application to statecraft. Politics he saw as the arena in which the conflict of interests rather than the struggle between right and wrong is resolved, either through mutual accommodation or through the triumph of superior force. Power and morality were two separate spheres whose only connecting link was the conscience of the statesman—his sense of responsibility for his actions, for the results they achieve, and for the effects they cause.[3]

In popular literature Bismarck is often labeled "the iron chancellor" or "the man of blood and iron," leaving the impression that he was a ruthless Machiavelli who exalted power and glorified violence. But this view is not justified either by his political attitudes or by his political conduct. He possessed an active conscience, grounded in his religious faith, which constantly weighed upon him and often limited his political actions. It prevented him from seeking power for its own sake and it preserved him from the frivolous waste of human life. In this respect he did indeed live in another world from that of Adolf Hitler.

It is questionable, nevertheless, whether the concept of responsibility, as illustrated in Bismarck, provides the kind of model from which contemporary Germans can gain more than limited benefits in their search for a new political orientation. As a total political philosophy it has the serious defect that it provides no other barrier to the misuse of power than the conscience of the statesman. And men's consciences vary, not to speak of their wisdom. By contrast, the western European and American political tradition has come to rely more upon legal and institutional checks upon the exercise of power than upon the ethical and oral character of statesmen.

[3] Although the literature on Bismarck's religious faith and its relationship to his political conduct is extensive, the most judicious analysis, notable for its insight and balanced judgment, is that of Hajo Holborn, "Bismarck's Realpolitik," *Journal of the History of Ideas,* XXI (1960), 84–98.

II

Certainly such checks are not absent from the German political tradition. Luther lived in a society in which political power was generally shared by the princes and the territorial estates. Yet Luther's denial of the right of resistance against even a tyrannical prince applied as much in the end to the estates as it did to rebellious peasants. By 1555 the Lutheran Reformation had lost what popular character it had possessed and had evolved into an instrument of princely authority. In this form it accelerated the decay of feudal dualism and the progress of the prince toward absolutism. Early in the nineteenth century a new kind of dualism emerged. The revival of feudal corporatism under the influence of romanticism and the spread of constitutionalism following the revolutions of 1830 and 1848 created new political structures of mixed powers. While the monarchs and their ministers continued to monopolize executive authority, they shared legislative power with bicameral legislatures whose upper chambers were chosen by heredity and royal appointment and whose lower chambers were elected by a limited suffrage.

Bismarck was a firm believer in the desirability of such a structure. In the late eighteenth century monarchical absolutism had given way to bureaucratic absolutism, and Bismarck had as poor an opinion of the wisdom of bureaucrats as Luther had of the integrity of princes. Parliaments were necessary to check their foibles and follies. While in power, nevertheless, Bismarck believed that folly was on the side of parliament and its political factions. During the constitutional conflict of the 1860s and again during the parliamentary struggles of the 1880s he considered the advisability of executing a *coup d'état*. His plans on these occasions and many of his actions during the constitutional conflict demonstrate that he valued the dictates of his conscience above the law. The greatest obstacle to "changes in the constitution," he complained in 1862, was the conscience of the king, who took seriously his oath to uphold it. The ministers as well had sworn "conscientiously" to uphold the constitution. "What if conscience bids me not to respect it?" In the debates of the Prussian Landtag Bismarck publicly disputed that he placed a higher value upon power than upon law, but his private remarks and his public actions at the most critical moments of his career show that the contrary was the case.[4]

At the other end of the political spectrum the German liberals were also deeply concerned throughout the nineteenth century with the problem of the responsibility of power. No other political term seems to appear as frequently in the deliberations of the Frankfurt Parliament, the Prussian Landtag, and the German Reichstag. Here the concept had a significance far closer to its western European meaning than that with which Bismarck was imbued and upon whose revival German historians place their hopes. To the German liberals the concept of responsibility was not merely moral. It was closely concerned with the problem of legal and institutional checks upon the exercise of political power.

During the 1840s, when the German liberal movement first began to prosper, it was split in many directions. Some were radical democrats, others were moderate reformers. There were advocates of republican and of monarchical constitutions, of universal and of limited suffrage, of social revolution and of the sanctity of private property. The ideal of German national unity was a synthetic force that tended to weld these disparate elements together; yet here too there was a division between those who valued freedom over unity and those who were willing to sacrifice the former to the latter. Whatever their disagreements on other points, one basic conviction was universally shared: a belief in the necessity of establishing the *Rechtsstaat,* a constitutional order guaranteeing the supremacy of law. In a divided country that for centuries had been ruled by swarms of princes and bureaucrats it was only natural that the abolition of arbitrary government should have been the loudest battle cry of reform. The goal of the *Rechtsstaat* survived the harsh disillusionment of the liberal failure in 1848–49, which destroyed radical liberalism in Germany for a half-century, and in the 1860s it became the rallying ground upon which the liberals fought and lost the constitutional conflict against Bismarck. Even after the capitulation of the liberal majority in 1866–67 it

[4] See the author's *Bismarck and the Development of Germany: The Period of Unification, 1815–1871* (Princeton, 1963), pp. 49–86, 207–12, 276–77.

lingered on as the last major principle of German liberalism.

The liberal concept of responsibility was an integral part of the principle of the *Rechtsstaat,* and the struggle for its realization in constitutional law was an enduring quest of liberals until the outbreak of the First World War. Certainly many other issues were involved in the effort to establish the *Rechtsstaat:* for example, the independence of the judiciary, the guarantee of the basic human rights, and the full and accurate accounting of public funds. Yet the establishment of the responsibility of cabinet ministers was generally regarded by liberals as the most essential aspect of constitutionalism. In the many debates upon the issue they constantly reiterated that ministerial responsibility was the "keystone" of the governmental structure. At other moments it was described as "the indispensable basis of all constitutional life," "the necessary postulate of political freedom," and even as an attribute of civilization.[5] Without it the constitution would never be secure and the *Rechtsstaat* would remain unrealized.

III

The kind of ministerial responsibility desired by most liberals was juridical rather than parliamentary. What they sought was not parliamentary control over the executive on the English model, but the establishment of the principle that ministers could be impeached, tried, and punished for violating the law.

This limited objective is apparent in the structure of the constitutions drafted for Prussia and Germany by the liberal assemblies in Berlin and Frankfurt following the revolution of 1848. In both cases the basic design was one of mixed powers. The best guarantee of political liberty was believed to lie in the division of powers between crown and parliament rather than in popular sovereignty. Through such an equilibrium the German liberals hoped to avoid the "tyranny" of either the monarch or the parliamentary majority. Naturally the critical question in this system was how to make certain that the executive and the legislature remained within their allotted spheres, particularly

---

[5] *Stenographische Berichte über die Verhandlungen des Landtages,* Zweite Kammer, 1850–51, II, 1155; Haus der Abgeordneten, 1861, II, 944, V, Nr. 156, p. 4.

where finances were concerned. The framers of the two constitutions sought to buttress parliament by giving it a voice in the
vital matters of taxation and expenditure. Yet this authority was
insecure as long as there was no assurance that ministers could
be compelled to adhere to the budget once it became law. For
this reason the paragraphs on the juridical responsibility of ministers were generally regarded as the most crucial in both constitutions.

At Frankfurt the issue of responsibility first arose in connection
with the creation of a provisional body to govern Germany until
the constitution could be drafted and go into effect. By a vote of
450 to 100 the deputies decided for a "non-responsible"
Reichsverweser and for a cabinet that was "responsible to the
national assembly" in the juridical sense. Yet the offenses that
could lead to impeachment were not listed, nor was the procedure outlined by which impeached ministers could be brought
to trial. Both questions were left to a "special law," which,
while drafted by a committee, was never enacted.[6] The completed constitution contained the following paragraph: "The person of the Kaiser is inviolate. The Kaiser exercises the power
entrusted to him through responsible ministers whom he appoints. All governmental acts of the Kaiser require for their
validation the countersignature of at least one of the Reich
ministers, who thereby assumes the responsibility."[7] Late in the
process of amendment a further clause was added that likewise
provided that a special law "shall be passed" defining responsibility and outlining the judicial procedure for impeachment
and trial.[8] Further than this the Frankfurt majority did not

[6] Franz Wigard, ed., *Stenographischer Bericht über die Verhandlungen
der deutschen constituirenden Nationalversammlung zu Frankfurt am Main*
(9 vols., Frankfurt am Main, 1848–49), pp. 356–535, 604–5, 611, 621–
22, 677, 716, 1574–75, 1597, 1816–17, 2342–43. In May 1849 the parliament passed a law making the temporary executive subject to removal on
a vote of non-confidence, but this came about after the withdrawal of the
moderate majority, which left the radical democrats in control. *Ibid.*, 6638–
39.

[7] The clauses dealing with ministerial responsibility in the constitutions
of 1848–49 were modeled after similar clauses in the constitutions of
France (1791, 1814, 1830), Nassau (1814), Bavaria (1818), Baden (1818),
Hesse-Darmstadt (1820), and Belgium (1831). For a history of the concept and its early application in Germany see Franz Schnabel, *Geschichte
der Ministerverantwortlichkeit in Baden* (Karlsruhe, 1922).

[8] Wigard, *Stenographischer Bericht*, pp. 4954, 4980.

venture. The Kaiser and all state officials were to be sworn "conscientiously" to uphold the constitution, but this obligation was purely moral, for no means was provided for its enforcement.

While more explicit, the Berlin constitution contained the same vital defect. The original draft (dated May 20, 1848) stemmed from the liberal government that had assumed power after the March uprising. While worded differently, the sense of its articles on the inviolability of the monarch and the responsibility of his ministers was the same as that of the Frankfurt constitution. Yet the government draft followed the English system by providing that the lower chamber could impeach and the upper chamber must try the accused ministers. Furthermore, a parliamentary committee headed by the democrat Benedikt Waldeck inserted an amendment specifying that the crimes to be punished were treason, malfeasance, and violation of the constitution. Either chamber could impeach, but the place of the trial was shifted from the upper chamber to a supreme court. In both drafts further details concerning judicial procedure and punishment were left to future legislation.[9]

The liberal parliaments in Berlin and Frankfurt were both frustrated in their efforts to provide Prussia and Germany with constitutions. The former fell victim to a counterrevolutionary coup in November 1848, while the latter was compelled to dissolve after Frederick William IV of Prussia refused to assume the crown it offered in April 1849. Yet the constitution decreed for Prussia by the counterrevolutionary government (December 5, 1848) retained the system of mixed powers and the clauses on ministerial responsibility as drafted by the Waldeck committee. Nor were these clauses changed in the final version of the constitution (January 30, 1850) framed by the conservative government. In November 1850, furthermore, that government actually introduced a bill for the "special law" promised in the constitution. After amendment and passage in the lower chamber, the bill was finally rejected in 1851 (72 to 59) by the

[9] For the Frankfurt and Prussian constitutions, including the amendments both proposed and adopted, see: Ludwig Bergstrasser, ed., *Die Verfassung des deutschen Reiches vom Jahre 1849 mit Vorentwürfen, Gegenvorschlägen und Modifikationen bis zum Erfurter Parlament* (Bonn, 1913) and Ludwig von Rönne, *Die Verfassungs-Urkunde für den Preussischen Staat,* vom 31. Januar 1850 (Berlin, 1859).

aristocratic upper chamber. In 1852, 1853, and 1854 the bill of 1851 was reintroduced in the Chamber of Deputies by the liberal minority, but on each occasion it died in the judiciary committee.[10]

After 1858 the succession of William I to the throne and the dismissal of the conservative government produced an environment more favorable to the passage of such a bill. Yet the chamber of deputies rejected in 1861 a motion that parliament seize the initiative in the matter and chose to wait on the "new era" cabinet to introduce its own measure. When finally presented to the House of Lords (January 1862) the government proposal called for amendments to the constitution requiring that both chambers, rather than merely the Chamber of Deputies, to approve a bill of impeachment and entrusting the trial of the accused to a special tribunal, rather than to the Supreme Court. While passed by the upper chamber, the measure was never debated in the Chamber of Deputies.[11] In any case it was unacceptable to the liberals, for it gave to the conservative majority in the upper chamber the power to frustrate any impeachment they might initiate.

The issue was far from hypothetical, for Prussia was then on the threshold of a "constitutional conflict" involving the very issues the clauses on ministerial responsibility had been intended to resolve. When the Chamber of Deputies refused to vote further money bills for a disputed reorganization of the Prussian army, the Bismarck cabinet, which assumed office in September 1862, proceeded to govern the country for four years without a legal budget. The deputies denounced his action as unconstitutional, but without a special law outlining procedures and punishments they believed themselves unable to impeach the cabinet. Although the bill of 1851 was again revived and passed the lower chamber (249 to 6) in April 1863, it died in the House of Lords. In 1866, following the Prussian victory over Austria,

[10] *Stenographische Berichte,* Zweite Kammer, 1850–51, I, 24, 128ff., 163, II, 1004, 1081ff., 1154ff., III, 10–12, 187ff., 219–21; 1851–52, I, 65; 1854–55, I, 405; Erste Kammer, 1851, II, 918ff., 1110ff.

[11] *Stenographische Berichte,* Haus der Abgeordneten, 1861, I, 417–18, 460, II, 937ff., VI, 955–58; 1862, I, 339–41, 389, II, 879ff.; Herrenhaus, 1862, I, 29ff., Drucksachen, Nr. 14. The chamber of deputies refused in July 1862 to consider the bill passed by the House of Lords on March 6 on the technical grounds that a dissolution on March 11 had broken the continuity of the Landtag session and automatically cancelled all pending bills.

a chastened Chamber of Deputies voted an "indemnity bill," which legalized the unconstitutional acts of the cabinet in the preceding years. Not until 1905 and 1910–12 was the attempt renewed to pass a Prussian law on ministerial responsibility, and again to no avail.[12]

Meanwhile, the issue had reappeared in somewhat different form in the German Reichstag. In Bismarck's original draft for the German constitution of 1867 the Bundesrat, composed of delegates from the state governments, was to perform the executive functions of the national government and also to share legislative power with the Reichstag, chosen by universal suffrage. Yet the liberals did succeed in inserting an amendment, moved by Rudolf von Bennigsen, that converted the Chancellor, originally but the presiding officer of the Bundesrat, into a "responsible" minister.[13] But Bismarck rejected their efforts to establish a full cabinet of responsible ministers and to provide for a special law "to regulate the responsibility and the procedure to be observed in making it effective."

Recent research[14] has suggested that Bismarck welcomed and may even have connived in the drafting of the *lex Bennigsen*. It provided him with the justification he sought to assume the position of Chancellor and enabled him to build that office into a monocratic executive body under his personal control. To have made this intention evident earlier would have excited the jealousy of his colleagues in the Prussian cabinet, who did not wish to be overshadowed, and the fears of the other state governments, which wanted as little centralization as possible. Through the

[12] *Stenographische Berichte,* Haus der Abgeordneten, 1863, I, 505, 541, II, 943ff., 980–82, III, 245–48, IV, 430–40; 1905, Anlagen, I Nr. 20; 1910, Anlagen, II, Nr. 32; 1911, Anlagen, II, Nr. 40; 1912, Anlagen, II, Nr. 41; Herrenhaus, 1912, I, 378.

[13] The final version of this clause (Article 17) read: "The ordinances and dispositions (*Verfügungen*) of the Confederate Presidency shall be issued in the name of the Confederation and shall require for their validation the countersignature of the Confederate chancellor, who thereby assumes the responsibility." For the debates which led to this result see *Stenographische Berichte,* Constituent Reichstag 1867, 103ff.

[14] See Otto Becker, *Bismarcks Ringen um Deutschlands Gestaltung* (Heidelberg, 1958), pp. 390ff., and "Wie Bismarck Kanzler wurde," in *Beiträge zur deutschen und nordischen Geschichte* (Schleswig, 1952), pp. 335–348. Rudolf Morsey has raised some doubts about the Becker thesis, known to him only through the article, but grants that it has "much probability." See his *Die oberste Reichsverwaltung unter Bismarck, 1867–1890* (Münster, 1957), pp. 25–28.

lex Bennigsen Bismarck escaped the collegial organization of the Prussian cabinet and gave to the Reich an executive organ of which there was no mention in the constitution.

Few features of the national constitution distressed the liberals so much in 1867 and afterward as the fact that the Reich possessed but a single minister rather than a cabinet of responsible ministers. Until the latter was achieved they could not even begin to agitate for a law on procedures and punishments.[15] In this respect, as in some others, the Reich constitution was even weaker than the Prussian. Yet the dominant National Liberal Party accepted the constitution in the expectation that the liberals would be able in the future to attain many of the objectives that had escaped them in 1867. They hammered away constantly at the absurdity that the Chancellor should presume to be fully conversant with all branches of the state administration and that the Reich officials or Prussian ministers who actually performed the administrative functions of the Reich were not independently responsible for their acts. In April 1869 the Reichstag passed a resolution calling for a national cabinet composed of "responsible ministries for foreign affairs, finance, war, navy, trade and communications." But Bismarck candidly informed the chamber that he had no intention of weakening his executive power by introducing into the central government the kind of collegial organization that existed in Prussia.[16]

Although they continued to agitate, the Reichstag liberals were impotent to achieve their objective without Bismarck's consent. Some of the force was taken out of their complaints by the appointment to the Bundesrat of high-ranking Reich officials and of the Prussian Ministers of War and Finance. As members of the upper chamber, they could appear in the Reichstag to defend bills emanating from their bureaus and ministries. A statute passed in March 1878, furthermore, provided that the Chancellor might delegate his responsibility to his principal subordinates, the Reich Secretaries of State. Yet these developments did not alter the fact that the German Reich possessed under the constitution but a single official with the attribute of a minister, bearing a responsibility undefined and uncontrolled.

[15] On this dilemma see the remarks by Karl Twesten in the budget debate of October 1867. *Stenographische Berichte,* Reichstag, 1867, I, 299–300.

[16] *Ibid.,* 1869, I, 389ff.

Certainly the term "responsibility" was not devoid of practical meaning. It provided an organizing principle for the Prussian and Reich administrations by designating which officials were to wield the executive power for the monarch. It could justify the resignation of a minister unable to square the monarch's decisions with his own conscience or judgment. Finally, it determined who had the primary obligation to defend government bills and policies and to answer interpellations in the Landtag and Reichstag. Only in this very limited sense could the responsibility of the Chancellor and Prussian ministers be regarded as "political" or "parliamentary." Otherwise the responsibility imposed was purely moral.[17] Neither in Prussia nor in Germany was the "keystone" ever placed in the constitutional arch.

IV

In retrospect the failure of the German liberals to establish the process of impeachment and trial of responsible ministers appears less tragic than it did to the participants in these struggles. As their conservative critics often pointed out, the crimes of treason and malfeasance were relatively unknown in Prussian history and, furthermore, such offenses were already covered by the Prussian code of criminal law. Certainly the liberals were right in assuming

[17] German authorities on constitutional law were never able to agree on the significance of the term *Verantwortlichkeit* as employed in the constitution of 1867. To some (Seydel, Hensel) it was merely a "phrase" devoid of meaning, to others (Joel, Laband) it had only a "moral" or "political" (in the sense used above in the text) character, while a third view (Meyer, Zorn) recognized the legal nature of the term but regarded it as *lex imperfecta* because of its noncoercive character. Preuss placed it in the category of "noncoercive law." For a summary of these opposing views see Hugo Preuss, *"Die organische Bedeutung der Art. 15 und 17 der Reichsverfassung," Zeitschrift für die gesamte Staatswissenschaft*, Vol. 45 (1889), 420–49. Most of these arguments are indicative of the kind of legal metaphysics in which the German *Staatsrechtslehrer* of the nineteenth century engaged. They theorized about the nature of legal relationships in the governmental structure, but paid little attention to the actual working relationships. In terms of the latter it is difficult to see that the responsibility of the chancellor was anything but moral. Recently E. R. Huber has defined the chancellor's responsibility as "parliamentary," but this merely confuses the matter further, for it is apparent from the context that what he has in mind is "political responsibility" in the sense of Joel and Laband, not "parliamentary responsibility" in the English sense. See his *Deutsche Verfassungsgeschichte*, Vol. III (Stuttgart, 1963), pp. 658–59, 898ff.

that there was a real danger of ministerial violations of the constitution. But they were wrong to believe that the danger could
be averted by judicial proceedings. This presumed that the constitution was firmly grounded in the moral concensus of Prussian
society and that those who possessed the power to subvert it
would never do so out of respect for the law. Yet that was not
the case. The grant of the Prussian constitution in 1848 was an
act of expediency by a counterrevolutionary regime whose aim
was to relieve popular discontent without impairing the aristocratic monarchical order. In his political testament Frederick William IV recommended that his successor refuse the oath to uphold the constitution. Although William I rejected the advice, he
fully expected to be released from his pledge by some overt act
of rebellion during the constitutional crisis of the 1860s.[18]

Some jurists maintained in 1863 that even without a law of
implementation the lower chamber possessed the power to impeach, and the Supreme Court the power to try, the Bismarck
cabinet.[19] The deputies were aware that in 1830 the French
parliament had impeached and convicted the ministers of Charles
X without the benefit of a law implementing the clauses on
ministerial responsibility in the French Charter of 1814. Yet that
action had occurred after a successful revolution and was im-
pelled by a public agitation, which overcame the scruples of the
parliamentary majority concerning its legality.[20] Neither of these
conditions existed in Prussia in 1863. Furthermore, the many
lawyers, jurists, and civil servants who sat in the Prussian chamber
were convinced that they must adhere strictly to the law if they
were to make a valid case against the government for violating
it. Nor could they have succeeded, even if they had undisputedly
possessed the power to impeach. The crown would have responded
by repeatedly dissolving parliament and, if necessary, by the
abolition or drastic revision of the constitution.[21]

That the liberals did not succeed in writing their version of

[18] Otto Hintze, *Die Hohenzollern und ihr Werk* (7th ed., Berlin, 1916),
p. 564.
[19] *Stenographische Berichte,* Haus der Abgeordneten, 1863, IV, 432.
[20] See Paul Bastid, *Les institutions politiques de la monarchie parle-
mentaire française* (1814–48) (Paris, 1954), pp. 328–29.
[21] See the author's *Bismarck and the Development of Germany,* pp.
207–12, 276–79.

ministerial responsibility into law is less significant than what their quest for it, and the importance they attached to it, reveals about the nature of liberal politics in nineteenth-century Germany. The numerous debates over the issue uniformly show not how remote, but how proximate were the positions of most liberals and conservatives on the fundamental issues of constitutionalism. On the fringes of both movements, to be sure, were extremists who were widely divergent in their political orientation. At one end of the political rainbow were romantic conservatives who dreamed of a resurrected feudalism and at the other were radical democrats with their visions of an egalitarian republic. Yet both extremes were small in numbers and after 1848 they dwindled in size and influence. Until the 1880s the arena of German politics was dominated by moderate conservatives and moderate liberals.

In the debates on ministerial responsibility the conservatives expressed their dedication to the principle of the *Rechtsstaat* almost as often as did the liberals.[22] The history of that principle shows that it was never an exclusively liberal concept. In fact, the term was first used in 1808 by Adam Müller, the philosopher of reactionary conservatism, and received its classic formulation in 1856 from Friedrich Julius Stahl, whose philosophy, by reconciling monarchism with constitutionalism, provided the doctrinal foundation for the conservative movement after 1848.[23] Because it focused upon the limits rather than upon the source of political power the concept of the *Rechtsstaat* could serve the needs of the moderates in both camps. While the conservative wished to preserve traditional rights and privileges from bureaucratic reform and revolutionary radicalism, the liberal was concerned with the abolition of arbitrary government and the guarantee of popular liberties. That the liberals succeeded in identifying the concept of the *Rechtsstaat* with themselves was owing not to its essential character, but to their development and more frequent use of it.

[22] See particularly *Stenographische Berichte,* Erste Kammer, 1851, II, 918.
[23] Friedrich J. Stahl, *Die Philosophie des Rechts,* Vol. II, part II (3rd ed., 1856), 137–38. On the history of the concept of the *Rechtsstaat* see Reimund Asanger, *Beiträge zur Lehre vom Rechtsstaat im 19. Jahrhundert* (Bochum, 1938) and Leonard Krieger, *The German Idea of Freedom* (Boston, 1957), pp. 252ff.

The proximity of moderate liberalism and moderate conservatism is also evident from the fact that both rejected absolutism and popular rule and advocated systems of mixed powers. Stahl advocated a modernized *Ständestaat* with a representative body based upon three estates (gentry, towns, and rural communes) and possessing weak legislative powers.[24] Friedrich Dahlmann, who was typical of the northern "classical school" of German liberal thought, was willing to accept corporate representation, but envisaged a parliament that would have a more positive share in the legislative process.[25] While the southern liberals tended to approve popular sovereignty in theory, they refused to reject in practice the existing mixed constitutional systems of Baden, Bavaria, and Württemberg. The philosophy of Karl von Rotteck was a desperate effort to harmonize the monism of the general will with the existing dualism of governmental structures in the south.[26] Although the act of a counterrevolutionary regime, the constitutional order imposed upon Prussia in 1848–50 was closer to the liberal than the conservative model. Nevertheless, the moderate conservatives were soon reconciled to it.

The issue of ministerial responsibility also demonstrates how close both schools of thought were on the fundamental questions of constitutionalism. In the first edition of his *Philosophie des Staatsrechts* (1837) Stahl, then a professor at the Bavarian University of Erlangen, found "the right of impeachment indispensable, if the representative body is to have any vigor, if it is actually to be a power." Without this right the power of the diet would be "ideal" rather than "real." In the second edition (1846), published after his appointment by King Frederick William IV to a professorship in Berlin, Stahl wrote that, while the right of impeachment was not contrary to the monarchical principle, it could not be regarded as "indispensable" in every situation, particularly where the diet was newly established.[27] Dahlmann was likewise besieged by caution the closer he got to the seat of power. In his principal theoretical work (1835) he de-

[24] *Die Philosophie des Rechts*, Vol. II, part II (2nd ed., Heidelberg, 1846), p. 352.

[25] *Die Politik auf den Grund und das Maass der gegebenen Zustände zurückgeführt*, Vol. I (Göttingen, 1835), 107ff.

[26] Krieger, *German Idea*, 242ff.

[27] *Philosophie des Rechts*, Vol. II, Part II (1st ed., Heidelberg, 1837), p. 176; (2nd ed., Heidelberg, 1846), pp. 344–45.

clared impeachment to be "the most extreme means of resistance
. . . the sword of the estates," not to be drawn frivolously, but
held as the final protection against arbitrary government. Three
things were necessary to make it effective: a court with jurisdiction, a law of procedure, and the renunciation or abolition of
the king's right of pardon.[28] Yet the constitutional committee of
which he was chairman left all three of these elements out of its
draft of the Frankfurt constitution of 1848, and Dahlmann
abruptly refused to reply to an interpellation requesting that the
committee elucidate what it meant by the "responsibility" of
ministers in the provisional government.[29] "Freedom," he was
fond of declaring, "has often emerged from order, but never
order from freedom."[30]

In the parliamentary debates of the 1850s and 1860s on the
subject of juridical responsibility the moderate conservatives (including Stahl) also employed the metaphor of the "keystone."[31]
The objections they voiced were not to the principle of responsibility as such, but to specific features of the bill of 1851,
which the liberals were constantly seeking to revive. In particular,
they were unwilling to concede to the lower chamber the exclusive right to impeach. Hence the government proposal of 1862
required that bills of impeachment also be approved by the House
of Lords as well. But there was also concern, furthermore, that
the Supreme Court might attain through its power to try the
accused a "position of political power, which would in some degree outweigh that of all other forces in the state and which
would be difficult to bring into harmony with its character as a
royal agency." To meet this objection the proposal of 1862 gave
jurisdiction in impeachment cases to a temporary court whose
judges were to be drawn by lot from the Prussian judiciary. It
was expected that such an *ad hoc* tribunal would be less subject
to political partisanship and political ambition.[32]

Even with these safeguards many conservatives remained op-

---

[28] *Die Politik auf den Grund und das Maass der gegebenen Zustände
zurückgeführt,* Vol. I (Göttingen, 1835), 97ff.

[29] Wigard, *Stenographischer Bericht,* I, 605–11.

[30] Dahlmann, *op. cit.,* I, 108.

[31] See particularly *Stenographische Berichte,* Erste Kammer, 1851, II,
922, 929, 935, and Haus der Abgeordneten, 1863, II, 961.

[32] *Ibid.,* Herrenhaus, 1862, Anlage Nr. 3, p. 11. See also Erste Kammer,
1851, II, 930, 941.

posed to any law implementing the constitutional clauses on ministerial responsibility. In 1846 Stahl had warned that the "monarchical principle" would not be safe unless the crown retained the final right to interpret the constitution.[33] In every debate some conservatives charged that juridical responsibility would inevitably be the entering wedge for parliamentary responsibility, that it would certainly upset the equilibrium of forces under the mixed system and eventually bring about the English system of parliamentary government. Even if blocked by the upper chamber, an attempt on the part of the chamber of deputies to impeach a minister would damage the prestige and authority of the crown. The best guarantee for the preservation of the constitution was the "conscience of the king and his ministers."[34]

Liberals were as insistent as conservatives that justice and politics were two different spheres, which must be kept clearly separate. Hence they vigorously and repeatedly denied that their goal was parliamentary responsibility on the English model or that this would be the practical outcome of a law on juridical responsibility. They maintained that the Chamber of Deputies was capable of acting as dispassionately as a state's attorney in bringing charges against cabinet members on the basis of law rather than of politics. In order to keep the juridical character of impeachment proceedings distinct, they rejected the efforts of Peter Reichensperger in 1863 and 1867 to make an unconstitutional act a civil rather than criminal offense, punishable merely by dismissal from public office rather than by imprisonment for twenty years as well.[35] Their purpose, the liberals asserted, was not to upset the equilibrium of forces under the constitution, but to make certain that the executive remained within its proper sphere.

Nevertheless, the conservatives were undoubtedly correct in their assumption that the spheres of politics and justice could not be kept rigidly apart if the Chamber of Deputies were ever

---

[33] Stahl, *op. cit.*, Vol. II, part II (2nd ed., 1847), 362.

[34] See particularly *Stenographische Berichte*, Erste Kammer, 1851, II, 931; Zweite Kammer, I, 129–30, 151; Haus der Abgeordneten, 1861, II, 956, V, Nr. 156, p. 3; Herrenhaus, 1862, I, 34; Haus der Abgeordneten, 1863, II, 959–61.

[35] *Ibid.*, Haus der Abgeordneten, 1863, II, 947ff.; *Stenographische Berichte*, Reichstag, 1867, I, 298ff.

made secure in its right of impeachment. In amending the constitution of 1848 the counterrevolutionary government had written into the document certain safeguards for autocratic rule which could have been jeopardized by a hostile parliament and unfavorable court decisions. The famous *"Lückentheorie"* was the most significant. No way was provided for the resolution of conflicts over the budget between crown and parliament, which enabled Bismarck to argue that in such cases the crown must govern without parliamentary approval, for the life of the state could not stand still. This hiatus in the constitution, as well as others dealing with public finance, was not accidental, but a refuge for autocratic authority which had been carefully prepared and often discussed long before the specific crisis of the 1860s arose.[36] Considered as a matter of law, the conservative case was good, and, if the liberals had dared to impeach Bismarck in 1863, it would have been on the basis of a questionable interpretation of the constitution.

With customary deftness Bismarck cut straight to the heart of the matter in a short speech during the debate of April 1863. In deciding against the reintroduction of the bill of 1862, he declared, the government had acted from the conviction that before such a law could be passed the constitution must offer an "indisputably clear and complete basis" for its enforcement. But this condition did not exist, for crown and parliament were deeply divided over the meaning of the constitution. Any court that might be given jurisdiction in the matter would inevitably arrogate to itself the "law-making power." By its judgment the court would "establish the future development of Prussian constitutional life." The vital issue of the distribution of power between the organs of the state, he concluded, could not be left to "the subjective opinion of the majority of those voting on the court."[37] What the government refused to grant to the judiciary it kept for itself—the power to interpret the constitution and thereby the power to augment it. This was the last reserve of the *Obrigkeitsstaat* and the final frustration of the *Rechtsstaat*.

[36] Bismarck himself first publicly expounded the *Lückentheorie* in 1850. Horst Kohl, ed., *Die politischen Reden des Fürsten Bismarck* (Stuttgart, 1892–1905), I, 312–21 and *Bismarck-Jahrbuch* (Berlin and Leipzig, 1894–99), III, 411–13. See also the remarks of Kleist-Retzow in 1851, *Stenographische Berichte*, Zweite Kammer, 1851, I, 129.

[37] *Stenographische Berichte*, Haus der Abgeordneten, 1863, II, 952.

That the German liberals could have regarded the juridical responsibility of ministers as the heart of constitutionalism demonstrates the limitations of their understanding of the constitutional systems of western Europe and America which they thought to emulate. They were aware that the power of impeachment had seldom been used in the west, even in Great Britain, which was their favorite model.[38] But rarely was it recognized that this was true because the western constitutional systems provided another channel for the resolution of the power struggle. What the German liberals did not choose to see was that the greatest issues of public life are political rather than legal, that the essence of western constitutionalism is not the supremacy of law, important though that is, but popular sovereignty.[39] The best guarantee for the lawful conduct of the executive is not the threat of the judicial process, but the possession of the right to repudiate the offending government and to turn it out of office. The power of impeachment can never be an adequate substitute for that of political control.

V

Writing in 1852 Robert von Mohl judged that the constitutional system of mixed powers was inherently unstable. Conflicts between crown and parliament were inevitable and from this dialectic must result either the "corruption" of the legislature by the executive or the establishment of parliamentary control over the latter.[40] Dualism must give way to monism, for sovereignty by its very nature is indivisible. The record of the nineteenth century does indeed suggest that Mohl was generally correct in his prediction. In France the constitutional balance, first established

[38] *Ibid.,* Zweite Kammer, 1851, I, 137; Erste Kammer, 1851, II, 933.

[39] In a significant study Reinhard Lamer has recently shown how fundamentally and persistently the German political theorists (particularly Rudolf Gneist), from whom the deputies gained their knowledge of the English system, misunderstood the actual character of English parliamentary life. *Der englische Parlamentarismus in der deutschen politischen Theorie im Zeitalter Bismarcks* (1857–90), Historische Studien, Vol. 387 (Lübeck and Hamburg, 1963).

[40] *"Das Repräsentativsystem, seine Mangel und die Heilmittel,"* reprinted in *Staatsrecht, Völkerrecht und Politik,* I (Tübingen, 1860), 395.

in the charter of 1814, fluctuated widely through successive regimes until the final triumph of parliament after 1870. Between 1848 and 1876 the Italian constitution, first established in Piedmont, evolved into a parliamentary system. Similarly the constitutions of the Netherlands and the Scandinavian countries were originally dualistic, but became by the end of the century parliamentary governments.

Yet in Germany the dualistic system had a greater durability than Mohl anticipated. During the Prussian constitutional crisis of the 1860s the possibility arose that parliament might erode the executive power. But Bismarck resolved the crisis by brilliant strokes in foreign policy and actually succeeded in strengthening the dualistic structure by making it the constitutional order of united Germany. By the end of the century, in fact, historians and political scientists had come to regard it as the uniquely German form of constitutional government.[41] Yet Mohl's prognosis was not entirely wrong so far as Germany was concerned, for the balance of power between crown and parliament did not remain static throughout this period. By his political manipulations during the 1870s and 1880s Bismarck sapped the vitality of the Reichstag. After his dismissal in 1890 the aging statesman, bitterly disappointed by the failure of parliament to check what he regarded as the unwise policies of his successors, complained about the "servility" of the Reichstag.[42] For a quarter of a century Germany had no adequate leadership and yet the parliament, even under the provocation of the *Daily Telegraph* and Zabern incidents, failed to seize the initiative against the government. In 1917 under the stress of war the constitutional balance was overthrown by the crown and Germany became in effect a military dictatorship.

During the Weimar period Carl Schmitt revived Mohl's thesis and concluded that Bismarck's achievement had merely postponed the inevitable decision between royal government and popular sovereignty. "Within each political union there can be only one source of constitutional power."[43] Yet history does not always proceed according to the rules of logic. The system

[41] Otto Hintze, *Staat und Verfassung, Gesammelte Abhandlungen zur allgemeinen Verfassungsgeschichte* (Leipzig, 1941), p. 349.

[42] *Die gesammelten Werke,* IX (Berlin, 1926), 119, 222, 347–51.

[43] *Verfassungslehre* (3rd ed., Berlin, 1957), p. 53.

was doomed not because of its inherent contradiction, as Mohl and Schmitt believed, but by the deterioration of its social foundations. The stability of the mixed constitutional order in Germany depended upon the preservation of the traditional social structure, but this was steadily being eroded by the progress of economic and social change. Everywhere in central and eastern Europe the old ruling élite, whose economic and social status depended primarily upon agriculture, was being undermined by the advance of industry and the growth of new social classes and new social interests. The vital question was not whether the old system of mixed powers would endure, but when and under what conditions it would dissolve and what would take its place. Military defeat and popular revolution in 1918 were catalysts that prematurely dissolved what would eventually have become an unstable compound.

The nostalgia of German historians for the old regime has delayed too long an earnest reassessment in Germany of Bismarck and his historical influence and of the German liberals and the inadequacy of their political insight. The works of the former and the limitations of the latter prevented Germany from evolving the kind of political order, through the dispersion of political responsibility and experience into the lower strata of German society, that could have assured an orderly transition from the old order to the new. Only through the sharing of political power and responsibility by widening circles of the population could the continuity of German political life have been assured. Certainly Bismarck's ethic of power has significance for contemporary Germans, but it ought to be merely the beginning point, not the final destination of a historical reassessment of the Bismarck era.

Chapter 10

BURCKHARDT'S *RENAISSANCE:*
BETWEEN RESPONSIBILITY AND POWER

Peter Gay

I

The Age of the Renaissance hovers uneasily between the Age of Responsibility and the Age of Power. The Middle Ages, no matter how unsuccessful it may have been in applying its model to life, sought to be a time of fixed and obvious responsibility: its master metaphor, the hierarchy, ordered life in a complex series of relationships that assigned both opportunities and duties to each member of each element, whether that element was the Church, the family, the city, nature, or the chain of all created beings. The master metaphor of the modern age, on the other hand, is the active individual, and its supreme problem is the taming of power—the restoration of the medieval ideal of responsibility in a totally new setting: a secular world governed by technology and hostile to the notion of formal hierarchy. Now, it was in the Renaissance that the medieval order of responsibility was first seriously attacked, and the modern idea of power first seriously broached. And it is the supreme merit of Burckhardt's *Kultur der Renaissance in Italien* to have grasped the nature of this attack, and to have taken upon itself the burden of its ambivalence—to have recognized that dawning modernity was a grave threat and a great opportunity.

There is nothing new in calling Burckhardt's *Renaissance* a masterpiece. Its analysis is audacious, its characterizations are apt, its prose is vigorous, its deployment of melodramatic incidents is shrewd, the logic of its organization is persuasive. Beyond this—and this too is well known—Burckhardt's *Renaissance* continues to command attention because it established a new historical period. Other historians had treated Italy from the fourteenth to the sixteenth century as the center of an admirable revival in painting, sculpture, architecture, and scholarship; Burckhardt raised these centuries to the status of an autonomous historical period in which the artistic and scholarly revivals were merely parts of a larger totality, parts of a period with its distinct cultural style.[1]

But beyond this, and above this, the power of the book lies in its superbly realized recognition of the historical function of the Renaissance. Burckhardt himself knew this; both in the book itself and in his letters he said that the Renaissance marked a break with the Middle Ages, and a rehearsal for our own; the Renaissance, he insisted, was the mother of our civilization, "the leader of our own epoch."[2] He saw it as the first period to encounter and formulate problems that we have not yet solved, to establish standards by which we still live, and to create human types that might be walking through nineteenth-century cities. The birth of modernity, then, is the subject matter of Burckhardt's *Renaissance;* it is, Burckhardt insists, about us.

But this, though far from trivial, is not all. Burckhardt's *Renaissance,* I think, survives in another, even more decisive respect. Our century is supremely, perhaps excessively, self-conscious and self-analytical; it is sensitive to the essential ambiguity of human experience, and inclined to see existence as a tragic puzzle whose solution (if a solution can be imagined at all) must be found in our own world. The proper problem for mankind is man. Terms like subtlety, ambivalence, irony, dialectic—all terms with a long, honorable history—have become the clichés of our time. For Burckhardt they were not clichés but presuppositions; they were his modes of perceiving the world of the past. And,

[1] For Burckhardt's predecessors and influence, see the reliable monograph by Wallace K. Ferguson, *The Renaissance in Historical Thought: Five Centuries of Interpretation* (1948); Werner Kaegi, *Jacob Burckhardt: Eine Biographie,* Vol. III, *Das Zeitalter der klassischen Werke* (1956); and the splendid bibliographical essay by Federico Chabod, "The Concept of the Renaissance," in *Machiavelli and the Renaissance* (tr. David Moore, 1958). For an authoritative modern appreciation of Burckhardt's masterpiece, see Hajo Holborn's 'Introduction' to the Modern Library edition (1954).

[2] *Die Kultur der Renaissance in Italien: Ein Versuch* (14th ed., based on the 2nd, by Walter Goetz, 1925), 527. The translations in this essay are my own, though I have occasionally borrowed a word or phrase from the standard translation by S. G. C. Middlemore (1878), which, though generally adequate, is often imprecise.

turning his perception on the Renaissance, he found what he was prepared to find: complexity, ambiguity, tragic grandeur.

I have spoken of the melodramatic incidents that punctuate Burckhardt's analysis; his book in fact is a well-made drama in which nothing has been left to chance. But it is something more than a melodrama or an urbane comedy. Burckhardt employed melodramatic incidents not to be sensational but to be truthful; was it his fault if his characters were often grotesque, their vices often hair-raising, their ambitions incredible to a tamer age? As he insisted—and had earned the right to insist—when he studied the past, he was "wholly prosaic."[3] And he also insisted that his readers must "comprehend the book as a whole," for, "it is the essential difficulty of cultural history that it is compelled to break up a large intellectual continuum into single, often apparently arbitrary categories, in order to portray it intelligibly at all."[4] The cultural totality could be grasped only indirectly; only the highest artifice could lead back to nature, to historical truth. Burckhardt treated style, selection, and organization as servants of his perception, and that perception pointed to the travail of Renaissance man as the central truth and identifying characteristic of Renaissance history.

Burckhardt was not an existentialist, but he saw man in the Renaissance confronting an extreme existential situation: Renaissance man was unshackled, endowed with fully elaborated capacities, at once threatened and importuned by his new possibilities, condemned to be free, thrown into a world he had not made and must dominate; he was therefore compelled to seek himself, his nature and his place, by testing his limits and probing his soul beyond the traditional boundaries of propriety or of good and evil. If Burckhardt's *Renaissance* is a drama, it is a tragedy, and a kind of tragedy in which our century has been particularly interested: a tragedy of the will.

For Burckhardt, then, the Renaissance was a time of perpetual

[3] See Burckhardt's letter to Emanuel Geibel, October 10, 1863: *"Ich werde allgemach ganz prosaisch bei der Erforschung der vergangenen Zeit . . ." Briefe* (ed. Max Burckhardt), Vol. IV (1961), 137. In the *Civilization of the Renaissance* itself, Burckhardt carefully distinguished between poetry and history, and criticized other historians for seeking to "excite, titillate, move their readers, as though history could take the place of poetry." *Renaissance,* 222.

[4] *Renaissance,* 3.

turmoil; having "escaped" from the Middle Ages, Renaissance men needed to interpret themselves: "Much that appears to us in their writings as commonplaces, was for them and their contemporaries a new, laboriously acquired view of things, about which there had been no discussion since antiquity."[5] At the beginning of the sixteenth century—precisely the time that the civilization of the Renaissance reached its height—"Italy was in a grave moral crisis, from which the best of men hardly saw a way out."[6] Tragedy ceased being play and became reality: "True tragedy, which then found no place on the stage, stepped mightily through palaces, streets, and public squares."[7] And just as true tragedy on the stage is possible only if the protagonist has grandeur, and fails, as fail he must, in the pursuit of great enterprises or great ideals, so the tragic Renaissance of Burckhardt's vision was both, and at once, great and terrible, terrible in its grandeur, and great in its terror. Renaissance man, the first modern individual, discovered a new sense of power at the same moment, and for the same reason, that he discarded medieval canons of responsibility. "Fully developed individualism," Burckhardt notes in a memorable phrase, is "the fundamental flaw" of the Italian character, but it "appears at the same time as the condition of its greatness."[8] It is here, in this clear-eyed, pitiless perception of the dialectical conflict at the heart of the Renaissance, that the enduring relevance of Burckhardt's book resides.

II

"The Italian of the Renaissance was compelled to endure the first mighty surging of this new epoch. With his talents and his passions he has become the most distinctive, most characteristic representative of all the heights and depths of that epoch. Side by side with deep depravity, there developed the noblest harmony of personality, and a glorious art which glorified individual life in a manner that neither antiquity nor the Middle Ages would or could achieve."[9] As the protagonist of Burckhardt's

5 *Ibid.*, 221.
6 *Ibid.*, 404–5.
7 *Ibid.*, 309.
8 *Ibid.*, 428.
9 *Ibid.*, 429.

drama, the Renaissance individual embodies and suffers the ambiguity of his age.

This Renaissance individual, Burckhardt argues, is an essentially new human type. There were some forceful personalities in the Middle Ages, but they were imperfect anticipations of fully developed Renaissance man; they had no real roots in their culture and were therefore, in a historical sense, freaks. "In the Middle Ages," Burckhardt writes in a famous passage, "both sides of consciousness—the side turned toward the world and that turned inward toward man—lay as it were beneath a common veil, dreaming or half-awake." It was through this distorting veil, which lent reality strange hues, a veil of "illusion and infantile preconceptions" that medieval man saw himself and his existence; he "recognized himself" only as member of some larger, corporate group, a "race, people, party, corporation, family." In Italy this veil first melted away, and there arose "an *objective* view and treatment of the state and of all things of this world in general." But "by its side," and with equal power, "there arose the *subjective.*" Man becomes a "self-conscious *individual,* and recognizes himself as such."[10] Thus Renaissance man strikes out in two distinct directions: toward objectivity and toward subjectivity; toward the clear, cool, logical grasp of the outer and inner world that is the product of detachment, and toward the passionate expression and indulgence of the self that is the product of engagement. The very Humanists who, as naturalists, philologists, critical historians, are the pioneers of the objective scientific spirit, are also, "the most striking exemplars and victims of unbridled subjectivity."[11]

There are moments, Burckhardt suggests, all the more precious for being rare, when a world-historical individual masters the contradictions that are the lot of others. So in the Renaissance: Dante writes "subjective lyrical poetry of wholly objective truth

[10] *Ibid.,* 123. Burckhardt speaks of a *geistiges* individual, and this adjective has been rendered, to my mind mistakenly, as "spiritual."

[11] *Ibid.,* 252. As Burckhardt recognized, any dialectical situation must contain not merely tensions but also bonds among its elements. Thus in the Renaissance the study and recognition of the self is at once enemy and ally of the development of the individual: the striving for self-awareness leads both to self-consciousness and to self-knowledge. Burckhardt in fact celebrates the profound understanding of man, and of men, as an achievement of the Renaissance to which we owe eternal gratitude (see *ibid.,* 284–85, 330).

and greatness."[12] But, being rare, such individuals are historically unrepresentative. They embody the ideal against which reality measures itself, only to fail. With its ideal, indeed—*l'uomo universale,* the man who possesses encyclopedic knowledge and harmoniously develops his varied talents—the Renaissance seemed to solve the contradictions inherent in its world. But this ideal, Burckhardt concedes, like any ideal, was the codification of a wish; it has historical value mainly in suggesting the aims of Renaissance culture, rather than its actual contours. The Italian Renaissance knew many versatile men—versatility was after all prized and cultivated—but "truly universal men" were "few."[13] They demanded a conjunction of circumstances and talents—a cooperation between *fortuna* and *virtù*—which niggardly fate was most reluctant to provide. There was Dante, there was Leonardo da Vinci; there was Leon Battista Alberti, to whose talents Burckhardt devotes several pages. Alberti, Burckhardt writes in some awe, was, with equal competence and grace, athlete, scientist, mathematician, painter, sculptor, architect, musician, psychologist, essayist, poet, wit, an enthusiastic lover of beauty, and a sensitive, sympathetic, "almost nervous" participant in all things of this world. A giant of a man like Alberti represents, not the tragedy, but the triumph of the will: "It goes without saying that the most intensive will power pervaded and sustained this whole personality; like the greatest men of the Renaissance he too said: 'Men can do everything on their own, as soon as they will it.' "[14]

Alberti, then, like a handful of others, is exempt from the ravages of contradiction; the universal men have harnessed the explosive, potentially mutually destructive, powers of personality into a harmonious whole. But most other, more ordinary men— and in the Italian Renaissance even men of striking gifts must be counted as ordinary—are subject to inner contradictions and struggles, to tragic disharmonies and often tragic fates. Burckhardt built up his portrait with the subtlest shadings at his command, but Renaissance man's central problem is pervasive

[12] *Ibid.,* 289.
[13] *Ibid.,* 128–30.
[14] *Ibid.,* 130–32. Burckhardt's term for Alberti—untranslatable—is *Gewaltmensch.*

and unvaried: each of his virtues produces its vice, each vice produces its antidote which is itself imperfect, so that the struggle of the individual is perpetual, and the result of his conduct ambiguous. The freedom of Renaissance man is a strange semi-slavery; it is half blessing, half curse.

The very law of individualism, the quality that makes the individual an individual, Burckhardt argues, drives the inherent contradictions of Renaissance man to its outermost limits. Renaissance man proudly cultivates that side of his personality that is most characteristic of him; he pursues the kind of literature he finds most congenial, wears the clothes that seem to express him most fully, attaches himself to men and causes that suit him. In consequence, Renaissance life presents an ever-varying chiaroscuro; it is never monotonous, always surprising. But precisely this overwhelming need for self-expression and self-expansion, issues in aggression, and leads to oddity and ruthlessness for their own sake. Artists are highly developed individuals, but then tyrants and *condottieri* also develop *their* individuality "to the highest degree."[15] The imagination that dominates Renaissance man presides over impressive invention and exhilarating originality, but over cruelty and crime as well. "The imagination, which governs this nation more than any other, is, then, one general reason why every passion took an extremely violent course and under some circumstances employed criminal methods. There is such a thing as a violence of weakness which is unable to control itself; but here we have a degeneracy of strength. This at times develops into the colossal; crime assumes its own personal quality."[16] There were romantic criminals before the Romantics; *actes gratuits* before Gide.

The lust for fame, Burckhardt suggests, follows this cult of personality like a shadow. Renaissance man, free from pious humility, seeks to establish his individuality by seeking renown; fame is a mirror that confirms self-esteem. This lust for fame is bound to produce both admirable and terrible consequences. Poets and painters may strive for the poet's crown or a papal commission that will give them immortality among generations of cultivated men, but there are many others who, lacking pacific artistic talents, seek public acclaim in less innocuous ways. What-

[15] *Ibid.,* 124.
[16] *Ibid.,* 420.

ever their capacities, Renaissance men were sure that it was better to be infamous than unknown. "How many," Burckhardt exclaims, "who could not gain distinction by praiseworthy acts, strove for it through disgraceful acts!" More than one responsible contemporary, he notes, records "striking and terrible" enterprises undertaken solely from the "burning desire to do something great and memorable." The Renaissance had drawn aside the veil of medieval conceptions of the world, but the paeans of hired writers, of "official" historians, wove a new, modern veil—the veil of publicity. But then, "now and again," this veil too was "drawn aside," and then we see, in truly frightful dimensions, "the most colossal ambition and thirst after greatness, independent of object or success." The stupendous crimes of the Renaissance, Burckhardt argues, are "not a mere degeneration of ordinary vanity, but something really daemonic"—they are committed by obsessed men, ready to use "the most extreme methods, and indifferent to success as such."[17]

Following its law, the Renaissance develops a countervailing power that holds the lust for fame in check—the feeling of honor. But by the same law, this sentiment is an antidote that kills as many as it cures. It is an incitement to self-control in some circumstances, and to abandon in others; it may be bar or invitation to crime. In one of those striking observations in which Burckhardt explicitly ties the world of the Renaissance to his own, he describes this "moral power," *Ehrgefühl*, as "that enigmatic compound of conscience and selfishness, which is left to modern man, even when he has lost (through his own fault or not), everything else: faith, love, and hope." The feeling of honor is "compatible with great egotism and great vices, and capable of incredible illusions; but then too, all the nobility that remains in a person may attach itself to it and draw new strength from this source."[18]

This dual nature of honor, Burckhardt suggests, is not surprising, for the feeling of honor is an aspect of that potent and neutral instrument, the will: consider Rabelais' abbey of Thélème, where men and women are goaded and guided by an "instinct and spur," which keeps them attached to virtue and

[17] *Ibid.*, 142.
[18] *Ibid.*, 405–6.

free from vice: *honneur*. Their rule is *Fay ce que vouldras,* but this freedom—do what you will—is not harmful, for those who are free from prejudice, noble in conduct, and thoroughly cultivated, set their own limits.[19] But by appealing to Rabelais' famous abbey Burckhardt means to exhibit the relative impotence of this inner check: Thélème after all is a Utopia. The reality is different—less cheerful and more complicated.

Fortunately, Burckhardt continues, honor is not the only check on unbridled egotism. Wit is another. Giants make large targets; wit humbles conceit and punctures pretensions; by fastening on particular limitations or vices—now more visible than ever—wit no longer expends itself harmlessly on corporate entities, but points its critique unmistakably at single individuals. Wit thus serves as the natural weapon against the vices attached to individualism; it is as much an invention of the Renaissance as individualism itself. It reached high forms of sophistication then; it was even subjected to theoretical analysis. But, Burckhardt insists, wit, like everything else in the Renaissance, exacted its price. At its best, it selects worthy victims, and remains amusing; at its worst, it is as unmeasured as its targets, as brutal as the brutalities it ridicules: the Renaissance in fact knew "much heartless and pointless malice."[20] Ironically, the most celebrated of Renaissance figures were also the most vulnerable, for they depended on the wits for their public reputation. But the race of wits was almost overrun by an underworld of buffoons and blackmailers: "The general high level of cultivation brought forth a terrible brood of clever powerless men, born carpers and slanderers, whose envy demanded its hetacombs."[21] Every famous man had to endure the grossest libels, and his response was (rarely) dignified silence, (more often) brutal retaliation, or (with Aretino, the most brilliant and most vicious slanderer of them all) abject bribes.

With a consistency worthy of the Renaissance wits themselves,

[19] *Ibid.*, 407. There is something poignant about Burckhardt's appeal to Rabelais, whom he does not like. Rabelais, he writes, shows us what the Renaissance would have been "without form and without beauty," but, true to his principle that the historian must use historical figures because they are revealing, even if they are distasteful, he devotes a significant paragraph to Rabelais.

[20] *Ibid.*, 145.

[21] *Ibid.*, 150.

Burckhardt carries his theme—the sacrifices exacted by the development of individualism—through to the end. One attractive aspect of this individualism, Burckhardt had suggested, is the cultivation of literature and the arts. Such cultivation required time: time to learn the ancient languages, to discover manuscripts, to perfect one's handwriting, and to converse, freely and at leisure, with one's peers. But, Burckhardt writes, in the Renaissance, there were many who developed this side of their nature only at the price of slavery and exile. It is especially among men of "involuntary leisure" that one finds the realization, and rational exposition, of fully formed "private life." The absence of political activity, of party struggles, "doubtless favors the rise of individual modes of thought"; indeed, "the politically indifferent private man with his partly serious, partly dilettante pursuits seems to have appeared, fully formed, in the despotisms of the fourteenth century." And just as this internal migration had ambiguous consequences, so did exile: "Above all, banishment has the characteristic of either wearing man out or developing him most completely."[22] In Burckhardt's hands, the irony of Renaissance individualism appears to be inexhaustible.

III

Burckhardt offers his analysis of Renaissance individualism in Section II of his book, but by the time he reaches it, he has prepared the ground with a collection of striking instances. Section I, "The State as Work of Art," is famous, partly for its shocking anecdotes, partly for its title. It is an introduction, a map of the Renaissance territory designed to orient the reader for the exploration to come, but it is more than that as well. Burckhardt's discussion of political forms and political action in Renaissance Italy makes a point which he himself stressed in a strategic place, the introductory paragraph of Section III: "We must insist, as one of the main propositions of this book," that it was not "the revival of antiquity alone," or even chiefly, that created the Renaissance, but the "intimate association" of that revival with "the spirit of the Italian people," a spirit expressed primarily in its political and social institutions. To be sure, Italian *Bildung* could

[22] *Ibid.,* 125–26.

not free itself from the mental world of the Middle Ages through mere experience—*blosse Empirie;* it needed the guidance of the antique vocabulary.[23] But, Burckhardt argues, experience remained decisive; it is the glory (even if it is a tragic glory) of Renaissance man that he constructed his distinctive personal style not from books but from life. To place his discussion of political realities first is to insist on their central role in the shaping of modern individualism.

But the main function of Section I, I think, is to offer the reader Renaissance man in his most outrageous shape—a gigantic caricature, monstrous like a shadow thrown on a wall, but like a shadow derived from reality. Renaissance statesmen, and the Renaissance states they dominate—states which in themselves loom as individuals acting out their destiny in the arenas of domestic and international politics—here exhibit the burdens of freedom. "Good and evil lie strangely mixed together in the Italian states of the fifteenth century. The personality of the ruler is so fully developed, often so significant, so characteristic for his position and task, that it is hard to make moral judgments."[24]

And Burckhardt implies, if it is hard for the detached historian, how much harder was it for the participants! The spectacular accounts of villainy that make up so much of Section I illustrate an unprecedented moral confusion. "An old anecdote (one of those that is nowhere and yet everywhere true) describes the situation somewhat as follows: Once the burghers of a city—Siena seems to be meant—had a general who had freed them from foreign pressure; they consulted daily how to reward him, and concluded that no reward in their power was large enough, not even if they made him lord of the city. At last one of them rose up and suggested: 'Let us kill him and worship him as our patron saint.' And so, we are told, they did."[25] It is a chilling and instructive story; it records not merely inhuman ingratitude, but a loss of standards reaching down to the very fundamentals of existence. Where all is possible, much will be done.

Here is the tragic aspect of Burckhardt's dialectical vision: this loss of standards, this failure of tradition, corrodes all in-

[23] *Ibid.*, 161, 165.
[24] *Ibid.*, 16.
[25] *Ibid.*, 21–22.

stitutions. Freedom offers opportunity to all men—and women—of talent regardless of social origins, but it also works toward the collapse of all loyalties; Renaissance states give unprecedented chances to bastards, opportunists, swindlers, criminals. "If only one could have trusted one's closest blood relations! But where all was illegitimate, no regular law of inheritance could develop, either for succession in power or division of property."[26] Lawful rulers are assassinated by their more energetic uncles or cousins; all that counts is effectiveness. Under these circumstances, soldiers of fortune—the *condottieri*—could aim at realizing their wildest ambitions. "Supremely characteristic for this century"—the fifteenth—"is the *condottieri's* striving for independent power, even for a dynasty; here was a further step on the road of pure objectivity and a high reward for talent as well as ruthlessness."[27] It is an age of pure calculation, complete disregard of all motives save ambition, a very state of nature, in which despots satisfy their insane cravings by playing at murderous pastimes; in which the corruption of the papacy shocks no one; in which a satanic personality like Cesare Borgia, who "isolates his father, murders his brother, his brother-in-law and other relatives and courtiers" as soon as they seem in any way troublesome,[28] may even elicit some admiring comment from his contemporaries.

Obviously, *this* form of individualism has nothing redeeming about it. Perhaps its most reprehensible consequence is that it destroys other individualities. The celebrated Emperor Frederick II, "the first modern man on the throne," who trained himself "to judge and treat matters with complete objectivity," develops his capacities at the expense of his suffering peoples. He degrades his nation through cruel taxation, centralized government, control of private life and even private convictions, and converts it into a "manipulable heap of subjects."[29] He is the first of the despots, and shows the way to later Renaissance despots "who allowed no individuality to grow and thrive other than their own and that of their most intimate servants."[30] This irony is worse

[26] *Ibid.*, 10.
[27] *Ibid.*, 15.
[28] *Ibid.*, 104.
[29] *Ibid.*, 6.
[30] *Ibid.*, 12.

than the irony I have mentioned before: in some despotic states, the impotent subjects are allowed to cultivate their personalities, provided that their cultivation remains politically innocuous; but in the worst of the despotic states, individuality is reserved to the ruler and his toadies.

The problematic individuality of rulers, Burckhardt argues, is matched by the problematic individuality of the state. True, Burckhardt called the Renaissance state a work of art. But *Kunstwerk* must not be taken as an approving epithet; its association with the only unambiguous glory of the Renaissance—its painting, sculpture, and architecture—is either coincidental or ironic. Burckhardt employs *Kunst* to evoke not aesthetic but craft associations; it means, not art but artifice. Burckhardt's own definition is clear, as always, and completely neutral: the state as work of art is "a conscious creation, the result of reflection, resting on precisely calculated visible foundations."[31] The Renaissance state, like Renaissance foreign policy or Renaissance warfare, is the creature of reason. But Burckhardt finds this, once again, a questionable advantage: reason enters because tradition has abdicated; reason is compelled to grapple with unprecedented situations. It is in the Renaissance, writes Burckhardt, that there appears "the modern European political spirit, yielding freely to its own instincts for the first time." The new states show, "often enough, unbridled selfishness in its most terrifying shape, mocking all law, stifling all sound cultivation in the bud." Yet fortunately there are exceptions; there are states where this particular tendency is overcome "or somehow balanced out," and then "a new living entity enters history: the state as calculated, conscious creation, as work of art."[32]

As Burckhardt sees it, even the finest creations of the Renaissance mind—the republics of Venice and Florence—must participate in the ambiguities of all Renaissance *Kunstwerke*. Venice, adroitly governed at home and brilliantly represented abroad, wealthy, enterprising, inventive in such rationalist arts as statistics, is yet poverty-stricken in the revival of classical literature and derivative in art; in Venice, quality has been sacrificed to quantity. And Florence, "the model and first expression" of the best in the modern world, the urban civilization in which quan-

[31] *Ibid.*, 83.
[32] *Ibid.*, 4.

tity is happily married to quality, accurate statistics coexisted
peacefully with magnificent works of art, is also a pioneer in the
"darker side" of modernity. "Dante had already compared Florence, steadily tinkering with its constitution, to a sick man who
continually changes his position to escape his pain, and with this
observation he notes a permanent characteristic of Florentine
political life. The great modern fallacy that one can *make* a constitution, manufacture it by calculating existing forces and tendencies, emerges in Florence again and again in times of crisis.
Even Machiavelli was not wholly free from it."[33] It is obvious
that Burckhardt is here glancing at modern rationalists, at the
philosophes and—he thought—their heirs, the French Revolutionaries; but his criticism of Florence also has universal application. Reason, like the will, is an uncertain weapon; it may
lead to perceptive clarity or cold rationalism, the good reasonable life or a mere mechanical existence.

IV

"The State as Work of Art" has troubled many readers. The
very length of the section, Burckhardt's evident relish in his
gruesome stories, his occasional credulity—the story of the Si-
enese *condottiere,* say, and the stories about Cesare Borgia,
rest on gossip and uncertain traditions—all this has suggested
that Burckhardt's declared aversion for these gigantic immoralists
rests on self-deception, and conceals a secret infatuation with
the forces that stand beyond good and evil. Perhaps, it has
been said, Burckhardt was closer to Nietzsche, briefly his colleague and his friend, than he himself recognized.

This reading of Section I may well be a clue to Burckhardt's
unconscious. But as to his conscious intentions, the manifest
evidence points uncontrovertibly the other way. Burckhardt al-
located space in his historical works not in proportion to his
approval, but in proportion to what he regarded as historical
relevance. No one can misread Burckhardt's extensive treatment of Aretino as an endorsement of Aretino's practices, or as
admiration, no matter how oblique, of Aretino's literary skills.
Burckhardt gave Aretino a hearing because this brilliant black-

[33] *Ibid.,* 78–79.

mailer offered invaluable testimony on the malformation of the Renaissance individual: "From the point of view of historical investigation"—but, we must add, from this point of view alone —"Aretino will always retain an important position."[34] The same holds true of the Renaissance despotisms: "Their crimes cry to the heavens, and history has recorded them circumstantially; but as wholly autonomous states, organized according to their own principle, they still retain a considerable interest."[35] A conscientious historian cannot ignore the unpleasant, no matter how unpleasant it may be.

In his letters, Burckhardt never wavered: the *terribles simplificateurs,* whom he saw hovering in the wings of his own century and threatening to engulf the traditional civilization he prized, were the heirs of the amoral despots, the gigantic criminals of "his" Renaissance. They were to be feared, but they could not be ignored. "Perverse genius is an invention of the devil— *versetzte Genialität aber ist vom Teufel,"* he wrote in 1849; it is worse than philistinism.[36] And not long before he began to write his *Renaissance in Italien,* he anxiously advised one of his young students to recognize the worship of Faust as an essentially adolescent aberration. He was ready to concede the failings of his century, he wrote, but he could not see that adopting the "ultra-Byronesque" posture of Faust would be a cure. On the contrary: all that talk of "divine spark," "striving for higher being," and so forth, did not conceal Faust's "odious character," his passivity, his dilettantism, his malice, and, above all, his lack of love: "Believe me, only the person who can still love something is interesting." If it is true, Burckhardt told his student, that you think yourself a "daemonic nature," then "I ask for only one thing: that you do not take pleasure in this thought— not for a moment."[37] It is for this reason that Burckhardt's relations to Nietzsche could never be intimate. In one of his last letters, to the Catholic historian Ludwig von Pastor, Burckhardt insisted on his distance from Nietzsche's vision of the super-

[34] *Ibid.,* 157.

[35] *Ibid.,* 7.

[36] Burckhardt to Hermann Schauenburg, September (14), 1849. *Briefe,* III (1955), 112.

[37] Burckhardt to Albert Brenner, December 2, 1855; to the same, March 18, 1856 *Briefe.* III. 232. 247.

man: as far as *"Gewaltmenschen"* or *"outlaws"* are concerned, he never had any admiration for them, but always considered them as *"Flagella Dei."*[38] And it was in this sense, as scourges of God, that Burckhardt treated them in his book on the Renaissance.

I insist on this point here not because I think the psychological dimension unimportant or psychoanalytic interpretation futile. It is certainly possible that the *Gewaltmenschen* of the Renaissance —in whom the id overrides the scruples of the superego and repudiates the organizing forces of the ego—represent some part of Burckhardt's unconscious ideal. Somewhere within him, Burckhardt, the repressed bachelor, the small-town patrician, the conventional anti-Semite, may have longed for the explosive lawlessness that he recorded in his book and did not experience in his own life. But as a reading of his masterpiece on the Renaissance, as an explication of its meaning, this psychoanalytical guess is unfortunate and, worse, misleading. Burckhardt's *Renaissance* is an intensely controlled, conscious, indeed self-conscious work, and its achievement springs not from its expressive quality. It springs, rather, from Burckhardt's supreme rigor and intellectual probity, from his ability to do without cardboard heroes and villains. For this: to be clear about muddle, unambiguous about ambiguity, is one of the more attractive aspects of that tattered thing we call modernity.

[38] Burckhardt to Ludwig von Pastor, January 13, 1896, in *Briefe,* Walther Rehm, ed. (1946), 93–94.

Chapter 11

POWER AND RESPONSIBILITY:
OTTO HINTZE'S PLACE
IN GERMAN HISTORIOGRAPHY

W. M. Simon

Friedrich Meinecke wrote to an inquiring American historian in 1949 that he ought to look at the work of his old friend Otto Hintze, who had died in 1940: "Hintze's magnificent essays ought to be much better known abroad."[1] Hajo Holborn himself, Meinecke's student, on several occasions about the same time went out of his way to call his own students' attention to Hintze's Hohenzollern book[2] and to his work in general. After a considerable lapse of time, there are now signs that Hintze's posthumous reputation is indeed beginning, at any rate in Germany, to catch up with Meinecke's own.[3] It may therefore be an ap-

[1] Meinecke to K. S. Pinson, 23.9.1949, in his *Ausgewählter Briefwechsel*, Ludwig Dehio and Peter Classen, eds. (Stuttgart, 1962), p. 300. (See also his letter to Walther Hofer, 8.3.1947, *ibid.*, p. 273.) Only one short extract from one of Hintze's historical essays has, to my knowledge, been published in English: "The Emergence of the Democratic Nation-State," in Heinz Lubasz, ed., *The Development of the Modern State* (New York and London, 1964), pp. 65–71. Secondary published material on Hintze is likewise scarce in English; a Ph.D. dissertation has been written on him at the University of Michigan (see below, n. 7) and another is in preparation at Washington University, St. Louis, by Leonard S. Smith.

[2] *Die Hohenzollern und ihr Werk: fünfhundert Jahre vaterländischer Geschichte* (9th ed., Berlin, 1916). Here and hereafter Hintze is the author when no other is cited. Translations from items cited in German are my own.

[3] Gerhard Oestreich is editing three volumes of *Gesammelte Abhandlungen* (hereafter *Ges. Abh.*). The first two volumes have been used in the preparation of the present essay: *Staat und Verfassung: gesammelte Abhandlungen zur allgemeinen Verfassungsgeschichte* and *Soziologie und Geschichte: gesammelte Abhandlungen zur Soziologie, Politik und Theorie der Geschichte* (Göttingen, 1962 and 1964). Unfortunately, publication of Vol. III has been delayed, but I am assured by the editor that it will contain nothing essential for my purposes that is not available elsewhere. I

propriate time to attempt an assessment of Hintze in relation to a few of his contemporaries and within the framework of the general topic of this volume.

In the light of hindsight at any rate, Hintze can be seen to have differed from most other well-known German historians— from Meinecke, for example—in the development of his political outlook. In the years before World War I he continued to defend the Bismarckian constitution with its "monarchical principle," while deploring William II's abuse of it, on the ground that Germany's situation in the world allowed no alternative. During the war he declined to join those colleagues who from 1916 or 1917 advocated a compromise peace. After the war he became only very slowly and reluctantly reconciled to the Weimar Republic, but also began belatedly to revise his opinions about the interaction of domestic and foreign affairs. My purpose, of course, is not to arraign Hintze for his political and historical judgments but to account for his divergence in these respects from such celebrated contemporaries as Meinecke, Ernst Troeltsch, and Max Weber with whom he was otherwise closely associated.

These contrasts, however, are often shaded rather than glaring, with many cross-currents and ambiguities, consisting really more of differences in the pace and order of Hintze's development than in its direction. They are not for that reason any the less important, but they require more detailed exploration. As so often in treatments of German historiography, we had better begin with Ranke. To an extent that is perhaps still not fully appreciated, Ranke cast his spell over German historical writing even beyond his own long lifetime, and Hintze did not escape it. Ranke had furnished at least the elements for a formulation of the problem of responsibility and power, of ethics and politics. If he had not provided the formulation itself, that was because he had not been conscious of any problem. He had thought to combine the historical idealism (the *Ideenlehre*) derived from Kant, Hegel, and most immediately from Wilhelm von Humboldt in a harmonious association with an emphasis on political and diplomatic history and on the "primacy of foreign policy" (also not his own formulation). In an imaginary early dialogue in which

should like to take this opportunity to thank Professor Oestreich for the kind assistance he has given me both orally and in writing.

Ranke achieved the *locus classicus* of this attempted combination[4] the chief protagonist overlays the necessity for a state to "fight for its rights" with an emphasis on its need for "moral energy" and with the characterization of states themselves as "spiritual creations," "thoughts of God." The other interlocutor, however (the "straight man"), warns of becoming "over-sublime," and many German historians in fact found themselves unable to accept Ranke's sanguine synthesis. The historical profession therefore tended, later in the century, to become divided very roughly into two schools, each emphasizing one side of the power-ethics dualism at the expense of the other. The so-called "Prussian School" of historiography, led by Heinrich von Treitschke, glorified Bismarck and wrote history to show that his unification of Germany was both right and inevitable; a smaller neo-idealist school of historians, political scientists, and philosophers emphasized the role of ideas in human affairs and often, at least by implication, repudiated Bismarck (as, indeed, did the old Ranke himself).[5] It was of this neo-idealist school that Friedrich Meinecke was the foremost representative among professional historians. Meinecke was a pupil of the great biographer of Frederick the Great, Reinhold Koser, who leaned toward the Prussian school; but he was also influenced by Wilhelm Dilthey, the neo-Kantian philosopher who, by example as well as by precept, powerfully affected the historical discipline too.

Otto Hintze, like his later friend Meinecke, inherited the problem of "ethics in a world of power"[6] through the mediation of two teachers. At the beginning of his professional career he found himself the protégé of Gustav Schmoller, the great administrative and economic historian of Prussia with whom he

[4] See his *Dialogue on Politics* (translated by Theodore H. von Laue and printed as an appendix to his *Leopold Ranke: The Formative Years* [Princeton, 1950]), pp. 167–69; cf. also p. 217 as well as passages in the essay on "The Great Powers," printed *ibid.*

[5] There was also an attempt to revive the "real" Ranke against the domination of Treitschke but, as a recent study has shown, its instigators themselves paradoxically resembled Treitschke more than they did Ranke. See Hans-Heinz Krill, *Die Rankerenaissance: Max Lenz und Erich Marcks. Ein Beitrag zum historisch-politischen Denken in Deutschland, 1880–1935* (Berlin, 1962).

[6] See the book by that title by Richard W. Sterling (Princeton, 1958). The subtitle is *The Political Ideas of Friedrich Meinecke;* Hintze is not mentioned. Sterling's interpretation of Meinecke is discussed below, n. 45.

collaborated on the monumental task of editing the *Acta Borus-sica*. As a student, however, he had been taught by J. G. Droy-sen, a philosophically inclined historian and an 1848 liberal who took his liberalism more seriously than the National Liberals of the stamp of Treitschke. It was to Droysen that Hintze later turned back to derive the inspiration with which to counter Schmoller's and, paradoxically, Droysen's own admiration of the Prussian state in past and present, by setting Prussian history in its European context and by insisting on a fusion of ideal and real factors.[7] Thus Hintze, like Meinecke, was brought face to face with the problem that Ranke had been able to avoid.

The immediate effect of casting doubt on the special merits of Prussia's internal development, however, was to stress the geopolitical situation that had forced her to produce (and now compelled her to retain) the institutions that distinguished her from other states, and therefore to bring to the fore problems of foreign policy and the connection between foreign policy and internal development—not only political but also economic and social. Hintze announced his emergence from under Schmoller's wing, tactfully but unmistakably, in a long review article on a book by one of Schmoller's colleagues in the field of economic history, Wilhelm Roscher.[8] It was time, Hintze declared, that the demands of national power-politics were once more given higher priority than social reform, as they had been at all successful moments in the Prussian and German past.[9] There had,

[7] See Hintze's two articles on Droysen now reprinted in Vol. II of the *Ges. Abh.*, esp. pp. 487–91, 501, 511, also the one on Schmoller, *ibid.*, pp. 519–43. Cf. also G. Oestreich's introduction, *ibid.*, pp. 36–37, 47; F. Hartung's introduction to Vol. I, pp. 17–18; Stephan Skalweit, *"Friedrich Wilhelm I. und die preussische Historie,"* Jahrbuch für die Geschichte Mittel- und Ostdeutschlands, VI (1957), 120–21; Milton Covensky, "Otto Hintze and Historicism: A Study in the Transformation of German Historical Thought" (Ph.D. dissertation, University of Michigan, 1953), pp. 55–56, 61, 79. On Hintze's view of Droysen see, further, his book review in *Forschungen zur brandenburgischen und preussischen Geschichte*, XVI (1903), 305. Hintze, like Ranke a very disciplined writer, disliked digressions and sometimes used book reviews to express important ideas that did not fit easily into the framework of longer and more formal essays.

[8] *"Roschers politische Entwickelungstheorie,"* Schmollers Jahrbuch, XXI (1897), 767–811 (now also in *Ges. Abh.*, II). It will be seen that Schmoller, for his part, gave Hintze space for his dissent.

[9] For particularly relevant passages from Hintze's historical analysis of earlier periods see the following: *"Geist und Epochen der preussischen*

he admitted, always been those who maintained that only a strong state could carry out social reforms—a reference that could easily be taken to include Schmoller. "But they have so far . . . emphasized ideas of social justice more than those of national power, which have surely always been the first consideration for the state. . . . Social reform is a prerequisite not only for economic progress and social justice but also for the development of national power."[10] From social justice Hintze went on to "the internal life of states" generally, which was "to a great extent dependent on the relations among states, on the pushing and shoving that prevails among them, on the rise and decline of neighboring states, on the higher or lower pressure, so to speak, of the whole political atmosphere." Certain internal constitutional forms corresponded to certain stages in the external growth of states.[11] Here is an authentic statement of the "primacy of foreign policy"[12] that Hintze was to repeat, sometimes in identical words, over and over again for many years.[13]

Hintze provided his views with a philosophical underpinning

Geschichte," in his *Historische und politische Aufsätze* (4 vols., Berlin, 1908), I, 16–18, 21, 32, 35, 40–41; "Der preussische Militär- und Beamtenstaat im 18. Jahrhundert," in his *Geist und Epochen der preussischen Geschichte: gesammelte Abhandlungen,* F. Hartung, ed. (Leipzig, 1943), pp. 453, 462; *Hohenzollern,* pp. vi, 200–4, and 253–54 (power and responsibility in the Great Elector and the beneficient triumph of *raison d'état*), 321–24; *Das politische Testament Friedrichs des Grossen von 1752* (Berlin, 1904), p. 10 (defense of Frederick II's invasion of Silesia on the ground of *raison d'état*); *"Friedrich der Grosse, Stein, Bismarck,"* *Hohenzollern-Jahrbuch,* XV (1911), 15, 17–18 (Bismarck in tradition of Frederick; Stein's ideals not realizable).

[10] "Roscher," p. 768.

[11] *Ibid.,* pp. 784, 800. The passage continues with a reference to Ranke.

[12] See the comment of Theodor Schieder, reviewing Vol. I of the *Ges. Abh.* in *Der Staat,* II (1963), 110: "With certain reservations one can even speak in Hintze's case of the primacy of foreign policy for social history, i.e. of a very broadly construed application of Ranke's principle to areas that Ranke had not included."

[13] For other statements of it before World War I, see the following essays, all now reprinted in Vol. I of the *Ges. Abh.:* "Staatenbildung und Verfassungsentwicklung" (1902), "Staatsverfassung und Heeresverfassung" (1906), "Das monarchische Prinzip und die konstitutionelle Verfassung" (1911), and particularly "Machtpolitik und Regierungsverfassung" (1913): "in the last resort it is power politics that has determined the social structure of states" (p. 438). See also George M. Schwarz, "Political Attitudes in the German Universities During the Reign of William II" (D. Phil. thesis, Oxford University, 1961), pp. 190–93.

by dissociating himself from the biological analogy according to which states grow like organisms. The growth of small states into large ones, he said, was attributable chiefly to political and military energy and organization.[14] But philosophical considerations were not uppermost in his mind: what preoccupied him was very specifically the international position of Germany at a time when, on the one hand, William II, as Hintze saw it, was undermining the bases of the Bismarckian constitution, and, on the other hand, power politics were being played no longer merely on a European but on a world stage—in the era of *Weltpolitik,* as William II himself had said, in the era when national European rivalries were fought out in imperial overseas struggles, in the era in which Germany had to assert her right to a "place in the sun" against the alleged threat of British world domination. Hintze had always been keenly interested in Britain for purposes of comparative political analysis as well as with reference to imperialism; indeed it was from a British historian, Sir John Seeley, that Hintze often quoted when formulating the principle of the primacy of foreign policy, and he was in the habit of contrasting the domestic effects of dependence on a land army with those of the ability to rely on sea power, which had historically permitted the development of far freer constitutions and institutions in Britain. Now, however, in Hintze's own day, Germany had to challenge Britain for the control of the seas, and Hintze like many members of the German professional classes was glad to be able to support Tirpitz's naval program as politically "liberal" as well as internationally necessary.[15] Hintze distinguished two senses of "imperialism": first, "the expansion of a state into a sea and world power, into a Great Power in the modern style which can play an active part in the international relations [*grossen Politik*], in the *Weltpolitik* of the future; in this sense it would be possible to speak of a German imperialism too; in this sense all states that wish to secure for themselves a place among the 'world powers' of the future, among the great powers of the new system of world states, pursue im-

[14] "Roscher," pp. 785, 797–98.
[15] See now particularly Jonathan Steinberg, "The Kaiser's Navy and German Society," *Past and Present,* No. 28 (July 1964), pp. 102–10; cf. Krill, *Rankerenaissance,* p. 185. For a typical reference to Seeley see, e.g., *Ges. Abh.,* I, 433.

perialistic policies"; secondly, a desire for sole power (*Alleinherr-schaft*) or supreme power (*Oberherrschaft*) in the world, which would upset the balance of power. Insofar as British imperialism was of the latter kind, Germany had a right and a duty to resist it, and the naval building program was essential to any resistance.[16]

In Rankean fashion Hintze idealized this political conception too, this time by declaring that imperialism and the drive for world power had always played an essential part in the progress of culture and civilization.[17] In this way, Hintze and other followers of Ranke "were giving the German cultural élite the welcome impression that the new policies did not . . . lead beyond the realms of previous experience and so could not possibly be a reckless embarkation upon a Sicilian expedition"[18]; by contrast with Treitschke's "national, emphatic view of power" Hintze was offering a "comparative-historical interpretation of the development of the power of European imperialism at the turn of the century."[19] But Hintze was very much more concerned with the specific impact of the phenomena under discussion on his own country than with philosophical disquisitions on the nature of power. That national power was worth defending and increasing was a self-evident proposition to him; on the one occasion when he raised the question whether nationalism itself was past its climax he immediately answered the question in the negative.[20] Moreover, he answered it with an emphatic reference to the need for a domestic policy attuned to the demands

[16] "Der britische Imperialismus und seine Probleme," *Zeitschrift für Politik*, I (1908), 297–98, 345; cf. also "Imperialismus und Weltpolitik" (1907), in *Ges. Abh.*, I, esp. pp. 463, 469; "Weltgeschichte und Weltpolitik: ein historischer Beitrag zum Verständnis der gegenwärtigen Lage," *Deutsche Monatsschrift für das gesamte Leben der Gegenwart*, I (1902), 684. On the well-known German ambivalence toward Britain, of which Hintze provides an excellent example, see now Gustav Schmidt, *Deutscher Historismus und der Übergang zur parlamentarischen Demokratie: Untersuchungen zu den politischen Gedanken von Meinecke, Troeltsch, Max Weber* (Lübeck and Hamburg, 1964), pp. 13–15.

[17] "Weltgeschichte und Weltpolitik," p. 672; "Roscher," p. 798; cf. Schwarz, "Political Attitudes," p. 306.

[18] Ludwig Dehio, *Germany and World Politics in the Twentieth Century* (tr. Dieter Pevsner, London, 1959), pp. 42 *et seq.*

[19] Oestreich, introduction to Vol. II of *Ges. Abh.*, p. 10.

[20] "Rasse und Nationalität und ihre Bedeutung für die Geschichte" (1903), *ibid.*, pp. 63–64; cf. Oestreich, *ibid.*, p. 12; Schwarz, "Political Attitudes," pp. 194–95, 307–9, 330–31.

of foreign policy: "There is no more urgent prerequisite . . . for an . . . expansionist *Weltpolitik* than a strong and firm national cohesiveness at home. Domestic policy . . . is the precondition for *Weltpolitik,*" especially a racial policy directed against Slav infiltration in the east.[21]

Ten years later Hintze was a good deal more worried about the capacity of Germany to maintain the sort of stability at home that would sustain *Weltpolitik*. The monarchy was necessary to maintain the "disciplined cohesion" required to resist the pressure on the frontiers. At the same time the rigidity of the military and bureaucratic structure that monarchy brought with it had introduced into the German party system hostility toward the state and other unhealthy features. A true parliamentary system, Hintze admitted, would be educational, but impossible in the existing condition of the parties and of Europe. Nevertheless, "the present system of government above parties is not the realization of an ideal but only a makeshift." The Bismarckian system had not been adapted to keep up with the times. But, true to the Rankean principle, Hintze found the key to the situation in foreign policy: "The internal situation is a result of the military and political pressure on our frontiers that has been growing for decades. Perhaps this oppressive bond . . . will have to be burst before our public life can move more freely."[22] In his last major essay written before the outbreak of war, Hintze's frustration, perhaps even desperation, is discernible in the increased stridency as well as the signs of inconsistency with which he reiterated his arguments.[23] He was caught in a vicious circle in which foreign policy was not adequately supported by domestic institutions, while at the same time the demands of foreign policy seemed to him not to allow time for constitutional reform. Hintze, the orthodox National Liberal, found himself moving toward the position of such a left-wing critic of Wilhelmian Germany as Max Weber but without the conviction that his criticism was constructive.[24]

[21] "Rasse und Nationalität," p. 64.

[22] "Machtpolitik und Regierungsverfassung," *Ges. Abh.,* I, 439, 454–56; cf. also "Das monarchische Prinzip," *ibid.,* 377.

[23] See "Das Verfassungsleben der heutigen Kulturstaaten," *ibid.,* 390–423.

[24] For an excellent analysis of Hintze's position at this time see Schwarz, "Political Attitudes," pp. 295–98.

All such criticism was temporarily stilled after the outbreak of war as the ranks closed and as intellectuals of many political stripes united in adopting what later became known as the "ideas of 1914," particularly the idea that the war would cement the cracks in German society. This idea in turn was predicated on the almost unquestioned assumption that Germany's cause in the war was just. Hintze was one of the editors and contributors of a volume designed to persuade Americans to take the same view. Here again he began with the same old refrain of the primacy of foreign policy:

> The spirit and character of a nation depend not alone upon its internal social structure, but in even greater degree upon the political necessities that spring from its geographical position and its relation to other states and Powers. . . . Germany in especial is subject to so relentless a pressure on her borders that, before all things, she is forced, through the imperative law of self-preservation, so to strengthen herself in a military sense as to be able, in case of necessity, to maintain herself in the face of a world of enemies. . . . The degree of political freedom permissible in the forms of government must evidently be inversely proportional to the political and military pressure exerted against the boundaries of the state.[25]

On these premises Hintze went on to defend "Prussian militarism"; to advocate, as he had done many times before, the slogan devised by a Prussian statesman of a century earlier, Baron Hardenberg, of "democratic institutions under a monarchical form of government"; and to reject, much more decisively than he had done just before the war, "a transformation that would place the government in the hands of changing majorities and subject the army to corrupt parliamentary influences. . . . France may indulge in such experiments; our position is too precarious to admit of the attempt."[26]

In writings for primarily domestic consumption during these early war years Hintze took much the same line. The war would have broken out many years earlier if it had not been for the steady love of peace on the part of William II and the majority

[25] *Modern Germany in Relation to the Great War* (W. Whitelock, tr., New York, 1916), pp. 9, 10, 12.

[26] *Ibid.*, pp. 14–15.

of the German people, which caused them to resist the provocation of the Allies, particularly of Britain, who hypocritically
tried to conceal her quest for world domination behind a mask of
pacifism and culture. Germans, for their part, were profoundly
convinced "that art and science can flourish only in the soil of a
strong and independent national life [*Volkstum*], of a strong
and self-sufficient political structure [*Staatsleben*]."[27] The need
for a large army required "strong monarchical leadership and
strict discipline in civilian life too," even in schools and in
industry. "I believe that our military constitution represents a
higher type of ethics and civilization than that of Great
Britain."[28] Gone are the doubts and hesitations of the years
1911–14. As late as 1917 Hintze still emphasized that "without
a political system [*Staatswesen*] that stands free and firm among
the nations even the most extreme democracy is nothing but a
cloak concealing the absence of freedom"[29]; but now he began
to use his earlier defensive interpretation of *Weltpolitik* to argue
that Germany could regard herself as victorious in the war if
enemy plans to annihilate her were frustrated and she was able
to maintain herself "in power and honor" with such a measure
of well-being as the destruction wrought by the war itself would
permit.[30] To be sure, the general guidelines that Hintze laid
down for Germany's war aims scarcely indicated a defensive
frame of mind or a willingness to compromise.[31]

After the collapse of 1918, however, Hintze reverted to the
doubts and hesitations of the immediate prewar years and even
went beyond them, though it would be untrue to say that he
underwent a real change of heart. He still maintained that a
"robust instinct for power" was necessary equipment for any

[27] "Deutschland, der Krieg und die Volksgemeinschaft," *Internationale
Monatsschrift für Wissenschaft, Kunst und Technik,* IX (1915), 27–40
(quotation from p. 37).

[28] "Unser Militarismus: ein Wort an Amerika," *ibid.,* 212–13, 220. See,
further, "Bismarck, die deutsche Politik und der Krieg," *ibid.,* 793–810,
and *Hohenzollern,* pp. 679, 682. Cf. Ludwig Dehio, "Gedanken über
die deutsche Sendung 1900–1918," *Historische Zeitschrift,* Vol. 174 (1952),
p. 490n.

[29] "Imperialismus und Weltpolitik," in a volume entitled *Die deutsche
Freiheit: fünf Vorträge* (Gotha, 1917), p. 169.

[30] *Ibid.,* pp. 116–17, 149.

[31] See *ibid.,* pp. 157–65.

statesman[32]; he was still inclined to assert the primacy of foreign policy (instancing the impact on Germany of paying reparations) although he was now more careful to point out that foreign affairs were only one determinant of internal constitutional and political life and that the relationship was a reciprocal one, and indeed went out of his way to repudiate the unconditional applicability of the slogan "the primacy of foreign policy." In his own prewar writings, Hintze insisted, perhaps disingenuously, he had not meant "that only the monarchical-military principle was capable of offering the kind of resistance to the pressure on our frontiers required for self-preservation"; he had always believed in the urgency of "a strong democratic substructure for the military monarchy" (which, if true, was not entirely relevant).[33] In one remarkable passage he even admitted that German foreign policy before the war had taken the wrong direction because it had been kept away from parliament and the responsible ministry.[34]

In rather similar and hesitant fashion Hintze began to denounce as "one-sided" an exclusive emphasis on power, especially military power, as the basis of states, and to oppose "nationalistic passions" while still calling for a strong, morally based "national feeling." Law, he argued, occupied an important place not only within the state but even among states, at least in the civilized world. Of course, he admitted, the active statesman was always

[32] Review of Karl Jaspers, *Max Weber,* in *Schmollers Jahrbuch,* Vol. 45 (1921), p. 293. Compare, however, Hintze's favorable treatment after the war of the nineteenth-century Prussian statesman Baron Stein, whom earlier he had been inclined to disparage for his lack of political realism and his neglect of foreign affairs. Now this neglect is still mentioned, but greater emphasis is placed on "the element of universalism that moderated his nationalism and saved it from degenerating into egotism." Review of Gerhard Ritter, *Stein,* in *Historische Zeitschrift,* Vol. 146 (1932), pp. 352–55; compare the earlier references in "Stein und der preussische Staat: eine Besprechung von Max Lehmanns Stein–Biographie I–II," *ibid.,* Vol. 94, pp. 427, 442, 444; "Friedrich der Grosse, Stein, Bismarck," pp. 11–13.

[33] "Liberalismus, Demokratie und auswärtige Politik" (1926), in *Ges. Abh.,* II, 200–1, 203; "Soziologische und geschichtliche Staatsauffassung: zu Franz Oppenheimers System der Soziologie" (1929), *ibid.,* 286. See also his reference to the nations defeated in the war being "oppressed and exploited" by the victors, review of R. M. MacIver, *The Modern State,* in *Zeitschrift für die gesamte Staatswissenschaft,* Vol. 86 (1929), p. 383.

[34] Review of F. Stieve, *Deutschland und Europa, 1890–1914,* in *Schmollers Jahrbuch,* Vol. 51 (1927), p. 166.

unscrupulous, "but the criticism of public opinion in which law plays a role not to be underestimated compels him to considerations that represent a very important element in politics." It was this factor of public opinion that Germany had neglected in 1914 in failing to put her enemies in the wrong. Now (1925), as a weak Power, Germany was in no position to fight force with force, and therefore it was in her interests, "if only for the sake of her moral self-preservation," to promote the use of law as a weapon in international relations. "Crude naturalism," Hintze concluded, "is not only scientifically untenable but also, things being as they are, in its practical effect the reverse of a sensible *Realpolitik.*"[35] Here is a strangely awkward, naïve, and tortured argument from a man once more not at peace with himself. Hintze now regretted the continuing advance of nationalism "in its harshest and most dangerous form, a brutal and exclusive mass egotism without any ethical element of self-restraint." He found a United States of Europe an attractive idea, especially for Germany in her weakened condition; but by the same token he thought it was an illusion, since Germany's adversaries desired not a federated Europe but an expanded France.[36] Federalism was a political principle of universal significance, based in turn on the principle of community, whereas modern *raison d'état* and imperialism were based on the principle of domination. "Our age suffers from an excessive reliance on the principle of *raison d'état,* whose chief standard-bearer is France."[37] Hintze distinguished between "a healthy and moderate national consciousness" after the manner of Bismarck and the excesses of Pan-Germanism which had given rise abroad to "a legend assiduously nurtured by enemy propaganda in the period of Germany's encirclement."[38] He thought that perhaps imperialism was beginning to decline, but federalism could replace it only when "reason and justice count for more in political life than, un-

[35] Review of books by Oswald Spengler and Otto Kollreuther, in *Zeitschrift für die gesamte Staatswissenschaft,* Vol. 79 (1925), pp. 546–47; cf. Oestreich in *Ges. Abh.,* II, 21–22, 26.
[36] "Nationale und europäische Orientierung in der heutigen politischen Welt" (1925), *ibid.,* 195–97.
[37] Review of Constantin Frantz, *Deutschland und der Föderalismus* (*et al.*), in *Schmollers Jahrbuch,* Vol. 49 (1925), p. 227.
[38] Review of M. S. Wertheimer, *The Pan-German League, 1890–1914,* in *Zeitschrift für die gesamte Staatswissenschaft,* Vol. 79 (1925), p. 548.

fortunately, they do at the moment."[39] He even went to the lengths of calling imperialism an ominous (*verhängnisvoll*) principle "which has achieved great things but has also done untold harm."[40]

But perhaps the most significant of all of these cautious and partial retreats from Hintze's previous positions concerned the nature of the state. He agreed with Max Weber that its monopoly of the legitimate use of force was the main hallmark of the state, and nobody should "imagine that they can have political freedom and self-determination without the elementary foundations of political power." But force was the precondition of law, not its contrary, and the state was "a hybrid of both force and law," not a mere "monster of filth and fire." A Hegelian view of the state as an embodiment of morality was, however, equally unacceptable: "We have no reason now," Hintze argued, again with that curious *ad hoc* logic, "to imitate . . . the political ideologies of our oppressors, intoxicated by victory."[41] The notion that the idea of *raison d'état* was a German monopoly had been put about by enemy propaganda and fostered within Germany by the proposition of Troeltsch and Meinecke that German thought had differed historically from that of the West.[42]

Meinecke, for his part, thought that he and Hintze had undergone a similar evolution in their political opinions: "The same man who published the book on the Hohenzollern in 1915 said to me in 1919 or 1920: 'We ought by now to have got as far as not being so anxious about the frontiers of states!' "[43] In fact, however, significant differences are discernible in the development of the two men. Meinecke had from the first concerned himself expressly with the problem of ethics and politics. Admittedly, in his earlier writings, Meinecke's emphasis on intel-

[39] "Föderalistischer Imperialismus" (1928), in *Ges. Abh.*, II, 210–15.

[40] "Soziologische und geschichtliche Staatsauffassung," p. 305. Cf. also "Wesen und Wandlung des modernen Staats" (1931), *Ges. Abh.*, I, 490, 496.

[41] "Soziologische und geschichtliche Staatsauffassung," pp. 274–75, 242; "Droysen und der deutsche Staatsgedanke," pp. 511, 518.

[42] "Troeltsch und die Probleme des Historismus," in *Ges. Abh.*, II, 327–29.

[43] Meinecke to Hofer, 8.3.1947, in his *Ausgewählter Briefwechsel*, p. 273; see also letter to Heinrich Brüning, 17.7.1953, *ibid.*, p. 300, and Meinecke's *Erlebtes 1862/1919* (Stuttgart, 1964), pp. 103, 105, 236, 250.

lectual history had tended to have the effect of lending an idealistic gloss to political history and to power politics. This gloss is particularly notable in his contribution to the collaborative propaganda volume of 1915, where his emphasis was on culture, not power. In apparent contrast to Hintze and to the notion of the "primacy of foreign policy," Meinecke asserted that it had been Germany's achievement to have attained, unlike England and France, a high level of culture "without the aid and support of a great political life. . . . It is absolutely false to declare that masterpieces of the mind can be produced only in a great and powerful national state." Nevertheless, a little "sunshine of political power and greatness . . . can be infinitely valuable to it," and about 1800 "German *Kultur* began to turn toward the state for the sake of its own completion." With an explicit reference to Ranke, Meinecke committed himself to a form of "historical realism" which would reveal new significance in "the egotism of states and nations": "It becomes the means for the development of all the latent forces in mankind. . . . Every nation possesses the natural and justifiable wish to assert the worth and the ideals of its own *Kultur* and to diffuse them in the world." Then, abandoning the theme of culture, Meinecke concluded: "It is nothing else but stern necessity that forces us to develop a maximum of military power. It is the only safe guarantee of our independence."[44]

But—and this is the second fundamental difference from Hintze—Meinecke's disillusionment with the stubborn refusal of the imperial government during the war to agree to constitutional reform caused him to despair of the idea that the forces that had founded a state could also maintain it in a progressive sense, and brought about in him a substantial political change of heart.[45]

[44] *Modern Germany in Relation to the Great War*, pp. 566–67, 578–79, 582.

[45] See now particularly Schmidt, *Deutscher Historismus*, esp. p. 124 and, on the "primacy of foreign policy," pp. 142–43, 156. Sterling, *Ethics in a World of Power*, denies any such change of heart, wishing to place it instead during World War II; but much of his own book nevertheless goes to prove one during World War I, and it seems difficult to avoid the conclusion that in fact Meinecke underwent two major political conversions. Sterling and Schmidt (pp. 70–71) agree, however, that Meinecke was working toward a resolution of the power-ethics dichotomy in terms of the paramount importance of the individual.

This in turn prompted him to change his categories of historical analysis, to arrive at new interpretations of such historical figures as Bismarck, and finally to suggest that Jacob Burckhardt was perhaps preferable to Ranke as a model historian.[46]

It was from his friend Ernst Troeltsch, the philosopher and historian of religion and of philosophy, that Meinecke had adopted the word "historicism" to denote the individualizing view of history to which both subscribed, of which Meinecke in turn wrote the "pre-history,"[47] and of which both tried to escape the relativistic and (allegedly) morally disturbing consequences. Their views of the nation, *raison d'état,* and the power-state before the war had been much the same, and much the same as Hintze's, all three being derived quite consciously from Ranke. In his contribution to the propaganda volume of 1915, Troeltsch was if anything more explicit than Hintze, certainly more so than Meinecke, in defense of the German political status quo:

> The nation is convinced that no independent German civilization is possible without the protection of a great and powerful state. . . . Great as may be the advantages of a parliamentary form of government for the discovery and training of political talent as well as for the political education of a people in general, it is a menace to the unity of the military and political leadership of a youthful state. . . . In the last analysis, national unity rests upon the army in the same manner as does the monarchy. All the ideal forces of education, science and technical training have been absorbed into the organism of the army: conversely, the military system furnishes the model and the requisite strength for the remarkable organization which prevails throughout the German nation and in which initiative of the individual and discipline of the whole are successfully united. All this is imposed on us by fate, which has placed us in the centre of Europe; of this necessity we have made a virtue.[48]

[46] These changes in Meinecke have been much discussed in the last twenty years, and considerations of space dictate extreme brevity here. See, in addition to Walther Hofer, *Geschichtschreibung und Weltanschauung: Betrachtungen zum Werk Friedrich Meineckes* (Munich, 1950), particularly Heinz Holldack, "Friedrich Meinecke: das Machtproblem in der neuesten deutschen Geschichte," *Hochland,* Vol. 46 (1953–54), pp. 437–51; and Schmidt, *Deutscher Historismus,* pp. 56–57.

[47] *Die Entstehung des Historismus* (2 vols., Munich and Berlin, 1936).

[48] *Modern Germany in Relation to the Great War,* pp. 69–71.

For all these reasons, Troeltsch argued, the idea of freedom had taken and still took a particular form in Germany.[49] It was from this assertion of the uniqueness of German intellectual development that Hintze later dissented.[50] But Troeltsch himself also soon abandoned many of his positions of 1915, although not this one. In fact his political development from 1917 was very similar to Meinecke's, both finishing up as *Vernunftre-publikaner*, supporters of the Weimar Republic on rational grounds while still emotionally committed to the monarchy.[51] Hintze never offered the Republic more than grudging toleration.

Even more active on behalf of the Republic in its early days than either Meinecke or Troeltsch was the famous sociologist Max Weber. This is not surprising, since Weber had been among the sharpest critics (outside the SPD) of the Wilhelmian empire and an advocate, before as well as during the war, of radical constitutional change in the direction of responsible government. Yet Weber combined this zeal for reform with an equally ardent pride in the power of the German state and an unquestioning insistence on the primacy of foreign policy: no amount of domestic reform, Weber declared in a classic phrase, was of any use "if the Cossacks are coming."[52] However, Weber's political views were all closely derived from the principal results of his

---

[49] *Ibid.*, p. 86; cf. Walther Köhler, *Ernst Troeltsch* (Tübingen, 1941), pp. 296, 306, 313; also, for general interest, Leonard Krieger, *The German Idea of Freedom* (Boston, 1957).

[50] See above, pp. 261.

[51] For a full discussion of Troeltsch and Meinecke see Schmidt, *Deutscher Historismus*, pp. 19–21, 47, 55, 63, 99–104, 106–7, 196 n.31, 205. On Troeltsch's last phase see, further, Eric C. Kollman, "Eine Diagnose der Weimarer Republik: Ernst Troeltschs politische Anschauungen," *Historische Zeitschrift*, Vol. 182 (1956), pp. 291–319, and Troeltsch's *Spektatorbriefe* (Tübingen, 1924).

[52] On Weber's politics J. P. Mayer, *Max Weber and German Politics: a Study in Political Sociology* (London, 1944) is available in English, but Wolfgang J. Mommsen, *Max Weber und die deutsche Politik, 1890–1920* (Tübingen, 1959), and Raymond Aron, "Max Weber und die Machtpolitik," *Zeitschrift für Politik*, n.s. XI (1964), 100–13, are much more searching. For a comparison of Weber with Meinecke see Gerhard Masur, "Max Weber und Friedrich Meinecke in ihrem Verhältnis zur politischen Macht," in *Studium Berolinense*, ed. Hans Leussink and others (Berlin, 1960), pp. 702–25; also Schmidt, *Deutscher Historismus*, pp. 241, 264.

historical and sociological research:[53] Weber was convinced that in an industrializing society "charismatic leadership" could be produced only by the competition of contending personalities in a democratic forum, and only such leadership could gain freedom for everybody against the incubus of a Parkinsonian bureaucracy. Thus Weber arrived by another route at what Troeltsch referred to as the characteristically German idea of freedom, where freedom depended on the exercise of the state's authority. Perhaps his study of Puritanism and the idea of Original Sin also contributed to what has been called "the almost insufferable placidity with which Max Weber treated the problem of violence in domestic politics." Equally, on the basis of his historical studies "Weber regarded . . . the struggle between nations and their values as a built-in factor of a dynamic world order."[54] These two main strands were combined into Weber's insistence that only a strong parliamentary democracy was capable of a strong foreign policy under the conditions of modern industrial society, and Weber was one of the few who could point without self-contradiction at the hollowness of the "ideas of 1914" and at the failure of the imperial regime to carry out a successful foreign policy even while giving it priority. In contrast to the tradition of the "primacy of foreign policy" from Ranke to Hintze, Weber attached that principle to the interests of the nation as a whole and not mainly to those of the monarchy.[55] Agreeing with Weber that historically the state was in the first place an instrument of power and that the world consisted of states engaged in a competition for power,[56] Hintze realized after 1918 that the German state in fact no longer answered to this description and found himself forced, painfully and reluctantly, to revise his analytical categories.

[53] See now the penetrating analysis of W. J. Mommsen, "Universalgeschichtliches und politisches Denken bei Max Weber," *Historische Zeitschrift,* Vol. 201 (1965), pp. 557–612, summarized in translation as "Max Weber's Political Sociology and His Philosophy of World History," *International Social Science Journal,* XVII (1965), 23–45. See also Gerhard Schulz, "Geschichtliche Theorie und politisches Denken bei Max Weber," *Vierteljahrshefte für Zeitgeschichte,* XII (1964), 325–50.

[54] Mommsen, "Max Weber's Political Sociology," pp. 41–42.

[55] See Schmidt, *Deutscher Historismus,* pp. 232–33, 235, 261–62; but Schmidt's attempt (pp. 235–36) to limit the operation of the principle in Weber seems to me sophistical.

[56] See Schwarz, "Political Attitudes," p. 222.

In this task he was considerably helped by another set of ideas borrowed from Max Weber. He and Meinecke were among the very few historians of their day to appreciate Weber's work and to bridge the persistent gap between their discipline and sociology. In the Weimar period Hintze wrote approvingly of Weber's advocacy and practice of "value-free scholarship," of his idea of the "Protestant Ethic," and of his comparative method, although he was at pains to point out that when practiced by a historian that method tends to produce sharper definitions and distinctions rather than the "ideal types" characteristic of Weber and sociologists generally. The sociologists' schematic approach failed signally, for example, to explain the appearance of the early representative constitutions of Europe, which Hintze insisted were characteristic of the Christian West alone and of the kind of states that had developed there.[57] On a smaller scale Hintze drew distinctions, for example, between the constitutional development of Prussia and France in the seventeenth and eighteenth centuries and attributed the differences to the Calvinistic asceticism of the Prussian rulers.[58]

Now Hintze had never ignored the political implications of Calvinism; he had long been interested in comparative constitutional history (especially, of course, in the comparison between Germany and Britain); and we know that he had always maintained that the external development of states was a major factor in their constitutional development. But if the comparative method and its applications were by no means new with him, his refinement of it in later years, inspired by Weber, is marked and his perseverance with it remarkable in view of his simultaneous preoccupation with rebutting the thesis of the unique evolution of political thought in Germany; for Hintze was also learning from Weber to emphasize the interdependence between "real" (political and economic) and "ideal" interests that, he said, Ranke's

[57] "Max Webers Religionssoziologie" (1922), in *Ges. Abh.*, II, 129; "Max Webers Soziologie" (1926), *ibid.*, 145–46; "Weltgeschichtliche Bedingungen der Repräsentativverfassung" (1931), *ibid.*, I, 178; cf. Theodor Schieder, "Möglichkeiten und Grenzen vergleichender Methoden in der Geschichtswissenschaft," *Historische Zeitschrift*, Vol. 200 (1965), pp. 542, 544.

[58] "Kalvinismus und Staatsräson in Brandenburg zu Beginn des 17. Jahrhunderts," *ibid.*, Vol. 144 (1931), p. 285.

Ideenlehre implied.[59] It was Weber's original appreciation of the importance of both historical continuity and historically caused divergences that enabled him to free sociology to a considerable extent from theoretical categories and abstract frameworks and thus make it accessible to an intellectually conservative historian such as Hintze; only then could Hintze in his turn attempt a new kind of synthesis of constitutional and social history in which the development of state and society were analyzed together and regarded as complementary rather than antagonistic[60] (reversing the opposite tendency that owed so much to Hegel).[61]

It seems justifiable, therefore, to contend that one essential dimension of Hintze's growth as a historian was a widening of his professional perspectives, a broader view of the nature and function of his discipline. This was not a radical process and did not of itself require him to discard any of his political opinions; for instance, the new analysis of state and society if anything reinforced the view (held, as we saw, by Weber too) that the state's requirements, of which the first was power, were paramount.[62] On the contrary: his feeling of a still firmer grasp of his historical material is likely to have strengthened rather than weakened his confidence in the political conclusions that he had drawn from his study of the past. In this respect Hintze must be contrasted with Meinecke and Troeltsch, who were much more ready not only to alter their political opinions in the light of current affairs but also to adapt their historical and social interpretations correspondingly. Some recent writers would see in this latter phenomenon a typical manifestation of the debilitating

---

[59] *Ibid.*, p. 232 (with specific reference to Weber); "Troeltsch und die Probleme des Historismus," pp. 352, 368; cf. Reinhard Bendix, "Max Weber's Sociology Today," *International Social Science Journal*, XVII (1965), 17 n.2.

[60] See Karl Bosl, "Der 'soziologische Aspekt' in der Geschichte: wertfreie Geschichtswissenschaft und Idealtypus," *Historische Zeitschrift*, Vol. 201 (1965), pp. 620, 629–630; Oestreich in *Ges. Abh.*, II, 28, 40.

[61] It may be remarked here, incidentally, that the so-called Hegelian apotheosis of the state is in part a legend (to which Hintze himself contributed, see above, p. 211).

[62] For the later Hintze on the state and power (in addition to passages already cited) see "Das Gesetz der Macht" (1926), in *Ges. Abh.*, II, 218–19, "Der Staat als Betrieb und die Verfassungsreform" (1927), *ibid.*, 206–7. For cogent objections to Hintze's confusion of "state" with "government" see Schwarz, "Political Attitudes," pp. 178–81.

effect of "historicism."[63] It is not necessary to subscribe to this view, however, to maintain that Meinecke's former superiority to Hintze in terms of a philosophical basis for historical thought was at least reduced by Hintze's partial acceptance from Weber of a different kind of philosophical substructure.

Weber, as we saw, had cause to change his political opinions very little, because his ideas on domestic reform, radical and extreme at the turn of the century, were by and large realized in the first year of the Weimar Republic, and because he died prematurely. Hintze, whose views had started out far to the right of Weber's and who lived longer, could not be quite so steadfast. Even before the war he had begun to question the inherent rightness of the Hohenzollern creation; after the defeat and amid the disillusionment of inflation and depression he was assailed by even stronger doubts. Yet, fortified by his new and more comprehensive historical analysis, he was most reluctant to admit that it could be leading him astray. This conflict, it may be suggested, is the source of the agonized inconsistencies scattered through much of Hintze's writing after 1918. Trapped by his own confident exegesis of Ranke, by the doctrine of the "primacy of foreign policy" and of the power-state (*Machtstaat*), he found it the more difficult after World War I to recognize what a German historian of a later generation, Gerhard Ritter, after the still greater disasters of World War II, called the "daemonic aspects of power."[64]

Hintze should not be taken too severely to task for his squirming. A foolish consistency is said to be the hobgoblin of little minds, and Hintze would certainly have been foolish to ignore the shortcomings of the Hohenzollern state, culminating in the failure of the Bismarckian empire to achieve its own goals. Yet

[63] The literature is by now considerable, but see above all Schmidt, *Deutscher Historismus*, pp. 31, 38, and *passim;* also Georg G. Iggers, "German Historical Thought and the Idea of Natural Law," *Cahiers d'histoire mondiale,* VIII (1964), 572–73. In another recent article, "The Dissolution of German Historism," in *Ideas in History: Essays Presented to Louis Gottschalk by His Former Students,* Richard Herr and Harold T. Parker, eds. (Durham, North Carolina, 1965), pp. 295–96, Iggers refers to the later Hintze's concern with institutional history as one escape route from the traditional "political values and historical concepts" of German historians.

[64] G. Ritter, *Die Dämonie der Macht* (Stuttgart, 1947), translated as *The Corrupting Influence of Power* (Hadleigh, Essex, 1952).

Hintze was not only by temperament rather inflexible—Meinecke admitted that his friend suffered from "innate inhibitions" and his share of "Prussian bureaucratic pedantry"[65]—but also an honest scholar who had built his politics on the foundations of his scholarship. He therefore found it hard to change his views on current affairs, and doubly hard and galling to change his historical analysis, since he was less ready than Meinecke to concede that scholarship might, on the contrary, be affected by politics.

Hintze's vacillation between adherence to and amendment of his own ideas is, in the final analysis, epitomized in his dual debt to Weber. In one sense assimilation of Weber made Hintze less adaptable by causing him to feel even more secure in his historiographical achievement. But in a quite different sense Weber's ideal of "value-free" scholarship perhaps helped Hintze at least to moderate his Rankean attachment of moral value to the state without having, like Meinecke, to search for moral values elsewhere.

[65] Meinecke, *Erlebtes*, p. 105.

Chapter 12

FREEDOM AND POWER IN HISTORY

Werner Kaegi
(Translated by Flora Kimmich)

When someone in the West reflects upon the fate of freedom in history, two figures will appear before him, one ancient, one modern, whose testimony is unforgettable. The first is the father of historiography, who, like the ancient poets, dedicated the volumes of his histories to the nine muses. In developing his theme he referred to all the countries of the world as he knew it. His one theme was the freedom of the Greeks—and thus of the Europeans—when it was threatened by an Asian power, the Persian empire. Herodotus, who took part in the events of which he writes, leaves us in no doubt as to how important he considered freedom—in this case the freedom of the city-states—to the outcome of the struggle. In about the middle of his voluminous work, he writes:

> Thus Athens went from strength to strength, and proved, if proof were needed, how noble a thing freedom is, not in one respect only, but in all; for while they were oppressed under a despotic government, they had no better success in war than any of their neighbours, yet, once the yoke was flung off, they proved the finest fighters in the world. This clearly shows that, so long as they were held down by authority, they deliberately shirked their duty in the field, as slaves shirk working for their masters; but when freedom was won, then every man amongst them longed to distinguish himself.[1]

In 1830, almost 2500 years after Herodotus, a German philosopher lectured for the last time on the role of reason in history. Looking back across time and events, he came to the conclusion

[1] Quoted from Herodotus, *The Histories,* Aubrey de Sélincourt, trans., Penguin Books, Baltimore, 1964.

that everything that had happened constituted progress in the consciousness of freedom, that in the Asian empires only the ruler had been free, that in the Greek and Roman states a group of men had been free. "We, however," he said, "know that all men are in fact intrinsically free; that man, as a human being, is free." These stages, Hegel believed, were the natural divisions of history itself, the course of actual events, and he saw this course of events not merely as progress, but also as change, which must be recognized as inevitable "necessity."

Since the middle of the last century, the man of average education has been wont to add to Hegel's concept of the necessity of progress in terms of his own idea of evolution and has turned to a natural law of history for proof that his belief in progress is correct. This natural law was thought to have found confirmation when, at the turn of the last century, the freest peoples on earth, the Europeans, were about to occupy the few areas of the non-European world that had not yet been incorporated into their system, to divide them by peaceful treaties, and by means of an enlightened, benevolent colonial rule to lead their populations to freedom. It seemed beyond all doubt that European hegemony as guarantor for general progress toward freedom was desirable, necessary, and in fact already assured.

Then came the turning point. Even in the past, intra-European struggles had precipitated the great crises of European colonial rule. For the areas outside the European continent the war of 1914 brought not only a crisis, but the beginning of the end of European domination. In the Western world itself one began to sense that the optimistic systems that had interpreted the course of history as a road to freedom were European systems and that in the future one would not be able to incorporate the far parts of the earth into a Western system, but rather would have to think in terms of a plurality of cultures and courses of history, whose connections would remain obscure for some time. At the same time, however, it became obvious in Europe that the arsenal of power had grown much more rapidly than the marshaling of individual freedom. The proprietor of this arsenal was the modern state. It had combined competence to tax, to administer justice, and to raise arms and had extended its amassed authority homogenously over wide areas, developed it, and thus formed nations. By universal military conscription this state had created a formidable instrument of force *vis-à-vis* its neighbors, but at the same time it had prepared for its own population the mass slaughter of dedicated persons that we have experienced in the wars of this century. On the battlefields of 1914–18 the freest of the free died in countless numbers; it was a mass slaughter of the self-sacrificing élites, of the creative talents. It was no less destructive of culture than the bombs of the Second World War; it opened that realm of silence in which the usurpers of 1933 could speak and act. In the meantime, obligatory schooling had made education a function of the large nation state; in critical times the state placed the press under its control and in important realms created a uniform and intimidated public opinion on crucial issues which reduced the individual to insignificance—all the more readily since in the inflation he lost what had heretofore been the main support of his independent existence, his modest possessions. The churches, too, came to feel the pressure of all this and acquiesced. When finally, concentration camps and new methods of torture were discovered and their use extended from wartime duress to the regular course of politics, then power assumed those terrible features that have characterized the history of our century for all time.

In the stillness that followed, when the noise of battle had died away and the wounds began to heal, the word freedom rang out with a different sound. Freedom could no longer be taken for granted; it was no longer the natural result of an historical process. It became again a gift of God, which, entrusted to man, is constantly endangered. Like the human personality, freedom was understood to be a precious and fragile product of history, which could be lost and destroyed. Can it be that the history of the Western world has again become a "special case: Europe," an historical curiosity, and that the events that take place on these foothills of Asia are incomprehensible and a matter of indifference to the rest of the world?

The history of freedom is not a peculiarly European phenomenon. In the seventeeth century the Dutch took the idea of independence across the seas, through storms and nameless deprivations, hunting down the oppressors of freedom wherever they could find them, and finally established a mighty empire on the other side of the earth, which, although it served their purposes, did not correspond to the spirit of Dutch freedom in every respect. There on the Moluccas the spirit of their homeland confronted them in the person of an Indonesian orankai. Without having studied natural law at a Western university, this nobleman found in the depths of his misery as a prisoner words of unforgettable pride: the gods had created the wind and the sea to help and further the Indonesian and the Dutchman alike. Though he well realized that in insight and wealth the Dutch were far superior to the native inhabitants of the islands, "nevertheless to love one's freedom was as indigenous to them as to the Dutch." Spoken by a man who opposed the colonial trade monopoly, this most excellent substantiation of the truth of Hugo Grotius' convictions about natural rights was recorded by a native of Basel, a soldier, whom the Dutch had appointed to speak with the prisoner.

The history of all parts of the earth and all cultures has confirmed that freedom belongs to the nature of man, but that it is at the same time a constantly endangered, subtle spiritual endowment which threatens to escape from him who possesses it just when he believes that he is defending it most effectively. To be sure, the archetypal experience of European freedom occurred in the struggle of the small Greek states against the Persian empire, and, to be sure, in modern times the threat to a free life derives from the nature of the modern state, which would draw everything into its service. But the small state itself has again and again gone through modifications, and in its own soil, sometimes simply in the process of growing wealthy, freedom developed into its opposite.

The discipline of history was founded in order to preserve these modifications in human memory. Awareness of such modifications has been a contributing factor whenever someone has undertaken to reflect more deeply upon events and to express his thoughts in the works of recorded history. The old Swiss citizen and the new one of Valerius Anshelm's time, the simple old Florentine and the new generation of those who gained riches quickly—*la gente nuova e i subiti guadagni*—of Dante's and Machiavelli's time, the old free Roman of Cato's mettle and the Roman of Tacitus' time, who had gained his pinnacle and become powerful but lost his freedom—these are the contrasts that have inspired some of the most important works of historiography. The essence of humanism itself took shape in these polarities.

The history of freedom presents a rich and variegated picture to the eyes of the historian. Freedom is no longer the glowing, iridescent sphere that hung like a mystical composition in the sunny afternoon sky of the time before 1914. It has become a spectrum, and each of its colors has been seen and experienced anew. Once again we can see the earliest form of freedom, the self-government of the small peoples of ancient times, and we can see how it was lost in the Roman Empire. Once again we can distinguish empires that preserved something of the freedom of conquered peoples or allowed this freedom to be revived, such as the imperia of the Middle Ages, of the Carolingians and Ottonians; and we think with new respect of the Holy Roman Empire of the German Nation with its pre-Napoleonic form, which, though scorned by the nineteenth century, had survived so much longer than its short-lived imitations in the decades after 1870. Within the nation states themselves we can see again the salutary survival of older, smaller forms of communal life; we recognize the duchies of southern France, the cities of Champagne, the imperial cities and provinces of Germany, in which Pirckheimer and Luther were born, in which Goethe ultimately was possible. Above all, however, the group of small states that in many parts of Europe have for centuries been the mainstays of healthy lawfulness, thriving economy, and brilliant culture lives with a new glow in our memory: the cities of Flanders and Brabant, Aragon and Castile, the cities of the Hanseatic League, and, most vividly, those small states of central and northern Italy, in Lombardy and Tuscany, which cultivated so much that still speaks directly to the spirit of our age.

The small state with its self-government and freedom, but also the small state as the discrete unit of the healthy nation state, a form that has its own group of equal, autonomous, free, and devoted men—this constitutes the beauty and dignity of the late Middle Ages and early modern times. To be sure, the systems of balances, which one encounters when one turns from the small and middle-sized states to the larger and largest states of Europe before this century, were a matter of *raison d'état* and self-interest. But the theory of balance was at the same time an idea of freedom, for it was conceived in the classical age of freedom and practiced by the two powers that, in an alliance that was strange if only by virtue of its disproportionateness, had to guarantee the independence of its individual members: Holland and England, the defenders of the politics of balance in the eighteenth century.

In the meantime, however, a wholly different conception of freedom had sprung up, which is more prominent in the mind of the average man than the freedom of a community of states: the idea of freedom of the individual. The legal liberties of the individual are not a late product of the Enlightenment, as is often believed. In the Middle Ages each little group of men had its own particular liberties of which it was proud, its privileges, as they were called. On the toll-free road, in the free faubourg, the tradesmen enjoyed liberties different from those of the episcopal city, the bourg. The seafaring merchant of one city paid toll whereas another was given free passage. Each person took pride and pleasure in such rights, which he regarded as individual rights. Even those liberties and rights that were later given the elevated name of human rights were originally privileges. As promulgated by the Magna Carta, protection from arbitrary arrest was a legal liberty accorded the English barons; in Luther's Germany, freedom of religion, the right to choose between the Catholic and the Lutheran confessions, was a privilege reserved for the sovereign of a given state. But these privileges of the governors were at the same time liberties—liberties in which the governed also took pleasure, because, by virtue of their rulers, they, too, could enjoy freedom. In the late sixteenth century there was, to be sure, a minority that deduced from the freedom of religion accorded the governors a freedom of religion for all. But this freedom was for the time being nothing more than the right to emigrate rather than pay with one's life when one had made an improvident choice of confession.

Every human right that the constitutions of the North American states later came to record and extend to all citizens of their respective states has its own proper, interesting history in the preceding experience of Europe. One would have to recount the history of the Western world in order to trace these rights to their roots. The British Isles have of course a particular place in the early history of human rights, for it was Anglo-Saxons who catalogued these rights in North America and prepared them to be adopted in the constitutions of revolutionary France. But there is not a country in Europe that does not appear at some point in the early history of these rights, whether by virtue of one man's contribution to the whole or by virtue of parallel developments in its own tradition.

In the course of the nineteenth and early twentieth centuries, human rights became the common property of all citizens of liberal states. This is tantamount, historically speaking, to an elevation of all persons into the nobility, the nobility of freedom. To take an example from the German: *"Herr"* was originally a title conferred only on a nobleman or a member of the clergy; now all adult males are called *"Herr."* *"Frau"* in its old form was reserved for a noble lady, who was the *domina,* the mistress, female counterpart of *"Herr,"* master. It is today the usual form of address for a woman. Great dignity and greatest danger are combined in this development. A right that is accorded to everyone changes from a special privilege to a matter of course. But one cannot summon much enthusiasm for a matter of course. It loses value. People begin to forget. It is always a dangerous moment when something for which men have fought long and hard has been won. Because in the twin concept of freedom and democracy the heavier accent continues to fall upon democracy, there is danger that the extraordinary quality of the history of legal liberties will be forgotten. With good reason, a catalogue of the rights of men and of citizens appears as a preamble to certain constitutions, preceding all the specific provisions of the constitution in question and occupying the place that older documents reserved for the invocation, the appeal to God. This implies that the legal liberties of the individual are not to be accorded at the discretion of a majority; they derive from a higher law and deserve particular respect because they are particularly endangered. What guarantees them? Only the belief of all persons in their dignity and necessity.

Since, however, the individual is no longer a citizen of medieval dignity but in most cases simply an inhabitant, since a people has become a population and the individual, at least at times, has become an insignificant constituent of the masses, it is not surprising that one hears serious and unquestionably sincere voices express the conviction that the belief in freedom is eroding.

Between the old doctrine and the new reality as we experience it something has intruded, which has crippled the old belief. Not everyone can find a proper response to the modern Satiricus who declares that in daily life freedom has been reduced to the possibility of crossing the street at a pedestrian crossing, with a green light, escorted by a policeman, and at a dead run. He who hesitates is lost. And, truly, how many faces that thirty years ago gazed unencumbered into the world are now distorted with fear, staring fixedly at the motorized citizen wondering if he will spare one's life? Something of this fear remains in the face of the modern city dweller until his death, even when he is not on the streets. Freedom and fear are opposites. Technology is power, and power is inimical to every form of freedom.

When a belief threatens to erode, it can be strengthened by deeds. One reads in the newspapers that in a country bordering on Switzerland 2200 children from one to fourteen years old are killed in traffic every year. How many are killed in all of Europe? How would it be if, by means of proper laws, we put an end to this Herodian infanticide, which takes place daily before our eyes? If we were prepared to value the lives of our children more than tourism, highway traffic, and promotion of the economy, it would be possible. How easy it would be if we really wanted to, and how difficult it is since so few want it.

The danger that threatens in the East is grantedly as great as that in the days of Herodotus, and perhaps greater. But freedom is not saved solely by staring in that direction and talking about a war of nerves. The particular lack of freedom that we know in modern times derives from a political technique discovered in the West, and its historical roots lie, not in the minds of 1917 and 1933, but deeper. Around 1921 one tended in Italy to describe Fascism as a movement of motorcyclists. The roots of this evil are still healthy and viable, even if they are hidden.

The all-too-intimate alliance of the modern state with the economy is not a matter of course, nor does it lie in the nature of things. We have yet to see whether this alliance can be brought into harmony with the preservation of the culture. The freedom of the church has not yet been discussed. In late antiquity and the Middle Ages, the church opposed the excessive power of the state. After this tension had been largely overcome in later times, and national and state churches had been founded everywhere, strong religious impulses in the nineteenth century were obliged once again to dissociate themselves from the state and to establish free churches, for the sake of schools, if for no other reason. For it was found that not only are piety and humility not always indigenous to the state, even politeness may not be.

Freedom of culture owes as much to the tradition of freedom of the church as it does to the state. The universities' struggle for freedom was directed as sharply against the state as against the church. And all cultural creativity derives ultimately from the mind of the individual. Jacob Burckhardt saw the essence of culture precisely in this spontaneity of the individual and in his freedom. "Basically," he wrote in 1876, "we are strangers everywhere, and our true home is a remarkable amalgam of the truly earthly and the spiritual and remote." Thus he was able to see the highest incarnation of freedom in the ascetics of the Egyptian desert, in the Greek philosophers of the Stoic and Pythagorean schools, and in Saint Severin at the time of the tribal migrations. For him, poverty, frugality, and simplicity in one's life were the surest guarantees of intellectual freedom and creative power.

The memories of freedom are so precious and so much endangered that in every age a group of men has found its life mission in collecting and examining them, and in keeping them accessible. In political matters, too, there is not enough greatness scattered about the earth for one people to be able to say, "We are sufficient unto ourselves." The discipline of history as a whole is one of the functions of the community, for whose sake William of Orange called the University of Leiden, when he founded it, a *praesidium libertatis,* a bulwark of freedom. Knowledge of the examples of freedom in all times and all parts of the earth is a spiritual patrimony that, although it can be distorted in certain places and certain peoples, cannot be obliterated. It proves its fruitfulness in each new generation that seeks to deduce the whole from intimations.

The historian believes in the power of memory because he knows that in every individual intellect there is a secret force that responds to truth. A sentence in one of Benedetto Croce's last books remains unforgettable:

The moral deed is not entitled to accommodate itself to what will happen next or to what has just happened; for even if one posits that the community of man will fall into slavery for one or two centuries or even a millennium, that it will be reduced to an exhausted, minimal freedom and to a minimum of creative intellect, nevertheless this incident—and it is an incident, for in the face of eternity it is only an instant—does not affect the moral deed in any way; it does not influence this deed's appointed task and cannot change it. For the appointed task of this deed is to ignite freedom and in each instance to use suitable means and suitable powers for this purpose.

The forms in which freedom lives are manifold and so various that they cannot be reduced to a single formula. Historical experience warns us not to identify freedom with a certain form of government and certainly not with a written constitution. There are peoples who have been free without written constitutions, and others who have had written constitutions yet lived in slavery. There are small democracies that have buried their freedom, as there are great nations in which freedom has flourished. The spirit of freedom, too, blows where it will. But it blows where men have contact with one another. It is a matter not only of forms and laws, but of the human beings who practice them.

PART III

THE DILEMMA OF POWER IN THE DEMOCRATIC AGE

Chapter 13

POLITICS IN A NEW KEY: SCHÖNERER

Carl E. Schorske

I

"People who were not born then," wrote Robert Musil of the Austrian *fin de siècle,* "will find it difficult to believe, but the fact is that even then time was moving faster than a cavalry camel. . . . But in those days, no one knew what it was moving towards. Nor," Musil continues, "could anyone quite distinguish between what was above and what below, between what was moving forward and what backward."[1]

The social forces that rose to challenge the liberal ascendancy could not fail to baffle an observer who viewed them through a liberal conceptual screen, and with a liberal's expectations of history. In the 1860s the Austrian liberals, though neither utopians nor believers in perfectibility, had rather clear notions of "what was above and what below, . . . what was moving forward and what backward." Socially, they believed that the aristocratic class, having been "above" through most of history, was either being liberalized or sinking into a harmless, ornamental hedonism. The principles and programs that made up the liberal creed were designed to supercede systematically those of "the feudals," as the aristocrats were pejoratively called. Constitutional monarchy would replace aristocratic absolutism; parliamentary centralism, aristocratic federalism. Science would replace religion. The German nationality would serve as tutor and teacher to bring up the subject peoples, rather than keep them ignorant bondsmen as the feudals had done. Thus nationality itself would ultimately serve as a principle of popular cohesion in a multi-

[1] Robert Musil, *The Man without Qualities,* Eithone Wilkins and Ernst Kaiser, trans. (London, 1953), p. 8.

national state. "The Germans in Austria," wrote the Liberal leader J. N. Berger in 1861, "should strive not for political hegemony, but for cultural hegemony among the peoples of Austria." They should "carry culture to the east, transmit the propaganda of German intellection, German science, German humanism."[2] Finally laissez faire would break the arbitrary rule of privilege in the economic sphere and make merit, rather than privilege or charity, the basis of economic reward.

In all these aspects of their program, the Austro-Liberals knew themselves to be combating the socially superior and the historically anterior: they saw themselves as leading what was below and moving forward against what was above and backward. If the common people could not yet be trusted, since they did not always understand, the spread of rational culture would one day provide the prerequisite for a broadly democratic order. Popular power would increase only as a function of rational responsibility.

Austrian society failed to respect these liberal coordinates of order and progress. During the last quarter of the nineteenth century, the program the liberals had devised against the upper classes occasioned the explosion of the lower. The liberals succeeded in releasing the political energies of the masses, but against themselves rather than against their ancient foes. Every shot aimed at the enemy above produced a hostile salvo from below. A German nationalism articulated against aristocratic cosmopolitans was answered by Slavic patriots clamoring for autonomy. When the liberals soft-pedaled their Germanism in the interest of the multinational state, they were branded as traitors to nationalism by an anti-liberal German *petite-bourgeoisie*. Laissez faire, devised to free the economy from the fetters of the past, called forth the Marxist revolutionaries of the future. Catholicism, routed from the school and the courthouse as the handmaiden of aristocratic oppression, returned as the ideology of peasant and artisan, for whom liberalism meant capitalism and capitalism meant Jew. By the end of the century even the Jews, to whom Austro-liberalism had offered emancipation, opportunity, and assimilation to modernity, began to turn their

---

[2] J. N. Berger, *Zur Lösung der oesterreichischen Verfassungsfrage* (Vienna, 1861), p. 19, cited in Richard Charmatz, *Adolf Fischhof* (Stuttgart and Berlin, 1910), p. 19.

backs on their benefactors. The failure of liberalism left the Jew a victim, and the most persuasive answer to victimization was the flight to a national home that Zionism proferred. Where other nationalists threatened the Austrian state with disruption, the Zionists threatened secession.

Far from rallying the masses against the old ruling class above, then, the liberals unwittingly summoned from the social deeps the forces of a general disintegration. Strong enough to dissolve the old political order, liberalism could not master the social forces that that dissolution released, and that generated new centrifugal thrust under liberalism's tolerant but inflexible aegis. The new anti-liberal mass movements—Czech nationalism, Pan-Germanism, Christian Socialism, Social Democracy and Zionism—rose from below to challenge the trusteeship of the educated middle class, to paralyze its political system, and to undermine its confidence in the rational structure of history.

Not all the new movements, national and ideological, which assaulted liberal ascendancy from the flanks and from below represented departures from liberal political culture. The non-German nationalist parties and the Social Democrats were the least difficult for the doctrinaire liberals to comprehend. Having been involved for half a century in a struggle for German national self-determination, the German liberals could understand, even when they deplored or rejected, the Czechs' increasingly radical demands for equality in legal and cultural institutions. The Social Democrats, formally founded as a party in 1889, likewise offered few conumdrums to the liberal mind. Indeed, of all the filial *révoltés* aspiring to replace the fathers, none bore the paternal features more pronouncedly than the Social Democrats. Their rhetoric was rationalist, their secularism militant, their faith in education virtually unlimited. True, the principal Social Democratic leader, Victor Adler, had rebelled against rationalism as a student, when he espoused German nationalism and Wagner's ideas of social integration on a folkish basis.[3] Yet in subsequently embracing the Marxist creed, Adler affirmed a fundamental allegiance to the rationalistic heritage of science and law.

[3] William J. McGrath, *Wagnerianism in Austria. The Regeneration of Culture through the Spirit of Music.* Unpublished Ph.D. dissertation (Berkeley, 1965), 8–17, 50–51.

The liberals themselves felt the socialists' affiliation to their culture across the issues that divided them. Liberals could condemn Social Democrats for their utopianism, for their absurd demands for a welfare state before "the most primitive prerequisites" of political enlightenment had yet been created.[4] But neither the impatient rationalism nor the excessive cosmopolitanism of the socialists destroyed the liberals' sense of kinship with them. Though one might reject a socialist's position, one could argue with him in the same language. To the liberal mind, the Social Democrat was unreasonable, but not irrational.

Other movements resulting from the liberal failure to bring the masses into the state represented a far more revolutionary break from the tradition of Austro-liberalism, and evoked a more traumatic response in the liberal community. These movements were Pan-Germanism, Christian Socialism, and—in answer to both of these—Zionism. Against the dry, rational politics of Austro-liberalism, the powerful leaders of these movements developed what became known as "the sharper key," a mode of political behavior at once more abrasive, more creative, and more satisfying to the life of feeling than the deliberative style of the liberals. Two leading virtuosi of the new key—Georg von Schönerer of the Pan-Germans and Karl Lueger of the Christian Socials—became the inspirers and political models of Adolf Hitler. A third, Theodor Herzl, pioneered in providing Hitler's victims with the most appealing and powerful political response yet devised to the gentile reign of terror. Thus even before Vienna's intellectual greats blazed trails to the twentieth century's higher culture, three of her sons pioneered in its post-rational politics.

Schönerer, Lueger, and Herzl all began their careers as political liberals and then apostasized to organize masses neglected or rejected by liberalism in ascendancy. All possessed the peculiar gift of answering the social and spiritual needs of their followers by composing ideological collages—collages put together of fragments of modernity, glimpses of futurity, and resurrected remnants of a half-forgotten past. In liberal eyes, these ideological mosaics were mystifying and repulsive, confounding the "above" with the "below," the "forward" with the "backward." Yet their political artists grasped a social psychological reality which the liberal could not see. They expressed in politics a rebellion against

[4] *Neue Freie Presse,* March 10, 1897.

reason and law which soon became more widespread. In their manner of secession from the liberal political tradition and in the form of the challenge they posed to its values, the new politicians adumbrated a concept of life and a mode of action that, transcending the purely political, constituted part of the wider cultural revolution that ushered in the twentieth century. We shall consider here the case of the man who pioneered this development, Georg von Schönerer.[5]

Georg von Schönerer organized the radical German nationalists in 1882, and led them into extreme anti-Semitic politics. Although he never succeeded in forming a powerful party, he elevated anti-Semitism into a major disruptive force in Austrian political life. Perhaps more than any other single figure, he was responsible for the new stridency in Austrian politics, the "sharper key" of raucous debate and street-brawling that marked the last decade of the nineteenth century.

A curious compound of gangster, philistine and aristocrat, von Schönerer conceived of himself as the militant knight-redeemer of the German *Volk*. He rejoiced in epithets redolent of chivalry: "Knight George," or—after his estate in Lower Austria— "the Knight of Rosenau." The official song of his party, *"Ritter Georg hoch!,"* was sung to the tune with which the Austrians traditionally honored their military hero, Prince Eugene of Savoy, "the Noble Knight" who had saved Austria from the Turk.[6] It is striking that Schönerer appealed to democratic students and to a frustrated lower middle and artisan class for his program of revolutionary national subversion in the archaistic garb of knight. His aristocratic pretension offers a clue both to psychological sources of his own rancorous rebellion against liberal culture and to the social sensibilities of the strata that he organized.

Georg von Schönerer acquired his title by honest inheritance, but he was far from an aristocrat of the blood. He came from the new industrial class. His father had received his patent of nobility from the hands of a grateful Emperor for services as an engineer and railway administrator. Georg was thus the son of

[5] An extended version of this essay, treating all three figures, may be found under the title "Politics in a New Key: an Austrian Triptych," in *Journal of Modern History*, XXXIX, No. 4 (December, 1967).

[6] Eduard Pichl, *Georg Schönerer*, 6 vols. in 3 (Oldenburg i.O./Berlin, 1938), Vol. II, p. 516.

a self-made man, "a man with qualities." He spent his life in oscillation between living up to his inheritance and living it down.

Matthias Schönerer: what a father, what an archetypical man of the early industrial era! In 1828, when only twenty-one, he built Austria's first railway—a horse-drawn affair—and thereafter several steam-powered lines.[7] From a study tour of railway engineering in the United States, he returned to Vienna in 1838 with the first steam locomotive, the "Philadelphia." He thereupon organized the first locomotive and car-building works to eliminate Austria's dependence on foreign equipment, and brought in American locomotive engineers to train native drivers.[8] Matthias' perquisites of office included a residence in Vienna's new South Station; in this very modern stable was born the future savior of German nationalism in 1842. The elder Schönerer displayed the talents of an administrator no less than those of a builder.[9] In an industry in which the closest collaboration between engineer and banker was called for, Schönerer developed excellent working relations with the great financial tycoons of the day. Whether through his diplomatic talent or his indispensability as a railway builder, he managed to work with two of the most bitter rivals in Austrian high finance: on the one hand, with the House of Rothschild, on the other with Baron Simon Sina, who was often associated in his railway ventures with the Jewish house of Arnstein and Eskeles. When the competition between these great private bankers took the more formidable form of a struggle between the colossal new joint stock banks— Sina's *Crédit mobilier* and the Rothschilds' *Oesterreichische Credi-*

---

[7] Schönerer's drive, business acumen, and ruthlessness emerged in this first venture, where he replaced the chief designer, his own teacher, by siding with economy-minded directors against him. See Oesterreichischer Eisenbahnbeamtenverein, *Geschichte der Eisenbahnen der Oesterreichisch-ungarischen Monarchie,* 5 vols. (Vienna, Teschen, Leipzig, 1897–1908), I, i, 99–101.

[8] *Ibid.,* 167–68, 174–75.

[9] An urn presented to Schönerer by his loyal personnel in 1846, when he was director of the Vienna-Gloggnitz Railway, celebrated his many talents with the iconographic variety characteristic of the age: Minerva stood for "Civil Engineering"; Mercury was elevated from his traditional role as trickster and divine messenger to represent "Administration"; a locomotive joined the pantheon to present "Railway Management"; while an anvil, labeled "Machine Construction," completed the quartet of symbols. Cf. Würzbach, *Oesterreichische Nationalbiographie,* Vol. XXXI, 149.

tanstalt,[10] Matthias Schönerer could be found high in the councils of the railway enterprises of both groups. In 1834, the
Rothschilds called upon him as an expert to determine whether
they should power their great projected *Nordbahn* by horse or
by steam.[11] It was this railroad that Schönerer's son was to
make the center of his anti-Semitic nationalization crusade in
1884. Schönerer senior achieved the height of his business career
as member of the Board of Directors of the Empress Elizabeth
Railway (built 1856–60). A Rothschild-dominated enterprise,
its board was thoroughly interlocked with that of the *Creditanstalt.*[12] The vigorous engineer became a wealthy man, collaborator of bankers, liberals, Jews, stock-jobbers and Imperial
bureaucrats: all those social types to whose destruction his son
Georg would devote his political life—after his father's death.

In 1860, on the occasion of the dedication of the Empress
Elizabeth Railway, the grateful Emperor honored Matthias
Schönerer for his services as railway builder with a patent of
nobility. Like others proud of his achievements in the world of
industry and trade, von Schönerer chose an escutcheon appropriate to his vocation: a winged wheel in the colors of technology,
silver and blue. His motto, too, *"Recta sequi* (to follow the
right)" conformed well to the ethic, if not always to the practice,
of his class and generation.[13] Less typical was Matthias' decision
to celebrate his social achievement by the purchase of a feudal
holding. He bought the manor of Rosenau near Zwettl, a four-
teenth-century estate with a charming castle from the era of
Maria Theresa. In England, time had hallowed the passage of the
merchant into the squirearchy via the country house. In Austria,
nobility for service had become common, but its normal badge
and accompaniment was higher culture, not a country seat. The
acquisition of a noble's estate was not in good taste; it would
carry some stigma of social presumptuousness.

[10] Creditanstalt-Bankverein, *Ein Jahrhundert Creditanstalt-Bankverein*
(Vienna, 1957), 2, 6–7. For the rivalry of the two giants in winning con-
trol of the railroads—from the government as well as each other—see
Oesterreichischer Eisenbahnbeamtenverein, *Geschichte,* I, i, 321–25.

[11] Schönerer counselled steam. Cf. *ibid.,* I, i, 133.

[12] *Ibid.,* I, i, 447–49; Creditanstalt-Bankverein, *Ein Jahrehundert,* 31.
See also the interesting account of the construction of the new company as
seen through the experience of the Hamburg entrepreneur, Ernst Merck,
in Percy Ernst Schramm, *Hamburg, Deutschland und die Welt* (Munich,
1943), 528–37.

[13] Würzbach, *op. cit.,* XXXI, 148–49.

The elder Schönerer felt untouched by such qualms. Nor did he, like other self-made men of his era, seem concerned to foster in his offspring the humanistic culture integral to the social style of Austria's *haute bourgeoisie* and especially of the service nobility which Schönerer now entered. The two of his five children about whom something is known were both intellectual middle-brows by the standards of their class. Alexandrine von Schönerer, Georg's sister, shared the organizing talents of her father and brother. But she also shared the ruling Viennese passion for the theater. After some experience as an actress, Alexandrine turned her talents and her substantial legacy to account as a theatrical entrepreneur. In 1889, she bought the *Theater an der Wien,* one of the oldest centers of popular folk theater. Under her management, it became the outstanding theater for operetta, with the hedonistic works of Johann Strauss and Millöcker replacing the more astringent social morality plays of Nestroy and Anzengruber. As a member of the Austrian cosmopolitan theatrical community which numbered many Jews, Alexandrine explicitly rejected her brother's anti-Semitic politics. Both as enthusiast for the theater-as-entertainment and as enterpreneurial spirit, she remained loyal to the culture of middle-brow Viennese liberalism.[14]

Georg seems to have suffered more deeply than his sister from the ambiguities bedeviling the child of an energetic parvenu. In Matthias Schönerer's education of his son, one again suspects a certain eccentricity in this otherwise regular royal entrepreneur. He sent the boy not to the *Gymnasium,* usual for his class, but to the technically oriented *Oberrealschule.* The fact that Georg changed schools several times suggests some kind of adjustment problem.[15] In 1859, Georg entered the school of commerce in Dresden. In the following years, when his father acquired knighthood and a landed estate, Georg changed course. He left the business school in 1861, and completed his education in two agricultural academies. In the spirit if not under the pressure of his father, Georg thus prepared himself for inheriting the newly

[14] Nagl, Zeidler and Castle, *Deutsch-Oesterreichische Literaturgeschichte,* 4 vols. (Vienna, 1899–1937), III, 798–800.

[15] Pichl states that Georg transferred from the *Oberrealschule* to a private school in Dresden as the result of a conflict with the instructor in religion. Pichl, *Schönerer,* I, 21–22.

acquired estate and title—and for making the life of a country squire pay. Aristocratic pretension and economic realism were to be harmonized in the second Ritter von Rosenau if not in the first.

It was appropriate therefore that Georg should have put the capstone on his education by serving as a steward or farm manager on the estates of Austria's greatest aristocratic entrepreneur, Johann Adolf Prince Schwarzenberg. Prince Schwarzenberg was to the economic modernization of the landed aristocracy what his gifted brother, Felix, Franz Joseph's mentor, had been to its political *aggiornamento* in 1848–52.[16] Educating himself in England in the latest techniques of capitalist agriculture, food processing, and mineral extraction, Johann Adolph transformed his ancient estates into a vastly profitable landed empire. He was called "the prince among farmers and the farmer among princes." As political leader in the Bohemian Diet, he was a pillar of extreme aristocratic conservatism, but as entrepreneur he operated in the same bourgeois circle of finance and industry in which Matthias Schönerer also moved. Prince Schwarzenberg served on the founding committee and as the first President of the Board of Directors (*Verwaltungsrat*) of the *Oesterreichische Creditanstalt,* which was so deeply intertwined with the Board of the Empress Elizabeth Railway.[17] Matthias Schönerer would have had ready access to the Prince through their many common financial associates. Though specific evidence is lacking, one may suppose that the father used his connections to secure so valuable an entree for his son into the technocratic aristocracy. In any event, the future Knight of Rosenau could scarcely have found a more promising apprenticeship than on the estates of Prince Schwarzenberg.

Where most sons of the successful middle class in Austria entered an urban vocation, Georg Schönerer thus became committed to becoming a modest replica of Prince Schwarzenberg, taking science and the entrepreneurial spirit to the land as a modern manor-lord. Whether this career emerged from the wishes

[16] Cf. "Die Grafen und Fürsten zu Schwarzenberg," *Oesterreichische Revue,* 4. Jhrg. (1866), No. 2, 85–167.

[17] Heinrich Benedikt, *Die wirtschaftliche Entwicklung in der Franz-Joseph-Zeit,* Wiener Historische Studien, Vol. IV (Vienna-Munich, 1958), 38, 42–43.

of the father or the ambitions of the son, we do not know.[18]

Certain it is that Georg strove with dogged if graceless conviction to fill the role of *grand seigneur*. Yet within the framework of the honest, "noble" life of Rosenau, he gradually prepared to rebel against virtually everything his father had built his life upon: Habsburg loyalty, capitalism, interracial tolerance, and financial speculation. As a frustrated psuedo-aristocrat, Georg prepared himself almost unconsciously to lead those social strata who chafted under the rule of the industrial bourgeoisie from which he himself sprang. Revolting masses and rebellious son would in due course find each other.

The process of transformation of the Knight of Rosenau into a nationalist demagogue proceeded slowly, and was completed only after his father's death in 1881. Thanks to his fortune, his energy, and his practical knowledge of rural needs, Schönerer first established in his home district a firm base for a political career. He formed and financed agricultural improvement associations, equivalents of the American grange, and volunteer fire departments. For his work in his own constituency, he chose the ideological symbol of the *Volkskaiser*, Joseph II, who had made it his policy to bring the fruits of science to the land and to build a strong peasantry. Schönerer erected plaques in various villages of his district showing Joseph with his hand on the plow.[19] Here the liberal cult of science and public welfare mingled with Habsburg loyalty: Schönerer was clearly still within the framework of the Austro-liberal Josephan tradition.

On this secure rural base, Schönerer began his parliamentary career. Elected to the *Reichsrat* in 1873, he joined the *Fortschrittsklub*,[20] the left-democratic wing of the liberal camp. He established an early reputation as a defender of the farmer's interest. Soon he came into conflict with the dominant liberal forces. Two issues first aroused Schönerer's dissatisfaction with

---

[18] All biographical information on the son here utilized derives from the fulsome but uncritical Pichl, who explores no problems which might alter the epic stature of his hero. Cf. Pichl, *Schönerer*, Vol. I, 21–26, unless otherwise indicated. Pichl's complete silence on Matthias' interests, character, and relations with Georg suggests the possibility of tension.

[19] Pichl, *Schönerer*, I, 23, note 2.

[20] The *Klub* was the basic unit of party organization within the parliament. A party was a loose structure generally composed of several such groups.

his colleagues: their indifference to social problems and their inadequate vigor in combating Slavic nationalism. On the latter front Schönerer scored his first great success in weakening Austroliberalism. The German Liberals as a whole were dividing on the nationality question. Concessions to the militant Czechs meant breaking the German middle class hold upon Bohemia and Moravia, and thus weakening liberalism. On the other hand, failure to make concessions might, by driving the Slavic peoples into still sharper reaction, threaten the Empire itself. Either way, the Liberals had no principle to bind together their national, their cosmopolitan, and their social loyalties. Their best defense seemed the maintenance of the restricted suffrage system, which kept the radical nationalist masses away from the polls.[21] If their national values suffered some loss, the integrity of the multinational empire could still be maintained, and their legal and social ascendancy only slightly weakened.

After the divided Liberals fell from power in 1879, Schönerer and an important group of young University intellectuals who had adopted him as their parliamentary representative openly rebelled against their party's line. They placed the principles of democracy and German nationalism ahead of imperial stability and middle-class oligarchy.[22] In the so-called Linz program (1882), this group formulated a platform which combined radical democracy, social reform, and nationalism in a manner resembling the contemporaneous phenomenon of Populism in the United States. In its support for home industries and "honest labor," a compulsory training certificate for artisans, and prohibition of house-to-house peddling, the program took account of the grievances of the anti-Semitic Viennese artisan associations. These were survivors of an earlier economic era now hard-pressed by the advent of the factory, the retail store, and the Jewish peddler who sold factory products to the former customers of the stationary artisan. The program was not, however, directly anti-Semitic.

[21] Cf. Ernst von Plener, *Erinnerungen*, 3 vols. (Stuttgart and Leipzig, 1911–21), III, 90–91.

[22] These included, among others, Victor Adler, later leader of Social Democracy; Robert Pattai, later Christian Social leader; Heinrich Friedjung, the liberal historian; and Engelbert Pernerstorfer. The group had its origins primarily in a University student organization, the *Leseverein der deutschen Studenten Wiens* (1871–78). See McGrath, *op. cit.*, Chs. I and IV.

The Linz program carried overtones of a *Grossdeutsch* orientation in its demands for a customs union and stronger treaty arrangements with the German Reich.[23] It did not, however, incorporate one aim that Schönerer had expressed in the Reichsrat in a moment of choler: "If only we already belonged to the German Empire!"[24] Schönerer's fellow nationalists in 1882 had not reached the point where they would wish to dissolve the Habsburg Empire entirely, and most of them never would. But they agreed with him in yoking together two of the great claims on the Austrian state which the liberals had unleashed but could neither curb nor satisfy: the demands for national ascendancy and social justice.

Schönerer expressed his synthesis of solvents in a manifesto to the *Verein der Deutschen Volkspartei* in 1881:

> We want to give lively expression to the feeling of solidarity of the German nation in Austria not only in contending with Slavdom, but also in a struggle against the exploitation of the noblest forces of the people [presumably the peasants and artisans] to the advantage of a few.[25]

Such a synthesis could encompass a rather broad front of Austro-German liberal nationalists concerned for social reform. But the front could not be stabilized. Schönerer himself pressed on to extend both terms of his synthesis to the point where they became wholly incompatible with Austro-liberalism. On the one hand he interpreted "the feeling of solidarity" to encompass not only "the Germans in Austria," but Germans everywhere. In one respect, Schönerer here revived the *Grossdeutsch* ideal of 1848, when German democratic revolutionaries sought to supplant the non-national monarchical states system with a unitary pan-German republic. During the Franco-Prussian War and with the founding of the German Empire in 1871, university students in Vienna and elsewhere had agitated for an extension of unification into the Habsburg lands. In 1878, Schönerer was elected honorary

[23] For a brief discussion of the origins of the Linz program and Schönerer's role in it, see R. G. J. Pulzer, *The Rise of Political Anti-Semitism in Germany and Austria, 1867–1938* (New York, 1964), 148–53. A deeper and more extensive analysis is to be found in McGrath, *op. cit.,* Ch. IV.

[24] December 18, 1878, cited in Pulzer, *Anti-Semitism,* 151.

[25] *Ibid.,* 152.

member of the student *Leseverein* at the same time as the aged chaplain of the Academic Legion of the 1848 Revolution. This coincidence reveals how difficult it was to distinguish "forward" from "backward," and how easily the older democratic nationalism could become reincarnated in new right-wing radical forms. Schönerer, for his part, aimed not a unitary German republic, like the democrats of 1848, but at the breakup of the "pre-slav" Habsburg monarchy in order that its western portion might be united with the Bismarckian monarchy. Not many left-wing Progressives could follow Schönerer into this conservative-revolutionary direction. But his development of anti-Austrian national loyalty found resounding echo in student circles. The universities, once centers of triumphant Austro-liberalism, became in the late seventies and eighties the scene of brawling nationalist agitation as the influence of the *Schönerianer* spread.[26]

Schönerer's second extension of his national-social program was into anti-Semitism. He made his first programatic statement against the Jews in an electoral platform in 1879. Here Schönerer characteristically linked aristocracy and people—"the interests of landed property and of productive hands" against "the heretofor privileged interests of mobile capital—and the . . . Semitic rule of money and the word [i.e., the press]. . . ." As if condemning his aged father and hence the sources of his own considerable fortune, he called for laws "against the moral and economic dangers arising out of the inadequate responsibility of founders of companies and corporation boards of directors."[27] Wider political opportunities for Schönerer as anti-Semitic radical soon opened up, and these coincided with his father's approaching death in 1881, which released his inhibited aggressions against all Matthias Schönerer stood for. The social base for his anti-liberal leadership and the psychological conditions for asserting it converged.

As in his pan-Germanism Schönerer had been anticipated by the nationalistic student associations, so in his social anti-Semitism

[26] For the Austrian student movement in general, see the nationalistic treatment by Paul Melisch, *Die deutschen Hochschulen in Oesterreich und die politisch-nationale Entwicklung nach 1848.* (Munich, 1922.) The specific question of Schönerer's connection with the student movement is best treated in McGrath, *op. cit.,* Chs. I and IV.

[27] The full text of this program is given in Pichl, *Schönerer,* I, 84–87.

he was anticipated by the artisan movement. In 1880, the first anti-Semitic "Society for the Defense of the Handworker" was founded in Vienna. In 1882, it was absorbed into the "Austrian Reform Union," at whose founding meeting Schönerer was the major speaker, declaring war on "the sucking vampire . . . that knocks . . . at the narrow-windowed house of the German farmer and craftsman"—the Jew.[28] The vicious "new key" of his rhetoric appealed to frustrated artisans no less than to Wagnerite students.

Schönerer achieved his greatest notoriety as parliamentarian in the years 1884–85, when he led the fight for the nationalization of the Nordbahn, the railway that his father had counseled the Rothschilds to construct years before. The franchise for this profitable line was due for renewal at the very time when the revolt against laissez faire was making itself felt in various strata of society. Turning the popular struggle against the bankers and brokers into anti-Semitic channels, Schönerer invested the issue with the explosive energy of his belated oedipal rebellion. He accused not only the liberals and ministers, but indirectly the court itself of "bowing before the power of the Rothschilds and their comrades," and threatened all with "colossal forcible overturns" at the hands of the people if that power were not now broken.[29] The return of the repressed in capitalist society had its analogue in the return of the repressed in Schönerer's psyche. The liberals, in the face of this outbreak of raw rancor, found themselves with their backs to the wall.

Schönerer's other targets in his anti-Semitic campaign he took more directly from the radicalized artisans of Vienna with whom he became identified. The Jewish peddler was the lower-class analogue to the Jewish department-store owner: both threatened the traditional small shopkeeper; both attracted the hostility as well as the custom of the small consumer. Finally Schönerer centered his campaign against the Jews in an attempt to restrict their emigration from Russia at the time of the pogroms. Where his father looked to American engineers for technical models for railway design, von Schönerer turned to the United States for a

---

[28] Ibid., II, 25–26; See also Hans Tietze, Die Juden Wiens (Vienna, 1933), 238–39.

[29] Cited from a speech in the Reichsrat, May 2, 1884, in Pichl, Schönerer, I, 232. For the wider issue, see ibid., 224–50; Oesterreichische Eisenbahnbeamtenverein, Geschichte, I, ii, 360–65.

legislative model for racial discrimination: the Chinese Exclusion Bill.

The anti-Semitism of Schönerer in some respects is much more central to understanding his disintegrating influence on liberal society than his nationalism as such. The Jews, as Hannah Arendt has rightly observed, were the "state-people" *par excellence* in Austria.[30] They did not constitute a nationality—not even a so-called "unhistoric" nationality like the Slovaks or Ukrainians. They owed their civic and economic existence not to their participation in a national community, such as the German or the Czech; on the contrary, their existence depended on not acquiring such a status. Even if they became assimilated completely to the culture of a given nationality, they could not outgrow the status of "converts" to that nationality. Neither allegiance to the Emperor nor allegiance to liberalism as a political system posed such difficulties. The Emperor and the liberal system offered status to the Jews without demanding nationality; they became the supranational people of the multinational state, the one folk that, in effect, stepped into the shoes of the earlier aristocracy. Their fortunes rose and fell with those of the liberal, cosmopolitan state. More important for our concerns, the fortunes of the liberal creed itself became entangled with the fate of the Jews. Thus to the degree that the nationalists tried to weaken the central power of the monarchy in their interest, the Jews were attacked in the name of every nation.

Schönerer was the strongest and most thoroughly consistent anti-Semite that Austria produced. He was equally and correspondingly the bitterest enemy of every principle of integration by which the multinational Empire could be held together: the enemy of liberalism, of socialism, of Catholicism, and of imperial authority. As a total nationalist, he could not rest content with the imperial state. The Emperor appeared to him, correctly, as compromising among the peoples into which his realm was nationally divided and the ideologies into which his realm was socially divided. If the Emperor was supranational, the Jews were subnational, the omnipresent folk-substance of the Empire, whose representatives could be found in every national and every credal grouping. In whatever group they functioned, the

[30] Hannah Arendt, *The Origins of Totalitarianism* (2nd ed., New York, 1958), especially Ch. II.

Jews never strove to dismember the Empire. That is why they became the victims of every centrifugal force as soon as, and only as long as, that force aimed to subvert the Empire.

Schönerer was the first leader of centrifugality *à outrance* to arise in the era of liberal ascendancy. No one ever espoused in such full measure *every* disruptive potentiality in the society: class, ideology, nationality, and constitution. Nationalism provided the positive center of Schönerer's faith; but since nationalism might have been satisfied without total disintegration, he needed a negative element to give coherence to his system. Anti-Semitism was that element, enabling him to be simultaneously anti-socialist, anti-capitalist, anti-Catholic, anti-liberal, and anti-Habsburg.

Schönerer never succeeded in building a great mass movement as his successors Lueger and Hitler did. His principal lasting impact was in the area of political deportment, in words and in action, where his style was as centrifugal as his ideology, but more contagious. Into the *Reichsrat,* center of liberal legality and dignity, Schönerer and his colleagues introjected the sharper key, with its raucous diapason of disorder and invective. That august body had to accustom itself to his diatribes against finance Jews, Northern Railway Jews, Jew peddlers, press Jews, Jew swindlers, and the like. These attacks on behalf of the "noble" German people were delivered in the presence of both Jews and Gentiles. It took some getting used to.

In June of 1886, Dr. Ernst von Plener, leader of the Liberal Party, a dignified lawyer and Anglophile gentleman, tried to put a term to the anti-Semitic agitation in the *Reichsrat*. He expressed his regret that the President (Speaker) "who otherwise . . . had cared so well for the dignity of the House" had permitted such vituperative tones to rend it. He hinted at a sterner use of the powers of the chair. Von Plener also proposed that the anti-Semites at last present their much-vaunted exhortations to curb the Jews in the form of legislative proposals. "Then," von Plener concluded, "we shall see what these gentlemen really intend, and then the . . . House will be given an opportunity to express its opinion concerning an agitation which is one of the most regrettable symptoms of our time."

Schönerer responded to the challenge with a vigorous combination of parliamentary action and the threat of force. He promised to bring in a variety of bills to curb the Jews. Between the promise and the fulfillment fell the threat: If the President of the House should follow the suggestion of von Plener to curb freedom of discussion on the Jewish question, "then this question could not be brought nearer to solution through proposals made and words spoken in the parliament; and in that case, the fists will have to go into action outside parliament."[31] While liberal parliamentarians condemned "the so-called anti-Semitic movement as unworthy of a civilized people," the Knight of Rosenau called for the "moral rebirth of the fatherland" by the elaboration of "legal restrictions on the Jewish exploiters of the people." Here again Schönerer used threatening rhetoric: He promised the *Reichsrat* in 1887 that if his movement did not succeed now, "the avengers will arise from our bones" and, "—to the terror of the Semitic oppressors and their hangers-on—," make good the principle, "'An eye for an eye, a tooth for a tooth.'"[32]

Political style and personal temperament in Schönerer both bore the marks of paranoia. Whether as accuser or accused, he became frequently involved in libel trials. Aggression, which brought him many followers, in the end proved his undoing. Less than a year after he had threatened the *Reichsrat* with "an eye for an eye," the noble knight broke into the offices of the *Neues Wiener Tagblatt,* and with the help of some colleagues, beat up the staff of this "Jewish rag." The editor of the paper, Moritz Szeps, was the intimate of Crown Prince Rudolf. As one of the more aggressive liberals, Szeps had been engaged in verbal and in legal duels with Schönerer before, and not always as the winner.[33] Schönerer's raid on the editorial office, however, was the first time the new style in politics took the form of trial by battle. The sharper tone in verbal combat was one thing; the *musique concrète* of physical assault another. The court sentenced Schönerer not only to a brief prison term but—most fatefully for his political career—to a suspension of political rights for five years.[34] Finally, the court decreed that Georg von

[31] Pichl, *Schönerer,* I, 300–1.

[32] *Ibid.,* 316, 318.

[33] In 1885, Szeps spent a month in jail as the result of a successful libel action brought against him by Schönerer. See Bertha Szeps-Zuckerkandl, *My Life and History,* John Sommerfield trans. (London, etc., 1938), 86, 91, 95.

[34] Oscar Karbach, "The Founder of Political Anti-Semitism," *Jewish Social Studies,* VII (1945), 20–22.

Schönerer was to be "von" no more. Losing his title, the Knight of Rosenau lost the one inheritance from his father that he had truly prized. In attempting to destroy his father's world, he destroyed the symbol of higher status that was the reward for success in it. Schönerer's career of political destruction ended in self-destruction. He soon returned to that oblivion whence his father had begun.

The perplexing combination of elements in Schönerer's makeup reminds us again of the serious historical content in Musil's ironic remark, that in that age no one quite knew how to distinguish between what was above and what below, between what was moving forward and what backward. Both in his person and in his ideology, Schönerer combined the most diverse and contradictory elements. Desperately aspiring to aristocracy, he might have succeeded as a Prussian Junker, but never as an Austrian cavalier. For the Austrian nobiliary tradition demanded a grace, a plasticity, and, one might add, a tolerance for the wrongs and ills of this world that were wholly foreign to Schönerer's makeup. Most socially aspiring sons of successful Viennese middle-class families, especially those of the service nobility, acquired aesthetic culture as an acceptable substitute for entry into the historical aristocracy of pedigree. Schönerer—or his father—tried a more drastic course, forcing the issue by acquiring a feudal estate and becoming a baronial technocrat. Not a cavalier, but a knight by *force majeur*. Correspondingly, Schönerer vented his political passion not against the aristocracy whose circles he failed to penetrate, but against his father's world of liberals, the higher bourgeoisie whom he had hoped to leave behind. His career of political destruction seems to have had its personal sources in the thwarted ambition of the undereducated and over-extended *arriviste* son of a *parvenu* father.

In the pursuit of his revolution of rancor, Schönerer constructed his ideology out of attitudes and values from many eras and many social strata: aristocratic élitism and enlightened despotism, anti-Semitism and democracy, 1848 *Grossdeutsch* democracy and Bismarckian nationalism, medieval chivalry and anti-Catholicism, guild restrictions and state ownership of public utilities. Every one of these pairs of values the nineteenth century liberal would have seen as contradictory. But there was a common denominator in this set of ideational fractions: total negation of the liberal élite and its values.

As Schönerer was an angry man, so his ideological *montage* appealed to angry people: artisans cheated out of their past with no comfort in the pieties of the present and no hope in the prospect of the future; students with the spirit of romantic rebellion unsatisfied by the flat homilies of the liberal-ethical tradition: these were the first of the rootless, the spiritual predecessors of decaying Europe's social jetsam whom Hitler and other rightist leaders would later organize. It was fitting that the deeply middle-class Knight of Rosenau, a belated and violent Don Quixote, should find in artisans and adolescents a pseudo-feudal retinue with whom to rehearse his brutal farce. One day that farce would take the stage as tragedy, with Schönerer's understudy, Adolf Hitler, in the leading role.

Chapter 14

BETHMANN HOLLWEG AND THE WAR: THE LIMITS OF RESPONSIBILITY

Fritz Stern

Bethmann Hollweg, philosopher-bureaucrat, a riddle to his contemporaries, has remained a subject of unending controversy for historians. His responsibility for the outbreak of the First World War and for Germany's conduct of it has been polemically debated for decades. A villain to the Allies, to the German military and their Pan-German allies, he was a weakling and the country's gravedigger. After 1918, German nationalist historians blamed his indecision and defeatism for hobbling Germany's war effort. His few defenders in the 1920s insisted that he had been a "military Chancellor,"[1] only more reticent and circumspect than the Pan-German extremists. The Third Reich interrupted the argument which, a few years ago, Fritz Fischer's massive *Griff nach der Weltmacht* revived. The roles have been reversed: Bethmann Hollweg's detractors now claim that he was an annexationist with philosophical veneer, and his defenders suggest that he was a noble, ill-cast bureaucrat, with occasional annexationist leanings.

Most often, and most ambiguously, he has been called the German Hamlet—as if there were but one Hamlet! Intended was convention's ineffectual Hamlet, torn by self-doubt. If it is to be Hamlet, then a better likeness is that of the prince, who, despite doubts and scruples, resorts to various strategems to dispatch enemies and friends, and leaves the stage littered with corpses.

The controversy is more than an academic exercise about an inscrutable individual. Bethmann Hollweg, Imperial Germany's

[1] *Bethmann Hollwegs Kriegsreden,* Dr. Friedrich Thimme, ed. (Stuttgart and Berlin, 1919), p. XXV.

last effective chancellor, led Germany into the First World War and left his office only after unrestricted submarine warfare and America's entry into the war had all but sealed Germany's fate. He necessarily is at the focus of all discussions concerning Germany's war guilt in 1914, her war aims during the war, and of the debate but recently started concerning the continuity of German history in the twentieth century. His chancellorship illuminates as well the mounting internal antagonisms of the Bismarckian Reich. The study of Bethmann, then, has ever been controversial, important, and politically explosive.

For decades he was made to serve as the anchor man in Germany's case for her own essential moderation. After Versailles, German historians were loath to indulge in criticism of the imperial regime that might bolster Allied charges against Germany. Indeed, they were reluctant to touch at all the "national-liberal" consensus which had virtually dominated German historiography before the November Revolution and which had become both anachronistic and inimical to the spirit of the new Republic. But then the historical guild—isolated exceptions notwithstanding—was more concerned with preserving the untarnished image of the Bismarckian state than with providing a Republic they disdained with an objective account of its origins.

In 1925, at the very beginning of his career, Hajo Holborn called upon historians to turn to the domestic history of the Bismarckian Reich—as against their cherished absorption with the minutiae of Bismarck's *Grosse Politik*.[2] An objective study of Germany's internal development, such as Hajo Holborn demanded, and unprejudiced studies of Germany's wartime and postwar foreign relations, such as his own work in 1932 on war guilt and reparations at Versailles exemplified, would have brought about a revision in this "national-liberal" consensus that kept the German past in the service of essentially conservative interests.[3] The struggle over a new historical consciousness in Germany was renewed after the second war—with greater acrimony because of the enforced delay and the intervening disasters.

This debate has recently centered on the First World War and

[2] Hajo Holborn, "Bismarck und Freiherr Georg von Werthern," *Archiv für Politik und Geschichte*, V (1925), p. 469.
[3] Hajo Holborn, *Kriegsschuld und Reparationen auf der Pariser Friedenskonferenz von 1919* (Leipzig 1932).

on Bethmann Hollweg. The legend of German innocence and Bethmann Hollweg's irenic passion has been effectively exploded; in some quarters, there is a tendency to create a legend in reverse by suggesting Germany's sole guilt, and thus to perpetuate the legend in a different form. What Germany did and Bethmann Hollweg said has now been quite thoroughly investigated—thanks to the impetus given by Fritz Fischer and Egmont Zechlin. The reasons for political decisions, however, are rarely as apparent as the decisions themselves. The present-day controversy over Bethmann Hollweg is marked by a distressing literal-mindedness, every "scrap of paper," every public document, has become sacrosanct and receives its own often exaggerated exegesis. To understand motives and decisions, however, one has to probe not only the conditions of political culture, the tangible pressures and conflicts, but also the less tangible elements of *milieu,* atmosphere, and private reasoning and character. Bethmann's thoughts and aspirations are difficult to reconstruct because his private papers were destroyed in 1945. The best remaining source is the diary of his longtime political assistant and secretary, Kurt Riezler, which I have been allowed to read and which is the principal source for these reflections.* The diary begins in July 1914, but a brief look at Bethmann's early career may be useful for an understanding of his later conduct.[4]

II

Theobald von Bethmann Hollweg, born in 1856, was a Prussian by birth, not tradition. His ancestors on the paternal side were rich merchants and bankers in Frankfurt; his grandfather became a professor of law in Prussia and in the liberal era under Prince William a Prussian minister. He resigned his post at the

* I am deeply grateful to Kurt Riezler's daughter, Maria White, and her husband, Professor Howard White, for permission to read the Riezler diary and for an opportunity to discuss it with them.

[4] An earlier interpretation of Bethmann on the basis of the Riezler diary, Karl Dietrich Erdmann, "Zur Beurteilung Bethmann Hollwegs," *Geschichte in Wissenschaft und Unterricht,* XV (1964), pp. 525–40, includes a few references to prewar entries. The copy I saw began with an entry of July 7, 1914.

beginning of the constitutional conflict in 1862. Bismarck's political adventurism revolted him, and a few hours before the outbreak of the Austro-Prussian war, he wrote the King, imploring him to remove the reckless Bismarck.[5] Time would be when Bismarck would be celebrated as the cautious statesman and Bethmann's grandson censured as the devious aggressor. Theobald's mother was a Swiss, Isabella de Rougemont. He was born on an estate his father had bought in Hohenfinow in the Mark Brandenburg; born in the Mark, but not wholly of it.

He studied jurisprudence, entered the civil service at the age of twenty-five, and in 1905 was named Prussian Minister of the Interior. In 1909 the Emperor appointed him Bülow's successor as Chancellor—and Bethmann had seen enough of politics in Imperial Germany to know the complexities and limitations of that office.

In fact, Imperial Germany could hardly be governed. Time and Bismarck had created a system of checks and imbalances, destined not to work. The political structure was cumbersome at best: a federal system in which Prussia held a central, but not unchallenged, position. The pseudo-constitutional state hid the locus of sovereignty. William, despite his occasional, disastrous outbursts of autocracy, had neither the constitutional prerogative nor the personal capacity to govern Germany. Parliaments, elected according to different systems of suffrage and therefore unequally representative, did not control the executive, though parliamentary approval was needed for the enactment of budgets and laws. The Chancellor's tenure was on the Emperor's sufferance; he was directly responsible to the Crown and indirectly dependent on the Reichstag which reflected the social composition—and cleavages —of an industrialized Germany. In theory, the Chancellor had to translate the Emperor's will—and sometimes whim—into effective political action, and when necessary, obtain parliament's approval. In practice, the Chancellor was caught between the conservative classes which, economically declining, were desperately clinging to their positions of power, and the liberal and radical groups, representative of a new society, that sought greater recognition of their own steadily increasing popular strength. The political system, already intricate and often unwieldy under Bis-

[5] Horst Kohl, ed., *Bismarck-Regesten,* I (Leipzig, 1891), pp. 286–89.

marck, had become incompatible with the social realities of the new age.

Bethmann's task was hard and his authority severely restricted. Political power had become much more fragmented after Bismarck's dismissal. The Chancellor had to contend with the military and naval leaders of the Reich who, fortified by their direct access to the Emperor, claimed not only autonomy in their *ressorts* but a strong voice in foreign policy as well. Antiquated court factions and modern pressure groups also sought to wield power or shape policy. In the years before the Great War, Germany faced immense problems at home and abroad. Internally, her industrial power provoked a steadily deepening antagonism between declining authoritarianism and a growing democratic movement. Externally, Germany's might aroused the fears of her neighbors, and her fitful, bullying policy, partly caused by her internal dissension, heightened these fears. Germany's worst problem was that its political system was virtually paralyzed and incapable of coping with these problems.

Bethmann intended to pursue a conciliatory course at home and abroad. He hoped to find a diagonal line, as he often put it, between conservative and liberal-radical pressures. "A clear conservative policy in the Reich was in fact an impossibility—the Right knew that best of all," he wrote after the war.[6] A consistently liberal policy, enhancing the power of the Reichstag, would have been equally impossible—for the Kaiser would not have tolerated it and the Reichstag could not have mustered a workable majority. Bethmann pushed meek measures meekly: he tried, for example, to reform the antiquated electoral system in Prussia which was the parliamentary bulwark of feudal dominance and as such sacrosanct to the conservatives and anathema to the left. He failed, inevitably, and in the process deeply antagonized both sides, also inevitably. He realized—as did most intelligent contemporaries—that the integration of the proletariat into the nation was the principal requirement of the age, but he saw no way of achieving it. In the years before the war, the antagonisms instead waxed stronger, and the opposing groups pushed each other into more radical and recalcitrant positions, as they did again during the war. The Socialists scored a great

[6] Th. von Bethmann Hollweg, *Betrachtungen zum Weltkriege,* I (Berlin, 1919), p. 98.

electoral triumph in 1912; a year later, the military flaunted their contempt for the *Rechtsstaat* in the Zabern affair, and enjoyed the Chancellor's full backing.[7]

Germany's external position was also precarious. The dangers were far more real than those Bismarck invoked to rally nation and Reichstag for military expenditures, and Bethmann always managed to obtain increasing army and navy appropriations. Foreign danger was sometimes a domestic convenience. It was always a source of the deepest worry to Bethmann who, unlike his predecessors, had had no military or diplomatic experience. The danger of war had mounted steadily since 1905, especially since the Bosnian crisis of 1908. Bethmann realized that Germany's exposed position between France and Russia had been rendered still more dangerous by its *Weltpolitik* and by its naval ambitions which had prompted England to seek closer ties with France and Russia. He found no comfort in Tirpitz's promises that his navy would frighten England into neutrality or negotiations, and in either case remove it as a threat to Germany in case of war. Instead he found England supporting France in the second Moroccan crisis and he heard with dismay of the Anglo-French naval conversations of 1912. His fear of German encirclement was genuine. He saw Germany, with decrepit Austria its only ally, surrounded by a ring of enemies, ready to block its continued growth. Bethmann certainly shared the nation's claustrophobia. He, too, had abandoned Bismarck's premise that Germany was a satiated power, and had embraced that curious blend of contradictory beliefs—social Darwinism, misunderstood romanticism, and cultural pessimism—all pointing to German expansion as the only alternative to stagnation. In January 1912, for example, he spoke privately of a great colonial empire in Africa, which Germany would be able to organize out of the Belgian Congo and the Dutch and Portuguese colonies.[8] Later that year, during the Balkan wars that clearly involved and damaged Austrian interests, he declared before the Reichstag: "If our allies while as-

[7] See Hans-Ulrich Wehler, "Der Fall Zabern. Rückblick auf eine Verfassungskrise des wilhelminischen Kaiserreichs," *Die Welt als Geschichte,* XXIII (1963), pp. 27–46.

[8] *Der Kaiser . . . Aufzeichnungen des Chefs des Marinekabinetts Admiral Georg Alexander v. Müller über die Ära Wilhelms II.,* Walter Görlitz, ed. (Göttingen, 1965), p. 107.

serting their interests should against all expectations be attacked by a third party, then we would have to come resolutely to their aid. And then we would fight for the maintenance of our own position in Europe and in defense of our future and security."[9] Germany's future in Bethmann's eyes, to say nothing of his colleagues', had to be open and dynamic, commensurate with its steadily growing economic power. Bethmann rejected the idea of a preventive war, but was determined to safeguard this expansionist future by all means, including war.

Germany's diplomatic position deteriorated during his tenure. At the time of the Haldane mission, he was already afraid of an Anglo-Russian naval convention, which would tighten the ring around Germany still more. He was ready to slow down German naval construction in return for a political agreement virtually involving an English withdrawal from Europe, giving Germany a free hand. Despite the failure of the Haldane mission, Anglo-German relations improved during the Balkan crisis. Austria's position, on the other hand, grew still more precarious and her reliability as an ally declined accordingly. The specter of an isolated Germany, gradually overshadowed by an ambitious, rapidly industrializing Russia, with its appalling multitudes, allied to France and probably England, haunted Bethmann and all German leaders.

Bethmann knew that in many quarters he was held responsible for Germany's mounting difficulties. In an age of national bombast and impetuosity, his plodding caution and conciliatoriness won grudging acceptance at best.

Berlin wits already called him *Bethmann soll Weg* (Bethmann should go), and there were always rumors of his impending ouster. The Crown Prince detested him, and the Kaiser, though respectful of him at most times and aware that he needed him, often railed against his *Schlappheit,* his brooding, and his philosophical airs. William's contempt for diplomats and civil servants was universally known, even if particularly crude outbursts against "stupid and anxiety-ridden diplomats, indeed [against] stupid civilians generally"[10] did not always make the rounds. The Kaiser preferred the often brainless virility, the *Schneidigkeit,* of soldiers.

[9] *Bethmann Hollwegs Kriegsreden, op. cit.,* p. xxiii.
[10] *Der Kaiser, op. cit.,* p. 68.

In this, too, he epitomized his age. Though tiresomely repeated, it is nevertheless true—and important to an understanding of Bethmann—that Germany was a thoroughly militaristic country in the years before the war. Gerhard Ritter cites one revealing instance: "It became good form even for higher state officials to wear military uniform at every conceivably fitting occasion. Thus Bethmann Hollweg in his first appearance as chancellor in the Reichstag appeared in a major's uniform—an exercise for which Bismarck with his endless masquerading as *Kürassier-general* certainly was not blameless. Only the person who could wear the uniform with the silver epaulettes counted as a real man [*ganzer Kerl*]."[11]

Outwardly Bethmann accepted the values of this system of creeping militarism, though he probably realized the attendant danger of eroding civilian control and political reason. At the same time, it seems probable that this exaltation of things military must have grated on his sensitive civilian soul.

It is generally agreed that Bethmann's abiding sense of responsibility and his brooding over every decision were his outstandingly attractive traits. What a contrast there was between the unevenly ebullient Kaiser, ever boastful of German prowess, so representative of his age, and Bethmann, the enigmatic, taciturn worrier! The slippery, smiling Bülow had certainly been more attuned to William's age and personality than his successor. As Riezler noted: "The Chancellor a child of the first half of the nineteenth century and of a better education [*Bildung*]. Strange that he with his old humanistic convictions, his seriousness, and his incapacity for all sham should have gained power in the new German *milieu* and should have been able to hold his own against parliamentarians and jobbers."[12]

The stark contrast in style and character between Bethmann and almost all the other leaders of Imperial Germany had encouraged the belief that there was a fundamental divergence of political aims as well. For this, however, the general consensus about Germany's national destiny was too broad and the Kaiser's tolerance for dissent too narrow: Bethmann Hollweg, as we will see, was perspicacious in his worries about Germany's course, but

---

[11] Gerhard Ritter, *Staatskunst und Kriegshandwerk*, II (2nd ed., Munich, 1965), p. 129.

[12] Riezler Diary, entry of July 7, 1914; hereafter referred to as R.D.

he had no alternative to propose and would have been powerless to implement one.

Bethmann resisted all efforts at the diminution of his office, and particularly all efforts to enhance the power of state secretaries. He had difficulties with his own appointee, Kiderlen-Wächter, who liked to conduct his foreign negotiations without informing him. Bethmann successfully resisted even the Kaiser's encroachments: in March 1912, at the time of the Anglo-German talks, William, impatient with what he thought Bethmann's dilatoriness, gave important orders directly to the ambassador in London and to the war minister in Berlin. Bethmann replied by submitting his resignation, warning the Emperor against a precipitous policy that in the end might force Germany into an attack on France in which the victim, but not the aggressor, would have the support of its allies. Bethmann argued that he could not take the responsibility for such a policy "and certainly not if Your Majesty informs an ambassador directly on such decisive measures as possible mobilization without listening to me first. By virtue of the office with which Your Majesty has entrusted me, I bear responsibility for the policies Your Majesty orders before God and country, before history and my own conscience. Even Your Majesty cannot relieve me of this responsibility."[13]

It was a manly avowal, and the Kaiser immediately retreated. Bethmann's letter points to a revealing distinction: he could reconcile himself more readily to a dangerous policy than to the imperial flouting of his authority. He would resign rather than accept both simultaneously. Bethmann's implicit distinction may help us to understand his complicated sense of the responsibility of power.

I have already suggested that he had a highly—in Imperial Germany, perhaps uniquely—developed sense of responsibility. He knew that future generations would hold him accountable for German policy, and his intelligence and realism made him recognize the potential dangers of that policy. He was cautious and circumspect and pondered the likely consequences of decisions. Often he appeared racked by doubts. Still, his sense of responsibility and his constant brooding did not paralyze him, as has

[13] *Kiderlen-Wächter, Der Staatsmann und Mensch,* E. Jäckh, ed., II (Stuttgart, 1924), pp. 159–61.

sometimes been suggested. They may have given him the psychological reassurance for action. He stared before he leapt, but he leapt nevertheless.

Bethmann's sense of responsibility was attenuated by his political ideas and experiences and by certain personal beliefs. He sensed intuitively what Max Weber posited in his celebrated "Politics as Vocation" immediately after the war, that a politician "allows himself to come into contact with diabolical powers lurking in every form of violence."* Bethmann probably would have agreed with a wartime observation by Riezler that "politics is really the art of doing evil and attaining the good— To be wise enough to know how everything is interlocked [and] through malice to lead the ill-intentioned [*die bösen Willen*] to something good."[14] He appreciated the ambiguity of power, and the distinction between private and public morality.

He had, moreover, suffered from the fragmentation of power in Imperial Germany, and he understood the limits on its exercise. Hence the responsibility of power was parceled out as well. Bethmann bent to the decisions of others in authority, often assuaging his conscience by the correct assumption that if he were to resign, his opponents would follow a still more reckless course, aided by a Chancellor less conscientious than himself. He defended, as I have suggested, his office more stoutly than his policy. A sign of diffidence, perhaps, but of something deeper also. Max Weber's distinction between the civil servant and politician is relevant: the politician's "conduct is subject to quite a different, indeed, exactly the opposite, principle of responsibility from that of the civil servant. The honor of the civil servant is vested in his ability to execute conscientiously the order of superior authorities, exactly as if the order agreed with his own conviction. This holds even if the order appears wrong to him and if, despite the civil servant's remonstrances, the authority insists on the order. Without this moral discipline and self-denial, in the highest sense, the whole apparatus would fall to pieces. The honor of the

---

* Weber, *Politische Schriften*, p. 447. Weber's lecture, delivered in 1919, recalls in so many ways the predicament of Bethmann, surrounded as he was by vain *Machtpolitiker*, that one wonders whether, unconsciously, he may not have been thinking of Bethmann as a tragic model of the politician without vocation.

[14] R.D., March 4, 1915.

political leader, of the leading statesman, however, lies precisely in an exclusive *personal* responsibility for what he does, a responsibility he cannot and must not reject or transfer."[15] Bethmann's sense of responsibility, I think, was an uncertain mixture of these two types.

A further point must be considered: Bethmann was by temperament and perhaps conviction a pessimist. As the Great War drew closer, he seems to have become a fatalist as well. This foreknowledge of disaster probably eased his sense of responsibility and reinforced the feeling of resigned duty that he had to stick to his job, however heavy the burden of decision, because a successor would be so much worse. In July 1914, his sense of responsibility, modified by these considerations, allowed him to take extreme risks and seek crafty subterfuges. For as the devoted but not uncritical Riezler wrote on July 7 and repeated later: "His cunning appears to be as great as his clumsiness. [*Seine Gerissenheit wohl ebenso gross wie sein Ungeschick.*][16]

III

The bulk of the Riezler diary pertains to the war itself, but the entries from July 7 to 23 offer unique insights into Bethmann's thoughts and conduct during the crisis weeks. They also record Riezler's gradual understanding of Bethmann's daring and complicated policy, designed to end what he thought was Germany's plight.[17]

On July 6, the two men traveled to Hohenfinow together, and Riezler was struck by Bethmann's melancholy, attributing it to his

[15] Max Weber, *Gesammelte Politische Schriften* (Munich, 1921), p. 415.
[16] R.D., July 7, 1914 and October 30, 1914.
[17] Ever since the Riezler diary was first introduced as an historical source by Karl Dietrich Erdmann, *op. cit.*, the present-day critics of Bethmann Hollweg have tended to damage Riezler's reputation as well by giving compressed and one-sided interpretations of his two prewar books. A balanced study of this sensitive scholar who for a decade was close to the center of German power would be desirable. The diary offers a rich source, of course, and incidentally contains some poignant hints about how it felt to belong to Germany's governing élite, with its undercurrents of anti-Semitism, and to marry during the war the daughter of the German Jewish painter, Max Liebermann.

wife's death a few weeks before. That night, Riezler learned of
the appalling dimensions of the crisis that had begun that morning with Germany's issuance of the "blank check" and her insistence that Austria honor it quickly and with aplomb. Bethmann
told the unsuspecting Riezler "the secret news . . . which
gives a shocking picture" of Germany's situation. Bethmann
began with the Anglo-Russian negotiations for a naval convention
and the prospect of a landing in Pomerania, "the last link in the
chain."[18] Russia was growing steadily stronger, Austria steadily
weaker and incapable of ever fighting "as an ally in a German
cause. The Entente knows that we are therefore entirely paralyzed."

The sequence of Bethmann's account makes it clear that his
response to the murder of Sarajevo was determined by what he
had long thought was Germany's precarious condition, not by the
immediate effects of the assassination itself. Sarajevo unrequited
would worsen Germany's situation; Sarajevo properly exploited
might lead to a dramatic escape from that situation.

On July 6, Bethmann spoke of "grave decisions." Official
Serbia was implicated in the assassination, Austria sought to rouse
herself, and Francis Joseph had asked the Emperor whether Germany considered the crisis as a *"casus foederis."* Bethmann
added: "Our old dilemma with every Austrian action in the
Balkans. If we encourage them, they say we pushed them into
it; if we discourage them, they say we left them in the lurch.
Then come the Western powers with open arms and we lose the
last powerful ally." This remark seems in odd, but not atypical,
contradiction to the fear that Austria was practically worthless as
a German ally anyhow.

Bethmann warned that "an action against Serbia can lead to
world war. The Chancellor expects that a war, whatever its
outcome, will result in the uprooting of everything that exists.
The existing [world] very antiquated, without ideas." He thought
it was a symptom of the general blindness that conservatives
hoped that a war would strengthen the monarchical order in
Germany. "Thick fog over the people. The same in all of Europe.

[18] On the importance Bethmann attached to these Anglo-Russian naval
negotiations, see Egmont Zechlin, "Deutschland zwischen Kabinettskrieg
und Wirtschaftskrieg. Politik und Kriegführung in den ersten Monaten des
Weltkrieges 1914," *Historische Zeitschrift,* CIC (1964), pp. 347–52.

The future belongs to Russia. . . . The Chancellor very pessimistic about the intellectual condition of Germany."[19]

What a strange mixture of motives and forebodings, of realism and pessimism! Yet this mixture constituted the background to Bethmann's decision to run the risk of war in July 1914.[20]

On July 8, Bethmann added that if the war "comes from the east" and Germany goes to Austria's help and not the other way around, "then we shall have prospects for winning it. If the war does not come, if the Czar does not want it, or France, thoroughly bewildered, counsels peace, then we still have prospects of breaking up the Entente through this action." The Riezler diary sustains the view that Bethmann in early July had resolved on a forward course; by means of forceful diplomacy and a local Austrian war against Serbia he intended to detach England or Russia from the Entente or—if that failed—to risk a general war over an opportune issue at a still opportune moment.

But Bethmann realized the dangers of a military showdown. Already on July 14, he correctly assessed the likely lineup of nations. "If in case of war, England starts at once, then Italy will under no circumstances come in." No wonder Riezler wrote on the same day: "Our situation is terrible."

On July 23, the Chancellor pointed out that if war came, it would come through precipitous Russian mobilization, before any negotiations. After mobilization, it would be too late for talks because the Germans would have to attack at once in order to have any chance of victory. "But then the whole people will feel the danger and will rise up." Bethmann envisioned the sequence of events that would lead up to a "defensive" war, provoked by Russia, which alone could unite the nation and perhaps even deceive other nations. Hence Bethmann was furious at the Crown Prince, who had sent bellicose messages to Pan-German groups. Such royal saber-rattling would obviously impair the credibility of this defensive war! In the same conversation he discussed the treatment of the socialists: in order to make sure of their support

[19] R.D., July 7, 1914.
[20] For an important and ingenious effort to relate Riezler's prewar writings to Bethmann's July policy, see Andreas Hillgruber, "Riezlers Theorie des kalkulierten Risikos und Bethmann Hollwegs politische Konzeption in der Julikrise 1914," *Historische Zeitschrift*, CCII (1966), pp. 333–51.

he would negotiate with them at once and in case of war forestall army action against them. Three days later, he was appalled at the recurrent idea of some generals to arrest all socialist leaders on the first day of war.[21] The principal components of Bethmann's tactics for the outbreak and conduct of war appear here for the first time with remarkable clarity: the war must be defensive, the utterances of the Pan-German chauvinists subdued, and the socialists wooed. During the war, he discovered that these tactics proved his only possible strategy.

In a sense, the most damaging evidence that the Riezler diary provides for the July crisis lies in what it does *not* say: it contains no hint or thought of any move by Bethmann to arrest the crisis, to save the peace. Why, we must then ask, did Bethmann opt for and persist in this forward course that he recognized from the beginning was fraught with danger? Riezler confirms what we would suppose: he chose this course regretfully, broodingly. On July 14, he said that a war would destroy the familiar world and that it represented for him "a leap in the dark and [his] hardest duty." Time and again, during the war, he worried over his responsibility for leading Germany into it. The "defensive" character of the war offered little solace to him.

Did it have to come to this? he asked on July 20. Should he have stuck to his resignation in 1912? But his successor—perhaps Tirpitz himself—would have been worse. Why was Germany in this predicament? "The earlier errors: simultaneously Turkish policy against Russia, Morocco against France, the navy against England—challenge everybody, put yourself in everybody's path, and actually weaken no one in this fashion. Reason: Aimlessness, the need for little prestige successes and solicitude for every current of public opinion. The 'national' parties which with their racket (*Radau*) about foreign policy want to preserve and strengthen their party position." A better analysis—or clearer indictment—of the fatality of Germany's prewar foreign policy could hardly have been made. It bears out completely a general observation that Riezler made in a prewar book: "The threat of war in our time lies . . . in the internal politics of those countries in which a weak government is confronted by a strong national-

---

[21] The Riezler diary reinforces the recent conclusions by Egmont Zechlin, "Bethmann Hollweg, Kriegsrisiko und SPD 1914," *Der Monat,* XVIII (January 1966), pp. 17–32.

ist movement."[22] Bethmann's judgment corresponds to Admiral von Müller's later view as to why the German government in July 1914 did not pursue a conciliatory policy: "The government, already weakened by domestic disunity, found itself inevitably under pressure from a great part of the German people which had been whipped into a high-grade chauvinism by Navalists [*Flottenvereinler*] and Pan-Germans."[23]

Bethmann overcame or suspended his doubts. In fact, once he had resolved on this forward course, he shook off his habitual hesitancy. Already on July 20, Riezler noted that the mood was serious, "the Chancellor resolute and silent." A week later, he recorded that Bethmann "sees doom [*Fatum*] greater than human power hanging over Europe and our own people," but added on the same day, "he is entirely changed, has no time to brood, and is therefore fresh, active, and lively, without any disquiet." The juxtaposition of fatalism and energy is not odd or unusual: Calvinists, too, believe in predestination and act decisively.

Obviously fatalism was a psychological condition, not a rational ground, for Bethmann's decision to run the risk of a world war. His fatalism went beyond the not uncommon assumption of the times that such a war was inevitable; he also believed that the world such a war would destroy was hopelessly superannuated, destined to be swept away. This, too, eased his sense of responsibility.

It has recently been suggested that Bethmann cherished expansionist aims, which he hoped to realize through war. Perhaps, but compelling evidence is lacking, and the Riezler diary offers no corroboration. Rather it suggests that his principal motive was fear for Germany's future. Bethmann's aims for the future were vague, his fears concrete, and the discrepancy allowed for the psychologically comforting half-truth that a war would be a defensive struggle. The diary does attest Bethmann's real terror at Russia's "growing demands and colossal explosive power." In a few years she would be supreme—and Germany her first, lonely victim.[24]

In his dread of the future he seems never to have reckoned with the fluidity of the European political system or the likely

[22] Quoted in Hillgruber, *op. cit.*, p. 339.
[23] *Der Kaiser, op. cit.*, p. 140.
[24] R.D., July 20, 1914.

workings of the balance of power. He feared the day when a thoroughly prepared Russia, supported by England, would crush Germany. But would England ever have supported the attack of a stronger Russia on a weaker Germany, thus establishing Russian hegemony in Europe? Or again: if Austria had in fact defected to the West, would not a return to a Russo-German alliance have offered a more than adequate counterweight? Bethmann barely considered these alternatives; in any case, he would not have persuaded the other rulers of Germany of their plausibility. Instead he remembered in those July days that Kiderlen-Wächter had always assumed the inevitability of war, and the implication was that Bethmann now at last accepted the dead man's judgment. Not that there was a dearth of living colleagues who urged him on.

Bethmann's anxiety about Germany's eventual isolation seems so exaggerated—as compared with even his own earlier estimates —that it may be legitimate to ask whether its intensity may in some small measure represent a kind of projection of his own melancholy stemming from his recent bereavement. His decision to risk war and his reluctance to do anything to save the peace was probably related to still another condition that combined personal and historical elements. For years he had been decried as a weakling. The military—but others too—frequently warned against another "Fashoda," which popular wisdom in those days, much like the indiscriminate warning against "Munich" today, adduced in order to preach a hard line against any compromise.[25] It is not likely that Bethmann's resolution in July 1914 was strengthened by a feeling that his policy of so-called conciliatoriness had yielded nothing, strengthened by the weariness of the civilian who had for so long been attacked by his tougher colleagues? It is a curious fact that in his postwar Memoirs he defended his July course by arguing that the opposite course—accommodation of Russia—would have amounted to "self-castration" (*Selbstentmannung*)—an unconscious allusion perhaps to the frequent charges of civilian effeminacy?[26] It is significant that two other principal actors of the July drama, Leopold Berchtold and Serge Sazanov, also smarted under their countrymen's

[25] *Der Kaiser, op. cit.,* pp. 74 and 140.
[26] Th. von Bethmann Hollweg, *Betrachtungen, op. cit.,* pp. 142–43.

allegations of earlier weakness.[27] It is difficult to assess the importance, if any, of such often unconscious factors, but it seems
arbitrary to ignore them altogether.

It is incontrovertible that Bethmann consciously risked a world
war, but there is no evidence that he did so in order to establish
German hegemony. It is naïve and excessively rationalistic to
suppose that aggression must spring from lust of conquest. Fear,
too, impels aggressive action, and if the action succeeds, then, as
Bethmann remarked in August 1914 about Moltke's war aims,
l'appétit vient en mangeant.[28]

IV

Kurt Riezler's notes from the war years offer a magnificent
mélange of events, impressions, and reflections, attesting his own
searching mind and his continuous proximity to power. During the
war he served as Bethmann's principal aide on domestic issues and
their relations became closer still. By training a classicist, by cast
of mind a philosopher and moralist, Riezler was an unlikely
partner for Germany's wartime Chancellor. Yet Bethmann clearly
found him congenial. He unburdened himself to Riezler as he
could to no one else, and he indulged his pessimism with seeming relish. We see a somber side of Bethmann then. The heart
of the diary remains their conversations, though Riezler's own
political education is mirrored in these pages as well. At the beginning of the war, he found himself still "dreamily uninterested"
in political matters, but his political sophistication and passion
grew steadily.[29] The diary consists of hastily composed, stylis-
tically compressed, often aphoristic entries, recording his thoughts,
not his daily duties or encounters. It has the double advantage of
political immediacy and philosophical detachment; it deserves to
be published.

Riezler's diary reflects a remarkable continuity of mood and
problems. Neither he nor the Chancellor experienced the great
exaltation that led Falkenhayn to say to Bethmann on August 4:
"even if we end in ruin, it was beautiful."[30] Despite moments of

[27] Luigi Albertini, *The Origins of the War of 1914,* II (Oxford, 1953),
pp. 124 and 181.
[28] R.D., August 20, 1914.
[29] R.D., September 25, 1914.
[30] R.D., November 22, 1914.

high hopes and a steady appreciation of the quiet heroism of the common people, Bethmann and Riezler persisted in their pessimism about Germany's future. They lamented the world without culture—the putative mass age *à l'américaine*—that would emerge from the war. For Germany, victory would bring spiritual corruption, defeat, political revolution. Still Bethmann saw no alternative but to continue the war and to attain for Germany the illusory goal of permanent security. With mounting anger and exasperation, they noted the ever-worsening internal problems: the encroachment of the military, the disintegration of unity, and the re-emergence of political divisions rendered worse by the demands of war.

The diary reveals neither the heady atmosphere of victory nor the certainty of some master plan of conquest; rather it suggests gloom, confusion, uninspired improvisation in planning, and endless wrangling in execution. Bethmann appears once again as racked by uncertainties and occasional self-recriminations. In his daily struggles, however, this "strange man," as Riezler habitually called him, acted with tenacity, discretion, and considerable finesse.

The question of Germany's war aims arose early and retained a central place in the preoccupations of Bethmann's entourage, as did the larger and vaguer question of the shape of the postwar world.[31] The first recorded discussions took place on August 21 at General Headquarters in Koblenz: "In the evening, long conversation about Poland and the possibility of a loose incorporation [*Angliederung*] of other states with the Reich—a Central European system of preferential tariffs. Greater Germany with Belgium, Holland, Poland as close, Austria as more distant satellite states [*Schutzstaaten*]." This clearly adumbrates the famous September program, published by Fritz Fischer, and its full discussion on August 21 and subsequent days rather explodes the ingenious

[31] In this essay I cannot deal with the present controversy about German war aims. The Riezler diary illuminates the atmosphere of the wartime debate, but contains no new hard facts that would resolve the question. If one had read the Riezler diary ten years ago, it would have come as a shock. After Fritz Fischer's book and the rash of recent works on the subject, it tends merely to amplify and confirm what we now know. The best analysis of the controversy is James Joll, "The 1914 Debate Continues," *Past and Present*, No. 34 (July 1966), pp. 100–13. Cf. also the articles by Klaus Epstein, Imanuel Geiss, and Wolfgang J. Mommsen in the issue on 1914 of *The Journal of Contemporary History*, I, 3 (July 1966).

idea of some of Fischer's critics that the September program was suddenly slapped together, as one would a list for Santa Claus.[32] Nor does it support the recent argument that German leadership embraced *Mitteleuropa* only after it realized that English resoluteness was turning a limited conflict into a world war.[33] On the other hand, Riezler never mentioned the September memorandum, which he presumably thought a provisional statement without any binding force.

In fact, the chief goal throughout the war remained *Mitteleuropa* as an economic union girded by political institutions guaranteeing German supremacy, even if details were refined, revised, and endlessly debated. Riezler believed that such a new order in Europe promised far greater permanency than the outright annexation of foreign territory. Others, he noted, wanted grandiose annexations; he preferred vassal nations to festering truncated states. Belgium and Poland should be turned into willing vassals, exposed to a gradual process of Germanization, as he often but ambiguously called it. Riezler and Bethmann knew what this "Middle-European Empire of the German Nation" really meant: "It was the European disguise of our will to power. (*Die europäische Verbrämung unseres Machtwillens.*)[34]

Riezler thought that the "petty" nationalisms of Central Europe could be supplanted by a kind of super-loyalty to this new Reich which would be dominated by *Grossdeutschland* as Imperial Germany had been by Prussia. He even spoke of the extinction of Prussia and *Kleindeutschland* and the return to the traditions of the Frankfurt Parliament of 1848.[35] Bethmann seems to have been more reticent in these matters, less given to grandiose schemes, but apparently never restrained, let alone rebuked, his more candid assistant. They often agreed concerning tactics; both, for example, feared that the military would insist on a formal assertion of German dominance: "hegemony itself can be enforced. The caudinian yoke of its formal recognition never."[36] The Riezler diary contradicts Gerhard Ritter's recent assertion

[32] Fritz Fischer, *Griff nach der Weltmacht. Die Kriegszielpolitik des kaiserlichen Deutschland 1914/18*, 3rd ed. (Düsseldorf, 1964), pp. 116–18.
[33] See Egmont Zechlin, "Deutschland zwischen Kabinettskrieg und Wirtschaftskrieg," *op. cit., passim.*
[34] R.D., April 18, 1915.
[35] R.D., November 22, 1916.
[36] R.D., December 2, 1916.

that Bethmann's policy toward war aims reached "a decisive turning point" in November 1914, after Falkenhayn's report that a
clear-cut military victory over all of Germany's enemies was no
longer possible.[37] As late as January 1917 Riezler wrote: "It is
clear, after all, that the insulated life of a small Germany in the
middle of Europe is tenable only for decades, that it remains
exposed to the greatest dangers and that it cannot have a very big
future."[38] A few days before the First Russian Revolution he
noted: "The policy of the Chancellor: to lead the German Reich
which by the methods of the Prussian territorial state . . . cannot
become a world power . . . to an imperialism of European form
[*Gebärde*], to organize the Continent from the center outward (Austria, Poland, Belgium) around our undemonstrative
[*stillen*] leadership . . ."[39] The major obstacles Riezler saw in
March 1917 were internal, that is, upper-class opposition to the
domestic complement of Bethmann's policy, democratic reform,
and military opposition to any policy that was not openly based
on German power.

The dream of a German *Mitteleuropa* died hard, if at all. When
the war went badly for Germany, the means shifted, not the end.
It persisted because it seemed to endow the war with some meaning. On September 4, 1914, Riezler lamented that "people today do not have a single idea that corresponds to the greatness
of the age. But it would be the ruin of Europe if on this occasion
it should not find a possible form of permanence and community."
The civilian's *Mitteleuropa* was the alternative to the military's
wild annexationism that would leave partitioned nations thirsting
for revenge. It was also the only means for safeguarding Germany's future. When Falkenhayn in November 1914 counseled
immediate peace with Russia, and Bethmann demurred, Riezler
noted: "If we make peace now, we will have to wage war in ten
years' time, alone and under entirely unfavorable conditions."[40]
The goal was to fight until Germany could create a new European
order that would render her inviolable from attack, and would
establish and, if possible, disguise German hegemony.

[37] Gerhard Ritter, "Bethmann Hollweg und die Machtträume deutscher
Patrioten im ersten Jahr des Weltkrieges," *Festschrift Percy Ernst Schramm
zu seinem siebzigsten Geburtstag von Schülern und Freunden zugeeignet*
(Wiesbaden, 1964), p. 210.
[38] R.D., January 6, 1917.
[39] R.D., March 11, 1917.
[40] R.D., November 26, 1914.

Would England—the most hated and envied country even in Bethmann's entourage—ever have accepted a Europe dominated by Germany? Riezler sensed the answer and dimly realized that the goal of permanent security could be attained only through a long war ending in England's defeat. In this way the limited goal of *Mitteleuropa* implied the unlimited, unwelcome goal of world dominance. This dizzy prospect was repeatedly invoked—casually, as an inevitable, indeed regrettable, consequence of the constellation Germany was fighting. Bethmann and Riezler discussed Germany's capacity for world dominance a month after the battle of the Marne.[41] Later they thought: "Perhaps the heroic attempt of this war to secure us an impregnable position of world power of the first order is half impossible and therefore the people's eagerness so moving and so tragic."[42] In August 1916, in a long disquisition about the war, Riezler noted that for Germany it had a "triple significance . . . defense against the France of today, preventive war against the Russia of tomorrow (as such too late), struggle with England over world dominance [*Weltherrschaft*]." German policy before 1914, he added, mistakenly pursued all three goals simultaneously.[43]

Riezler's cryptic sentences should not be overinterpreted: he did not believe that Germany had entered the war to attain these goals, merely that they had been intermittent and contradictory motives during the prewar era. The war itself joined them together, and Riezler as well as Bethmann was appalled by the magnitude of the stakes. They feared that "England's tragic error might consist of compelling us to rally all our strength, to exploit all our possibilities, to drive us into worldwide problems, to force upon us—against our wills—a desire for world dominance."[44] Some might dismiss this as self-exonerating bombast. They would I think, be wrong. Bethmann and Riezler genuinely believed that fate or a concatenation of deep forces in world history was thrusting world dominance upon Germany. Bethmann found the prospect uncongenial; as Riezler once remarked, the Pan-Germans were right in sensing that world dominance was repugnant to the Chancellor.[45] I doubt if Bethmann and Riezler regarded such

[41] R.D., October 11, 1914.
[42] R.D., November 22, 1914.
[43] R.D., August 1, 1916.
[44] R.D., October 4, 1915.
[45] R.D., July 16, 1915.

dominance as intrinsically evil or undesirable; they merely feared that Germany would perish in the effort. Already in August 1914, Riezler noted: "The difficulty for the German to accustom himself to the mien of world dominance which he *must* wear after a victory."[46] In December 1914 he wrote of "the tragedy in the development of modern Germany: if it is victorious, all its energies will be absorbed in tasks for which Germans have no talent—world dominance, which is contrary to its spirit and greatness."[47] Finally, in April 1918, he still thought: "Never was a people more capable of conquering the world, and less capable of ruling it."[48]

Bethmann hid from himself the fact that Germany could gain permanent security, which he wanted, only by defeating England and by establishing world dominance which he neither wanted nor thought feasible. Once again, he failed to reckon with the unwanted consequences of Germany's ambitions, as he had in July 1914. It is perhaps a common convenience for statesmen to believe quite genuinely that goals not wanted in the mind cannot be goals implicit in their actions and decisions. For Bethmann it was enough that he and Riezler knew, and said to each other countless times, that Germany was totally incapable of ruling the world, of ruling Europe—or herself.

Their despair over Germany's political incompetence may have been tinged by their *Weltuntergangstimmung,* but it was gallingly confirmed in Bethmann's daily struggles. The bureaucratic chancellor and his idealistic assistant were at one in their horror at the daily face of German politics: intrigues, party jockeying, false and reckless promises. They expected, especially in wartime, order, rationality, and public rectitude—and they encountered virtual chaos and mounting unreason. They feared that Germany would perish because of the political *Unbildung* of its people.

The foremost cause of discord was the continuous struggle between Bethmann and the military, though the latter fought among themselves as well.[49] The prewar fragmentation of power had turned into the bitter competition for power during the war,

---

[46] R.D., August 21, 1914.
[47] R.D., December 13, 1914.
[48] R.D., April 15, 1918.
[49] Karl-Heinz Janssen, *Der Kanzler und der General. Die Führungskrise um Bethmann Hollweg und Falkenhayn (1914–1916)* (Göttingen, 1967), appeared unfortunately after my article was finished, and hence I could not use it.

with the final arbiter, William, gradually relinquishing his leadership altogether. A brilliant French officer, who was himself to become something of an expert on the question of political authority in his own country, wrote in 1924 about a particular instance of William's fickleness: "Extraordinary retreat of the supreme power, indisputable proof of that crisis of authority which was despite certain appearances the true spiritual cause of the defeat of the Empire."[50] The military continually expanded their sphere of control and as early as September 1914 Riezler lamented, "the concept of the purely military concern is having a field day here."[51] The soldiers lacked, however, all political intelligence, and Riezler's diary is the record of mounting exasperation and anger at these powerful incompetents in uniform and their blind, brutish faith in force. By harassing the natives, they wrecked Germany's chances in Belgium and Poland. By their alliance with conservatives, industrialists, and Pan-Germans, they poisoned Germany's internal politics. They understood neither friend nor foe, and they meddled in realms where even their technical knowledge was inadequate. "It is a real wonder that this dilettantism, in which the German people has unshakable faith because it wears a uniform, does not ruin it."[52]

There were individual culprits, too. Tirpitz was the arch-villain, dubbed "the liar," "the father of the lie," or the "Jesuit." He and his uncompromising policy against England were responsible for the war. Bethmann knew that Tirpitz was a charter member of the *fronde* against him and that the Admiral was intermittently plotting for his removal. Most generals were political infants, and the party leaders a disaster.

Bethmann and Riezler saw beyond personalities. They were appalled by the political immaturity of all Germans, by the antagonisms within Germany, by the hopelessness of governing the country under such conditions. Time and again they complained of "insane political unreason, of the dominance of blind passion."[53] The ruling classes were the worst. Bethmann despaired of any future with the Thyssens, the *Krautjunker,* and the Hohenzollerns in whom "the intellectual decline of the day finds its most

[50] Charles de Gaulle, *La discorde chez l'ennemi,* 2nd ed. (Paris, 1944), p. 51.
[51] R.D., September 20, 1914.
[52] R.D., January 9, 1917.
[53] R.D., April 28, 1915.

rapid expression. . . . He does not know how the new Germany of power and finance supremacy could find its harmony with Goethe."[54]

The somewhat lofty, even snobbish, tone should not disguise the very practical import of Bethmann's thoughts. He feared that the war—and most especially a victory—would brutalize the ruling élites still further, making them still more uncultured, selfish, and blind, and still less able to govern the country. Bethmann was genuinely impressed by "the idealistic strength of the common people," by the idealism of the trade unionists.[55] But he feared that the loyal left would be goaded into revolution by the selfish, chauvinistic right, and he spoke of "the incubus of the postwar Revolution which oppressed him."[56]

Bethmann had to contend with the political stupidity and power-drunk arrogance of Germany's ruling classes throughout the war. The worst struggle occurred over the use of the submarine—a struggle that began in 1915 and ended with the fatal announcement of unrestricted submarine warfare in February 1917.[57] From 1915 on, Tirpitz and his colleagues at the Admiralty boasted that their "miracle weapon," if fully unleashed, not hedged in by restrictions about who could be torpedoed and how, would bring England to the negotiating table—or to her knees—in a matter of months. Bethmann, supported at first by Falkenhayn and Admiral von Müller, the Kaiser's chief of naval cabinet, opposed indiscriminate sea warfare because he rightly thought that Germany had too few submarines to wage an effective campaign, and he feared that the only certain result would be the enmity of the remaining neutrals. Bethmann persuaded the Kaiser to stave off unrestricted submarine warfare. Thwarted by the Chancellor, the naval clique launched a great and mendacious propaganda campaign promising a *Siegfrieden* through submarines. The bourgeois public, incited by renowned academics and by most of the non-socialist deputies, proved thoroughly receptive, and Bethmann found himself in a crossfire between putative experts of the Admiralty and an aroused, greedy public. Riezler records the stages

[54] R.D., July 28, 1915.
[55] R.D., July 28, 1915 and March 4, 1915.
[56] R. D., June 14, 1916.
[57] For a comprehensive survey of this struggle, see Gerhard Ritter, *Staatskunst und Kriegshandwerk* (Munich, 1964), III, Chs. 5 and 8, and Karl E. Birnbaum, *Peace Moves and U-Boat Warfare. A Study of Imperial Germany's Policy towards the United States April 18, 1916–January 9, 1917* (Stockholm, 1958).

of the conflict and provides a chorus for the unfolding of the tragedy.

In February 1916, the Chancellor weighed once again the arguments for and against the full use of submarines. He hesitated a long time, realizing that without them, England could not be decisively beaten, and hence would refuse concessions. Riezler feared he would yield: "My suspicion that the main argument— unconsciously—is his fear of rejecting the weapon that all the Emperor's military advisers contend they cannot do without, while not being able to present anything which will end the war in 1916."[58] The vilification of Bethmann mounted: in six weeks' time, his opponents claimed, England could be finished, "but the requisite courage is lacking"—in Bethmann.[59] Riezler hoped Bethmann would resign rather than accept a defeat on this issue. "His style is caution and intelligent reflection. . . . If he lets himself be forced into something which is against his conviction and style, he is lost. . . . For some, the unrestricted submarine warfare is like an orgy of ruthless force which intoxicates them. Their clamor almost confirms what the English always say: the Germans have become mad."[60] In February 1916, Bethmann once more prevailed. As an aftermath of this exhausting struggle, Tirpitz resigned, his hatred for Bethmann hardly diminished, and the agitation gathered new strength in his wretched *Vaterlandspartei*.

The submarine issue hung fire all through 1916. Germany's chances for a victory on land seemed nil; even her chances to hold out in a defensive position were rapidly diminishing. As more submarines became available, their unrestricted use made more sense. The question was: could total warfare knock out Britain or would her losses be offset by America's entry into the war? Would the submarines then merely clinch Britain's resolution to destroy German power and give her the American means to do so? The dilemma was real, and the Chancellor sighed that the U-boats would follow him to the grave: "It will always remain the great enigma what would have happened if they had been unleashed without restrictions."[61]

The public howl for their full use never ceased, and Bethmann gradually weakened. Did he share Riezler's view that the Pan-

[58] R.D., February 4, 1916.
[59] R.D., February 11, 1916.
[60] R.D., February 22, 1916.
[61] R.D., August 10, 1916.

German madness could never be overcome "save it be permitted once to run wild so that the damage could be seen"?[62] Would unrestricted warfare bring total victory over all enemies—or necessary catharsis for the Germans themselves? In the event, it brought neither.

Bethmann had urged the Kaiser to replace Falkenhayn by the immensely popular Hindenburg and Ludendorff, hoping that perhaps Hindenburg would make a reasonable peace respectable. Instead the new military leaders became champions of the U-boats, and Bethmann was caught between folk heroes promising victory and politicians branding caution treason and cowardice. Bethmann weakened in his opposition, partly because the promises of the military had begun to impress him, too. On January 9, 1917, he surrendered to the military. Their victory marked the virtual end of the Bismarckian Empire, for power had slipped from civilian into military hands. The next day Riezler wrote: "Despite all vows of the navy, a leap in the dark. We all have the feeling that this question hangs over us like a doom [*Fatum*]. If history follows the laws of tragedy, then Germany should be destroyed by this fatal mistake which embodies all her earlier tragic mistakes." A few days later, in a slightly different vein: "We have signed a piece of paper without knowing whether it contains our own death sentence or the acceptance of a legacy of millions, William the Very Great or William the Last."[63]

Bethmann had now agreed to play what a year earlier he had called "a game of *va banque*, the stakes being our existence as a great power and our entire national future."[64] If he had stuck to his refusal but a few months longer, Germany's chances for a favorable peace would have been excellent. Seven years after the disastrous decision, de Gaulle wrote: "If it had not been for American intervention and the hope it inspired in the Entente, the Reich would have been placed by the Russian Revolution and peace a few months later, by the failure of the French spring offensive with the moral crisis that ensued as a consequence, and by the efforts in London of the Lansdownes and Ramsay Macdonalds in very favorable conditions for negotiating peace, with the help of mediation that President Wilson had just offered."[65]

---

[62] R.D., March 22, 1916.
[63] R.D., January 31, 1917.
[64] Quoted in Karl E. Birnbaum, *op. cit.*, p. 59.
[65] Charles de Gaulle, *op. cit.*, pp. 26–27.

The decision, however, had become ineluctable—given the internal politics of Germany—and Bethmann hoped that the desperate gamble might pay off. But could it—without sanctifying militarism and perpetuating its rule? Riezler probably spoke for both men when the U-boat agitation made him cry out: "Germany is like a person reeling (*Taumelnder*), staggering along the abyss, wishing for nothing more fervently than to throw himself into it."[66]

The submarine crisis deepened Bethmann's disillusionment with Germany's ruling classes and parties. Only the Social Democrats, he had thought, retained any idealism, and this almost aesthetic appreciation turned practical when he realized that sensible policies could be made only with the left, never with the right.[67] The Social Democrats, he said, could teach all other parties the meaning of *Staatsraison,* and he was grateful for their restraint and rationality. He needed their support and they deserved his solicitude—and yet what a necessary gulf remained between them. In private, Bethmann could bewail the selfish idiocy of Germany's élites; in public, he was their representative and protector. In private, he could say to Riezler that "to change East Elbia is an impossibility; [it] must be broken . . . disappear."[68] But he worried lest the socialists should publicly expose the chauvinism and selfishness of the upper classes. In his relations with the socialists, Bethmann had something of the *grand seigneur* who liked his servants better than his equals, treated them accordingly in private, and was much pleased by his own largesse. Some of the socialists were impressed and flattered, too.

But Bethmann knew that more tangible rewards for socialist loyalty were needed. As early as 1914 he realized the inevitability of postwar reform at home, and he told Riezler he would resign after the war rather than abandon the reform of the Prussian suffrage. The sacrifices of the lower classes and their mounting suspicion of the war aims and postwar plans of the ruling classes made it increasingly difficult to postpone reforms until later. Even the promise of reform, however, was anathema to the right. It was Bethmann's task to keep the two extremes from open warfare: he could not govern in defiance of the right nor could Germany carry on the war without support of the left. Bethmann's

[66] R.D., April 24, 1916.
[67] R.D., November 3, 1916.
[68] R.D., June 14, 1916.

sympathies in the short run were with the socialists; in the long run, he feared both sides for he had little faith in a parliamentary-democratic future.

Bethmann's surrender on the submarine question threatened his tie to the socialists. He strove hard to keep them in line. Predictably, the U-boat decision merely emboldened his foes: "The whole *Kanzler-fronde* apparently full of fear that the war might be coming to a successful end before they succeed in overthrowing the Chancellor."[69] The socialists were accommodating at first: "Touching—the modesty of the socialists and touching their patriotism."[70]

Still the lines were drawn clearly: on the right, Pan-German war aims, unrestricted submarine warfare, and die-hard resistance to domestic reform; on the left, demands for a compromise peace, democratic reform, and skepticism or opposition concerning submarine warfare. The surface calm was shattered by reactionary moves in the *Herrenhaus,* which Bethmann countered on March 14 with the forthright promise of internal reforms after the war. The next day came the news of the Russian Revolution, and Riezler noted that Bethmann's speech had come at the last possible moment: after the Revolution, his promises would have been branded as weakness. The Russian Revolution acted as a sudden gale fanning Germany's discord: the conservatives and industrialists saw the Revolution as the harbinger of things to come in Germany, especially if Bethmann were allowed to continue his conciliatory policy. The socialists demanded immediate reforms —and needed them, if they were to keep even their moderate supporters in line. Bethmann promised them, but was defeated by his ministers who feared that the promulgation of a democratic franchise in Prussia would mean "that one would not be able to work any more with the bourgeois parties, great agitation of the League of Farmers against the cities—dire consequences for the food supply."[71] Once more Bethmann had to retreat and the socialists had to be disappointed because the King's ministers, themselves opposed to reform, conjured up the specter of upper-class sabotage! No wonder Riezler sighed: "Only a few sense how closely we brush catastrophe all the time."[72]

[69] R.D., February 18, 1917.
[70] R.D., February 25, 1917.
[71] R.D., April 6, 1917.
[72] R.D., April 10, 1917.

The mood remained grim throughout the spring: Riezler thought it would be a miracle if Germany survived the madness of its ruling classes. "The Chancellor's heroic struggle against the soldiers—but the great policies we could be carrying out are ruined by it."[73] The Chancellor's position was rapidly weakening even before the final crisis in July: "If the people identify the Supreme Army Command with the Pan-Germans, if it leaks out that the Chancellor has lost all his political freedom of movement in internal and external affairs because of the army leaders, then will come the rebellion against the rule of militarism and the beginning of the collapse."[74] But before the Chancellor's captivity was realized, rebellion and intrigue finally felled him.

A newly constructed Reichstag majority grew impatient of Bethmann's temporizing and sought to develop its own initiative in the form of the peace resolution. Ludendorff exploited the disaffection of the moderates in order at last to get rid of Bethmann. Despite everything, the Kaiser probably regretted having to part with his Chancellor. De Gaulle's portrait of their relationship was amazingly apt: "Bethmann, moderate without weakness, hardworking without ostentation, respectful without servility, was the very model of a good servant, and this character pleased William whose superficial authoritarianism and prickly prestige he did not vex."[75] In taking leave of the Kaiser at the end, Bethmann did not mention "the true reason [for his resignation], Ludendorff's blackmail, in order to spare the Emperor, already *de facto* abdicated." He merely complained that his telephone had been tapped and that when he hears the click he shouts into it, "What *Schweinehund* is listening in?"[76] Shaken when Bethmann yielded on submarine warfare, Bismarck's Empire ended when Ludendorff and Hindenburg, banking on their glory and backed by their nationalist allies, imposed their will and finally their dictatorship on Emperor and populace.

Riezler's notes on the July crisis apparently were lost, but his predictions during the final eighteen months of the war attested his clairvoyant pessimism. In April 1917 he thought the Allies might soon announce their willingness to negotiate with the Ger-

[73] R.D., May 8, 1917.
[74] R.D., June 9, 1917.
[75] Charles de Gaulle, *op. cit.,* p. 155.
[76] R.D., August 4, 1917.

man people, not the Hohenzollerns.[77] He foresaw the internal
consequences of defeat: "If we collapse because of hunger and the
agitation of Haase and comrades—or if it looks that way—then
the bad peace will be blamed on the workers, everything will be
misconstrued in favor of the right, and Germany, mortally
wounded physically, will have her soul completely confounded as
well."[78] After Bethmann's departure, he sensed the beginning of a
reactionary plot to "goad and provoke the socialists by all possible means—the war demagogy [*Kriegshetze*], etc. serves this
purpose principally, the socialists should be forced to turn their
hatred of the *Vaterlandspartei* against the state . . . and in this
way should be pushed from the state."[79] Bethmann's feeble
successor could hardly maintain his laborious efforts to coax and
bully the socialists into the state. Agrarians and industrialists,
parliamentarians of the right and rabid annexationists, always
urged on by Ludendorff, preferred to keep the nation cleanly
divided: either our state or theirs. In victory, the upper classes
were resolved to hold on to their own, and make no concessions; in
defeat, they were determined to accuse the left of treason, spreading spiritual poison, which would corrupt all public order.

On October 1, 1918, Riezler grasped the totality of Germany's
defeat and dreaded its implications: "The defeat in its worst
form—if no miracle intervenes, or if the enemy coalition does not
become disorganized, we will practically have to accept *das
Diktat*. Slavery for a hundred years. The dream about the world
[*Welttraum*] finished forever. The end of all hubris. The
dispersion of Germans around the world. Fate of the Jews."

V

Riezler was a perspicacious judge of people and situations.
His impressions of Bethmann, however, may have been occasionally distorted by loyalty and admiration, for he was devoted to
his chief, as young advisers to men of power often are. Riezler's
Bethmann may have been wiser, more detached, than he appeared to most others. Sometimes Riezler was critical and im-

[77] R.D., April 13, 1917.
[78] R.D., April 19, 1917.
[79] R.D., February 11, 1918.

patient, but he was always puzzled by "this strange man." To some extent, we still are.

Before the July 1914 crisis, Riezler thought of Bethmann as a highly intelligent and cultivated civil servant. The July crisis made him disavow that judgment: "He is great—as a man and because of the breadth and independence of his mind. He is entirely free of all prejudice and pettiness and entirely independent of public opinion and suggestion. His judgment is autonomous. . . . If only he did not have the dreadful habit of pretending doubts even when he has firmly formulated his own opinion, of saying things that he himself does not believe only to hear the contradictions of others."[80] At the beginning of the war, Bethmann's *Gejammer*, his stubborn anxiety, his reluctance "to think big," exasperated Riezler who longed for something more dynamic, more inspiring—who longed in fact for the charismatic leader that Weber depicted after the war. He wished the Chancellor would cease playing *advocatus diaboli*, would fortify his will to power, would gain some of that passion and magnetism that would inflame the people. He praised his defensive energy, his toughness and tenacity, his caution and perspicacity, but hoped he would occasionally seize the initiative. Toward the end of the chancellorship, Riezler's admiration rose and silenced all criticism. He saw Bethmann, lonely, ever unbefriended, heroic, martyr-like. The Chancellor had always been at his best when things were at their worst; when optimists collapsed, he was calm and confident. Perhaps a critical situation confirmed his private view of the world, and he could adapt to it more readily. His defeat left his dignity unimpaired and indeed something like nobility clung to him as he departed. Riezler once wrote and always believed: "He is superior to others in human as well as intellectual qualities. [*Seine menschliche Überlegenheit über die anderen tritt zu der geistigen.*]"[81]

With this judgment there can be no quarrel, though the competition for greatness in wartime Germany was obviously not keen. Riezler's impressions of Bethmann are invaluable, though the historian's perspective and questions are necessarily different. We are not principally concerned with Bethmann's person, but with the statesman and his relations to society.

[80] R.D., July 20, 1914.
[81] R.D., March 7, 1916.

Perhaps the most extraordinary quality that emerges from Riezler's portrait is the realism and reasoned pessimism of Bethmann's views about Germany. He understood the divisions and antagonisms of German society, and he feared that the struggle between blind ruling classes and aspiring lower classes would lead to revolution, particularly under the stress of war. He saw in wartime Germany the same danger of violent upheaval that he had seen in prewar Europe. His commitment in the struggle with foreign nations, however, had been unambiguously national whereas his sympathies in a divided nation were not so easily identified. He admired the socialists as they were during the war, but feared a social-democratic future as jeopardizing authority and culture. He detested the wartime politics of agrarians and national bourgeoisie, doubted that they would ever reacquire the qualities of leadership, and yet by background and tradition belonged to them. At his best, Bethmann had no political home in Germany.

He clung to the only course he could find: conciliation, the policy of the diagonal, which in the end, fleetingly, united the two opposites against himself. Perhaps there was no other way, save revolution, which was anathema to the monarchical, bureaucratic Bethmann. Slightly lugubrious by temperament, he was hardly buoyed up by his vision of the future. "To fear the worst often cures the worst" did not apply to Bethmann.

He was a Puritan gambler: he worried about plunging his country into war, but he took the leap nevertheless; he feared Pan-Germanism in its effects at home and abroad, and he consented to the submarine gamble anyway. His personal weakness has been blamed for his failure to defend his cautious course—and to some small extent, with justice. There were weightier reasons for his repeated, if disguised capitulations: it must be remembered that to a large extent, he accepted the values of the very system he criticized. Much as he railed against individual generals, he probably shared his countryman's excessive faith in the authority of the uniform. Much as he inveighed—in private—against the *Unbildung und Verblendung* of his colleagues and compatriots, he too had a fatal blind spot when it came to appraising Germany's place in the world or the likely effect on others of her "defensive" ambitions. The chief reason, of course, for his failure to achieve his goals at home was the political system itself. The upper strata of German society had enough power and resolution to block their own political enfeeblement. The system kept Bethmann confined to a very narrow area of maneuverability, and the fact that he himself hesitated to move beyond that area was secondary. Personal hesitancy was functional: the system enjoined it.

The remarkable thing about Bethmann was not his failure to achieve pacification at home, for no man could have done that. Rather it was the fact that this seeming moderate, so clearly hounded by his sense of responsibility, could cover with his own authority such fateful decisions as the forward course of July 1914 and the submarine war of 1917. As Chancellor he presided over the subversion of political authority by the military. On several occasions, he thought of resigning—the traditional means of disavowing responsibility for the political acts of others. In the end, he always shrank back—and certainly not for love of power. His devotion to the monarch—whatever his thoughts about William or the affronts he suffered at court—made him hesitate to leave his post in wartime. His patriotism and his pessimism combined to keep him in his office: he knew that his successor would abandon his conciliatory, moderate course altogether. He was psychologically prepared for unpalatable decisions because he expected the worst anyhow. His pessimism, too, had its functional aspects.

Thus it came about that this moral man became the uniquely useful agent of reckless, selfish leaders. Unwittingly, probably unconsciously, he slid into the position of being a front for the very forces he detested. Riezler saw this tragic irony: "there persists the strange paradox: that we can follow such a foolhardy policy in the domestic and foreign realm is made possible exclusively [by the fact that we have] the most cautious and circumspect man at the helm who alone can make it credible. This paradox from the beginning of the war."[82] And again, "All his bad qualities have one advantage. The people outside politics have confidence that if this man demands something it is really necessary. . . . This was already an important asset at the outbreak of the war."[83] Or again, "strange irony of fate, that this great hard man, earnest and prudent, with the warmest heart must conduct and cover the most foolhardy policy—that the only accomplishment of him who had the best interests of Germany at

[82] R.D., February 14, 1917.
[83] R.D., April 28, 1915.

heart is to keep the mass of the people—the only thing that is great and worthy of respect in today's Germany—in line with the policy of Ludendorff, Tirpitz, etc."[84] Bethmann meant to be a brake on political irresponsibility, but at critical moments he served as the mask of conscience and character for the very devils he detested—and without which they would have been far less effective.

Worse still, Bethmann could have rendered a signal service to the pacification of Germany after the war and revolution if he had rendered an honest account of his years as Chancellor. As early as 1916, Riezler hoped that Bethmann's struggles against the military would be described precisely, "after the war, as an example for the Germans to learn from."[85] Later he cried out: "Will the history of this U-boat war, this profoundest [*imgeheimsten*] lie, ever be written? If yes, then it must unmask the *Unbildung,* stupidity of militarism, and the rottenness of the whole chauvinist upper strata."[86]

Bethmann's Memoirs went but halfway. He gently criticized Tirpitz and Ludendorff, who had already vilified him. But he could not bring himself to write a full, objective, and hence scathing account of how German leadership was corrupted during the war and why. His motives were undoubtedly mixed and honorable. A full account would have substantiated Allied charges of German militarism and imperialism. He shrank from denouncing Germany's erstwhile leaders for fear of deepening the divisions within Germany. But he knew better than most men the quality of those who were already poisoning the life of Germany by their infamous stab-in-the-back legend and their cries of treason. Perhaps Bethmann's most culpable act was to have seen and understood so much and to have said so little. His semisilence, though understandable, facilitated the second and worse triumph of the very passions he deplored.

Despite his personal integrity, his biting sense of responsibility, and his own exceptional intelligence, his historic role abetted the disastrous course of Germany's history in this century. To say that he was more a victim than a villain is an obvious tribute that puts him in a class with most well-intentioned, unsuccessful statesmen of modern Germany.

[84] R.D., January 31, 1917.
[85] R.D., December 2, 1916.
[86] R.D., April 13, 1917.

Chapter 15

DOMESTIC CAUSES OF
THE FIRST WORLD WAR

Arno J. Mayer

When analyzing the origins of the Great War, diplomatic historians continue to focus on two sets of underlying and precipitant causes: those rooted in the dysfunctions of the international system and those rooted in the mistakes, miscalculations, and vagaries of the principal foreign policy actors. These historians assume that in a multiple-state system the balancing of power is a natural and essential method of control, notwithstanding its inherent uncertainties. In other words, they do not question or criticize the balancing-of-power system or process as such. Instead, they tilt their lances at four developments that complicated, if not obstructed, its smooth operation: 1. the alliance system, which became increasingly polarized and rigidified, thereby threatening to transform any limited, local conflict into an unlimited, general war; 2. the attendant armaments race, which exacerbated mutual hostility, fear, and distrust; 3. the new military metaphysics, which inclined civilian foreign-policy actors to become increasingly responsive to the military leaders and their iron-clad timetables; and 4. public opinion, expressed and mobilized through the daily press, notably the yellow and jingoist dailies, which were impatient with accommodation.

In addition to diagnosing these four dysfunctions in the balancing-of-power system or process, diplomatic historians also probe into the personal attitudes, motives, and objectives of the principal foreign-policy actors—heads of state, chief executives, foreign ministers, permanent foreign office officials, ambassadors, and military and naval officers. Not surprisingly, each major historian tends to have his favorite villain. Rather than indict entire nations, scholars tend to return verdicts against individual actors of a given nation or alliance. Three categories of charges are most commonly preferred: 1. that they made grave mistakes in diplomatic tactics; 2. that they miscalculated the responses of potential enemies; and 3. that they pursued objectives that were incompatible with the maintenance of the European equilibrium. But whatever the charge, in the last analysis their actions and judgments are said to have been warped by personal ambition, caprice, pique, or lack of backbone in the face of ruthless warmongers.

Admittedly, this framework of orthodox diplomatic history, tempered by amateur psychology, has been used to good advantage. It has served to uncover a great deal about the origins of the First World War in particular, and about the causes of international conflict in general.

Just the same, this time-honored approach has some rather grave limitations. In particular, it slides over 1. the proclivity of key foreign-policy actors to risk war in general, and preventive war in particular; 2. the degree to which they realized that any localized conflict was likely to develop into a major all-European or even world war; and 3. the extent to which they entertained recourse to external war for internal political purposes.

This third limitation stems very largely from the diplomatic historian's disposition to detach foreign policy hermetically from domestic politics; and to disconnect foreign-policy and diplomatic actors rigorously from the political and social context from which they originate and in which they operate.

Admittedly, this twofold dissociation, for analytic purposes, may not fatally handicap the study of the international politics of the relatively calm and elitist mid-eighteenth century. There seems little doubt, however, that this dual disjunction hinders the examination and understanding of foreign policy and diplomacy in such revolutionary eras as 1789 to 1815 and in such brief revolutionary spasms as 1848–50.

This interconnection of domestic politics and foreign policy is exceptionally intense under prerevolutionary and revolutionary conditions. Characteristically, in the prewar years domestic tensions rose sharply at the same time that the international system became increasingly strained. Moreover, this symbiotic growth of domestic and international tensions occurred in that part of the world in which, for the first time in recorded history, government policies, including foreign policies, were shaped in the crucible of organized party, pressure, and interest politics.

In other words, on the eve of war the major European polities were far from quiescent; and both the making and the conduct of foreign policy had ceased to be the private preserve of an encapsulated élite free of political pressures and neutral in the explosive domestic controversies of their respective societies. Accordingly, the 50 per cent increase in military spending in the five prewar years may not have been exclusively a function of mounting international distrust, insecurity, and hostility. In some measure it may also have been a by-product of the resolve by conservatives and ultraconservatives to foster their political position by rallying the citizenry around the flag; and to reduce the politically unsettling cyclical fluctuations of the capitalist economies by raising armaments expenditures. In this same connection it should be stressed that the chief villains of July–August 1914— those foreign-policy actors whom diplomatic historians identify as having practiced reckless brinkmanship—were intimately tied in with those social, economic, and political strata that were battling either to maintain the domestic status quo or to steer an outright reactionary course.

To attenuate if not overcome the limitations of diplomatic history's conventional approach to the causes of war its analytic framework should be recast to accommodate three aspects of the historical and immediate crisis that conditioned and precipitated hostilities in July–August 1914: 1. the dysfunctions in the international system; 2. the domestic dysfunctions in the would-be belligerent nations; and 3. the inextricable interplay between these two sets of dysfunctions.

Whereas the dysfunctions in the international system and the diplomatic rivalries among the major powers have been studied exhaustively and are well-known, the same cannot be said about the prewar domestic dysfunctions, notably about their all-European scope.

During the decade, including the weeks immediately preceding July–August 1914, the European nations experienced more than routine political and social disturbances. Even Britain, that paradigm of ordered change and constitutionalism, was approaching the threshold of civil war. Judging by the Curragh incident, Carson and the Ulster volunteers had the sympathy if not outright cooperation of influential civil and military leaders in their defiance of Parliament; and the Triple Alliance of railwaymen, miners, and transport workers, among whom militant syndicalists were ascendant, threatened a paralyzing general strike in case their minimum demands were not met by the fall of 1914. Whereas Ulster became the rallying issue and symbol for an influential conglomeration of conservatives and reactionaries, the strike project of the Triple Alliance roused extensive support throughout the restless Labour movement. The resulting polarization, along with the shift from debate in Westminster to direct action in the streets, eroded the vital center so essential for the politics of compromise and accommodation. Indeed, historians have wondered whether if external war had not come in 1914 England might not have become caught up in civil strife, with fatal damage to her time-honored parliamentary system.

In France, meanwhile, the struggle between the right and the left raged with unabated intensity around the twin issues of the three-year draft and the progressive income tax. As in England, the center of the political spectrum, which in France was multiparty in nature, was being eroded in favor of the two opposing extremes. In particular, the left's strident antimilitarism, which the right construed as a pressing social threat, frightened not only moderate republicans but also radicals into a common political front with the right. In turn, the *enragés* of the left made it increasingly difficult for the socialists to cooperate with the center-left, which stood accused of truckling to antirepublicanism. And, indeed, the right and center joined forces in support of the three-year draft, capitalizing on the appeals of nationalism to impugn the patriotism of the socialists, who advocated a two-year draft. This reordering of political partnerships was reflected in acute cabinet instability and in the antirepublican and protofascist right becoming the backstop for a conservative-leaning regime putting order and defense ahead of reform.

In Italy prewar political and labor disturbances culminated in the explosive Red Week of early June 1914. Especially once this strike wave subsided, and as usually happens in the wake of misfired rebellions, the Italian middle-class nationalists assumed a position of intransigent hostility to the left—including the moderate left—which in 1915 took the form of taking Italy into the war against the will of the vast majority of the Italian nation.

As for Germany's semi-parliamentary system, which was the privileged preserve of conservative nationalists, it was heavily besieged by those parties—the Social Democrats, the *Zentrum,* the Progressives, and the moderate wing of the National Liberals—that denounced Prussia's three-class franchise and clamored for the cabinet's subordination to the Reichstag. Paradoxically, the mounting militancy in certain key trade unions scared off potential converts to political reform. In any case, according to Arthur Rosenberg, the political and social tensions in prewar Germany were "typical of a pre-revolutionary period," and if Germany had not gone to war in 1914 "the conflict between the Imperial Government and the majority of the German nation would have continued to intensify to a point at which a revolutionary situation would have been created."[1]

The power élites in both halves of the Dual Monarchy faced increasingly explosive nationalistic unrest which, in itself, was an expression of spiraling political, economic, and social dysfunctions. Both Otto Bauer and Victor Bibl have argued convincingly that fear of southern Slav insurgency and of intensifying Austro-Czech tensions drove Vienna's political class into trying to overcome its permanent internal crisis by recourse to external war.

Simultaneously the Russian government, firmly controlled by unbending conservatives, confronted rising labor unrest in the major industrial centers alongside heightened restlessness among the peripheral national minorities. It was a sign of the times that during the first seven months of 1914 industrial unrest reached unparalleled scope and intensity, much of it politically and socially rather than economically motivated.

Great care must be taken to distinguish between, on the one hand, the actual scope and intensity of these internal tensions and disturbances, and, on the other hand, their perception, evaluation, and exploitation by the political contestants of the time. It is characteristic of prerevolutionary situations that hardened conservatives and counterrevolutionaries deliberately exaggerate all disorders, including the imminence of their transmutation into full-scale insurrection, in order to press and justify energetic precautionary measures. In turn, advanced reformers and revolutionaries similarly distort and distrust the intentions and actions of their domestic antagonists, charging them with pre-emptive counter-revolutionary designs. But this mutual misrepresentation itself

---

[1] Arthur Rosenberg, *Imperial Germany: The Birth of the German Republic, 1871–1918* (London, 1931), p. 58.

contributed to the polarization between the intransigent forces of order and the revolutionary forces of change, at the expense of the moderate, compromise-seeking center.

In Britain, France, and Italy parliamentary liberalism—the locus of this vital center—was heavily besieged, if not on the verge of collapse. The moderately reformist administrations of all three countries found it increasingly difficult to secure governing majorities. They were buffeted constantly by the parliamentary as well as extraparliamentary pressures of the militant counterrevolutionary right and the militant revolutionary left. In Germany, Austria-Hungary, and Russia, where the ruling power élite considered even the advocates of integral parliamentarism dangerous revolutionaries, the vital center was almost completely emasculated.

It would seem that in these as in other prerevolutionary eras, the specter of revolution precipitated an active counterrevolutionary response among vulnerable status groups—the landed aristocracy, the petty nobility, the petite-bourgeoisie, the artisans, and the bypassed entrepreneurs. In fact, there may well be a certain parallelism between the attitudes and actions of such crisis strata in domestic politics and the attitudes and actions of foreign-policy actors who consider their nation's international power and prestige to be declining. In both instances the threatened parties are particularly prone to force a pre-emptive showdown—armed repression or insurrection at home or preventive war abroad—with the resolve of thereby arresting or reversing the course of history, which they claim to be turning against them.

Admittedly, much has been written about the antiwar agitation that was such a prominent aspect of the prewar thunder on the left. Considerably less is known about the superpatriotic agitation that was so central to the corresponding thunder on the right. To be sure, conventional diplomatic historians have noted the upsurge of nationalism before the war, and its further inflammation during and immediately following the July crisis. Few, however, have bothered to examine systematically the social, economic, and political background of the political organizers and social carriers of this nationalist revival. Surely it is not without significance that nearly all the superpatriots who clamored for preparedness and foreign-policy pugnacity held reactionary, ultraconservative, or protofascist views on domestic affairs. Before the war there were few if any liberal conservatives or reformers in the Navy League, the Tariff Reform League, and the pro-Entente wing of the Unionist and Liberal parties in England; in the *Action française,* the *Ligue des patriotes,* and the *Fédération des gauches* in France; in the Nationalist Party and the *fasci* in Italy; in the Pan-German League and the Conservative Party in Germany; in the war party centering around the Archduke in Austria-Hungary; and in the Assembly of the Russian People and the Black Hundreds in Russia.

Evidently foreign-policy issues became highly politicized, since notwithstanding governmental appeals, the primacy of foreign policy is inoperative under prerevolutionary conditions. Whereas the campaign against the arms race was an integral part of the struggle against the forces of order, the campaign for preparedness was a central feature of the struggle against the forces of change. All along the superpatriots of the two opposing camps did each other's bidding in that they exploited and fomented the mutual suspicion, fear, hostility and insecurity that quickened the European arms race. The Pan-German League and the *Action française* unwittingly helped each other at the expense of heightening international tensions. Domestically, meanwhile, they were instrumental in frightening liberal conservatives and reformists into supporting national preparedness, thereby eroding the vital center. In the parliamentary nations of Western Europe as well as in the autocratic empires of Central and Eastern Europe the prewar governments were particularly responsive to superpatriotic blandishments whenever moderate and advanced reformists threatened a united front, as was the case when Caillaux and Jaurès explored the basis for cooperation. In brief, the center increasingly relied on the right as a backstop, with the powerful encouragement of the upper echelons of the army, the foreign offices, the diplomatic corps, the ministry of the interior, and—in most cases—the church. Almost without exception these time-honored institutions were strongholds of the threatened and intransigent crisis strata rather than of the self-confident and supple business and banking grande-bourgeoisie.

To a not inconsiderable degree, then, throughout Europe the rising international tensions were accompanied by rising internal tensions—by mounting social, political, and economic struggles that radicalized the extremes, eroded the center, and inclined the governments to push preparedness and diplomatic obduracy as part of their efforts to maintain a precarious domestic status quo.

II

These unsettling domestic developments were not without influence on the international situation. Judging by the experience of 1856 and 1870–71, military defeat promised to benefit the forces of change, while victory promised to benefit the forces of order. By 1887 Bismarck cautioned the monarchies to avoid war, since defeat, which could never be excluded, would rebound to the advantage of democratic, possibly even socialist forces. Once the reverses in the Russo-Japanese War threw Russia into revolutionary turmoil, thereby demonstrating the wisdom of Bismarck's admonition, Europe's statesmen, politicians, diplomatists, and editorialists began to face up to this relationship between external and internal war. At the conservative end of the political spectrum only select far-rightists and conservatives in Russia and Austria-Hungary warned against subjecting the brittle eastern empires to the rigors of modern war. Most others—Carson, Poincaré, von Westarp, Conrad von Hötzendorff, Maklakov—inclined to view war as an antidote to revolution. Left of the center of the political spectrum Grey, Morley, Giolitti, and Bethmann Hollweg tended to be afraid of war as a precipitant of social revolution, while Wilson, Lloyd George, Jaurès, and Caillaux feared it as a breeding ground of reaction. Needless to say, especially those political actors who contemplated recourse to external war as a diversion from domestic troubles thought in terms of a short, victorious rather than a protracted, unsuccessful conflict.

These views of the relationship of war and revolution seem to have left their imprint on the Sarajevo crisis of July 1914. Each government's foreign-policy course was affected by other than purely diplomatic, military, and security considerations. The principal foreign-policy actors in the executive could not ignore the political battle surrounding the question of war or peace: there were those individuals, pressure groups, factions, and parties that firmly resisted brinkmanship; those that actively pressed for accommodation or appeasement; and those that energetically opposed accommodation, to the point of actually urging recourse to war. Moreover, the ambassadors of the major powers were instructed to report home about the course of this partisan struggle in the country to which they were accredited.

At first the German Foreign Ministry assumed that "if only for reasons of domestic policy Russia would think well before provoking a European war, whose outcome was doubtful."[2] Bethmann Hollweg and his advisers assumed, furthermore, that because France was so sharply divided internally, Paris "would do everything to restrain Russia from intervention."[3]

By July 25, 1914, however, Pourtalès, the German Ambassador in St. Petersburg, informed Bethmann Hollweg that "the question said to have been discussed at yesterday's Ministerial Council was whether Russia's present *internal* situation was such that the country could look forward to *external* complications without uneasiness in this direction. The majority of the ministers present are said to have expressed themselves to the effect that Russia did not need to shun complications of that nature on account of the *internal* situation."[4] Three days later Sir George Buchanan, the British Ambassador in St. Petersburg, wired Foreign Secretary Grey that Sazonov, the Russian Foreign Minister, had "today received a telegram from the Minister of the Interior, who was making a tour of the provinces, telling him that he need have no fear concerning internal disturbances, and that in the event of war the whole nation would be behind the Government."[5] Should repressive measures be required, the Tsarist Government might draw courage from Izvolsky's wire of July 29 to the effect that if need be Viviani and Poincaré were prepared to deal resolutely with French pacifists.[6] Eventually Pourtalès reported that Maklakov, the Interior Minister, who was so reassuring about the provinces, was said to be part of a cabal "clique of chauvinists" which urged general mobilization less

[2] Koester, Baden's Chargé in Berlin, to Dusch, Baden's Foreign Minister, July 20, 1914, cited in Luigi Albertini, *The Origins of the War of 1914*, II (London, 1953), p. 59.

[3] Bethmann Hollweg to Riedern, Secretary of State for Alsace-Lorraine, July 16, 1914, cited in *ibid.*, p. 160.

[4] Cited in Max Montgelas and Walther Schücking (eds.), *Outbreak of the World War: German Documents Collected by Karl Kautsky* (London, 1924), p. 215 [italics mine].

[5] G. P. Gooch and Harold Temperley (eds.), *British Documents on the Origins of the War, 1894–1914*, XI (London, 1926), p. 162.

[6] See Albertini, *op. cit.*, pp. 600–1.

as a military measure than as a pre-emptive antidote to industrial disturbances and autonomist movements.[7]

In Vienna, nearly the entire political class wanted war, primarily in the hope that a quick but decisive military victory would raise its prestige at home and abroad. In its judgment, as in the judgment of so many of Napoleon III's advisers in 1869–70, even a striking diplomatic success, such as the thorough humiliation of Serbia, could not produce this twofold tonic. This predisposition to run the incredible risk of turning a local into a general crisis was reinforced by military and diplomatic experts who urged Berchtold to force a showdown before Russia completed her program of railway construction and army modernization and France implemented the three-year draft. General Conrad von Hötzendorff was a leading brinkman in spite of his own awareness that "in 1908–9 [war] would have been a [card] game in which we could see all the cards . . . ; in 1912–13 it would have been a [card] game with some chances of success . . . ; now it was *ein va-banque Speil.*"[8] On July 28 Shebeko, the Russian Ambassador in Vienna, advised Sazonov that the Austrian Government had decided to strike at Serbia "in order to raise its prestige on the Balkans *and at home,*" all the time calculating that German support and the inclination to appeasement of the other powers would keep the conflict localized.[9] It was feared that to forego decisive and dramatic action would further accelerate and intensify the growth of centrifugal pressures and movements that were undermining the Austrian monarchy and élites.

The Hungarian Prime Minister, Count Tisza, clearly saw that Austria's conservative political class was eager to seize upon the assassination in Sarajevo to precipitate a war that they hoped would shore up if not salvage their internal position. But Tisza had sound reasons for advising extreme caution. He realized that the primacy of the Magyar propertied and ruling class was contingent on the maintenance of Hungary's privileged status in

[7] J. F. Scott, *Five Weeks: The Surge of Public Opinion on the Eve of the Great War* (New York, 1927), p. 166, and Jean Stengers, "July 1914: Some Reflections," in *L'Annuaire de l'Institut de Philologie et d'Histoire Orientales et Slaves,* XVII (Brussels, 1963–65), pp. 105–48.

[8] Cited in Albertini, *op. cit.,* p. 122.

[9] Otto Hoetzsch (ed.), *Die Internationalen Beziehungen im Zeitalter des Imperialismus: Dokumente aus den Archiven der Zarischen und Provisorischen Regierung,* 1st. ser., V (Berlin, 1934), p. 143.

the Dual Monarchy which, in its turn, was the prime beneficiary of the existing European equilibrium. Whatever the outcome, war would upset this twofold balance. Whereas victory would lead to Hungary's subordination to a reinforced Austria and Germany, defeat—which Tisza considered the more likely eventuality—would pave the way for the reduction of Hungary to a narrow Magyar core. By mid-July Tisza abandoned his objections to Berchtold's deliberately provocative course, but he did so only following concerted pressure from Berlin.[10]

Indeed, the Berlin authorities encouraged rather than restrained those Austrian officials who thought that this opportunity for preemptive action should not be missed. It was von Jagow, the Secretary of State for Foreign Affairs, who as early as July 18 wired Lichnowsky, the German Ambassador in London, that since Austria-Hungary "hardly counted any longer as a really Great Power" Germany could not deprive her of her "last chance of political rehabilitation . . . [otherwise] the process of wasting away and of her *internal* decay would still be further accelerated." In this same dispatch von Jagow went on to relate Austria-Hungary's double-edged dilemma not only to Germany's international position but also to her own internal future.

> . . . the absolute establishment of the Russian hegemony in the Balkans is, indirectly, not permissible even for us. The maintenance of Austria, and, in fact, of the most powerful Austria possible, is a necessity for us both for *internal* and *external* reasons. That she cannot be maintained forever I will willingly admit. But in the meantime we may perhaps be able to arrange other combinations. . . . The more boldness Austria displays, the more strongly we support her, the more likely is Russia to keep quiet. There is certain to be some blustering in St. Petersburg, but at bottom Russia in not now ready to strike. France and England do not want war now. In a few years according to all expert opinion Russia will be ready to strike. . . . I have no wish for a *preventive* war, but if the fight offers itself, we dare not flinch. . . .[11]

In his reply of July 23 Lichnowsky met the issue of the interplay of domestic conditions and international politics head on.

> In the alliance [with Austria-Hungary] we must be the leading not the bleeding partner. . . . Austria's value as an ally depends

---

[10] See Albertini, *op. cit.*, pp. 126–33.
[11] Cited in Montgelas and Schücking (eds.), *op. cit.*, pp. 131–32, [italics mine].

above all else on her military capability, and not on her prestige abroad. . . . I believe as little in the imminent collapse of Austria as I believe in the possibility of *mastering internal troubles by prosecuting an active foreign policy*. . . . An active policy by Austria will only stimulate the nationalist feelings of the Southern Slavs and drive the Balkan nations even closer into the arms of Russia. . . . As far as localization of the struggle is concerned, you will have to admit that [it] . . . belongs in the realm of pious wishes. . . .[12]

It is still unclear whether and to what extent Bethmann Hollweg and imperial ruling circles inclined to bridge over or master Germany's own domestic entanglements with a brash foreign policy. Meanwhile, however, there is evidence to suggest that once he was satisfied that the Social Democrats would not oppose war by strike—and the German Government took the same systematic soundings of and precautions against antiwar pressures as the Russian, French, and Italian governments—he readily either yielded to or agreed with those of his civil and military advisers—and William II—who looked to a smashing diplomatic or military triumph to consolidate the monarchy, to perpetuate Prussia's three-class franchise, and to check both reformists and revolutionaries. Of course, Bethmann Hollweg tried all along to maneuver Russia into making the first overt military move, in the hope of casting her in a provocative role. Russian pugnaciousness would help not only to transmute the SPD's passive neutrality into active war enthusiasm but also to rally the antiwar elements in France and Britain, more particularly in the British cabinet. These same considerations prompted Berlin, at the very last minute and unsuccessfully, to urge Vienna not to reject Grey's mediation proposal out of hand and, still later, to ask Russia to cancel her partial mobilization.[13]

Similarly, Viviani and Poincaré, while assuring St. Petersburg of unqualified solidarity, sought to expose and dramatize Germany's aggressiveness for the benefit of the Radical Socialists and socialists in France and their counterparts in Britain. Certainly these political considerations weighed heavily in the decision of August 1 to pull back French troops from the Franco-German border by some 10 kilometers, thereby gravely endangering the

[12] Cited *ibid.,* pp. 188–89 [italics mine].
[13] See Fritz Fischer, *Griff nach der Weltmacht,* 3rd rev. ed. (Düsseldorf, Droste, 1964), Chs. 1–2.

critical Briey basin. In any case, the hard-liners both inside and outside the French cabinet, army, and foreign office pulled more weight than the unnerved socialists, particularly once the Radical and Radical Socialist deputies, on July 29, upon Poincaré's return to Paris from St. Petersburg, formally assured Premier Viviani of their full support for a collision course.[14] Since in addition to being internally divided the socialists were now completely isolated, the assassination of Jaurès was hardly needed to complete the paralysis of France's antiwar forces.

Sir Edward Grey still stands accused of a grave diplomatic blunder for not serving explicit and timely notice, especially to Berlin, that England would stand by France in the event his mediation miscarried and the Austro-Serbian conflict became generalized. There is no gainsaying his abhorrence of war, which may have unsteadied even an otherwise tenacious statesman. After all, it was Grey who repeatedly warned both Vienna and Berlin that in modern nations war would generate costs and dislocations that would "mean a state of things worse than that of 1848; . . . [that] irrespective of who were the victors in the war, many things might be completely swept away"; and that by going to war Europe would court economic bankruptcy.[15]

Even so, Grey's reluctance or failure unequivocally to declare Britain's intentions in time to give pause to Berlin and Vienna was due neither to diplomatic ineptitude nor to concern for the established European order. The Foreign Secretary's policy was a function of elementary political rather than diplomatic considerations.[16] He and Asquith were working with a cabinet that was split three ways: an important group of waverers, led by Lloyd George, held the balance between interventionists and anti-interventionists. In addition to being careful not to affront the mercurial Lloyd George with precipitate action, Asquith and Grey were worried about parliamentary support, since more than half the Liberal and all the Labour MP's allegedly were opposed

[14] E. Malcolm Carroll, *French Public Opinion and Foreign Affairs, 1870–1914* (New York, 1931), pp. 299–300.

[15] Montgelas and Schücking (eds.), *op. cit.*, pp. 184, 321–22; Gooch and Temperley (eds.), *op. cit.*, pp. 70–71; Ludwig Bittner, Alfred Pribram, et al. (eds), *Oesterreich-Ungarns Aussenpolitik von der Bosnischen Krise 1908 bis zum Kriegsausbruch 1914*, VIII (Vienna, 1930), pp. 602–3, 878.

[16] Cf. Albertini, *op. cit.*, p. 215.

to an interventionist course. Outside the cabinet and Parliament neutrality or extreme caution were stridently advocated by the Liberal and Radical press, the Labour movement at large, influential segments of the financial and business community, and various committees of intellectuals.

Who, then, urged that the informal but honor-binding diplomatic, naval, and military pledges to France be implemented? In the cabinet above all Asquith, Grey, and Churchill, with the first two trembling for the unity and survival of the Liberal Party; at the Foreign Office Arthur Nicolson and Eyre Crowe; and in the military establishment General Sir Henry Wilson.

These stalwarts of intervention eventually found their most vocal support among Unionists and Liberal Imperialists both inside and outside Commons; in such national conservative and/or superpatriotic papers like the *Times,* the *Daily Mail,* the *Morning Post,* and the *National Review;* and in patriotic and imperialist organizations. Having backed Grey's pro-French policy over the years, in part because the Foreign Secretary also served to keep the Radicals in check, the Unionists were expected to rally to his side.

It was Winston Churchill, the interventionist First Lord of the Admiralty, who with the consent of Asquith approached F. E. Smith to inquire whether if anti-interventionist Liberals resigned their Cabinet seats Unionists would fill them. Simultaneously Paul Cambon, the French Ambassador in London, who was on exceptionally close terms with Nicolson, notified a prominent Unionist—George Lloyd—that Grey "was pleading the attitude of the opposition as an excuse for inaction."[17] At any rate, between July 31 and August 2 the high command of the Unionist Party—Bonar Law, Amery, Chamberlain, Lansdowne, Balfour, and Carson—decided to back Grey against his own back-benchers without, however, reacting to the coalition feeler. In his letter of August 2 Bonar Law formally assured the Prime Minister of the united support of the Opposition, insisting that "any hesitation in supporting France and Russia would be fatal to the honor and the future security of the United Kingdom."[18] Incidentally, no mention was made of Belgian neutrality, the Unionists being concerned with Britain's informal understanding with France and with Brit-

[17] See Sir Austen Chamberlain, *Down the Years* (London, 1935), pp. 93ff.
[18] Cited *ibid.,* p. 99.

ain's isolation in case of a military victory by the Central Powers. For the conservatives this was essentially a matter of national interest—balance of power and security of Empire—rather than of moral obligation.

Asquith and Grey used this Unionist reinsurance, which carried a coalition threat, to win over the waverers and all but two of the anti-interventionists in the cabinet. Moreover, certain of Unionist support, when addressing Commons on August 3 Grey sought to rally the left opposition. Accordingly he studiously avoided any mention either of the balance of power or of Russia, both being anathema to Radicals and Labourites; and he devoted the second half of his speech to Belgian neutrality, thereby providing Lib-Lab dissenters with a moral justification and purpose for war. Even so, whereas his declaration was cheered wildly on Liberal Imperialist, Conservative, and Tory benches, large segments of the Liberal side of the House, not to speak of the Labour benches, remained undemonstrative. With Grey they sensed that the "lights were going out all over Europe" and that the great Liberal Party—that symbol of Europe's crumbling vital center—was lying down to die. Indeed, they had good cause to sit in solemn silence.[19]

It would seem, then, that any analysis of prewar foreign policy and diplomacy without careful attention to domestic variables is likely to leave a distorted picture not only of the long-run and immediate causes of the Great War but also of the place of that war in the international civil war of the twentieth century. Both the Great War and this civil war dramatize the degree to which the vital center ceased to be viable. Whereas the influences of the left on the politics and diplomacy of prewar Europe have been examined, these have not been studied alongside and in interaction with the attendant upsurge of their right-wing antithesis. In the immediate aftermath of the war defeat strengthened the forces of revolutionary change in the three defunct empires of Central and Eastern Europe while victory promoted their right-wing antithesis in the Allied and Associated nations.[20]

[19] See Francis R. Flournoy, *Parliament and War* (London, 1927), pp. 244ff.

[20] See Arno J. Mayer, *The Politics and Diplomacy of Peacemaking: Containment and Counter-Revolution at Versailles, 1918–1919* (New York, 1967), *passim*.

Chapter 16

NAUMANN AND RATHENAU: THEIR PATHS TO THE WEIMAR REPUBLIC*

Henry Cord Meyer

Walther Rathenau's last work, the text of a sophisticated address on the foreign policy of the Weimar Republic, was published in June 1922 in a magazine founded three decades earlier by Friedrich Naumann to convey his early message of the social gospel. Within that generation both of these men became widely known in Germany as political commentators. Naumann first attracted national attention at the turn of the century when he launched a movement which sought a comprehensive political solution for the national and social problems of his era. In subsequent years his continuing articles, books, and addresses gave him a public identity in prewar Wilhelmian Germany comparable to that of Walter Lippmann in modern America. Rathenau's journalistic career was meteoric by comparison, reaching its brilliance in the years from 1917 to 1920. Both men were troubled by the political immaturity and ineffectiveness of the Germans. Both felt that maturation and further experience for their nation would develop with reforms that took account of massive social and technological changes in modern society. Each eventually played a significant role in the early Weimar Republic. Death came to both as they were about to reach the culmination of their political careers. How did they conceive of politics and power? By what routes did they arrive at their responsibilities in the Weimar Republic?[1]

* This essay is an aspect of a larger study of German society in the era of Naumann and Rathenau, as seen through their writings and careers. The writer wishes to express his thanks to the John Simon Guggenheim Memorial Foundation and the American Philosophical Society for research grants during 1960–61 and the summer of 1963.

[1] Basic materials used in this essay include various major works of Naumann; *Die Hilfe*, 1918–19, *passim;* Theodor Heuss, *Friedrich Nau-*

These were, indeed, very different men by background and temperament. As Naumann grew up in the rustic limitations of rural Saxony, Rathenau came of age in a cultured Jewish milieu of Berlin, close to the mainstream of nineteenth-century intellectual developments. In 1883, shortly after Rathenau's father had established the German General Electric Company and laid the basis of his family's fortune, Naumann arrived as a young theologian in proletarian Hamburg to work with destitute children. For the next fifteen years he studied the whole range of social and political problems of the new German Empire. In the same period Rathenau finished his university education, torn between aesthetics and science as a vocation, and completed his managerial internship abroad and in Germany. By 1900 Rathenau had embarked on the fabulous business career that would place him, as he saw it, among the few hundred men who controlled the destiny of the Western world. At this time he also began to publish anonymously various belletristic pieces on art, morals, and society. For Naumann these were years of practical learning and maturation: struggles with conservative church authorities, the failures of his first political movement, and widening influence on German academic youth. During the prewar decade he was elected to the Reichstag and wrestled with social, economic, and foreign policy issues. He seldom missed a weekly contribution to the *Hilfe,* was often away on lectures and was always pressed to the full utilization of his capacities. Simultaneously Rathenau moved easily in the best circles of the Empire. He enjoyed friendships with Ballin, Hauptmann, Rilke, Liebermann, and Edvard Munch; there was association even with the Kaiser himself. Although both men were frequently in Berlin, there is no indication Naumann and Rathenau ever met before the war or were seriously aware of each other's endeavors.

Sometimes similarly, often very differently, these two men expressed their awareness of Germany's dilemmas and concern for her future. Initially Naumann spoke with almost primitive Germanic vehemence and competitive enthusiasm about nationalism

mann . . . (Stuttgart, 1937); various major writings of Rathenau; M. von Eynern, ed., *Walther Rathenau. Ein preussischer Europäer. Briefe* (Berlin, 1955); Hellmuth M. Boettcher, *Walther Rathenau* . . . (Bonn, 1958); Harry Kessler, *Walther Rathenau. His Life and Work* (London, 1929); James Joll, *Intellectuals in Politics: Blum, Rathenau, Marinetti* (London, 1960).

and imperialism; in later years he moderated these attitudes considerably. He was consumed with work and propagation of his ideas: articles in a dozen different papers; speeches to all sorts of groups; addresses in the Reichstag and work on its committees. Lujo von Brentano, who sometimes supplied Naumann with economic data, once commented that the man was so busy pouring out his analyses and proposals that he hardly had time to master the essential information.[2] No doubt Naumann was a simplifier (though hardly a terrible one, in Burckhardt's sense), and initially he was naïvely sentimental about many cultural and political issues. Yet, with restless energy and full personal commitment he would come to grips with any one of a dozen issues and often several simultaneously. This vitality came from a man fundamentally at peace with himself, trying to improve human relationships in a workaday world and in the context of Christian idealism.

Rathenau was a much more complicated personality. He ran the gamut of "boundless optimism to depths of black, all-embracing pessimism."[3] A key to his character, and the source of some of his frustration, was his effort to meld the essence of the Hebrew ethic with the spirit of romantic German nationalism. He possessed a social conscience derived from the Old Testament prophets, yet he savored the refinements and comfortable material setting of Prussian classicism. He suffered from an awareness of the Jewish situation, which he hoped to resolve by making the Jews into Germans, "like Saxons, Bavarians or Wends," who would "live and die in Germany, and for Germany, as our fathers did before us."[4] Business attracted much of his energy between 1890 and 1914, but there is little evidence as to how he conducted these affairs or developed his techniques of administration. The Rathenau we know is the man of arts and letters, the thwarted humanist. No doubt he had a more capable and refined intellect than Naumann; yet his acute analytical powers apparently did not give him a satisfactory sense of self-fulfillment. His letters convey the sense of a man under constant self-restraint, of a would-be philosopher in a world of mechanization, of an ambitious man pulling a taut rein on his acknowledged will to

[2] Lujo Brentano, *Mein Leben* (Jena, 1931), p. 276.
[3] Joll, p. 60.
[4] Quoted in Joll, p. 66.

power. Naumann could fully immerse himself in his causes and usually had some sense of response from the various groups with which he communicated. Ratheau's correspondence, even in the final year of relative political success, reveals a man who felt he was not recognized for his real worth, who suffered from being misunderstood, who yearned for more appreciation than he had so far earned.

Each of the two men had a distinctive style of communication and concept of political action. From his Christian convictions Naumann carried an emotional momentum that expressed itself as joyous zeal in a political offensive and provided a spiritual resource in times of trouble or retreat. Rathenau probably overcompensated intellectually for his fine sensitivity and basic emotion; he knew that as a Jew in Germany he was always potentially a stranger in a hostile land. Naumann had an instinctive talent for effective contact with men in all walks of life; he was gregarious, with perhaps a touch of charisma on occasion. Rathenau was essentially a loner. He always resented being a subordinate member of a group and expressed confidence that his abilities lay in technical and organizational tasks, in being able "to recognize human capacities and see through people, to associate, talk, write and arrange various combinations with human beings."[5] But he used these capacities intellectually, not empathetically. Naumann could earn the trust and confidence of hundreds; Rathenau's personal influence seldom went beyond individual friendships.

The art of politics and the character of power assumed different specifications in the minds of these two men. Commitment and struggle were essential ingredients of politics and power in Naumann's view. Early in the century he published *Demokratie und Kaisertum,* a survey of German problems and potentialities resolved in the naïve hope that a firm and wise monarch would preside over a successful struggle to realize genuine parliamentary government. "But let us not imagine," wrote Naumann, "that pursuit of politics necessarily means measurably improving the welfare of each individual human being; nor would we believe the political struggle makes us personally happier. . . . We know that when we win, others must lose. Yet this fact should not keep

[5] Letter to Frau Rathenau, January 1, 1893, in v. Eynern, p. 58.

us from wanting to win. He who would not triumph over anyone
. . . may be a model human being and Christian, but he will
hardly qualify as politically creative."[6] Politics are related to the
power stance of the nation. "Foreign policy is more important
and more difficult than internal policy. . . . Both are different
manifestations of the same quality. . . . But foreign policy has
at any given moment greater responsibility, because internal reforms, freedom, prosperity all diminish and fragment when the
outward thrust of power fails." "Never will a great nation let
itself be guided by leaders who are not absolutely trustworthy
in their own confidence in power. . . . Here lies the key to all
other political problems."[7] Naumann could hardly have surmised
that two decades later he would play a formative role in a new
German state that had to achieve reform in a milieu certainly not
without internal struggle, but that was also defeated and bereft
of any outward thrust of power.

From his vantage point as a business manager Rathenau developed other concepts of power. In 1904 he wrote to a friend
that physical power was no longer decisive. "The strong man no
longer plays a role in this world. . . . Personal courage does not
influence decisions in the Far Eastern war; these stem from the
wisdom of the naval engineers and supply organizers, from discipline based on fear—and money. . . . Bourgeois life is determined solely by reason. The sagacious man combines and organ-
izes; he works, strives and achieves. . . . True power is wielded
by those who have cleverly risen from the ranks. Vanderbilt,
Rockefeller, Carnegie and Krupp are the kings and fate of our
time."[8] A decade later he wrote in a similar vein: "It is not the
physical power of the battalions in themselves, but this power
multiplied by the degree of business capacity, that decides a nation's position in the world."[9] As the organizer of Germany's raw
materials during World War I, Rathenau gave measurable effect
to these conceptions. But as Foreign Minister of the Weimar
Republic in 1922, though he dealt precisely with business and
management on an international scale, he must have sensed that
power had more primitive dimensions.

[6] From *Demokratie und Kaisertum,* quoted in Heuss, p. 173.
[7] *Ibid.,* as quoted in Heuss, p. 175.
[8] Letter to F. Wedekind, November 21, 1904, in v. Eynern, p. 66.
[9] Quoted in Kessler, p. 162.

During the war both men vaulted into prominence. Early in the conflict Rathenau gave the decisive turn to German war economics, whose effects changed the socio-economic pattern of the nation. Contacts with men like Bethmann Hollweg and Ludendorff kept him in touch with decision-making at the highest levels under politically simplified circumstances. His conception of postwar continental economic integration is thought to have given significant direction to German war aims.[10] Concurrently Naumann achieved his greatest fame with the publication of his wartime best seller, *Mitteleuropa*. With this concept he went beyond Rathenau's ideas of a customs union and economic rationalization for Europe. Naumann attempted to lift German sights from narrower nationalism, war-aims quarrels, and annexations to survey a postwar German society interrelated with other nations of Middle Europe and living with them in a new context of social and cultural relationships. By 1917 Naumann was completely caught up in the political cross-currents of the era; Rathenau by that time was largely disengaged from official tasks and turned to the most active phase of his career as a political commentator.

By what paths did these two men then come to the Weimar Republic?

Naumann's way was much more direct than Rathenau's and his sojourn there was brief. During the latter part of the war he focused his interest primarily on internal affairs. No longer was he the chauvinistic nationalist of 1898; his devotion to country and people was expressed with pride in their wartime sacrifices and with apprehensive concern that they realize their finer potentialities. From the beginning Naumann had sought to reconcile bourgeoisie and workers, had denounced the inequities of Prussia's suffrage and the stupidities of her agrarian policies, including the struggle with the Poles. As he envisioned a *Volksstaat,* it might still be the monarchy he had once sentimentally acclaimed in his first major book, but now the emphasis was firmly placed upon parliamentary democracy. His major themes recur: realization of elemental justice in social and economic relationships; education of Germans to meaningful political participation in the affairs of state; cooperation of masses and classes in a nation-state representing their finest ethical and cultural achievements; and,

[10] See Fritz Fischer, *Griff nach der Weltmacht,* 2nd ed. (Düsseldorf, 1962), pp. 107–13.

finally, a crucial role for Christianity as the force that maintains the individual spiritually and sustains him in the face of modern mass pressures.

The collapse of 1918 found Naumann on a speaking tour among soldiers. Like all Germans, he was overwhelmed by the suddenness of events, and was bewildered and fearful. Then he reappraised the situation: the soldiers had done their part, now it was the civilians' turn. Primarily he feared interruption of Germany's political continuity and loss of her unity. He gave whatever support he could to the Moderate Socialists and their leaders. "It would be hardly bearable," he wrote, "if we survived the armistice and our defeat without a fundamental renewal of the state."[11]

Political changes also produced a new organization, the German Democratic Party, which drew significant support from the circles where Naumann's ideas had long been popular. He became their leading, and winning, candidate from Berlin for election to the National Assembly. Next to the Moderate Socialists, this party drew the strongest support in Germany. Until the end, Naumann continued at Weimar his characteristic efforts at rapprochement with the socialists, seeking to draw their support for the nation and a left-of-center synthesis that stood off sharply from the right as well as from Bolshevism. When seriously considered for the Presidency, he declined, indicating it should go to Ebert in order to strengthen the involvement of the socialists in the state and foster their sense of responsibility for it. He might have moved into the Foreign Office, but in consultation with his party caucus he decided to stay with the greater challenges at Weimar. He wrote with characteristic metaphor in the *Hilfe:* "Those who expected to greet the Republic in the sparkling light of a struggle for freedom, will have to withhold their palm fronds a little longer. [Instead] our Republic has come to us in the ordinary houseclothes of daily cares and duties. Every day her health has been somewhat uncertain. But thus we have all learned to look after her as a fragile child."[12]

Many of the issues that had long attracted Naumann became items of deliberation at Weimar. He would have preferred a fed-

[11] *Die Hilfe,* December 5, 1918.
[12] *Ibid.,* March 6, 1919.

eral state, like the American union, with a strong executive power. Failing in this endeavor, he turned his energies to another aspect of the emerging constitution—the major section on Fundamental Rights and Duties of Germans. Recalling the spirit in which the first Declaration of the Rights of Man and the Citizen had appeared in 1789, Naumann sought to make an impact in Germany that would be ideological as well as legal. Often bills of rights in the nineteenth century were catalogues of grievances. He wanted to be more positive, to awaken the citizen to his obligations, to indicate areas of future creative development for a people just emerging into the freedom of self-government. Obviously the Weimar Constitution was the result of many minds and influences, but the mark of Naumann's lifelong endeavor is stamped on the Fundamental Rights and Duties. It expressed the pride of a German citizen, free under law (Art. 109). Marriage and the family were related both to individual personality and the interest of the nation (Arts. 119–22). Property was viewed as more than just a right. It was identified as entailing responsibilities meaningful to the individual *and* the community; rural and municipal land reform were seen as duties that a landlord owed his community (Arts. 153–55). And, finally, there was Article 165, for which Naumann fought especially hard. It anticipated the kind of community he saw evolving in the twentieth century, where new kinds of group action and group relationships were needed to take the place of anarchic individualism: Statutory bodies representative of workmen and employees were to be created for the protection of their social and economic interests at various levels in the new state.[13]

Another set of issues attracted Naumann's earnest attention and commitment: the interrelationship of church, school, and state. These were the areas of concern that had originally prompted his move from parish into public life. In these matters he again found himself at Weimar in a crucial position to mediate between left and right. The socialists originally desired to relegate religion to the category of personal hobbies, but they wished to supervise education carefully. The conservatives desired to retain as much as possible of the imperial structure of church and school

[13] Heinrich Oppenheimer, *The Constitution of the German Republic* (London, 1923), pp. 244–57; in general, Heuss, pp. 603–21.

relationships. Naumann wanted the church to have full opportunity to develop in the community; but he did not wish to see it a part of the new state or as strongly influenced by the upper church bureaucracy, which had stressed particularism at the expense of the nation. He envisioned a united Protestant church, living alongside other faiths, which could respond to more liberal and creative influences in clerical and lay membership. Naumann wanted to modernize schools in subject matter and cultural spirit, but he also sought a secure place in the curriculum for emphasis on religious ethics, without which he felt no man could be whole. Church reorganization proceeded generally as he wished, but he lost his struggle to integrate religious ethics with the heart of public education.[14]

Naumann did not survive the summer of 1919. He had weakened physically in the later war years; the psychological shock of national defeat and disorderly change hastened his death. One senses the change in his writings: the convictions are still there, but not the vigor; his characteristic enthusiasm gives way to forced effort and anxieties of duty. Naumann lived to see the Promised Land of a new German state before him, incomplete and distorted; but he did not enter into it.

Rathenau, unlike Naumann, did not move directly into the great issues of his time, as it were, on the street level. He gives instead the impression of descending from Olympian heights of aesthetics and intellect. Prior to 1912, his works appear as impressions, aphorisms, and reflections. His views on economics and society emanate from executive offices, largely uninfluenced by contact with workshop, laboratory, or discussion with labor. Rathenau expressed dismay at the "impudent folly," the "arrogance of materialized life," and "the disgraceful affairs" of the semi-absolutist Empire.[15] He also sought an alternative in a *Volksstaat,* a romanticized conception of the German nation sustained by a trained, almost self-denying and self-governing middle class, into which the better men of the masses might rise by talent and accomplishment. Just before the war he wrote *Kritik der Zeit* and *Mechanik des Geistes,* works that philosophically underlie all his subsequent writing. They reflect the continuing tension between the heart of a poet, the spirit of a prophet,

[14] Heuss, pp. 621–31.
[15] *In Days to Come* (New York, 1921), pp. 184–85.

and the head of an administrator. His penetrating comments on current issues were enshrouded in a haze of mysticism that rejected materialism and conjured up profounder spiritual values. His readers found shrewd analyses of Germany's ills combined with alternatives that defied practical fulfillment.

Between 1917 and 1919, Rathenau published a succession of appeals and pronouncements: *In Days to Come, The New Economy, To Germany's Youth, The New State, The New Society*. He opened the first of these works with these words: "This book treats of material things, but treats of them for the sake of the spirit. . . . All earthly activities and aims find their justification in the expansion of the soul and its realm."[16] Man must search through doubt, exhaustion, and despair in order to find the courage to establish values and speak of change and future work. In his heart he will then find the "transcendental conditions" that require new language, new imagery, and fresh illumination for the tasks ahead. "When we turn from mechanization as an objective fact, and when we comprehend it from within as a spiritual revolution, [then] we realize most intensely that we primarily need a redirection of the spiritual, not the mechanical [factors in life]."[17]

What sort of community did Rathenau envisage? He was convinced that the existing capitalist order would give way to a new type of integrated socio-economic organization. That new society would still contain the power of tradition, a role for authority, and a sense of nation and *Volk;* it would appeal to austere self-discipline and be uncorrupted by the enervating rivalries of competing groups. The changes he called for were intended to strengthen the power and competence of a new, moral society. It would become the focal center of all economic life and assume the power now wielded by the managerial class. Spiritual forces would have an opportunity to develop. Existing follies of production and irresponsibilities of consumption—including the manifold vanities of women—would be curbed; the energies thus saved would be guided into channels supporting the new state and its defense. It was to be a people's state: "every group of the population shall secure a due share of influence, every legitimate peculi-

16 *Ibid.*, p. 11.
17 *Ibid.*, p. 43.

arity shall find expression, every available spirit shall have its appropriate method of service. As in a well-ordered household, labor authority, relationships and responsibility, disposition, expenditure, communal sentiment and mutual confidence must cooperate in harmonious union."[18] Tradition, intellect, and expertise were to be the guiding hands in a society with freedom for full participation of all according to talent and accomplishment.

Rathenau's *Volksstaat* would not be a product of institutions, would not be created by written laws and a constitution; it would be born of the spirit and the will. When the right public attitude of mind had developed, then institutions—so far as these were necessary—would be created. The supreme power of state would be entrusted to responsible leadership that stood above all striving, desire, and temptation of common life. The people of the society would hopefully have the fine qualities that Rathenau saw in the Prussians: the breeding of true aristocracy and the plasticity of the masses, which latter group had produced the "two great Prussian organizations," the army and social democracy.[19] Calling upon Germany's youth, Rathenau pleaded for national reawakening in a Germany that would be the leader of a new economic and social order in the Western world. "Our way of life will be new, [as will be] our economy, our social structure and the form of our state. The relations between states will be new, as will be world trade and politics. Our learning and even our speech will be new. . . . The great ones of the past have had their say. It is now time for the common man to speak."[20] But how would Rathenau close the gap between his philosophic élitism and sincere concern for a reformed common man?

When the German revolution came in 1918, Rathenau wrote: "I welcome it and have no doubts about our future, in spite of all the internal and external pressures upon us."[21] He turned to practical political tasks, founded a Democratic Peoples' Union, and drew up a manifesto that was refreshingly clear in contrast to his characteristic writing. It supported the revolution, attacked reaction, called for a constitutional democratic state, proclaimed equality in education and work, and demanded limitations on

[18] *Ibid.*, p. 203.
[19] *Ibid.*, pp. 205–20.
[20] *An Deutschlands Jugend* (Berlin, 1918), pp. 74, 90.
[21] Letter to Curt Bran, December 16, 1918, in v. Eynern, p. 292.

property and income. Finally, the old Spartan theme reappeared:

> Industry is not a private concern of individuals; it concerns everyone. Production must be increased by avoiding waste. . . . Nationalization should take place where suitable. The import and consumption of luxuries should be taxed and restricted. . . . Life must be made more simple.[22]

The Democratic Peoples' Union was stillborn. Rathenau tried to run for the National Assembly in the German Democratic Party—and lost. He blamed these political defeats on various groups: on the hidebound middle class that refused to consider social problems seriously; on the socialists, whom he considered incarnations of soul-destroying mechanization and materialism. But the dimensions of opposition to him were more complicated than these simple explanations. Labor suspected him not only because of his attacks on Marx and socialism; they identified him as a prominent element of big business. His fellow businessmen considered him a renegade. To the racists he was simply a Jew; but many Jews opposed his views on the Jewish question in Germany. Despite the wide circulation of his writings, or because of them, Rathenau aroused no political enthusiasm and found few adherents for his cause.

The German Revolution ran its course through the winter of 1918–19. Several governmental commissions deliberated at length on measures of socialization for the new state, the new economy, and the new society; Rathenau played no role in these matters, was not even summoned as a consultant. Major foreign policy decisions arose in connection with the Versailles Treaty and required initial German responses. Rathenau's only connection with these events was the gossip that linked him with a potential list of war criminals whom the Allies were expected to demand for trial. "I realize without any feeling of sadness and resignation," he wrote in that winter, "that I myself will not contribute to this future [of Germany]. My writings have made me an enemy of the old middle class; the new powers-that-be do not welcome me as one of themselves, but, for some reason or other that I do not know, they regard me as an opponent."[23] Later he was

[22] In Kessler, pp. 260–61.
[23] Letter to Curt Bran, December 16, 1918, in v. Eynern, p. 292.

resigned: "We have been dreaming, dreaming there was a revolution. We awake, find ourselves in a democracy and do not know what has happened to us."[24]

Rathenau was finally called to government service in early 1920, to work with the Second Socialization Commission. In these deliberations he stood with a gradualist majority against more radical socialist proposals. Echoing his earlier distrust of socialist politics, which he saw as continuing evidence of the "fruitless old party and agitation system," he indicated that "care must be taken to avoid premature formation of political systems for which the [ethical] driving force has not yet been developed."[25] This contact was his one, superficial involvement with the reconstitution of German society, about which he had thought and written so much.

In the spring of 1920, through a growing friendship with Finance Minister Josef Wirth (and in face of strong opposition), Rathenau joined the delegation of German experts attached to continuing conferences with the Allies on problems of reparations. Thus began his one, meaningful, and final association with the German Republic. At last Rathenau was on home ground in intimate, personal, and expert relationship with major men and issues relating to political-economic problems on an international scale. He could now bring his broad business experience and intellectual brilliance to bear on German foreign policy and international economic complications. Yet even here he experienced no real sense of accomplishment. The basic political decisions at home were made by others; the Allied representatives abroad were no more inclined to respond to his bold economic proposals than they had earlier to suggestions by John Maynard Keynes.[26] A brief term of office in the summer of 1921, as Minister of Reconstruction, firmly established his public identity with a program of fulfilling the onerous reparations demands but gave no time for the longer-range results of this policy to bear fruit. His appointment as Foreign Minister in 1922 came not as a tribute of public confidence. Rathenau reluctantly assumed the responsibility in the absence of willingness by any politically oriented per-

[24] Quoted in Boettcher, p. 202.
[25] Quoted in Boettcher, p. 119.
[26] On Rathenau in foreign affairs see Eric C. Kollman, "Walther Rathenau and German Foreign Policy: Thoughts and Actions," *Journal of Modern History,* XXIV (1952), 127–42.

sonality to take the unpopular job. Arrived at last, almost by default, in a position of crucial significance for the German nation, Rathenau was still thwarted by circumstances and then struck down by assassination.

By very different paths Naumann and Rathenau came to the Weimar Republic. Naumann was certainly not the most influential man at Weimar; but events bear the clear stamp of his role in the working politics of the German Democratic Party, in the various discussions at Weimar, and in significant aspects of the new German constitution. In the same era, in relation to the same interests, Rathenau was a bystander—constantly thinking and writing, often read, generally rejected or ignored. Naumann's impact was finally mature, emotionally convincing, and politically effective. Rathenau, who was intellectually overwhelming and technically brilliant, made no significant political impact. His efforts in foreign policy remained unfulfilled because of his untimely death; but considering the circumstances, the issues, and the man, there is ample reason to doubt they could ever have been successful. There was a constant thread in Naumann's political striving (whatever the weaknesses of his various proposals and projects) that was woven into the fabric of the Weimar Republic and is still discernible a generation later. Rathenau never really entered into the political edifice of the Republic. His conceptions of internal reform remain as thought-provoking philosophical sermons; his foreign policy appears as a fragment of a bygone era. Each of these men will probably be remembered as long as the other, but with this distinction: Naumann was in the political mainstream of his time; Rathenau was always an outsider.

Chapter 17

FRIEDRICH EBERT AND THE
GERMAN REVOLUTION OF 1918

Richard N. Hunt

I

The November Revolution of 1918 was one of the critical turning points of German history, although perhaps a turning point where—as A. J. P. Taylor said of 1848—German history failed to turn. Certain it was that the semi-absolutist empire of the Hohenzollerns would not survive military collapse without internal transformation. By the autumn of 1918 the forces that held it together were defeated and demoralized, while the pressures for change, both from within Germany and from without, had grown irresistible. But what sort of transformation would occur? Would Germany emerge from the war as a democratized constitutional monarchy? Would it follow the Russian path to Communist dictatorship? Or would it produce (as it actually did) a democratic republic tragically shackled to the surviving twin pillars of Prussian authoritarianism—the army and the bureaucracy? Or was there perhaps still another alternative, a republic not so shackled but based on a more thoroughly democratized governmental apparatus and social structure? Upon Germany's political leaders of 1918–19 fell the primary responsibility for determining which of these historically possible futures would become actuality.

The German November Revolution produced no great charismatic leader, no Cromwell, Robespierre, or Lenin. What leadership it had was provided almost entirely by the Social Democratic Party (SPD), headed by an earnest but relatively colorless official, Friedrich Ebert. It was Ebert whose choices and actions, more than those of any other single individual, set Germany's course through the revolution and into the unsettled era which followed. To make a fresh examination of these choices and actions, of Ebert's values and his use of power, is the task of this study.

Ebert's political values can perhaps be summed up in three key words—patriotism, democracy, socialism. Ebert loved his country and had supported it loyally throughout the war, but he wanted to see its government democratized and its social structure reformed in an egalitarian direction. These three values, however compatible in the abstract, tended to produce conflicting responsibilities for the exercise of power in the concrete historical situation Ebert faced. With his country defeated and surrounded by hostile powers, patriotism suggested collaboration with the old ruling establishment, at the expense of democratic and socialist aspirations. After the revolution and the failure of his party to win an electoral majority, democratic values seemed to preclude the execution of a socialist program. Alternately, the temptation of power and the desire for socialism might have led Ebert—as it had Lenin—to sacrifice democratic principles as well as the territorial integrity of his country. These conflicting claims of conscience posed agonizing choices that would have staggered even an experienced and self-confident political leader.

Friedrich Ebert, however, was singularly unsuited for the role he assumed, which adds still another dimension to the problem of historical assessment. On his own abilities he had become, prior to the war, a Social Democratic party secretary, and in other times he might well have served out his years in that modest capacity. A series of fateful accidents elevated him first to the chairmanship of his party, then to the leadership of the revolutionary provisional government, and ultimately to the Presidency of the Weimar Republic. He was not born to power, nor did he seek it; rather it was thrust upon him. As a former bureaucrat, reluctantly turned revolutionary, he was instinctively inclined to use power conservatively and collaborate with previously existing authorities.

Mixing together the limited historical possibilities inherent in the situation, the conflicting claims of Ebert's political principles, and finally his inexperience and limitations as a political leader, one has the necessary ingredients for a discussion of responsibility and power in the German Revolution of 1918.

Friedrich Ebert was born in 1871, the son of a Heidelberg

master tailor.[1] After a primary school education and an apprenticeship in the saddling trade, he found work in Mannheim where his father's stepbrother first introduced him to Lassallean socialist ideas. The eighteen-year-old Ebert joined the Social Democratic Party and the saddlers' union. He wandered to northern Germany, doing organizational work for the union, and eventually settled in Bremen. From the beginning Ebert was disposed toward a practical and reformist socialism. In addition to his union activities, he busied himself during the Bremen years (1891–1905) editing the local SPD newspaper, organizing a bakers' cooperative, and creating a labor secretariat to advise workers on their legal rights, especially in social welfare matters. He was also the first Social Democrat elected to the Bremen city council, where he worked for improved social legislation and for the democratization of the franchise. Never a great theoretician or popular orator, Ebert's activity in these formative years revealed his boundless energy and considerable administrative talent, as well as his inclination to work within existing institutions in collaboration with existing authorities.

Meanwhile Ebert also rose within the Social Democratic organization. Representing Bremen at the annual party congresses, he eventually attracted national attention and in 1904 was considered for a post on the party executive, but was vetoed by the ruling patriarch of the SPD, August Bebel, as standing too far to the right. The very next year, however, he was elected over Bebel's opposition because of the energetic support given him by the reformist-minded trade unions. At this time the executive consisted of two chairmen, a treasurer, and (with Ebert) four secretaries. Moving to Berlin in early 1906, Ebert soon found himself busy developing and rationalizing the party apparatus in accordance with a newly adopted organizational statute. He introduced modern office methods in party headquarters, appointed paid functionaries to staff new regional organizations, and required regular reports from both regional and local units. In a

---

[1] The most comprehensive, but uncritical, biography of Ebert is Georg Kotowski, *Friedrich Ebert, Eine politische Biographie* (Wiesbaden, Steiner, 1963), of which only the first volume has appeared to date. More thought-provoking, but very brief, is Waldemar Besson, *Friedrich Ebert, Verdienst und Grenze* (Göttingen, Musterschmidt, 1963). The facts of Ebert's life I have taken from these two works.

large sense Ebert was the creator of the famous SPD bureaucracy.[2]

It was perhaps the central tragedy of German Social Democracy that no first-rate younger leaders were able to grow up in
the broad shadow of August Bebel. His death in 1913 (combined with the death of his co-chairman, Paul Singer, two years
earlier) left a vacuum that had to be filled by men who should
never have taken such important posts. When Singer died in 1911,
the trade unions proposed Ebert to replace him, but Bebel—
though impressed by Ebert's administrative accomplishments—
gave his decisive support to Hugo Haase, a mild-mannered and
rather ineffectual Königsberg lawyer who stood closer to the center
of political gravity within the party. When Bebel himself died two
years later, however, there was no one but Ebert to fill the
vacant co-chairmanship. The two new chairman divided the work
appropriately between them: Haase, with his legal training and
greater parliamentary experience, would assume the political leadership of the movement; Ebert would look after the party apparatus. Even for this lesser responsibility Ebert felt himself inadequate, and he accepted the position with genuine reluctance.

The schism precipitated in German Social Democracy by World
War I carried Ebert to still greater heights. Taken by surprise
when the war broke out in August 1914, Ebert quickly joined
the great majority of Social Democratic leaders who supported
the government in what seemed to them a war of self-defense. As
it happened, the pacifist-inclined Haase belonged to the minority
that opposed the war from the outset. By 1917 the growing antiwar minority had separated from the majority and, under Haase's
leadership, formed the new Independent Social Democratic Party
(USPD). This schism, which Ebert tried for a long time to avert,
had the incidental effect of leaving him in command of the old
party. At the Würzburg congress of 1917, Ebert became the
senior co-chairman, with Philipp Scheidemann elected to the second chairmanship.

Thus was Ebert lifted to the leadership of Germany's largest
party as the Empire approached its critical hour. Shortly he would

[2] On this point see especially Carl E. Schorske, *German Social Democracy, 1905–1917* (Cambridge, Harvard, 1955), pp. 122–27. Schorske's
description of Ebert: "Colorless, cool, determined, industrious, and intensely practical, Ebert had all those characteristics which were to make
of him, *mutatis mutandis,* the Stalin of Social Democracy" (p. 124).

have to make political decisions of the gravest consequence. In late September 1918, General Erich Ludendorff concluded that the war was lost and decided to create a parliamentary government to replace his own quasi-dictatorship. He did this mainly in the hope of securing more favorable peace terms from the victorious Western democracies, but also in the hope of averting the more profound political and social alterations that conservatives feared might follow the collapse of German arms. The liberal Prince Max of Baden was picked to become chancellor, but he could not form a majority government without Social Democratic support. The party had to decide. Against Scheidemann's urgings that it was foolhardy to enter a "bankrupt concern," Ebert convinced the party leaders to join Prince Max's coalition. "If you consider the interest of the party," he told them, "you must oppose participation in the government; but if on the contrary you believe that the collapse of our country cannot be a matter of indifference to us, then consider most seriously if we should not take the risk upon ourselves."[3] The wisdom of this move, which allowed the military to shift the burden of defeat from its own shoulders, will doubtless always be a matter of controversy. But no one doubts Ebert's deep sense of political responsibility, his readiness to place the needs of his country, as he understood them, above the interest of his party.

If joining Prince Max's government bore with it the onerous responsibility of accepting the victors' peace terms, it also offered the positive prospect of participating in Germany's democratization. One by one, in October 1918, the democratic reforms long demanded by the SPD and long resisted by the ruling classes were put into effect: parliamentary control over the cabinet, over war and peace, over military appointments, together with elimination of the three-class system of voting in Prussia. These major reforms, the "October Revolution," satisfied the basic political demands of Ebert and the Majority Social Democratic leaders. Although theoretically republicans, they preferred not to press that issue now. Indeed, they saw positive advantages in retaining a figurehead monarchy to help preserve order in the difficult transition from war to peace. And they had no desire to bring to life a royalist opposition such as plagued the early years of the

[3] Quoted in Wilhelm Keil, *Erlebnisse eines Sozialdemokraten* (Stuttgart, Deutsche Verlags-Anstalt, 1947), I, 448.

French Third Republic. In his last speech before the old Reichstag, Ebert spoke warmly of the October reforms as the "birth of
German democracy," and also expressed his hope for a mild
peace.[4] He clearly looked forward, not to revolution, but to an
influential position for his party in the postwar governing coalition
of a democratized constitutional monarchy.

Thus Ebert belonged to that broad segment of moderate opinion that, at the war's end, pressed for democratic reform but
sought to retain legal continuity with the past, especially through
the institution of the monarchy. Many historians have subsequently expressed regret that Germany did not follow this path.[5]
It offered the prospect of a stronger central authority to guide the
nation through the exceedingly difficult postwar period. Perhaps
most important in light of later developments, it offered the hope
of retaining the loyal cooperation of the traditional élites—army,
administration, landowners, industrialists, educators, and clergy—
which the Weimar Republic, for the most part, so conspicuously
lacked. In a monarchical Germany, so it is argued, these groups
would never have considered giving Hitler power, nor would
the Nazis have won such widespread support among the masses.
Attractive as these considerations are, one must remind oneself
of the difficulties: neither William II nor the crown prince
was a likely candidate for a figurehead monarchy, and a regency
would lack much of the desired authority. With the executive
apparatus of the old regime basically intact, would formal parliamentary controls have been any more effective than they were in
the Weimar Republic? How long would the center-left coalition
have retained its majority and its control of the cabinet? And if
traditional conservatives managed to retain or regain effective
power, would they have pursued in foreign affairs the fulfillment
policy of Gustav Stresemann?

In any event, this first possible future for Germany—as a
democratized constitutional monarchy—was soon pushed aside by
the rush of events. It depended, at least after Wilson's third note

---

[4] Speech of October 22, 1918, in Friedrich Ebert, *Schriften, Aufzeichnungen, Reden* (Dresden, Reissner, 1926), II, 72–93.

[5] See for example Friedrich Meinecke, "Die Revolution, Ursachen und
Tatsachen," *Handbuch des Deutschen Staatsrechts,* Gerhard Anschütz and
Richard Thoma, eds. (Tübingen, Mohr, 1930), I, 95–119; and Erich Eyck,
A History of the Weimar Republic, Harlan P. Hanson and Robert G. L.
Waite, trans. (Cambridge, Harvard, 1962), I, 37–46.

(October 23), on the willingness of William II to abdicate, and this he steadfastly refused to do. Between the blindness of the emperor and the rising revolutionary mood of the war-weary masses, the Social Democratic leaders were caught in the middle, unwilling to abandon the government of Prince Max but also unable to watch their followers desert wholesale to the Independents. "Unless the Kaiser abdicates," Ebert told the chancellor on November 7, "the Social Revolution is inevitable. But I will have none of it; I hate it like sin."[6] Nonetheless the party was forced to associate itself with the giant revolutionary demonstrations in Berlin on November 9. As a last desperate expedient, on that day, Prince Max assumed the responsibility of announcing the emperor's abdication and the prospect of a regency, meanwhile appointing Ebert chancellor. Through this device, an extremely dubious legal continuity was preserved and Ebert became the last chancellor of the Bismarckian Reich.

While Prince Max and Ebert were thus conspiring to make the revolution legal, the more impetuous Scheidemann, fearful of losing the masses altogether, took it upon himself to proclaim a republic. Ebert was furious when he confronted Scheidemann afterward: "You have no right to proclaim the Republic," he shouted.[7] But the deed could not be undone—the Social Democrats had become revolutionaries in spite of themselves. The next day Ebert became chairman of a six-man provisional government, calling itself the council of people's representatives, and basing its authority upon the soldiers' and workers' councils that had been formed in Berlin. The Independents obtained parity representation on this body, a move Ebert supported because the Independents would be less dangerous as partners than as a revolutionary opposition.

Thus the man who five years before had qualms of inadequacy about becoming a co-chairman of his party suddenly found himself head of a provisional government possessed of sovereign power and overwhelming popular support. It was tragic that the leadership of the German Revolution fell upon a man whose rise beyond the party bureaucracy had been largely accidental, a reluctant revolutionary who hated revolution "like sin," a repub-

[6] *The Memoirs of Prince Max of Baden,* W. M. Calder and C. W. H. Sutton, trans. (London, Constable, 1928), II, 312.

[7] Philipp Scheidemann, *The Making of New Germany,* J. E. Michell, trans. (New York, Appleton, 1929), II, 264. Scheidemann might have inquired with equal justice what right Ebert had to call himself chancellor.

lican who preferred constitutional monarchy and saw no "right" in proclaiming the Republic. But whatever his reluctance and personal limitations, Ebert now possessed the power and responsibility of a head of state. Given the failure of his preferred alternative, a constitutional monarchy, what future would he seek for Germany? To Ebert and most of his contemporaries there now appeared only two historical possibilities: a parliamentary republic or Bolshevik dictatorship.

Radical elements in the revolution were working for a development to the left. They demanded immediate socialization of industry and a "proletarian dictatorship," i.e., a government based on workers' and soldiers' councils after the Soviet model. Opposing these conceptions vehemently, Ebert held that the provisional government had only caretaker functions: to bring the armistice negotiations to a successful conclusion and, domestically, to maintain law and order until a National Assembly could be elected to determine the nation's future. There can be no question of Ebert's democratic intentions. For the sake of maintaining order, however, he made decisions that determined the nation's future at least as much as the National Assembly. He called upon the military and administrative apparatus of the old regime, thus assuring the survival of these authoritarian monarchist institutions in the new democratic Republic and perhaps crippling German democracy from the outset. Were these decisions a tragic necessity forced upon Ebert by the extreme conditions of the time, most particularly by the acute danger of a Communist "second revolution"?

Most of Ebert's contemporaries, and most historians since that time, have contended that Germany narrowly averted communism in 1918–19. They point to the collapse of traditional authorities, the mood of bitter disappointment that came with the full realization of Germany's defeat, the conditions of near starvation imposed by the blockade, and the chaotic state of the economy at the war's end, aggravated by the return of masses of servicemen. This explosive mixture, combined with the catalyst of Bolshevik success in Russia, seemed to give the Communists an unparalleled opportunity to seize power in Germany. Recent historical investigation, however, has emphasized the extreme weakness and fragmentation of the radical forces in Germany, making a successful Communist revolution seem extremely improbable.[8]

Although Lenin's victory in Russia is often depicted as the work of a tiny conspiratorial group, the Bolshevik Party had upwards of a quarter of a million members by the time of the November Revolution. More important, an absolute majority of Bolshevik supporters (60 per cent) were elected on the eve of Lenin's coup to the Second All-Russian Congress of Soviets. The only test of Bolshevik strength by universal suffrage came with the Constituent Assembly elections, which Lenin permitted to be held in late November. Here the party won nine million votes, or 25 per cent of the total, but one must add to this the strength of the Left Social Revolutionaries who shared power in the first Bolshevik government. Although no one knows for sure, it is quite possible that Lenin's government initially enjoyed the support of a majority of the Russian people.

In sharp contrast, the radical forces in Germany were without significant popular support and were fragmented into several factions, from the intermediate Ledebour grouping, to the so-called revolutionary shop stewards, the Spartacists, the ultra-radical Bremen Left, and other smaller groups. The German Communist Party (KPD), organized by the Spartacists and the Bremen Left in December 1918, numbered no more than a few thousand members at the time of its bid for power in January 1919. At the National Congress of Councils, meeting on December 16, the Spartacists claimed only 2.5 per cent of the delegates. The combined strength of all radical elements at this congress is revealed in the crucial vote of 344 to 98 to call a National Assembly and transfer sovereignty to it. By this act the council movement voluntarily committed suicide, yet it was opposed by only 22 per cent of the delegates. Nothing illustrates so well the weakness of the radicals among the very social forces that carried out the revolution. The first test of German Communist popularity by universal suffrage came in June 1920 when the party received a scant 2.1 per cent in the Reichstag elections. Had they taken part in the National Assembly elections of January 1919, Arthur

[8] See especially Eric Waldman, *The Spartacist Uprising of 1919* (Milwaukee, Marquette, 1958). Also: Eberhard Kolb, *Die Arbeiterräte in der deutschen Innenpolitik, 1918–1919* (Düsseldorf, Droste, 1962); Peter von Oertzen, *Betriebsräte in der Novemberrevolution* (Düsseldorf, Droste, 1963); and Werner T. Angress, *Stillborn Revolution, The Communist Bid for Power in Germany, 1921–1923* (Princeton, Princeton, 1963).

Rosenberg estimates the Communists would have won "a couple of hundred thousand" votes, or less than 1 per cent of the total.[9]

Of course, from correspondingly weak beginnings in Russia the Bolsheviks made colossal gains between March and November 1917, by attracting masses of war-weary soldiers and land-hungry peasants to their cause. But the German radicals had no such growth potential. There was no question of continuing the war, which ended two days after the initial revolution, and the soldiers' councils remained relatively conservative. Neither was Germany's rural population a revolutionary force in 1918–19; this was undoubtedly the greatest social difference between the two revolutions. German Communists could recruit a mass following only among industrial workers, but here the deep roots of Social Democracy and the Free Trade Unions created loyalties that were hard to sever, as illustrated by the subsequent electoral history of the KPD. In November 1932, during the depth of the depression, and when the rival SPD seemed completely discredited, the Communists reached their Weimar maximum of 16.9 per cent, still less than the Social Democratic figure of 20.4 per cent and smaller than the Communist minorities France and Italy have endured for many years.

In the 1918–19 period, then, the weakness of the radical forces alone would seem to preclude a successful second revolution. But there were other differences between German and Russian communism that made the prospect even more remote. Whereas Lenin had little confidence in the undirected efforts of the masses and had organized a tightly structured vanguard party to lead them, Rosa Luxemburg, the intellectual founder of German communism, had an almost unlimited faith in the masses. A spontaneous uprising involving the bulk of the population was her conception of the proletarian revolution. The KPD was organized accordingly along ultrademocratic lines, with a maximum of local autonomy, open membership, and a minimum of professionals—an utterly un-Leninist party, and utterly incapable of engineering a coup without mass support, as we shall see. Because of her belief in a mass "democratic" revolution, Luxemburg vigorously (but vainly) warned her followers against ir-

[9] *A History of the German Republic,* Ian F. D. Morrow and L. Marie Sieveking, trans. (London, Methuen, 1936), p. 18.

responsible putschism. "It would be a criminal error to seize power now," she told the founding congress of the KPD in December 1918.[10] She reckoned on a preparatory period of at least six months before the masses would stand mobilized behind the party's banners, during which time the KPD would organize street demonstrations and "partial actions" to attract support and harass the Ebert regime.

Despite the relative restraint of Luxemburg and most of the German Communist leadership, the party did become involved in a minority putsch in January 1919.[11] The coup was not planned in advance, however, but incredibly undertaken from one day to the next as an overenthusiastic response to the success of a radical demonstration on January 5, protesting the dismissal of the sympathetic USPD Berlin police chief. Among the seventy-odd demonstration leaders who decided that evening to overthrow Ebert, there were two prominent Communists—Karl Liebknecht and Wilhelm Pieck. Significantly, when these two brought back word of their action to the KPD central committee, Luxemburg was furious and all the remaining members condemned the undertaking as foolhardy. But the deed had been done and they felt obliged to go along. On the next morning leaflets proclaimed, "Down with the Ebert-Scheidemann government!" but none of the prominent government buildings were seized. Nothing had been planned and the radicals had no organized military force at their disposal. There were no coordinated revolutions in the provinces, merely scattered demonstrations of support. After the first day only a few thousand intransigents remained, and even they became increasingly disposed to negotiate their way out of the fiasco. The "Soviet Republic" proclaimed in Munich during April 1919 had an equally pathetic history.[12] The radical minority in the German Revolution harassed the Ebert government and created

[10] Quoted in Ruth Fischer, *Stalin and German Communism* (Cambridge, Harvard, 1948), p. 74. Also note the warning Luxemburg wrote into the party program itself: "The Spartacist League will never assume governmental power unless it is supported by the clear, decisive will of the great majority of the proletariat in Germany, and in no other way except with their conscious acceptance of the ideas, objectives, and fighting methods of the Spartacist League." (Quoted in Waldman, *Spartacist Uprising*, p. 133.)

[11] A full narrative and analysis of this putsch can be found in Waldman's remarkably dispassionate study (see note 8).

[12] See Allan Mitchell, *Revolution in Bavaria, 1918–1919* (Princeton, Princeton, 1965).

confusion in the streets, but it could not seriously contend for power.

If communism was not a real historical possibility in 1918–19, there was nothing unreal about the hysterical fear of communism that engulfed the more conservative elements of German society, including the leaders of Social Democracy. Unfortunately, it cannot even be said on their behalf that they were ignorant of radical strength or of the organizational and ideological differences between German and Russian communism. Certainly after the elections to the National Congress of Councils in December, which the Majority Social Democrats were confident of winning, the weakness of the radicals became a matter of public knowledge. Most party leaders were just as sure they would win an absolute majority in the National Assembly elections.[13] The Social Democratic leaders had confidence in their numbers; what they lacked was confidence in themselves.

To be sure, the noisy disorder of the radicals was not the only problem they faced. Germany had to conclude an extremely difficult peace, bring home and demobilize a mass army while protecting the government and defending the Eastern frontier against pre-treaty Polish encroachments, guard against separatist tendencies, feed the population through the long winter with the blockade still in effect, and reconvert an exhausted economic plant to peacetime production. It is hardly surprising, under such trying circumstances, that the inexperienced Social Democrats felt unequal to the task and were tempted to seek aid from established governmental authorities, even though this might involve risks.

Of the possible alternatives for Germany's future, a constitutional monarchy was excluded after November 9, and communism never had a chance. The real political and moral dilemma confronting Ebert and his lieutenants in the exercise of their power was this: should they turn to the old establishment for help in meeting the grave problems they faced, thus gambling with the future of democracy; or should they forego that help and break up the old establishment, thus gambling with the political and economic chaos that would attend failure?

Ebert, of course, chose the first alternative. With the assist-

[13] For examples of this confidence, see Scheidemann, *New Germany*, II, 285; and Ebert, *Schriften*, II, 125.

ance he received, he was able to bring the country successfully through its immediate postwar difficulties. The National Assembly, elected in January 1919 with an 85 per cent pro-republican majority, made Ebert president and created a constitution giving Germany the most advanced parliamentary government in Europe, including a comprehensive system of social insurance and a secure position for the trade unions. But the promising constitutional forms of this modern democratic welfare state were built upon old governmental institutions and a social structure hardly compatible with healthy democracy. Ebert's alliance partners—the old state bureaucracy, the judiciary, above all the army—survived the revolution almost unchanged. Moreover, given the depleted condition of the economy and the acute food shortage, the Social Democrats thought it unwise to undertake any large-scale "experiments" in socialization or land reform. Among the political and social forces thus left intact arose a powerful conservative opposition to the Weimar Republic which would eventually collaborate with Hitler to destroy it. Choosing the first alternative, Ebert gambled with the future of democracy . . . and lost.

But did he really have any other option? Some historians have argued that he did, that there was another historical possibility for Germany, a "third way" between Bolshevism and the tragic compromises of the Weimar Republic. Classically expounded in the work of Arthur Rosenberg, this view has long been popular in America and has recently found new scholarly support in Germany.[14] According to this thesis, Ebert and his lieutenants neglected a genuine opportunity to create a pro-republican armed force, to use the councils as instruments of democratization (especially in administration), and to inaugurate a substantial program of socialization and land reform. Only by means of a real social revolution, so it is argued, by destroying the power of the old authoritarian establishment, could a secure and stable democracy be built in Germany. Let us single out the area of military reform—the most crucial and controversial—for a closer look at both the possibilities and the difficulties that confronted Ebert as he made his fateful choices.

On the day the provisional government was organized (Novem-

---

[14] See the major works of Kolb and Oertzen cited in note 8 above; also Peter von Oertzen, "Die grossen Streiks der Ruhrarbeiterschaft im Frühjahr 1919," *Vierteljahrshefte für Zeitgeschichte*, VI (1958), 231–62.

ber 10), General Wilhelm Groener, who had replaced Ludendorff in the Supreme Command, telephoned Ebert offering him the
services of the army for "combating Bolshevism," in exchange
for the new government's help in preserving "order and discipline in the army." By allying himself to the moderate elements
in the revolution, Groener hoped both to ward off the radical
danger and to preserve his army intact. "We hoped to win for
the army and the officer corps a share of power in the new state;
if we succeeded, then, despite the revolution, the best and strongest element of old Prussiandom would be rescued and preserved
for the new Germany."[15] Ebert did not hesitate in accepting
Groener's offer. To bring the army back from France within the
rigid armistice time limit and to supervise its demobilization, as
well as to provide protection for his government, he felt the indispensable need of the Supreme Command. Groener promised to
send ten divisions to Berlin. This was the historic Ebert-Groener
alliance.

In the event, Groener had promised more than he could deliver.
The field army maintained discipline only until it reached German soil. Then the weary conscripts, who had no stomach for
more fighting, especially in the Christmas season, began to desert
in great masses. Of the ten divisions promised for Berlin, only
about eighteen hundred men showed up, and even these disappeared in the course of their first domestic engagement against
the sailors' mutiny on December 24. For all practical purposes,
by Christmas Day 1918, the proud army of Imperial Germany—
"the best and strongest element of old Prussiandom"—had ceased
to exist. The officers at Supreme Command headquarters no longer
had any soldiers to obey their commands. In broad historical
terms, here lay a unique opportunity for the revolutionaries. It is
quite difficult to reform an army in being and quite rare for an
army to disappear. In this temporary vacuum perhaps a new
republican army could be organized.

Certainly there was mass support for such action. Germany
was swept in these months by a wave of antimilitarist feeling
more pervasive and profound than one could have imagined
a few years before. Soldiers displaced their officers, formed councils, deserted in droves. Officers who walked in the streets risked

[15] Wilhelm Groener, *Lebenserinnerungen* (Göttingen, Vandenhoeck &
Ruprecht, 1957), pp. 467–69.

having their epaulets and insignia torn off. These sentiments were not confined merely to the radical fringe. The National Congress of Councils, which had shown its moderation by voting overwhelmingly for a National Assembly, also demonstrated its complete revulsion against the old military by voting unanimously for the so-called Hamburg Points. This seven-point program instructed the provisional government to take over the powers of the Supreme Command and inaugurate sweeping changes in the old army (election of officers, elimination of insignia of rank, etc.), but also to demobilize this old army as quickly as possible and create a new popular militia (*Volkswehr*). Outraged, Hindenburg and Groener threatened to resign. Again, Ebert did not hesitate to choose: he ignored and sabotaged these instructions from the presumably sovereign National Congress, thus mollifying his military partners and preserving the alliance of November 10.

For the creation of a new army General Groener already had his own ideas. Throughout December, "in agreement with Ebert," he was working "under cover" toward the organization of volunteer units, *Freikorps,* to be formed by salvaging the most "dependable" elements from the vanishing field army.[16] The first of these new units, Maercker's Rifles, was officially sanctioned on December 16 and others followed in short order. Needless to say, the *Freikorps* attracted primarily conservative-monarchist officers, while the ranks were filled out largely by embittered front-soldiers enamored of violence and the "enticing urge to destroy."[17] These were the troops Ebert used to put down the January uprising in Berlin and thereafter to suppress the radicals all over Germany. *Freikorps* officers and men provided the core of the later Reichswehr and, by means of this transitional form, the old army (as Groener had hoped) did indeed survive the revolution and become a major power in the new state.

Instead of giving German militarism a new lease on life, could Ebert have created a republican militia? Certain steps were taken in this direction. On December 12, at the insistence of the Independents, the provisional government authorized the

---

[16] *Ibid.,* p. 473.

[17] Expression of Friedrich Wilhelm Heinz, member of the notorious Ehrhardt Brigade and later one of Hitler's SA leaders, as quoted in Robert G. L. Waite's excellent study of the Freikorps, *Vanguard of Nazism* (Cambridge, Harvard, 1952), p. 42.

formation of a Volkswehr, a move subsequently endorsed in the Hamburg Points of the National Congress of Councils. But the project never really got off the ground.[18] And its projected strength, which Ebert set at eleven thousand men, made it a token force compared to the ten divisions Ebert was then expecting Groener to deliver, or compared to the two hundred thousand to four hundred thousand *Freikorps* troops that were roaming over Germany by mid-1919.

Even with the best of wills, however, Ebert would not have found it easy to create a dependable and efficient *Volkswehr*. At the outset of the revolution, pro-republican sailors had formed a People's Naval Division of several thousand men to protect the new government in Berlin. But the sailors proved undisciplined and unreliable. On December 23 they mutinied in an effort to secure back pay, and they refused to defend the government in the January uprising. The Berlin police force—some forty-five hundred men—was in the hands of the left-wing Independent, Emil Eichhorn, and likewise remained neutral in January. As a counter to Eichhorn's police, two Majority Social Democrats, Otto Wels and Anton Fischer, had organized a Republican Defense Corps, projected at twelve thousand men, but it was soon infected by radicalism and also left the government in the lurch. Workers seemed to have little stomach for fighting other workers, or for the discipline of military life in general. And if the workers stood aloof, perhaps the government had no choice but to call upon the professional soldiers of the old regime.[19]

Yet the picture is more complex. The Social Democratic workers were not entirely pacifist or disinterested. They stood ready to defend the government against right-wing counterrevolution, as they demonstrated most effectively during the Kapp Putsch of 1920, and later when some 3½ million of them joined the pro-republican paramilitary defense organization, the

[18] Ebert's footdragging on this question is revealed in the unpublished minutes of the meetings of the provisional government, *Protokolle des Rats der Volksbeauftragten*, International Institute for Social History, Amsterdam, I, 57–58, 68, 144; II, 23, 68–69.

[19] This is of course Gustav Noske's argument in *Von Kiel bis Kapp* (Berlin, Verlag für Politik und Wirtschaft, 1920), pp. 70–73; for more extensive documentation of these difficulties, see Harold J. Gordon, Jr. *The Reichswehr and the German Republic, 1919–1926* (Princeton, Princeton, 1957), pp. 15–52.

Reichsbanner Schwarz-Rot-Gold. That these same workers did not flock to join the *Freikorps,* or later the regular Reichswehr, is scarcely surprising. The real question is whether the government could have recruited substantial numbers of them into a popular militia reliable and efficient enough to defend it against insurrection from the left. It cannot be denied that the job would have been difficult and the results uncertain; neither can it be denied that Ebert's efforts in this direction were dilatory in the extreme, and conceived as a sop to the Independents rather than as a substitute for the Groener alliance.

An interesting light is thrown on this question by the events of the January uprising. On the first day of the insurrection (January 6), the only day on which it had a chance of even momentary success in Berlin, the government found itself entirely without troops. There was as yet no *Freikorps* in the city; the military units that were in Berlin refused to fight. The Social Democratic leaders had no choice but to call on their mass following, in what turned out to be the most imaginative political stroke of the entire ill-starred revolution. Friedrich Meinecke describes their action:

> In the morning they summoned forth their supporters in the city, who streamed together unarmed into the Wilhemstrasse and there formed a living wall around the Reich chancery. For hours they stood there, while on Unter den Linden—the author saw it with his own eyes—bands of Spartacists with machine guns moved along and could have begun a fight at any moment. But once again, and this time to the advantage of the government, the old adage proved itself, that workers do not shoot on workers. The revolutionary committee (Ledebour, Liebknecht, etc.) did not find the courage to signal an attack on the government. Their successes were confined to the occupation of several newspaper and office buildings in the city and to the terror in the streets.[20]

To their government leaders assembled inside the chancery, the Social Democratic masses shouted, "Arms! Arms! Give us arms!"[21] But inside, Ebert was appointing Gustav Noske as military commandant, authorizing him, not to arm the workers, but to call in the *Freikorps.* Some of the demonstrators nonetheless

[20] *Handbuch,* I, 116–17.
[21] Quoted in Eduard Bernstein, *Die deutsche Revolution* (Berlin, Verlag Gesellschaft und Erziehung, 1921), p. 144; and confirmed by Noske, *Kiel bis Kapp,* p. 68.

found weapons and, together with handfuls of pro-republican soldiers, had reoccupied most of the city by the time Noske's troops arrived in force on January 11. It was actually the Social Democratic masses, not the *Freikorps,* who saved the government in the January uprising.[22]

Ebert's defenders have argued that the military alliance was a tragic necessity forced upon him by the reckless insurrectionary policy of the Communists, who should bear the real blame for the revival of German militarism.[23] It is hard to see the basis for such an argument. Ebert made the alliance on the second day of the revolution, long before any Communist move against him. The Communists were not strong enough to seize and hold power; their policies were disorderly but not insurrectionary; the January uprising came more by accident than by sinister design, and in any event was warded off by the Social Democratic masses, not by the old military. Indeed, it can be argued that what little strength the radicals possessed stemmed largely from Ebert's military policy. Just as it drove the Independents from the provisional government in late December, so it must have provoked many workers and soldiers into joining the radicals. Ebert's brother Social Democrats in Austria, under roughly parallel circumstances, eschewed alliance with the disintegrating Hapsburg army, successfully created a Volkswehr, and had correspondingly less trouble with left-wing violence. They managed to maintain law and order effectively with a force of no more than sixteen thousand republican volunteers.[24]

Further, Ebert's defenders imply that, but for the tragic necessity, he would have preferred to see the disappearance of the old army and the establishment of a *Volkswehr.* There is no evidence to support this implication. Ebert did not hesitate when Groener made his offer on November 10, nor did he reveal any inner struggle when reaffirming the military alliance in mid-December against the instruction of the Hamburg Points. Neither does anyone report moral qualms in late December when Ebert

[22] This is candidly acknowledged by the conservative historian and former army officer, Erich Volkmann, in *Revolution über Deutschland* (Oldenburg, Stalling, 1930), p. 185.

[23] See Eyck, *Weimar Republic,* I, 51–52; and Koppel S. Pinson, *Modern Germany* (New York, Macmillan, 1953), pp. 378–91.

[24] See the excellent evaluation of Charles A. Gulick, *Austria from Habsburg to Hitler* (Berkeley and Los Angeles, California, 1948), I, 69–83.

was forced to choose between the generals and his Independent coalition partners. In Prince Max's government, before the revolution, Ebert had proposed dismantling the military cabinet and subordinating the army to a responsible parliamentary minister of war, but he demanded no reform of the army itself.[25] In the Weimar Republic essentially this program was put into effect: the old army was placed under formal (but quite ineffective) parliamentary control. There is no reason to suppose that Ebert ever wanted or imagined anything more than this.

Indeed, what distresses one most about Ebert's behavior during the revolution is precisely the absence of any moral agonizing over the choices he was making.[26] His patriotism, his belief in democracy, and his socialist aspirations certainly made conflicting demands upon him in a cruelly difficult situation. Yet his choices, in the light of his behavior, appear not so much the agonized decisions of a principled leader torn between incompatible values. Far more they appear the instinctive reflexes of a party secretary loaded with responsibilities beyond his capacity. There is no indication, for example, that Ebert saw the military alliance as a tragic choice between conflicting values, or even understood the enormous gamble he was taking with the future of democracy. "Militarism," he inauspiciously announced to the opening of the National Assembly, "is shattered to pieces and will not arise again."[27]

Perhaps Scheidemann unwittingly hit the nail on the head when he later testified at the Munich stab-in-the-back trial, "We turned *naturally* to professionals, to officers like General Groener"[28] (emphasis added). In truth, turning to "professionals" was the first resort, not the last resort; it was the "natural" choice for Ebert, the party secretary. He possessed all the virtues of

[25] Reichstag speech of October 22, 1918, *Schriften,* II, 78.

[26] Significantly, even in later years, what haunted Ebert's mind and drove him to an early grave was not the left-wing charge that he had betrayed democracy and socialism, but the right-wing taunt that he had committed treason against his country.

[27] February 6, 1919, *Ibid.,* II, 150. Noske even praises the alliance as a *positive* development: if it only had come sooner, "Germany's position in the world would have been more favorable." *Erlebtes aus Aufstieg und Niedergang einer Demokratie* (Offenbach, Bollwerk, 1947), pp. 88–89.

[28] Scheidemann's testimony is reproduced in Lothar Berthold and Helmut Neef, *Militarismus und Opportunismus gegen die Novemberrevolution* (Berlin, Rütten & Loening, 1958), p. 211.

a bureaucrat—administrative skill, level-headedness, and ability
to compromise—but also all the defects—a narrow and legalistic
vision, a blind trust in experts, and an unreasoning horror of
disorder. In a party secretary these faults were no doubt negli-
gible, but history had called Ebert to lead the German November
Revolution. It was not that he lacked a sense of responsibility
in the exercise of his power, for everyone testifies to the contrary.
It was not even so much a want of governmental experience,
for surely he had more of that than Lenin or Trotsky. What
Ebert lacked was the imagination and the confidence, both in
himself and in his followers, to try the other gamble, to rule
without turning for help to the professionals of the old regime.

The failure of the German Revolution was in the first instance
a failure of its leadership. The masses did everything that could
be expected of them: they rose up and displaced the old authorities, including the military authorities; at the same time
they resisted in their great majority the allure of communism;
they stood ready to back their leaders in the creation of a
genuinely democratic government. But their leaders lacked the
stature to grapple successfully with the enormous tasks thrust
upon them. The cry "Arms! Arms! Give us arms!" remains to
tease the imagination of those who wish German history might
have reached this critical turning point, and turned more decisively.

Chapter 18

LENIN AND POWER

Henry L. Roberts

The image of Lenin, at least in the non-Communist world, is that of the revolutionary genius, the uncompromising opponent and destroyer of the old order. Indeed, the hyphenate term Marxism-Leninism largely connotes the revolutionary elements in Marx together with Lenin's own additions, chiefly out of the Russian revolutionary tradition: a tightly disciplined body of professional revolutionaries, a stress upon underground and illegal activity, and a resolute refusal to compromise with "revisionists" or those who would seek an evolutionary path to the reform of the existing order.

And yet there is a respectable body of opinion that sees Lenin's genius not as that of the destroyer and uprooter but rather as the organizer, the creator, or at least as the man who achieved mastery over the elemental chaos of revolutionary Russia. Three writers, of rather different views, may be cited to indicate this picture.

Thus, E. H. Carr, in his *Studies in Revolution,* has a chapter on "Lenin: The Master Builder":

Lenin, for all his fame as a revolutionary leader, was a creator rather than a destroyer. He played no personal part in the events of 1905 or in the February revolution of 1917, nor were Bolshevik ideas an important contributory factor. What Lenin achieved in October 1917 was not the overthrow of the provisional government—that followed logically from all that had gone before, and was bound to happen—but the construction of something to take its place. The decisive moment of the revolution came when, at the first congress of Soviets in June 1917, an orator remarked from the platform that there was no revolutionary party willing to take over the responsibilities of government, and Lenin, amid mocking laughter retorted from his place in the hall, "There is such a party." Only when the new regime had taken over did Lenin rise to his full stature as administrator, head of government, organizer and supreme political tactician.[1]

Adam Ulam, in his study of the Bolsheviks, offers an interpretation that is somewhat similar:

> The Bolsheviks did not seize power in this year of revolutions. They picked it up. First autocracy, then democracy capitulated to the forces of anarchy. Any group of determined men could have done what the Bolsheviks did in Petrograd in October 1917: seize the few key points of the city and proclaim themselves the government. . . . Thus the Bolsheviks' achievement in 1917, great though it was, pales in comparison with the enormous task they accomplished in the next five years in conquering the very anarchy they had helped to create and in building out of the most anarchistic of the revolutions the most authoritarian state in the world. It is not in the maker of the revolution that we can see Lenin's genius in its fullest; far greater is his achievement as its conqueror.[2]

In speaking of Lenin in power Louis Fischer, in his biography, suggests, too, that the years of authority were the period of Lenin's real greatness, up to the moment when he was smitten by the illness that was to kill him. Speaking of 1922 Fischer remarks:

> Yet during the year that preceded the mental collapse which ended Lenin's career, his intellectual grasp remained supreme and he dominated Soviet Russia as never before. His prestige grew and so did his command of persons and situations. Nobody could have suspected in those twelve months from March, 1922, to March, 1923, that they were seeing the flaming tail of a comet and not the rising sun. . . . In fact, Lenin's last year was his greatest. It was probably also his saddest for it is impossible to suppose, judging by what he said, that he failed to realize where he had failed.[3]

These observations, by serious and well-informed students of Lenin and the revolution, that Lenin is most appropriately to

[1] E. H. Carr, *Studies in Revolution* (New York, 1964: first published by Macmillan, 1950), pp. 134–35.
[2] Adam B. Ulam, *The Bolsheviks* (New York, Macmillan, 1965), p. 314.
[3] Louis Fischer, *The Life of Lenin* (New York, 1964), p. 566.

be regarded as a creator or a ruler rather than as a destroyer, and that his last years, when power had been achieved and in considerable measure consolidated, represented the "highest phase" of his life, lead to some extremely intricate problems relating to the theme of this book, "power and responsibility." In the case of a great revolutionary figure, as Lenin undoubtedly was, both the terms "power" and "responsibility" take on a rather ambiguous flavor. By "power" are we thinking of the seizure of power or its application in running a political order? By "responsibility" do we mean responsibility for the course of events, responsibility to some sector of society, responsibility to a set of ideas, or responsibility in the sense of rational political behavior?

This essay, which does not pretend to resolve these ambiguities—the evaluation of Lenin and his inheritance remains one of the great questions of our times—will try to offer some reflections on three themes: 1. The contradiction and dilemmas confronting the revolutionary before and after he has come to power; 2. The nature of his sense of responsibility, to whom or to what; and 3. The criteria of "responsible" behavior of an explicitly, indeed blatantly, revolutionary regime.

I

First, a minimum of historical stage-setting is required. The picture of Lenin as the person who chanced to come to power in November 1917—in the way an alert person happens to pick up a penny in the street—while having a certain element of truth, does justice neither to Lenin's revolutionary achievement nor to the complexity of the peculiar historical situation that led to Russian power being, in a sense, something to pick up.

Admittedly, Russia, between the collapse of the monarchy in March to the Bolshevik victory in November, does increasingly give one the sense—though with ups and downs and moments of apparent recovery—of a situation in which "power" was there for the taking, whatever this "power" might turn out to be. In the last couple of months, particularly, and notably after the Kornilov affair, one has, in reading the records of the time, a curious feeling of emptiness, as though political structure and political meaning had evaporated. There is a marked falling off in local voting, no longer a rush to the polls as there had been in many areas in the earlier months of the revolutionary period. One has the impression that the Provisional Government is operating in a void, and a strange question comes to mind: Where is everybody? One explanation, of course, is that the masses of the discontented, disillusioned with a fumbling regime, were preparing themselves for the final assault. Such certainly is the common picture of the cities and of the diminution of delegated authority in the countryside.

Yet, I have the impression that such was not the process, at least not for the bulk of the population, but rather that a great vacuum was setting in—anarchy if you choose, though perhaps that is too active a term—that a general societal disintergration was in train, that the Great Russian society, except in its smaller and more intimate units, was ceasing to exist. One feels this in the army, in the factories with the rise to shop committees as against trade unions, in the unorganized peasant activities which were rapidly mounting at this time, and in the movement toward autonomy or separation among the nationalities on the fringe of the Empire.

In other words, the assertion that power *was* there, to be picked up like a penny, is itself open to question. As efforts to define "power" in the political setting have demonstrated, it is a most elusive entity: at one moment present, awesome, and commanding vast instrumentalities for its realization, at the next it evaporates or seems to be an epiphenomenon derived from a complex of social and political circumstances. This very uncertainty about the reality of power leads us to question *how* this situation could have come to pass in Russia. How does a community become this strange emptiness in such short order? It clearly operates against our sense of social processes and the usual pattern of history that such disintegration should proceed so far so fast.

For this we must consider, very briefly, the much-disputed issue of the state of health of prerevolutionary, or prewar Russia. The "viability" of imperial Russia, had the First World War not slashed across the scene, has long been the subject of intense and passionate dispute. Here we can only summarize certain propositions: 1. The dynasty as such seems to have been beyond recovery as an autocratic force; whatever the course of events the Romanovs seemed slated to disappear from the scene or, at most, to become *rois fainéants*. 2. Russia, even in peacetime, and noticeably in the years after 1911, was facing a major domestic crisis, not of stagnation or lethargy, but of disequilibrating growth and change. One can pick from the wild mélange of evidence "proofs" of imminent crisis, of potential crisis, or of likely convalescence from the upheavals of 1905—but my own reading is that this was indeed a highly problematic situation in which an enormous variety of outcomes might have occurred. It does seem clear, however, that some sort of crisis in the old order was taking shape and not just because of dynastic ineptitude. 3. One has the sense, as in fact one has also for the Dual Monarchy and for Wilhelmian Germany, that a set of contradictory impulses was becoming increasingly dynamic, that the existing constitutional order, even had it been run by abler men, was not in a position to cope with. The introduction of universal suffrage in the Austrian half of the Monarchy in 1907 had not eased the national problem, but exacerbated it. It was evident that the German Social Democratic victories in the elections of 1912 were not something to be absorbed into the Bismarckian Constitution—something was going to have to give way. So, too, in Russia, though the form of the problem was different, one feels a structural crisis of the political system darkening the horizon, a crisis that "progressive" evidence, such as renewed and very rapid industrial expansion, the growth of private as against state entrepreneurial initiative, the likelihood of greater vigor and life in the Fourth Duma, would sharpen rather than dampen. 4. Whether these implied short-term crises that might have been met by in-system solutions (whether, for example, the mounting wave of strikes would have slackened and the new working class have been harnessed to urbanization), or whether they were indicators of deep-rooted maladies, bound to get worse until a general explosion occurred, is difficult to say. Indeed, I think it is impossible to say, because of the vast number of contingent influences that could have affected the scene with each day of history.

II

It is into this dynamic, crisis-ridden, but highly problematic situation of late imperial Russia that we must try to fit Lenin—Lenin the revolutionary before his access to power. It should not be forgotten that Lenin's great hour in 1917 was when he was forty-seven, and it would be reasonable to assume that the essential man and political outlook, whatever adaptations, changes, or reversals the acquisition of power might occasion, had been formed. Here again, only some very general and perhaps dogmatic characterizations can be made:

1. From a very early date—and the ultimate psychological and social roots can be argued endlessly—Lenin was aiming at a "revolutionary" rather than an "evolutionary" resolution to the evils, as he saw them, in the existing Russian order. This was a basic, personal impulse, operative in his analysis of Russian society, in his evaluation of the explosive potentialities of its various sectors and classes, and in his views on the organization of the requisite political party.

2. Between Lenin, who was a serious and, to his mind, orthodox Marxist, with a belief in a pattern of historical progession, and this revolutionary impulse existed a basic tension that he never really resolved on the level of articulated political theory. Some of Lenin's most difficult and elusive political concepts—the democratic dictatorship of the proletariat and peasantry, his insistence upon "stages," his formula of democratic centralism for his party, his doctrine concerning nationalities, his pronouncements on the relation of war and revolution—can all, I believe, be related to an effort to put into coherent political formulation this underlying tension.

3. Despite this problem of finding an appropriate "ideological" formulation and the often observed anomaly between, say, *What Is to Be Done?* with its stress on the Party, and *State and Revolution,* in which the Party is not even mentioned, Lenin's writings cannot be dismissed as manipulative *pièces d'occasion,* though certainly some of his writings bear that mark, but can be regarded as serious pieces in the sense that he *was striving* for a coherent and explicit theory of revolutionary action. It is more likely that

the reason for the peculiar difficulties one encounters in analyzing his writings lies in the inadequacy of the particular intellectual categories within which Lenin was obliged, or had elected, to work. But—and this is of decisive importance—below this "literary" level, Lenin had, even during his long absences from the Russian scene, some basic and essentially consistent views and intentions that were not fantasies of cloud-cuckoo land but very much in touch with "reality," however distorted and ambiguous their overt expression may appear to have been.

4. Among these basically realistic insights and aims one might include the following: First, Lenin never had any intention of permitting a real period of "bourgeois" power to follow the fall or overthrow of "feudal" tsarism. He may, as Haimson pointed out some years ago,[4] have been obliged to give a rather peculiar definition, at least in Marxist terms, to the bourgeoisie, but surely his instinct was not far from the mark in feeling that the Russian bourgeoisie had neither the strength nor the will to assume power (indeed, the late Joseph Schumpeter doubted whether they ever had anywhere), and hence that if social eruption occurred, he was going to be in on it and see that it moved toward his goals. Much of his confusing and shifting policy with respect to the peasantry—the vast majority of the Russian population—is intimately related to this consideration. Second, Lenin had a real sense both of the "blind" forces of spontaneous combustion that were present in Russian society and were profoundly difficult if not impossible to compose by in-system reforms, and of the obstacles presented by inertial drift and habit and by the advantages that are enjoyed, partly for that reason, on the part of the "powers that be." It is from this double realization—both facets of which strike me as sound insights into the structure and behavior of societies— that we find through much of Lenin's writing and action a fear both of being outflanked by anarchy and spontaneous *buntarstvo* and of becoming involved in "adventures," premature actions. It is Lenin's quite reasonable appreciation—given his aims—of this twofold danger that accounts for some of his disconcerting swings to the left as well as to his periodic hesitancies to take decisive action. The problem, however one chooses to formulate

[4] Leopold H. Haimson, *The Russian Marxists and The Origins of Bolshevism* (Cambridge, Mass., 1955).

it, was a real one, and a man with a strong sense of reality had to be looking in both directions at once. If you permit your party and your goals to be swept along by the unmeasured force of spontaneous Russian resentment, you may well be engulfed and lose any control over a wild tide sweeping across the land. On the other hand, if you are obsessed by concern for his danger and disregard the *vis inertiae,* you may become equally isolated, dispersed, undermined if not destroyed by the habitual and residual strength of the existing order. For a rational revolutionary there is no pat solution to this most difficult of quandaries. It is so bound up with the "balance of forces" of the moment that an abstract revolutionary theory will not do; one must have a feel for the particular configuration at any given moment of time. And this talent Lenin possessed, though it was often cloaked in the vocabulary and jargon the Russian left required.

Finally, there is the question of Russia and the outside world. I would submit that Lenin had his basic impulse—a revolution in Russia—tempered with a perfectly rational recognition of the dangers involved in a relatively backward country making the sudden leap into socialism. Here, as in so many of his writings, one encounters contradictions: the formal analysis of *Imperialism* in conjunction with his 1917 writings on the matter of a separate peace and defeatism, and the harsh reality of Brest-Litovsk. But again, it would seem that for all the historical and analytical holes one can punch in Lenin's characterization of imperialism and for the far more important question whether it was luck or insight that enabled him to survive Brest-Litovsk without Russia's falling under permanent German hegemony, Lenin was, in his Zimmerwald formulas and in his general position on the war, trying to meet, with an acute sense of reality, an almost insoluble problem (I may say that I think that in this particular area Lenin was luckier than insightful). Without doubt, the outbreak of the First World War *did* represent a mortal crisis for the old European order—we still live in the shadow of its consequences—and also the Second International, to use Schumpeter's adaptation from Dante, did commit *lo gran rifiuto.* Lenin was probably right in his sense that the war presented a fundamental crisis—as is illustrated by the increasing inability of the European governments, at least from 1916 on, to make sense of the war for their citizenry. The outburst of radicalism, in both hemispheres, suggests the failure of the effort to make this hideous bloodletting intelligible to the people, whatever the perfectly "rational" diplomatic or strategic reasons for the various abortive campaigns may have been.

It is not surprising, then, that Lenin, with his instinct for the jugular, should have felt that this was *the crisis*—which Russia alone might or might not have produced through its own internal difficulties—and hence that from the outset he generalized and combined war and revolution. I think that this was a point where his analysis went astray, but the point here is simply that, however inadequate Lenin's theory of imperialism may have been, he was working against a real possibility in which, as it turned out, a number of contingencies—the timing and outcome of military actions, the entry of the United States, and the like—pushed events in a direction different from what he had not unreasonably anticipated.

Whatever the external opportunities or accidents, it seems clear that Lenin, from the onset of the Revolution, was driving for a seizure of power, an overturn that would bring his party and his views into the saddle. Admittedly there are moments of hesitation, as in the confusion during the June and the July days, the anomalies in *State and Revolution* written while he was in hiding, and even very late in the day, after the Kornilov affair, in his interesting article "On Compromises," suggesting still the possibility of cooperation with other sections of the Russian left in a non-violent solution. Still, in general, his temper in these months of 1917 is unmistakable, and upon hearing of the Kornilov affair his instinct that *now* was the time burst froth like an erupting volcano. Despite his being in hiding, despite Trotsky's success in working through the Soviet and the Military Revolutionary Committee, one can probably accept the latter's verdict that without the driving power of Lenin the Bolsheviks would not have made their own revolution. It is quite possible that they would have assumed office, possibly along the lines variously envisaged by Trotsky, or even by Zinoviev and Kamenev, but that would have been a quite different situation and very likely with a quite different outcome.

This leads in turn to a consideration of Lenin's situation as the wielder of power, the ruler of a state. It can and has been argued that Lenin, in authority, "inherited" a very difficult situation and that much of the brutality of the years of civil war and war communism, which presumably shaped many of the lasting features of the Soviet regime, should be seen as the necessary acts of a head of state fighting both domestic and foreign enemies. This argument is not wholly without foundation; certainly we cannot hold Lenin responsible for all the problems the new regime faced: the war, imperial mismanagement, the economic crisis, plus the whole background of an outdated autocracy would have assured a terribly tough job for any ruler of Russia. And yet, I do not think that Lenin can be let off this hook so easily. While the problems he faced were not by any means all of his own making, it can hardly be denied that he was, in fact, now obliged to face the consequences of much that he had desired and willed to happen, whether or not his intentions and will had been the major causal factors in bringing about the actual course of events. For example, the disintegration of the Russian army was, despite the claims of friends and foes, probably something that would have occurred in any case at that stage of the war. But certainly Lenin's efforts, so far as his effectiveness went, were in the direction of increasing and promoting this disintegration. The same can be said with respect to the peasant problem, the upsurge of the nationalities, and so on. In other words, Lenin's chickens were coming home to roost, whether Lenin had set them loose or not. In that fact lies, I believe, an essential element of ir-responsibility—in the meaning of non-rationality—that was to plague Lenin throughout his years of power and that has been built into much of the subsequent history of the Soviet system.

III

The fact, then, is that Lenin is centrally responsible for the willingness, under admittedly difficult circumstances, to assume a Bolshevik monopoly of power, seized by violence, and purposely so. Lenin did not want to be bound by constitutional fictions or hampered by questions of "legitimacy." Still, this was no free-booting power-grab of a robber baron or a competent warlord. To repeat, Lenin was serious. And at the time he was at odds with Zinoviev and Kamenev as to whether the situation was ripe for revolution, he hotly denied their contention that the Bolsheviks were in the minority. He insisted that the Bolsheviks did represent the majority of the Russian people. This, of course, raises an interesting question. That the Bolsheviks were, by nose-counting, a distinct minority is evident, as was subsequently demonstrated arithmetically by the vote for the Constituent Assembly shortly after the Bolsheviks seized power and in which they received approximately a quarter of the vote.

Trotsky, in his history of the Revolution argues, while admitting the fact of the voting, that Lenin was correct as against Zinoviev and Kamenev. His argument, on Lenin's behalf, was that one had to take a dynamic view of public support, that the Bolsheviks had won over the "advanced" sectors—the capital city in particular—that the drift of support was clearly in their direction, and hence that it was only a matter of time for the rear to catch up with the vanguard. Now while this argument is a bit questionable, it cannot be dismissed entirely. The analysis that Oliver Radkey has given to the elections suggests that this argument was not wholly spurious.[5] An examination of the election returns indicates that Bolshevik influence was clearly radiating outward from the capital and other industrial centers and progressively affecting the surrounding areas, including even some predominantly agrarian regions in western Russia. Admittedly, it would be hard to imagine just how one could develop a coherent set of political standards from Trotsky's kind of argument: it is perilous to give the mandate to what is, at the time, only a possible "wave of the future."

But a more interesting feature is that this rather convenient if questionable line of argument is *not* the defense that Lenin himself used. On the contrary, in refuting Zinoviev and Kamenev, he pursued a quite different pattern of reasoning: the Bolsheviks represented the majority because that majority, including now the aroused peasantry, was behaving "objectively" in a manner that made the Bolsheviks the majority party. In other words, in respect to the question of the relationship between the taking of power and responsibility to the population—constituency is too precise a term in these chaotic circumstances—Lenin

[5] Oliver Henry Radkey, *The Election to the Russian Constituent Assembly of 1917* (Cambridge, Mass., 1950).

followed neither the classical democratic legitimation of power through the ballot nor even Trotsky's notion of justification by the future (and Trotsky clearly felt this need—that sooner or later the people would swing around in *conscious* support), but in his own and, so far as I know unique, belief in the "objective" identity of interests—necessarily as he conceived of them.

This view, while ultimately destructive of any true democracy or responsibility, has a central bearing on the question of Lenin *in* power; it helps to explain, indeed it may be the central clue to his capacity to make the transition from the destroyer of a political order to the creator of a new one, a pair of tasks rarely carried out by the same person in the course of a major revolution.

IV

What, then, are the criteria of "responsible" behavior in a totally chaotic situation, to some measure of one's making or desire, but to a large degree a consequence of the brutal and disastrous course of events, the full causes of which are of infinite complexity? I should say that, despite Lenin's sense of reality and of the contradictoriness of reality, and despite the fact that a Russian upheaval, by 1917 at any rate, of a deeply chaotic character was in the cards, with or without Lenin, his behavior was irresponsible or non-responsible: in his uncompromising will to recognize no responsibility to an entity, be it a party or a person, outside the frame of his own will and thought, cloaked perhaps as loyalty to a revolutionary ideal (and this can be combined with personal modesty and the absence of overt egotism—it was all disconcertingly impersonal, this feature of his personality). Conversely, or correspondingly, in seeking instrumentalities for the achievement of his will and his revolution he exploited—again with an uncanny feel for "reality"—impulses, rages, frustrations, social flaws—which it is precisely the act of true responsibility to correct, repair, or alleviate. This is not meant in any Metternichian sense or even in the formulae of classical political liberalism. It is rather a matter that lies at the very heart of social, human, or humane, organization. It is charged that throughout 1917 Lenin played the demagogue in advancing crude slogans—peace, bread, and land—incapable of real achieve-

ment, to poison, paralyze, and disrupt the uncertain and increasingly chaotic "dark masses." I am not particularly impressed
by the criticism put thus—there was, or could have been, a
positive and creative content in all these slogans even if they
represented massive oversimplifications of the complex problems
Russia faced. Rather I have the impression of almost demonic
quality, often expressed overtly in his drumming on slogans,
to play upon an even deeper layer of disruptiveness—the profound resentment of people, and more particularly the Russian
masses, against (and this may seem a trivial symptom) the
"rudeness" of their "betters." This plaint in the demands that
seem to recur as a *leitmotiv* in prewar strike slogans, in the
flavor and actual content of the famous Soviet Order No. 1, in
the evident popular mistrust not only of the Duma and the
Provisional Government, but even of the Petrograd Soviet (as
in the July days), has struck me as a singularly malignant
symptom, since it cannot be satisfied by fiat. One cannot legislate a man out of his "rudeness"; he can merely make its manifestations more subtle—but both sides will understand what is
going on. In other words, the necessary element of brotherhood,
fraternité—that indispensable third part of the French revolutionary triad as a link between the other two—was in 1917 lacking,
and Lenin, for all his rhetoric about the common interests of the
masses, was plucking away at that raw spot. In so doing—and
I rather suspect that his effectiveness in 1917 may lie here rather
than in the supposed superior qualities of Bolshevik organization
—he was, to be sure, in touch with reality, but a destructive
and ugly, and ultimately insatiable one.

In this respect, Lenin's drive to power was an historical act
of the profoundest irresponsibility in its willingness to unchain,
with all their unknown, unknowable, but surely and predictably
cataclysmic consequences, the truly dark forces—not those of
Satan but rather those of a tortured Caliban. The genius of Lenin
lay perhaps in his capacity to behave "responsibly," and not in
panic or in frenzy, within this tumultuous universe he was helping
to bring into being. This gets us, admittedly, into some deep
and uncertain waters, but some such appraisal seems necessary
for a comprehension of the quality of "responsible" behavior
in the next and final stage of his career—as the man in power.

One of the salient features of Lenin's actions after the seizure of power is the number of reversals of policy that quickly followed and that seemed in such blatant contrast to his 1917 writings and actions. *State and Revolution* did not come to serve as a blueprint for the new order; indeed, Lenin cheerfully granted that many of the ideas advanced in 1917 concerning the economic and fiscal management of a society had been simplistic or plainly erroneous. Workers' control of industry was soon dropped as unworkable. The peasantry did not join in the anticipated alliance, but rather a form of tension re-emerged between town and country that has persisted to this day. The doctrine of national self-determination, including the right of separation, while never formally abandoned, rapidly became emptied of content as conflict flared up between the Bolsheviks and the various national groups, above all the Ukrainians, that sought full independence. Above all, despite Lenin's pledges not to make a separate peace with the imperialist German enemy, he was obliged, amid perhaps the severest crisis within the Party, to force through acceptance of the terms of Brest-Litovsk. With the draconic measures of war communism, to be followed by the admitted retreat to NEP—and all this in a world that, while hostile, had failed to provide the hoped-for revolutionary backdrop—one might argue that Lenin, once in power, had betrayed, or failed in his responsibility to, the revolutionary ideal that had sustained him for so many decades.

It is true that the Party remained intact, indeed became an even more tightly organized body with the provision against factionalism at the Tenth Party Congress in 1921. It is true, too, that such potentially disruptive challenges as those provided by the Workers' Opposition, the Democratic Centralists, the rebellious peasants of Tambov, the sailors of Kronstadt, and the nationalist movements in the Ukraine and the Caucasus had been put down, defeated, or driven into the wilderness, but these, unlike the successes in the conflict against the "Whites," the interventionists, and the Poles, were bitter victories. Meanwhile the "state" was re-emerging in full panoply, the old Russian demon of "bureaucracy" was coming back into its own. And Great Russian chauvinism, as displayed by Stalin in his activities in his native Georgia was clearly reappearing, to Lenin's dismay and anger.

And yet, if our view of Lenin is correct, these marked changes that occurred, once the Bolsheviks were in power and had to fight for the preservation, consolidation, and re-extension of their writ, should not, perhaps, be regarded ultimately as either betrayals or a belated recognition of harsh fact. For if, as we have suggested, the key to Lenin as a political figure lies below the level of articulated political theory but encompasses a sense of reality, of politics as the art of the possible, then these palpable shifts in the years 1918–22, while representing "betrayal" to left communists and auguries of a "return of normalcy" to hopeful outside observers, were in fact neither, but simply a continuation in a period of power and authority of essentially the same perceptions and insights that we find in Lenin during the pre-revolutionary period. For *if* the regime he had managed to bring into power were to survive, most if not all of these changes were unavoidable.

If one examines the various alternative plans and schemes against which Lenin fought, from the crisis of Brest-Litovsk through to the tensions of the critical year 1921, one can only conclude, unless one is bound by ideological preconceptions or a dedication to *fiat justitia,* that they would all have failed, in the sense of destroying what they were supposed to support and strengthen—the Bolshevik regime.

This is not to posit, of course, a justification of Lenin's positions while in power, except in the Hobbesian sense that if such and such a goal is premised, then certain acts follow; otherwise a self-destroying contradiction sets in. It might well be maintained that there was no manifest reason *why* the Leninist system should survive to become the core of the Soviet state (which it was, whatever happened later under Stalin). Indeed, one could argue—though it would be risky because it would be difficult indeed to trace the infinitude of domestic and foreign consequences, that it would have been for the best if this *tour de force* had explicitly failed and if Russia had undergone in due course a Restoration of sorts (doubtless without Romanovs). One need not be put in the position of asserting the necessity of the Soviet system. Possibly a breakup of Russia into a variety of national entities might have led to a more stable international situation—though it is not hard to advance arguments to the contrary (for example, the implications of an independent Ukraine and its vast resources, vis-à-vis a revived Germany in the 1930s; the scenario becomes too complex for useful reconstruction).

The only point to be stressed is that Lenin in power behaved "responsibly" as a practical political being—but within the frame of the basic irresponsibility I have sketched in the preceding pages. I have tried to bring out above what seems to have lain in the very creation of the Soviet system—the decision to wrest and maintain power—in the service of a revolutionary ideal of which Lenin felt himself to be the sole custodian. And it is this particular feature of the Soviet system, though its survival even in Lenin's day involved doing violence to aspects of that ideal, that seems to have become part of its very fiber as it has evolved over the last half-century, and that full emergence, or emancipation, from which still appears to be a major problem for Russia's future. *Tempora mutantur et nos mutamur in illis,* perhaps, but against this comforting notion that time changes all—with new generations, new problems, perhaps even a new culture— there seems still to reside in the Soviet Union of today a certain quality embedded by Lenin before, during, and after the actual revolution itself, derived in part from earlier Russian history, or portions thereof, but crystallized or precipitated by Lenin's own genius. It is not just a question of authoritarianism—this is but symptomatic—but rather something deeper, more than purely habitual or historical: the juxtaposition within one person—perhaps more than a juxtaposition; a powerful and lasting amalgam —of the hater of external, autocratic power being at the same time profoundly unwilling to accept *vox populi,* fighting the former in the name of the latter, but with himself, and his extension, the Party, sole mediator to bridge the abyss.

V

This leads, in turn, to a final question, that of Lenin's sense of failure at the end of his life. As I have said above, I am somewhat skeptical, at least on the superficial level, of the verdict that things had not turned out as utopian as some of Lenin's writings might, in our reading, have led him to anticipate. In this respect he was a realist throughout. More may be said of the view of the impact of sheer physical impairment, the ebbing of the tremendous will to make the moribund body perform while the mind still perceived. Here one can well imagine Lenin's anguish and the poignancy of the communications, long-suppressed, relating to his mounting concern and anger about the figure of Stalin. Lenin surely sensed his physical, and perhaps organizational, impotence against this looming figure.

But perhaps there is more to be said than simply the familiar story of the "old bull," the day past when "Not another dared him then, Dared him and again defied." For along with Stalin, Death, too, was stalking Lenin, and I would suggest that it was not merely death in its universal role as the oncoming destroyer of the physical being of the Bolshevik leader, but the fact of death itself (human mortality is still 100 per cent sooner or later) that suggests the ultimate irreconcilability between power and responsibility in Lenin, whether he was aware of this or not, and in subsequent Leninism. For human mortality—whatever one's beliefs about immortality or an afterlife may be—is *the* one sure, common possession, or fate, of us all. Unlike taxes, there is no reprieve or evasion. Hence any responsible position toward the question of political power, including that of state-building, must take this universal fate into consideration—in this plight, or release, is the one indubitably common quality of all members of mankind. From this, certain consequences follow. It does not necessarily mean the creation of a heaven—though some would argue so; it does not even mean, necessarily, the refusal to take life—though others have argued so and with some cogency; one may still have a well-reasoned doctrine of the "just war." But at the very least it does entail that, unless the human being is to become pure "object," in which case power ultimately operates in a meaningless waste, one must come to terms, as best one can in this world, with a recognition of the common rights arising from a common fate. One's fellow, even if one's enemy, is a "subject." And here, it would seem to me, lies the ultimate irresponsibility of Leninism in power. Not that Lenin was inhuman personally in this regard, as is evidenced by his sadness over Martov who was dying at the same time, but in the hideous—the word is strong but intended—disjunction between those human sentiments Lenin certainly felt and his political ruthlessness. If a person is beyond the pale politically, then sentiment cannot interfere, and then the use of the "instrument," be it the Cheka or whatever, moves in as a matter of logical consequence. What in Lenin's psyche ultimately created or permitted this disjunction I am unable to say. But as a central constituent of a power apparatus it is more than drumhead justice or revolutionary *élan;* it is something much colder and more inhuman. It is a commonplace that the Bolsheviks have always had trouble coming to terms with Death: it makes the New Soviet Man slightly, but decisively, less than an ideal model. But the failure to absorb and grant this, among other unavoidable human foibles, was productive, under Stalin, of the dreadful and reverse meaning that was to be given to Engels' hopeful statement that in the new order the "government of persons is replaced by the administration of things."

Chapter 19

NEVILLE CHAMBERLAIN AND MUNICH:
TWO ASPECTS OF POWER

William E. Scott

Munich has become such a damning symbol that the personality and policies of Neville Chamberlain may never be fairly judged.[1] On the Munich Pact itself there can be no doubt—it cried out the weakness of France and Britain.[2] But it is false to carry over the aura of that capitulation to the man. He was a strong man, an activist, and his primary motives stemmed not from anxiety but from confidence that what he was doing was "right." What hurt Chamberlain was not weakness but miscalculation.

Chamberlain was ill-served by the cartoonists, whose use of his famous umbrella, held over his prim, tight-lipped face, give no hint of the iron in the man. Another approach plays on his age, describing Chamberlain at the climax of the Munich crisis as an "aged, weary and broken man."[3] These timid, feeble images are nonsense.

Neville Chamberlain ran his government in a forceful, almost autocratic manner. His "most dominant characteristics were an

[1] The best biographies of Chamberlain are those by Keith Feiling, *The Life of Neville Chamberlain* (London, 1946) and Iain Macleod, *Neville Chamberlain* (London, 1961). I am indebted to Sir Alec Douglas-Home, Mr. Chamberlain's Principal Parliamentary Secretary, 1937–39, for a very helpful interview, July 14, 1966.

[2] On the Munich crisis see: Sir John W. Wheeler-Bennett, *Munich, Prologue to Tragedy* (New York, 1948); Keith Eubank, *Munich*, (Norman, 1963); R. G. D. Laffan, *Survey of International Affairs*, 1938, II (London, 1951); Pierre Renouvin, *Histoire des Relations Internationales*, Tome 8, *Les Crises du XXe Siecle*, II, 1929–45, pp. 120–39; Henri Noguères, Munich, ou la drôle de paix (Paris, 1963); Boris Celovsky, *Das Münchener Abkommen von 1938* (Stuttgart, 1958).

[3] Frank P. Chambers, *This Age of Conflict* (New York, 1962), p. 485.

unshakeable reliance on his own judgment and ruthless single-mindedness in the execution of that judgment."[4] Sir Samuel Hoare noticed an instant effect. "Chamberlain seemed at once to crystallize all the fluid forces in the cabinet. His clearcut mind and concrete outlook had an astringent effect upon opinions and preferences that had hitherto been only sentiments and impressions."[5]

Not only vigor but courage was there. When Chamberlain disclosed his idea of flying to see Hitler, Hoare's reaction was that he would be taking "a great political risk by personally intervening in a way that was quite likely to fail." Chamberlain replied that "he would never forgive himself if war broke out and he had not tried every expedient for averting it."[6] Although he was sure of the rightness of his course, there was no guarantee that it would work. Yet he did not hesitate to commit himself completely and so to risk his career and his reputation. It was Winston Churchill who wrote that "the course which he [Chamberlain] followed required the highest degree of moral courage. . . . He did not shrink either from the responsibility which he incurred or from the personal exertions required."[7]

Chamberlain took very seriously one aspect of the responsibility of power—the necessity to use it. That is not to say that power must be used simply because it is there, although that proposition might be argued, but it is to say that every statesman has a duty to use his power to deal with any major threat to the state. Such a threat existed—the danger of war posed by the ambitions of Nazi Germany. Unlike his predecessor, Chamberlain faced it squarely. He tried to deal with it by a clear, intelligible policy, and he had the courage to commit himself deeply to that policy. In this area, there is not the gulf between Chamberlain and Churchill that is widely believed. Both men were movers, doers, interfering everywhere, often too much so, incapable of merely drifting.

[4] D. C. Watt, *Personalities and Policies; Studies in the Formulation of British Foreign Policy in the Twentieth Century* (Notre Dame, 1965), p. 163.

[5] Viscount Templewood (Sir Samuel Hoare), *Nine Troubled Years* (London, 1954), p. 167.

[6] *Ibid.*, p. 300.

[7] Winston Churchill, *The Gathering Storm* (London, 1948), pp. 292, 269.

II

When Neville Chamberlain became Prime Minister, May 25, 1937, he inherited a barren legacy in foreign policy. Churchill called the period from 1931 to 1935 "the years that the locust hath eaten." Actually the locust consumed two more years. Not until February 1938 did a definite British policy toward Germany emerge.[8]

Why were these years left open to the locust? So far as any individual is concerned, the blame lies on Stanley Baldwin, the most powerful politician in England from August 1931 until his retirement in May 1937 and Prime Minister from June 7, 1935 on.[9] Baldwin was a kind, sensitive man who took pleasure in good books and good food and had a deep love for the English countryside. Extremely skillful as a politician, he was preoccupied with the strength of the pacifist movement in England. He was afraid that all-out rearmament and a vigorous campaign of resistance to Hitler would be regarded by millions, especially in the Labour Party, as a cynical device to divert attention from social reform. Baldwin was probably correct in this belief, but it was an excuse, not a cause. It was a pretext to cover the fact that he was bored with foreign affairs.

> He was a man of many virtues charged with supreme responsibility in the wrong age. . . . He was remarkably ignorant of foreign politics, to him a terra incognita which he regarded as the domain of the experts, and he avoided them whenever possible, as a man avoids tampering with the electricity in his house, preferring to rely on an electrician.[10]

[8] On British foreign policy in the 1930s see: A. J. P. Taylor, *English History, 1914–1945* (Oxford, 1965), pp. 351–476; W. N. Medlicott, *The Coming of War in 1939* (London, 1963); Martin Gilbert and Richard Gott, *The Appeasers* (London, 1963); P. A. Reynolds, *British Foreign Policy in the Interwar Years* (London, 1954). Margaret George, *The Warped Vision; British Foreign Policy, 1933–1939* (Pittsburgh, 1965).

[9] From 1931–35 Baldwin voluntarily relinquished the post of Prime Minister to James Ramsay MacDonald, the Labour leader who had broken with his own party to form a 'National' coalition with the Conservatives and Liberals. But, although nominally only Lord President of the Council, Baldwin was by far the most powerful man in the cabinet, the leader of 471 Conservatives to MacDonald's 13 National Laborites.

[10] The Earl of Birkenhead, *The Life of Lord Halifax* (London, 1965), p. 361.

Baldwin's lethargy and indifference have been revealed by his Welsh confidant, Thomas Jones, and by his two Foreign Secretaries, Sir Samuel Hoare and Anthony Eden. When Hoare sought out Baldwin for guidance on his famous speech to the League of Nations during the tense Ethiopian crisis in 1935, they talked about the English countryside, walked around the garden, and had tea. Then the Prime Minister said: "'You have got a speech to make, and you have brought me the draft. Let me have a look at it.' . . . He gave it a quick glance and said. . . . 'That is all right. It must have taken you a long time to make it up' and that was all."[11]

Anthony Eden, who succeeded Hoare in December 1935, developed a policy of his own, but he could not get Baldwin to take him seriously. Eden, who twice had had long talks with Hitler, lost all faith in the latter's solemn promises after the remilitarization of the Rhineland. He decided that the British government must start to prepare for a showdown with Nazi Germany. But Eden was too young and too much indebted to Baldwin's patronage to push the Prime Minister hard. All that he could do was to reason, and he failed to rouse the Prime Minister from his inertia. What an epitaph for Baldwin, to have told Eden in the autumn of 1936: "I hope that you will try not to trouble me too much with foreign affairs just now."[12]

Baldwin's confidant, Thomas Jones, who was a convinced appeaser, had no more success than did Eden. Jones went to Germany in May 1936, and came back to beg Baldwin to accept Hitler's wish for a "face-to-face" meeting. Baldwin expressed mild interest, dwelt on the objections, and retreated to playing patience for hours on end, "as the only means of stopping himself from thinking." Jones never could get him to commit himself and the meeting fell through. The Prime Minister revealed the bankruptcy of his policy in a remark to Jones in April 1936: "With two lunatics like Mussolini and Hitler you can never be sure of anything. But I am determined to keep the country out of war."[13]

On rearmament, Baldwin's record was only slightly better.

[11] Viscount Templewood, *Nine Troubled Years*, p. 167.
[12] The Earl of Avon, *The Eden Memoirs, Facing the Dictators* (London, 1954), p. 167.
[13] Thomas Jones, *A Diary with Letters, 1931–1950* (London, 1954), pp. 207, 191.

In 1933 the British Army and Air Force were pathetically small and ill-equipped. Baldwin knew it and clearly sensed the danger, but was so cautious about affronting pacifistic opinion that his rearmament program was small and very slow-paced.

When Stanley Baldwin retired, no intelligent observer, let alone the man in the street, could have drawn any meaningful conclusion about British foreign policy. Policy could not be judged because no policy had been followed long enough to be recognized. Chamberlain, incidentally, knew this full well; in July 1936, he wrote in his diary "we have no policy."[14] Baldwin simply turned his back on foreign affairs and, in this area, refused to accept the responsibility of power.

III

On May 25, 1937, Neville Chamberlain succeeded Baldwin as Prime Minister. For nine months, while he settled into office, Chamberlain allowed Eden to stay on at the Foreign Office despite a growing disagreement. But such a blurring of issues was alien to Chamberlain's character, and in January and February 1938 he twice imposed his policy and Eden resigned. They broke over basic policy to the dictators—resistance or appeasement—and over Chamberlain's rebuff of Roosevelt's secret overture for Anglo-American cooperation. After a long argument, Eden noted: "Fundamentally the difficulty is that Neville believes that he is a man with a mission to come to terms with the dictators."[15] Eden's successor was Lord Halifax, who agreed with Chamberlain's policy but whose greater sense of dignity and openness to contrary advice sometimes saved him from the more embarrassing nuances of appeasement. Chamberlain and Halifax frequently called in for consultation Sir John Simon and Sir Samuel Hoare, both former Foreign Secretaries; these four formed the "inner cabinet," which met almost every day in September 1938. They were eased down the road to appeasement by Sir Nevile Henderson, British Ambassador in Berlin, Geoffrey Dawson, Editor of the London *Times,* and Sir Horace Wilson, Chamberlain's personal adviser. Only Halifax could turn

---

[14] Quoted in Feiling, *Chamberlain*, p. 295.
[15] The Earl of Avon, *Facing the Dictators*, p. 559.

the Prime Minister from his course; the others merely gave advice and provided a sounding board.

Neville Chamberlain's policy of appeasement and its dramatic application at Munich are well-known. Not so well known are the reasons why. Let us look carefully at Chamberlain's principal motives, in the following rough order, for priority is very important. First was his hatred of war, his desire to avoid it at almost any price. Hoare says that Chamberlain was "overwhelmingly convinced that a world war would be an appalling disaster, and that it was his responsibility to try to prevent it."[16] Chamberlain himself said that

> even if it [Munich] were to fail, I should still say that it was right to attempt it. For the only alternative was war, and I would never take that awful responsibility upon my shoulders unless it were forced upon me by the madness of others.[17]

He shared the revulsion of so many men at the staggering losses of World War I. "When I think . . . of the 7 million of young men who were cut off in their prime, the 13 million who were maimed and mutilated, the misery and the suffering of the mothers or the fathers. . . . In war there are no winners, but all are losers."[18] But the deepest reason for his hatred of war was that it was such a frightful waste. He had a vision of social reform on which he had made some great beginnings as Minister of Health from 1924–29. He had not a twinge of the boyish delight in war that made Churchill such a great war leader. For Chamberlain war was a total loss, without any redeeming features. "To me the very idea that the hard-won savings of our people, which ought to be devoted to the alleviation of suffering, to the opening out of fresh institutions and recreations, to the care of the old, to the development of the minds and bodies of the young—the thought that these savings should have to be dissipated upon the construction of weapons of war is hateful and damnable."[19] Despite this deep loathing of war, he was not a pacifist in the classical sense of the word; as Chancellor of the Exchequer he had vigorously supported Baldwin's rearmament program and even had pushed for a more rapid pace.

[16] Viscount Templewood, *Nine Troubled Years,* p. 297.
[17] Quoted in Feiling, *Chamberlain,* p. 359.
[18] Quoted *ibid.,* p. 320.
[19] Speech at Birmingham, April 9, 1938, reprinted in Neville Chamberlain, *In Search of Peace* (London, 1939), p. 176.

Chamberlain's second motive—that Czechoslovakia was not worth going to war for—is entangled with the first. War was so repulsive to him that he would only undertake it for an over-riding "vital" cause, and, to him, Czechoslovakia was not such a cause. He thought that the peace treaties had made a travesty of self-determination by placing three million Germans in Czechoslovakia. It was one of the "trouble spots" of Europe that eventually would have to be revised in order to set up a stable basis for peace. When he first met Hitler, at Berchtes-gaden, the latter said that negotiation was possible only "if the British Government were prepared to accept cession [of the Sudeten Germans] in principle and to say so. . . ." With no hesitation, Chamberlain said so: "On principle I had nothing to say against the separation of the Sudeten Germans from the rest of Czechoslovakia. . . ."[20] Four days later, Chamberlain told the United States Ambassador, "I can see no rhyme nor reason in fighting for a cause that, if I went to war for it, I would have to settle after it was over in about the same way I suggest settling it now."[21]

Chamberlain's third motive, again involved in the first, was the belief that appeasement of Germany's "legitimate grievances" would satisfy Hitler, would turn him from aggression. The Prime Minister had in mind a wide-ranging negotiation in which the Germans were to be offered economic and colonial concessions in addition to the peaceful domination of Central and Eastern Europe.[22] Munich was only to be the first step, because his primary motive was peace and he understood that no momentary retreat, only a comprehensive settlement, would create good con-ditions for peace.

It was this desire to settle the Czech question at almost any price, in order to use it as the prelude to a general negotiation, that led Chamberlain to his weakest hour. When he returned to see Hitler at Bad Godesberg, the latter arrogantly brushed aside his own Berchtesgaden proposals and upped his price.[23]

[20] *Documents on British Foreign Policy, 1919–1939* (hereafter cited as *B.F.P.*) Third Series, II (London, 1949), p. 341.

[21] Conversation with Ambassador Kennedy, September 19, 1938, *Foreign Relations of the United States* (hereafter cited as *F.R.U.S.*), 1938, I (Washington, 1955), p. 622.

[22] See, for example, the note in Chamberlain's papers, November 26, 1937, quoted in Feiling, *Chamberlain*, pp. 332–33.

[23] On the Bad Godesberg talks, September 22–23, 1938, consult: *B.F.P.*, Third Series, II, pp. 463–508; *Documents on German Foreign*

The British Prime Minister at first was indignant, but by the time he returned to London, he had decided that Hitler's new demands should be accepted. His apologists ignore or gloss over this embarrassing moment.[24] The fact has been known for some time, but the sources have been men hostile to Chamberlain and, in any case, not members of the "inner cabinet."[25] We now have confirmation from the unpublished diary of Sir Alexander Cadogan, Permanent Under-Secretary of the Foreign Office, who was an eyewitness of Chamberlain's report to the "inner cabinet."

> P.M. [Chamberlain] returned [from Bad Godesberg] by lunchtime. Meeting of the "Inner Cabinet" at 3:30 and P.M. made his report to us. I was completely horrified—he was quite calmly for total surrender. More horrified still to find that Hitler has evidently hypnotized him to a point. Still more horrified to find that P.M. has hypnotized Halifax who capitulates totally.[26]

This time, when he proposed acceptance to the full Cabinet, Chamberlain met shocked resistance, led by Alfred Duff Cooper, First Lord of the Admiralty. But in no way did this revolt shake Chamberlain's resolve. The mover was Lord Halifax, whom Chamberlain trusted completely. The Foreign Minister, after "a sleepless night," with Cadogan's "horrified" criticism working at his conscience, told the Prime Minister that the British government should not accept Hitler's ultimatum and, above all, should

---

Policy, 1918–1945 (hereafter cited as *G.F.P.*), Series D, II (London, 1950), pp. 870–910; Paul Schmidt, *Statist auf diplomatischer Bühne* (Bonn, 1949), pp. 400–7; Sir Ivone Kirkpatrick, *The Inner Circle* (London, 1959), pp. 112–22.

[24] Viscount Templewood (Sir Samuel Hoare) blandly wrote in his memoirs: "When Chamberlain returned to London, the issue, therefore, was stark and rigid. The meeting of the four Ministers at once decided that Hitler's new demands were unacceptable. Our view was strongly confirmed by the Cabinet." *Nine Troubled Years*, p. 312. Iain Macleod, in his biography of Chamberlain, accepts Hoare's account against that of Duff Cooper, on the normally sound ground that Hoare was "much closer to the events." *Chamberlain*, p. 246. Hoare was closer to Chamberlain, but his account is quite false.

[25] These earlier sources were Alfred Duff Cooper, *Old Men Forget* (London, 1953), pp. 234–37; Leslie Hore-Belisha, Secretary of State for War, in R. J. Minney, *The Private Papers of Hore-Belisha* (London, 1960), pp. 144–47; and Lord Winterton, Chancellor of the Duchy of Lancaster, quoted in L. S. Amery, *The Angry Years* (London, 1955), pp. 268–69. See also confirmation in the biography of Walter Elliot, Minister of Health, by Colin Coote, *A Companion of Honour* (London, 1965), p. 171.

[26] Quoted in Birkenhead, *Halifax*, p. 399. Sir Alexander Cadogan was an adviser to the inner cabinet.

not try to coerce the Czechs into accepting it. Chamberlain tried to win back Halifax but, failing to do so and finding that the French Cabinet was also opposed, he reluctantly decided to reject the Godesberg demands.[27]

Chamberlain's fourth motive was to gain time to rearm. That England was not militarily ready to go to war was a fact—and it came out when the French at last pinned down the British ministers on their contribution to a land war. Two divisions and 150 airplanes were all the British could put on the continent of Europe in September 1938! Just after the Anschluss, Chamberlain was told by the Chiefs of Staff that the country was not ready for war, and that "any involvement in a war with Germany at this stage could well lead to an ultimate defeat. . . ." Commander P. K. Kemp claims that here at last we have the "true background" to Munich. This warning placed Chamberlain in a position "from which there was no escape; national prestige, national honour, the obloquy of future generations, none of these could weigh against his overriding duty to his country, to gain time."[28] It sounds grand, but the evidence will not fit. Chamberlain was not a martyr to necessity. He was well aware of British military weakness and eager to gain time. That was why he spoke of "the double line" of appeasement and rearmament. But the two were not equal; one was a matter of the heart. The search for peace came first.

Fortunately, there are three excellent confirmations of this priority. Sir Samuel Hoare, deeply implicated in Munich and therefore one who should welcome such a patriotic excuse, writes that military weakness

> was never absent from our minds. . . . Nonetheless, it would not be correct to say that our military weakness was the principal cause of the Munich Agreement. The over-riding consideration with Chamberlain and his colleagues was that the very complicated problem of Czechoslovakia ought not to lead to a world war, and must at almost any price be settled by peaceful means.[29]

[27] Chamberlain wrote a note to Halifax, September 25, 1938. "Your complete change of view since I saw you last night is a horrible blow to me, but of course you must form your opinions for yourself." Quoted *ibid.*, p. 400.

[28] P. K. Kemp, *Key to Victory: The Triumph of British Sea Power in World War II* (London, 1957), pp. 25–26.

[29] Viscount Templewood, *Nine Troubled Years,* p. 289.

Keith Feiling, his biographer, who might have delighted in rehabilitating the fallen hero, mutely enduring unmerited slander for doing his duty, did not find the evidence as he went through Chamberlain's private papers. He concludes:

> Many have spoken, and written, as if Chamberlain's first object at Munich was to gain time to arm against an inevitable war. He would, indeed, have been unfit for his position if that had not been in his mind. . . . But it was never his first motive, which was plain enough, simply the rightness of peace and the wrongness of war.[30]

Just before the parliamentary debate on the Munich Pact, Lord Swinton, who had been Secretary for Air under Chamberlain until May 1938, went to see the Prime Minister. "I will support you, Prime Minister," he said, "if you are quite sure in your mind that you have only been buying time for our rearmament." Chamberlain drew out the declaration he had signed with Hitler and protested: "But don't you understand? I have brought back peace."[31]

These were Neville Chamberlain's principal motives. Many other things were in his mind: his sensitivity to the reluctance, and, in some cases, the vehement opposition of the Dominions to war in support of Czechoslovakia[32]; his belief that the British people were profoundly eager to avoid war; his hope of detaching Italy from Germany; his sense of the military weakness and moral decadence of France; his acute suspicion of Stalin's intentions; his belief that the United States was incorrigibly isolationist.

IV

The most striking aspects of Chamberlain's motives are his misunderstanding of Hitler and his almost total disregard of

[30] Feiling, *Chamberlain,* p. 359.

[31] Lord Swinton, to Ian Colvin, quoted in the latter's study, *Vansittart in Office* (London, 1965), p. 276.

[32] D. C. Watt has shown in an important essay that Chamberlain and Halifax received very strong and persistent warnings, notably in the last week of the crisis, from the Dominions. Had the British government gone to war "they would have lost the backing of South Africa, have found Australia divided and unhappy and might well have put the Canadian Government in a very difficult position . . ." *Personalities and Policies,* p. 173.

strategical factors. There is no evidence to show that Chamberlain liked Hitler; he spoke of his "rather disagreeable" expression and found him entirely "undistinguished" in looks. But Chamberlain did decide that under certain circumstances Hitler could be trusted. He confided to his elder sister, on his return from Berchtesgaden, that "in spite of the hardness and ruthlessness I thought I saw in his face, I got the impression that here was a man who could be relied upon when he had given his word."[33] The Prime Minister allowed far too much latitude to his impressions of the moment. After only one interview, again Berchtesgaden, Chamberlain came to the conclusion that "though Hitler was determined, his objectives were strictly limited."[34] Yet *Mein Kampf* is a monument to Hitler's contempt for limited objectives! Appeasement was based on the assumption that the Nazis would be satisfied with peaceful penetration, with diplomatic and economic spheres of influence. Chamberlain found it impossible to believe that anyone would go to war for what he could get in large part without war. What the Birmingham businessman and parliamentarian utterly failed to recognize was that Hitler's glorification of war, violence, and struggle was sincere. As Hajo Holborn has said, "the foremost error of this policy was its fallacious appraisal of Hitler."[35]

But let us suppose, for the sake of argument, that Hitler would have been satisfied for a few years with what Chamberlain wanted to give him—peaceful domination of Central and Eastern Europe. The absence of a strategical analysis of the consequences of this change is hard to believe. Chamberlain had no sense of the balance of power, none of that strategical cast of mind which enabled Winston Churchill easily to imagine the potential menace of Germany. As Harold Nicolson said in the House of Commons after Munich, the Prime Minister gave the impression that Britain had abandoned her policy of preventing "the dominance

[33] Letter of September 19, 1938, quoted in Feiling, *Chamberlain*, p. 367. Chamberlain told Daladier and Bonnet the day before that he "had derived the impression, whilst he was watching Herr Hitler and talking to him, that he would be better rather than worse than his word . . ." *B.F.P.*, Third Series, II, p. 378.
[34] Entry for September 17, 1938, unpublished diary of a Cabinet Minister.
[35] Hajo Holborn, *The Political Collapse of Europe* (New York, 1954), p. 152.

of Europe by any single Power or group of Powers."[36] Chamberlain could rattle off sentences about German dominance of Central and Eastern Europe with apparently no thought that there were other parts of Europe. Did he not fear that, once having expanded to the East, Hitler could turn back to the West and sweep over Holland, Belgium, and France? Apparently not. Where then would England be? A vulnerable island, 20 miles off the coast of Europe, just as she was from June 1940 to June 1941.

Chamberlain did recognize the strategical importance of France to British security. When, in the tense days between Godesberg and Munich, war seemed imminent, he pledged English assistance to France if the latter were involved in war. But he made no connection between Czechoslovakia and French security, and therefore he could make none between Czechoslovakia and British security.

V

Munich has become a symbol for the appeasement of aggression. It need not have been so. One of the reasons for this result is the priority of Chamberlain's motives, the fact that for him peace and appeasement were more important than gaining time to rearm. But one can conceive of other men conducting a Munich policy—the essence, the sacrifice of Czechoslovakia—from a different priority of motives. For some of Chamberlain's secondary motives were powerful and based on an accurate reading of realities. He was right in thinking that the British nation was not ready to go to war, militarily or morally. He was right about France. Mr. Churchill, with his great sense of honor, badgered the Cabinet with pleas for sending an ultimatum to Hitler, based on his belief that, if Czechoslovakia defended herself, "France would have moved to . . . [her] aid in a surge of national passion. . . ."[37] He was sure, he told Hoare, that "the French and the Russians were ready for an offensive

[36] House of Commons, October 5, 1938, Parliamentary Debates, Fifth Series, Vol. 339, col. 433.
[37] Churchill, *The Gathering Storm*, p. 302.

against Germany."[38] All honor to Churchill's desire to fight Hitler, but he was wrong to count on the French at this point. There was no "national passion" to surge forth, not the slightest possibility of a French offensive to aid Czechoslovakia. Because of its rigidly defensive organization, the French Army was incapable of undertaking an offensive against Germany. Chamberlain knew that—at one point he pinned down Daladier to admit it—and he sensed the crisis of French will power.[39]

Probably Chamberlain also was right and Churchill wrong about Russia. Stalin would not have thrown an offensive against Germany unless he were sure that the French also would do so.[40] He had no intention of doing the fighting for France and England. Had war broken out on September 28, 1938, France would have manned the Maginot Line, England would have sent to France two divisions and 150 airplanes. Probably Stalin would have watched. The result almost certainly would have been a lonely Czech defense overwhelmed by the Wehrmacht in one or two months.

Looked at strictly in terms of the conditions existing in September 1938, Chamberlain's decision not to fight was right, *but* right for the wrong reasons. A tough-minded realist, less moved by honor than Churchill, might have looked at the tiny British Army and the rising, but still small Royal Air Force, at the rigidly defensive French Army, at Stalin's inscrutable face and Roosevelt's vague smiles of good will, and decided that this was no time to fight. "Run away, the better to fight some other day."

We find something of this disenchanted realism in the diaries

[38] Viscount Templewood, *Nine Troubled Years,* p. 302.

[39] On the defensive nature of French strategy and organization see Charles de Gaulle, *Vers l'Armée de Metier* (Paris, 1934) and *Mémoires,* I, *L'Appel* (Paris, 1954), Ch. 1; Maurice Gamelin, *Servir,* 3 vols. (Paris, 1946, 1947); Paul Reynaud, *Mémoires,* 2 vols. (Paris, 1961, 1963); P. E. Tournoux, *Défense des Frontières, Haut-Commandement, Gouvernement, 1919–1939* (Paris, 1960); A. Goutard, *The Battle of France* (London, 1958); Richard Challener, *The French Theory of the Nation in Arms, 1866–1939* (New York, 1955).

[40] This is not the place to discuss this still obscure question in detail; consult the books cited in footnote 2 above and the reports from Moscow in *G.F.P.,* Series D, II and IV, p. 602; *B.F.P.,* Third Series, II; and *F.R.U.S.,* 1938, I; also *New Documents on the History of Munich* (Prague and Moscow, 1958); William V. Wallace, "New Documents on the History of Munich" in *International Affairs,* XXXV (1959).

of General Sir Edmund Ironside, although he wrongly assumed that Chamberlain shared it. "We have had an exciting few days and have ended with one of the greatest humiliations we could have suffered. Chamberlain is, of course, right. We have not the means of defending ourselves and he knows it."[41] Lord Swinton was another unhappy realist; he supported Munich to gain time for rearmament, ". . . but I had no illusions about peace."[42]

That is the point. The realist would have had no illusions. There would have been no "peace in our time," no little pieces of paper to wave, no hypocrisy that all this somehow was good for the Czechs. The realist would have known that the Sudeten Germans were only one of the German colonies in the East, that in sacrificing Czechoslovakia he was making it easier for Hitler to take the next step into Rumania or Poland. "Had Mr. Chamberlain returned to London, not with garlands but in sack cloth, and urged Britain to embark upon a policy of 'blood, sweat, toil and tears,' our national record would have been cleaner and we should have been better prepared, both morally and materially, for the ultimate conflict."[43] And then Munich would not have become such a craven symbol. It would have been retreat, even flight, but not appeasement of aggression.

VI

Because Chamberlain's primary motives were the wrong ones, the breathing space gained by the sacrifice of Czechoslovakia was only halfheartedly used. After Munich, the Prime Minister tried to make further agreements with Hitler, especially in the field of economic and financial cooperation. Simultaneously, by his obvious lack of interest in negotiating the guarantee of the remainder of Czechoslovakia and by his willingness to allow Germany and Italy alone to decide the extent of Czech cessions to Hungary and Poland, he showed that he accepted Germany's hegemony in Central Europe. He did give orders to speed up rearmament in case Munich did not live up to his hopes. But the

---

[41] General Sir Edmund Ironside, *The Ironside Diaries, 1937–1940* (London, 1963), p. 62.
[42] The Earl of Swinton, "Lord Swinton on the Prime Ministers" in the *Sunday Times,* October 24, 1965.
[43] Sir John W. Wheeler-Bennett, *Munich,* p. 293.

acceleration was only partial, not close to all-out rearmament. Finally, Chamberlain made no attempt whatsoever to prepare his countrymen morally for the likelihood of war.

British advances drew no response from Hitler. Instead Hitler proceeded to destroy what remained of the Czechoslovak state. Using Slovakian separatism as a pretext, he sent German troops into Bohemia and Moravia on March 15, 1939, annexed these provinces, and set up Slovakia as a German satellite. These events were a shock to Chamberlain, but initially he did not intend to change his policy.[44] However, rumors of a Nazi coup in Rumania and angry criticism in the House of Commons and in the press created a turbulent situation which could not be ignored.

It was Halifax again who, in the words of his biographer, "asserted himself and imposed his will on the Prime Minister." He told Chamberlain that

> the moment had come when Britain's attitude to further German aggression must be forcefully proclaimed, and that the [Conservative] Party, the House of Commons and above all the British people demanded that this should be done with no further delay. . . . If he failed to do so he must expect insurrection both in the Conservative Party and the House of Commons.[45]

At Halifax's insistence, the Prime Minister amended a speech and at Birmingham, on March 17, he criticized Hitler for his violation of the Munich Pact and gave the warning that "any demand to dominate the world by force was one which the democracies must resist."[46] Chamberlain and Halifax now began to search for a "danger signal" which would warn Hitler off any new adventures. Under the influence of a rumor of an immediate Nazi threat to Poland, the Prime Minister hastily announced the famous Polish Guarantee to the House of Commons on March 31, 1939. If Poland resisted a threat to her independence, England would go to her assistance. England and France gave the same guarantee to Rumania and Greece two weeks later. In May Chamberlain pushed through conscription, against bitter Labour opposition.

[44] See his remarks in the House of Commons, March 15, 1939, *Parliamentary Debates*, 5th Series, Vol. 345, cols. 435–40.

[45] The Earl of Birkenhead, *Halifax*, p. 432.

[46] *Documents on International Affairs, 1939–1946*, I (London, 1951), pp. 66–71.

It took, then, Hitler's brutal Prague Action, angry jibes in the House of Commons, and the determined persuasion of Lord Halifax to disenchant Neville Chamberlain. He did not lead opinion; he followed it. March 1939 was not a conversion but the reluctant recognition of unpleasant facts. The result was a change of tactics, which he hoped might still serve his principal motive: peace.

Despite its far-reaching nature, the British guarantee to Poland was not meant by Chamberlain as a sign that England accepted inevitable war. (This paradox is explained by the lack of the strategical factor in Chamberlain's thinking.) First of all it was a political move to satisfy the aroused show-us mood of the House of Commons. As far as Germany was concerned, Chamberlain meant the guarantee as a warning, that clear warning that had not been given to Germany in 1914. He cherished the hope that Hitler would recognize the danger signal and slow down, as may be seen from an entry in his diary:

> I feel that something of the kind is needed, and though I can't predict the reactions in Berlin I have an idea that it won't bring us to an acute crisis, at any rate at once. . . . As always, I want to gain time, for I never accept the view that war is inevitable.[47]

During the spring and summer of 1939, the Prime Minister took many steps to prepare for war, but he never changed over to a policy of deep, irrevocable opposition to Hitler's ambitions. He retained a residue of hope and allowed it to influence his policy in several ways; refusal to bring into the Cabinet the men who were symbols of resistance to Hitler—Churchill and Eden; refusal to bid strongly for Russia as an ally; pressure on the Poles to negotiate with the Germans; and allowing his personal adviser, Sir Horace Wilson, to make a secret proposal to a visiting German economic official, Herr Wohltat, in July 1939. The last was a wide-ranging scheme including a "Joint Anglo-German declaration not to use aggression."[48]

[47] Diary note of March 19, 1939, four days after Hitler's occupation of Bohemia and Moravia. Quoted in Feiling, *Chamberlain*, p. 401. At this moment Chamberlain was referring to a proposed Anglo-French-Russian-Polish Consultative Pact. After this proposal was rejected by the Poles, Chamberlain and Halifax shifted over to the idea of a guarantee to Poland.

[48] The Wilson-Wohltat talks took place in London, July 18 and 21, 1939, *G.F.P.*, Series D, VI, pp. 977–83.

The end came with the German invasion of Poland on September 1, 1939. When Chamberlain finally told the House of Commons on September 3 that Great Britain was at war with Germany, his choice of words revealed how deep was his commitment to peace: "Everything that I have worked for, everything that I have hoped for, everything that I have believed in during my public life, has crashed into ruins."[49]

VII

Neville Chamberlain failed to appease Hitler. He also failed as a war leader, and was replaced by Winston Churchill on May 10, 1940. Six months later he died a broken-hearted and reviled man. Did he succeed in anything? Yes, but it was the opposite of what he intended.

In foreign policy Chamberlain badly neglected one aspect of the responsibility of power: the duty to be well-informed and to keep an open mind to unpleasant advice. His miscalculations about Hitler and the nature of Nazism were common to the decade, but he held to them very late in the game, in the face of much evidence and advice to the contrary. He had, however, the courage to accept another side of the responsibility of power —the duty to use it—and out of that came his redemption. Stanley Baldwin tried nothing and therefore demonstrated nothing. He would not use his talents. Chamberlain tried something —to appease Hitler—and when Hitler slapped his face the whole British nation felt it. Thereby, Chamberlain purged a large part of the British people of the illusion he shared with them—that never again could there be a just war. Sometimes, success is an ironic mistress. Instead of peace, Chamberlain created an invincible morale for war.

[49] Speech at noon, September 3, 1939, House of Commons, *Parliamentary Debates,* 5th Series, Vol. 351, cols. 291–92. Anyone looking at Chamberlain's choice of words will be struck by the extent to which he personalized the declaration of war. When he announced the news to the nation in a radio broadcast at 11 A.M., September 3, he said: "You can imagine what a bitter blow it is to me that all my long struggle to win peace has failed. Yet I cannot believe that there is anything more or anything different that I could have done." *Documents on International Affairs, 1939–1946,* I, p. 522.

Chapter 20

REINHOLD NIEBUHR: PROPHET IN POLITICS

J. H. Nichols

Between the two World Wars a revolution occurred in American thinking on the relation of morals to politics. Historical events were doubtless most persuasive in this transition, but the most important individual intellectual contribution was surely that of Reinhold Niebuhr, who emerged in the 1930s as America's foremost political philosopher. The focus of his work was the exploration of the dimensions of responsibility in relation to power, so much so, indeed, as to limit his relevance as a moralist for that great part of world Christianity with a minimum access to power. But the scope of Niebuhr's American impact was the greater because it coincided with the reluctant American acceptance of the responsibilities of a world power.

The debate occurred within a nominally Christian society and cannot be understood without reference to the diverse tendencies of Christian political ethics. Divergencies had been apparent even in the first century. The Sermon on the Mount was politically irresponsible on the face of it, oriented to a nonpolitical realm. Paul's advice to the Christians in Rome to be submissive politically since "the powers that be are ordained of God" provided a text for generations of preachers. A contrasting hostility and lust for revenge on those "powers" was scarcely concealed in the visions of the Apocalypse of "Babylon," fallen in smoking ruin. Christians scarcely came in sight of the moral problems associated with the exercise of political power until the fourth century. Then it was Ambrose and Augustine who first formulated an ethic for Christian statesmen, appropriating themes from Greek and Roman, especially Stoic, jurists and political moralists. Their conceptions here provided a framework for discussion ever since, along with the continuing influence of the various Biblical views.

Reinhold Niebuhr's brother Richard has proposed in *Christ and Culture* a useful typology of some five historically recurrent patterns of adjustment of the rival claims of Christ and of cultural and political responsibilities. They range from an otherworldly renunciation of cultural responsibility to a domestication of the Christ within the cultural perspective. Three intermediate patterns are distinguished in which both poles are taken seriously in various ways. The five patterns are severally designated as "the Christ of culture," "Christ above culture," "Christ transforming culture," "Christ and culture in unresolved tension," and "Christ against culture."

The revolution in American ethics identified with Reinhold Niebuhr may be roughly defined as a movement across the scale of these types. The American liberal tradition had effectively identified the religious absolute with the cultural pattern of humanitarian democracy. "Identification" is too static a term, however, since the distinctive aspect of the conception was its preoccupation with the progressive tendency of history, permitting a disregard of distinctions and conflicts. Christians came to terms with American culture rather as tending toward the Christian norm. In effect the dominant American view thus approximated to the Christ of culture or (Thomistic) Christ above culture.

The shift articulated by Reinhold Niebuhr meant a rejection of these patterns at the assimilationist pole of the scale. In their place he urged a view in which the claim of Christ was seen in sharper contrast to that of the culture, occupying ground represented classically by Luther and Calvin, of Christ in tension with culture or, to a degree, transforming it. The perspectives of Reformation thought were thus brought to bear on American life as they had not been for generations, redefining the meaning of responsibility.

Hajo Holborn came from Germany to the United States about the same time as Paul Tillich, who was to be Niebuhr's colleague at Union Theological Seminary. Tillich once compared the German situation of the early thirties with the American. Germans, he felt, were immobilized before Nazi criminality, caught between Marxist utopianism and the pessimistic transcendentalism of Lutheranism. Tillich found the Americans, by contrast, at least in university and seminary circles, everywhere preoccupied with a naïve pacifism.

Just a decade earlier two of these options, German Lutheranism and the American social gospel, had first confronted each other on a broad field. The world conference on "Christian Life and Work" in 1925 gathered on the neutral ground of Stockholm for the first time since the war representatives of the Protestant churches of the world. Wartime resentments were transcended only with difficulty, and no doubt heightened the theoretical antagonisms. Most conspicuous of these was the debate between the Americans, eager to "build the Kingdom" on prohibition, the League of Nations, and good will in general, and the tight-lipped Germans, more than skeptical of all three and wholly pessimistic about the possibility of any human contribution to God's Reign.

Reinhold Niebuhr, who followed German developments as closely as any American thinker, was to effect a creative interplay of just those Lutheran and Marxist traditions Tillich had found so hopelessly opposed in Germany, in such a way as to torpedo the whole rationale of the American social gospel in which he had begun his own career. Critical as he was of Lutheran docility under despotism and of Marxist illusions, Niebuhr was still susceptible of description as "a Lutheran with an open eye for the reasons why Marxism arose and conquered half the world."[1]

It is probably significant that in his search for guidance in the analysis of the ethics of power, Niebuhr could not find help in modern Christian thinkers. Augustine and Pascal taught him much, especially in relation to his own introspective analysis of the self, but for the social analysis he turned to Marx. He was selective in his Marxism, accepting neither its utopianism nor its moral cynicism. For that matter, he was free and selective in all his borrowings. The historical traditions we have used to pigeonhole him are only rough approximations; he was an independent and non-academic thinker, shaping his ideas more to concrete issues than to schools of thought.

It may also be useful to analyze Niebuhr's achievement in terms of role. Daniel Bell once critized Eugene Debs for ir-

[1] Richard Kroner, in *Reinhold Niebuhr, His Religious, Social and Political Thought*, C. W. Kegley and R. W. Bretall, eds., 180.

responsibility, utilizing Max Scheler's simile of the prophet who stands on the mountain as a signpost. The prophet points the way, Scheler had observed, but cannot go himself, for if he did, there would no longer be a sign. But it is the function of the politician, Bell added, to carry the sign with him into the valley.[2] Whatever is to be said of Debs, we have in this last image a fair picture of Reinhold Niebuhr, who insisted on a realistic confrontation with the moral ambiguities of politics, in part to clarify the testimony to moral absolutes in their purity.

How could the prophet keep his integrity in politics and avoid falling into either rudderless pragmatism or irrelevant absolutism? Perhaps it is pushing a point to call Niebuhr a politician. He did not seek or hold political or civil office. But as a political commentator for a quarter of a century, in the *World Tomorrow, Nation, Radical Religion, New Leader,* and *Christianity and Crisis* he submitted to the discipline of making vicarious political decisions to meet press deadlines. Such a commentator, of course, has more freedom than a politician to pick his issues, is less hemmed in by the tug and press and by the momentum of previous decisions. But he is as close to the life of a politician as can be without being one. Niebuhr was also an advocate of scores of causes, of groups and individuals. One suspects his office at Union Seminary must at times have resembled that of a ward alderman, he was so generous with his time and energy.

Again, how is one to acclaim as a politician one who for two decades pursued the marsh gas of a third party, voting the Socialist ticket for much of it, hoping in the 1930s for the rise of a "Protestant proletariat" in the South, who looked with patronizing contempt on the political achievement of the New Deal, demonstrating its inadequacies by categories derived from European experience? Yet it can be argued that in this apparent political ineptitude Niebuhr was a profound instructor in the dimensions of political responsibility, relating effectively the prophet's signpost to the confusing decisions in the valley.

For a full assessment of Niebuhr's achievement we need perhaps a third character in the simile, the philosopher, meditating apart in the shade, with a good view alike of the mountaintop

[2] "The Background and Development of Socialism in the United States," in *Socialism in American Life,* D. D. Egbert and S. Persons, eds., I, 302.

and of the ebb and flow below. This role also we will find
Niebuhr occupying in his later years after the Second World
War.

II

It is a measure of Niebuhr's achievement that his political
ethic today seems so obvious, and that it calls for a strenuous effort of historical imagination to comprehend the liberal social
gospel out of which he sprang and which he largely replaced.
Some attempt at such comprehension must be made.

The liberal social gospel is to be identified in its political
program with pre-World War Progressivism and populism. It
was a middle-class reforming movement, expressing the reaction
of the older, more organic society of the small Protestant town
and countryside to the impersonal rapacity of the new mass industry, the "trusts," Wall Street, and the great concentrations of
exploited immigrant labor. The social gospel represented only a
small minority in the churches, of course, and most laymen were
hardly aware of it. It was largely confined to urban ministers of
the industrial northeast. But it was influential far beyond its
numbers because of the eminence of its leaders in the church,
and their opportunities for influence among the powerful. Among
the most noted names were Washington Gladden, Josiah Strong,
George Herron, W. D. Bliss, Walter Rauschenbusch, and Francis
McConnell. By the 1920s its most representative agency was
the Federal Council of Churches, and most widely read organ,
C. C. Morrison's *Christian Century*. As a Detroit pastor in the
1920s Reinhold Niebuhr was a recognized spokesman of the
movement.

For a grasp of the deeper dynamics of the social gospel,
however, one must go back to the first half of the nineteenth
century. This had been the truly formative epoch of American
religious life, in which was shaped that distinctive synthesis of
American culture and "evangelical" Protestantism that was to
define the "mainstream" of American religion well into the
twentieth century. In the enormous population expansion and
church extension of the second quarter of the century, older institutional structures and patterns of thought were swamped by

the new methods and conceptions evolved in the generation of Lyman Beecher and Charles G. Finney. The social gospel, which emerged in the last quarter of the century, was just one coloration of this evangelical synthesis and cannot be understood apart from it.

The generation that saw the final disestablishment of New England Congregationalism witnessed the creation of a strategy consciously designed to maintain Christian leadership in American society in other ways. It was sufficiently successful to startle Tocqueville as he compared the influence of religion in America with that in Europe. The rapidly expanding and westward-moving population forced the churches to count heavily on a device for assembling individuals by an emotional appeal, the revival. A whole series of voluntary societies similarly channeled the kindled energies of awakened Christians for moral reform, evangelism, and philanthropy: the American Temperance Society, the American Anti-Slavery Society, the American Board of Commissioners for Foreign Missions, the American Home Missionary Society, and others. The use of the word "American" in these names states an implicit claim to a representative status in the national community. Most of the societies were shaped in New England and represented an etherealized notion of the New England ecclesiastical establishment, now on a broader denominational base and intended to reach the whole national geographic community. These pretensions were resisted by a few opponents of religion in general, by various religious bodies that did not find the theological orientation congenial, such as Universalists and in part Methodists, and by Westerners resenting eastern paternalism. But the pretension was strong enough to constitute a "mainstream." Immigration, meanwhile, was building enormous colonies and ghettoes of Roman Catholics and Lutherans, as yet virtually passive in the political community of the nation, but who were also to challenge the pretensions of the "mainstream" after the First World War.

The pretension can scarcely be understood apart from the expectations nurtured by revivalist excitement. It seemed at times that the whole national community was about to be swept up in one great revival. Indeed, evangelical missionaries set forth overseas in unprecedented numbers actually looking for the conversion of the world. A new age was imminent in which the world would become the Kingdom of Christ. This eschatological expectation was matched or followed by secular counterparts in the various nuances of the faith in Progress. Many European countries also breathed this heady air in the 1840s, but the reaction after the Revolution of 1848 gave them little encouragement. The holocaust of the Civil War in America similarly left a nation morally exhausted and bitter, but the utopian expectation revived again in America to heights unequaled elsewhere.

The notion of an increasing approximation in time to the ideal was a form of theological perfectionism, and perfectionism is perhaps the most revealing trait of the evangelical synthesis. At this point came the sharpest break with the older American theology. Colonial Protestantism generally held, in the words of the Westminster Confession, that in this life "some remnants of corruption" would remain, and indeed at times "must prevail" even in the lives of the saints. But the Finney revivals produced perfectionist views repeatedly even before Finney espoused them personally. Congregationalists and Presbyterians at first attempted to discipline such opinions, but by the middle of the century they had given up. Lutheran immigrants were scandalized to find Americans using the word "evangelical" to refer to a perfectionist moralism scarcely compatible with justification by grace. Methodism, of course, had been oriented this way from the beginning.

The social gospel was one response of this evangelical synthesis to the ethical and social problems of the new industrialism. There was the same conjunction of personal conversion and moral endeavor, what Rauschenbusch described as a "dumbbell theology." George Herron and Walter Rauschenbusch preached fervently to congregations of businessmen to give themselves sacrificially for the shaping of the cooperative commonwealth, the "Christianizing of business." The "Men and Religion Forward Movement" of 1912, that climax of the prewar social gospel, was at once the most massive evangelistic effort in American history, and a social service campaign. It sought to win "the personal acceptance of Jesus Christ" and consequent "permanent enlistment in the program of Jesus Christ," especially in terms of social service. Voluntary agencies were created, like the Methodist Federation for Social Service, "to do for our day what the early temperance societies and the Abolition Society did for their era."[3] In some quarters, to be sure, revivalistic fervor was cooling to sentimental moralism. But one depended still on oratory to induce a voluntary renunciation of the sinful practice. Great confidence was now placed on the new "social science" as the resource by which the Christian idealist might master the ills of industrialism. And the perfectionist and eschatological dimension remained conspicuous. The postwar Federal Council tract, *The Church and Industrial Reconstruction,* acknowledged a "radical evil" in human nature, but it was evidently not radical enough to be able to withstand a sustained moral pressure. "The entire social order must be Christianized . . . this ideal can, indeed, be realized."[4]

Several weaknesses of the perfectionist ethic of the evangelical culture religion were exposed in the struggle over prohibition. The concern with "temperance" had been characteristic of evangelical Protestantism since the 1820s, and by the twentieth century all the major American denominations save the ethnically separate Lutherans and the Episcopalians (in some areas explicitly "the drinkers' church") were committed to the temperance cause. The concern united both the ascetic discipline of conservative evangelicalism (along with hard work, thrift, business honesty) and the progressive reaction against a corrupt and corrupting industry (along with efforts for the abolition of child labor, the protection of working women, and the "abatement and prevention of poverty").[5]

The churches generally had identified this "area" of life as one to be "Christianized" by voluntary and denominational agencies, and at length by legislation. The practice itself of using or trading in alcohol was identified as the sin to be renounced. The victory had been won. What were they to do when faced in the 1920s with a counterattack?

The counterattack came from the cultural aliens concentrated in the new metropolitan centers, the Roman Catholics, Orthodox, and Lutherans to whom both the American Sunday and the temperance movement were impositions, with no moral claim on them whatever. Their problems were the new problems of in-

[3] Cited in D. B. Meyer, *The Protestant Search for Political Realism 1919–1941,* 39.

[4] 114f., 6, 32.

[5] See the "Social Creed" of 1912, in J. A. Hutchinson, *We Are Not Divided,* 103.

dustrial civilization, the issues that the social gospel leaders of Protestantism wished to address responsibly. But the conflict in mores lay heavy across the effective cooperation of the social gospel with urban labor in particular. The social gospel, for its own reasons, was at least as dry as the Protestant community generally. It was not going to achieve any very cordial alliance with labor until it learned to drink beer. For it was the new urban society that was growing and the older small-town culture that was declining. The census of 1920 showed that the scales had already tipped.

The extent of the distortion of the Protestant social ethic was dramatized in the presidential elections of 1928 and 1932. Al Smith represented the triumph of the new metropolitan wing of the Democratic party and promised the more constructive approach to social issues generally, as the *Christian Century* observed. But the churches had served notice that they would oppose a wet candidate of either party, and Smith was wet. The *Century* was typical of Protestantism in throwing its weight to Hoover on this one issue. Anti-Catholicism was also significant, but secondary. Millions of Protestants voted on the sincere conviction that prohibition was the great moral issue of the election. By that act they stood convicted of irresponsibility by very large sections of the nation, including important proportions of their own children.

The distortion continued in the election of 1932. To take an extreme case, the Chicago area conference of the Methodist Episcopal Church unanimously adopted a "socialistic" resolution in 1932, and then the members dispersed to vote 4 to 1 for Hoover! Few Protestants would have voted socialist in any case, but not till repeal was a significant migration of progressive Protestants to the Democratic party possible.

Sociological analysis reveals some relations that were not familiar to social gospel leaders, and that they would have found very disturbing. The ministerial leadership of the social gospel came largely from the predominantly upper-class denominations with relatively high standards of ministerial training, the Congregationalists, Episcopalians, and Presbyterians. To these must be added a somewhat atypical urban wing of Methodism. These were also the denominations whose laymen were politically most conservative. The Baptists, on the other hand, who probably had fewer conspicuous social gospel spokesmen than any other major body save the Lutherans, were as strong for the New Deal at the polls as the Congregationalists were against it. The laymen, in short, recognized no significant connection between their religion and their politics, and generally voted according to socio-economic status and interest. The social gospel pastors were generally in management-oriented churches, appealing to bankers, industrialists, and merchants to regulate or restrain their acquisitive impulses.

An unacknowledged *modus operandi* had evolved, whereby the laymen tolerated a certain amount of atypical social opinion from the pulpit or in denominational resolutions and publications provided they were equally free to express contrary views in action. There are numerous instances of preposterously unrepresentative declarations, as when the arch-Republican Congregational General Council voted in 1934 for "abolition of . . . our present competitive profit-seeking economy." Methodism produced perhaps the largest number of these irresponsible proclamations. It is also significant that the typical social gospel ministers were not pastors who had to maintain a basis for ministry to their people, but men at one remove from the pastorate—editors, lecturers, teachers, staff executives of religious agencies.

The fundamentalist movement, which threatened a schism in several denominations in the 1920s, can be partly understood in this relation. Fundamentalism was a movement of reaction in the social realm almost as much as is the theological. It was in considerable measure a lay reaction against the social and theological tendencies of the better-educated ministers, seminary teachers, denominational officials, and especially the interdenominational agencies such as the Federal Council. Not infrequently conservative businessmen subsidized fundamentalist preachers in mill or mining towns to keep religion other-worldly.

III

Such was the tradition of Protestant social ethics out of which Niebuhr came and against which he reacted. It seemed to him doubly irresponsible. It was irresponsible as prophecy because its perfectionism was not perfect enough. It was irresponsible in politics because its policy was not realistic enough. He was attacking the American evangelical synthesis with the weapons of two of the greatest critics of the Hegelian-Lutheran-Germanic synthesis of a century earlier, Marx and Kierkegaard.

It was the shock of the Depression that finally produced a movement of revolt against the social gospel. But Niebuhr had been for some years straining at the limits of the tradition. The social gospel counted essentially on preaching to change the mentality of businessmen in the pews. It proceeded as if there were great masses ready to hear the call to repentance from acquisitiveness, as they had with slavery and the liquor traffic. But as Niebuhr reflected on the death of Bishop Williams in 1924, a man "who knew how to interpret the Christian religion so that it meant something in terms of an industrial civilization," he had to admit "that he didn't change the prevailing attitude of Detroit industry by a hair's breadth."[6] Whether in or out of the Protestant community, the great part of the leaders of American industry acknowledged no authority in the social gospel ministry and were impermeable to moral exhortation in this area. Nor, for that matter, were the masses of labor open to guidance by the culturally remote leaders of the social gospel.

It was at this point that Niebuhr adopted the Marxian class analysis of the social conflict. It meant only a particular application of a type of thinking that was native to him. In one of his earliest articles he had already set forth a theory of social conflict, arguing that all social groups have a predatory character. And the samples from his early journal given us in his *Leaves from the Notebook of a Tamed Cynic* show a mind unusually acute to detect self-interest in his own motivations.

To adopt the Marxian class analysis was to enter territory the social gospel liberals had characteristically avoided. Their hope was to widen the circle of relations of the family type to ever-larger social units, preserving always the model of domestic harmony and cooperation. The "socialism" of the Federal Council, for example, usually signified this conception of a cooperative fraternal order. The Marxist put no hope in such appeals to self-sacrifice. In his mind the way to restrict or redirect power was not to preach at it, but to counterweight it with another power. Class conflict was indispensable in the achievement of justice.

[6] *Leaves from the Notebook of a Tamed Cynic*, 93.

Only Walter Rauschenbusch of the prewar generation had admitted class struggle as essential to his strategy. Now Niebuhr revived Rauschenbusch's policy after a decade and set it in a different theological context. Niebuhr knew how discipline was maintained in the Ford plant in Detroit. He doubted whether justice and brotherhood were attainable there without the organization of labor strength as counterweight. On the issue of the use of force in industrial conflict Niebuhr resigned in 1934 from the Fellowship of Reconciliation. The majority, while identified with the labor cause, remained strict pacifists.

The Marxian analysis also questioned social-gospel assumptions about the neutrality of government and church alike. Was it true that they were genuinely "third parties"? Were not both really captive to a certain power structure? Was not "neutrality" usually a device for supporting the status quo and avoiding the question of its justice? In these matters Niebuhr's use of Marxism could and did mean a gain in responsibility. It forced many to accept responsibility for what they had been doing when they supposed they were doing nothing.

The political case was argued in Niebuhr's most striking book, *Moral Man and Immoral Society* (1932). There was no escape in history, he contended, from the struggle for power between rival groups and states. Justice, when achieved, was always in part the result of self-interest, and was never more than approximate and temporary. Repentance, humility, pacifism were not courses of action open to great corporations or governments. The responsible man must acknowledge these moral limitations of the policies of the social bodies to which he belonged.

The argument also struck at the social gospel philosophy of history, the faith in a Progress that would in the future remove the difficulties now before us. Niebuhr no longer believed that the essential elements of the human situation could be expected to change. If one lost the hope that the world was progressively approximating the Kingdom of God, the divergent purposes and character of the religious and political communities became more distinct. The Reign was increasingly seen to have transpolitical aspects, and to involve the resolution of ills not simply political. Here also Niebuhr was building on insights of long standing. In his autobiography he describes how he had "relearned the essentials of the Christian faith" at the bedside of a dying parishioner in the form of a hope that was not merely political.[7]

There was thus a less obvious sense in which even in his apparently political argument Niebuhr was being a prophetic witness to the claim of the absolute. Was it not a thirst for the absolute, a perfectionist trait, that sharpened his insight into hypocrisy? Who else so flagellates himself and his fellows? It is notable that Niebuhr's image of the Christ was less bourgeois than the usual liberal Jesus. One would not have expected in him anything like the best-selling blasphemy of Bruce Barton, but it is striking that he fastened on the exegesis of Francis of Assisi, the rebel against the acquisitive and commercial ethos in church and society, and that his Jesus was precisely the most "impossible" and transcendent symbol over against the American way of life.

The hidden religious meaning of Niebuhr's new turn was not explicit until the last chapter of *Reflections on the End of an Era,* entitled "The Assurance of Grace," written in 1934. His earnest probing of the limits of political morality had led him to recognize the actuality of a fulfillment beyond morality. He had rediscovered the force of Luther's *simul iustus et peccator,* that the sinner is "justified" even though his sin is not overcome. "The apprehension of perfection is at once the means of seeing one's imperfection and the consoling assurance of grace which makes this realization bearable."[8] Here was the religious basis that, though less frequently articulated, lay behind the unremitting exposure of moral self-deception and illusion in these years. Niebuhr probably muted this note in part because he recognized in it certain perils to the socio-moral passion. Others of his contemporaries who had entered on this path seemed inclined to political quietism: Karl Barth, Paul Tillich, his own brother Richard. The religion of grace sometimes, but not always, lives in a relation of mutual support with ethical passion. And Niebuhr's vocation was that of a political moralist.

A further dimension of the Niebuhrian contribution to responsibility came in relation to foreign affairs. He was a major factor in persuading the leaders of ethical opinion in America that, whether they liked it or not, America had become a world power and could no longer evade responsibility for the con-

[7] Kegley and Bretall, *op. cit.,* 6f.
[8] *Reflections,* 285.

sequences of her decisions, whether for action or inaction. The virgin innocence of the nineteenth century could not possibly be maintained; to attempt it would entail undesired international consequences of appalling dimensions. Yet precisely in this harsh challenge Niebuhr was able to define another dimension or opportunity of human responsibility than the merely moral.

Through the nineteenth century, Washington's advice about avoiding entangling alliances had made good sense. A small state on the fringe of Western civilization could afford to concentrate on domestic tasks, especially when it was to the interest of British sea power to shield her former colony from Continental interventions. The Civil War, of course, was an abyss of horror in the American experience, but in foreign affairs the United States never had to discipline its thought and emotion to the burdens and terrors of world politics. Probably most people in every country expand their horizons from domestic affairs only under pressure, and only certain classes of special training and experience can be expected to maintain a continuing intelligent interest in foreign affairs. But this universal local-mindedness had developed a special dimension of self-righteous optimism in America. The happy isolation of America from world affairs was interpreted by many as the appropriate consequence of American good will and rectitude. The outbreak of the First World War was incredible in this perspective, such a frustration of the natural tendency of history as could be intelligible only as the work of particularly evil men. Only to punish them and "to end war" could most Americans have been persuaded to enter the world conflict. Even into the peace consultations President Wilson sustained the illusion that the world had "left behind the days of the balance of power."

In the general disillusion that followed, and the withdrawal from responsibility, the Protestant churches probably maintained the best record in the national community. The social-gospel leaders never abandoned their concern for world order and peace, and maintained a formidable propaganda of conferences, lectures, and literature. They campaigned for American participation in the League, in the disarmament conferences, for the World Court, for the Kellogg pact, for some limits to reparations, and a concern for the viability of a democratic Germany. There was in all this considerable naïveté but also more intelligence and interest than in most comparable sections of the population. The country would probably have been more responsibly and intelligently guided in these matters by the Federal Council of Churches, for example, than it actually was by the U. S. Senate.

The pressure of events in Ethiopia, the Saar, and Spain, however, forced new decisions and sharp disagreements on the Protestant peace movement in the second half of the 1930s. It became increasingly difficult to pursue at the same time the hope of order through the League and the World Court, with the commitment to sanctions this implied, and, on the other hand, the course of neutrality and arms embargoes. Supporters of the latter course were driven, step by step, into isolationism, something new for social-gospel spokesmen. C. C. Morison of the *Christian Century* was the representative case here. Supporters of the former alternative were driven, step by step, toward active involvement in another world war as the only alternative to a terrible tyranny.

The most powerful advocate of this camp was Reinhold Niebuhr. He was eventually to employ in this connection the same argument he had used with regard to industrial conflict in the early 1930s, but it took him half a decade to establish the continuity. In *Moral Man and Immoral Society* there was no suggestion that there might be a "rough justice" between nations that would morally warrant support for the self-interest of some as against others. Nor did the *Interpretation of Christian Ethics* (1936) transfer to international affairs the ethical analysis applied to the class struggle. But Niebuhr entered into the German experience with growing anxiety and horror. Munich was his decisive crisis, and thereafter he attacked the neutralism of the *Christian Century* with ferocious indignation. He did not advocate actual intervention, but feared the moral position of those who would preserve both their virtue and their prosperity at the expense of the rape of Europe. He scorned those "who is one moment try to persuade themselves that America is made of different stuff from other nations and in the next moment seek to throttle every impulse of sympathy and every sense of common responsibility which might establish a common humanity among us rather than a unique guiltlessness."[9]

In the community of guilt and forgiveness, on the other hand,

[9] *Christianity and Power Politics*, 41.

there was a potential for even political community and action. When the Oxford Conference on Life and Work in 1937 had written to the German Church that, in the enforced absence of their representatives, the sense of fellowship was stronger than ever before, they were stating a sensible fact. It was widely felt in Germany also. The Council had gone on to declare in its message that "if war breaks out . . . fellowship of prayer must at all costs remain unbroken." The calling of the Christian was now being stated, not in terms of the pursuit of justice, but of identification and *présence*.

So Donald Meyer described the movement of Niebuhr's thought:

> In the dissolution of all alternatives in tears, there was identification with the "other," and with that identification, a new sort of will emerged, the will to use whatever freedom the self possessed to move closer to the other; Americans who wept recognized the essence of European tragedy within themselves, and wished to lend themselves as Americans. The switch from political to religious criteria for choosing a political course of action occurred at this juncture.[10]

It is doubtful whether the new American school of realists in world affairs who honor Niebuhr's name draw much on this strain of his thought. This is a dimension of responsibility not likely to be a major factor in politics, although it found classical American expression in Lincoln. But many have learned from Niebuhr responsibility in the sense of realism about the national interest and national capabilities in an interdependent world.

A similar distinction can be made with regard to Niebuhr's interpretation of domestic politics in the 1930s. Arthur Schlesinger ended a fine tribute by acclaiming Niebuhr as the belated theorist of the New Deal, one who restated the democratic faith for an industrialized mass society.[11] This last he surely did, but was it his greatest achievement? And should it be attached to the New Deal? One might question how much the New Deal expressed any political theory and how much it was a mixture of brilliant improvisation, desperation, and liberal naïveté. And in so far as there was a theory, was it not closer, as FDR himself suggested, to the progressivist agenda of the Federal Council

[10] Meyer, *op. cit.*, 459.
[11] Kegley and Bretall, *op. cit.*

than to the tragic vision of Niebuhr? Both at the beginning of the war, also, and in the insistence on "unconditional surrender," Roosevelt seemed closer to the naïve Anglophiles than to Niebuhr. And on the other side should we not say frankly that Niebuhr was by comparison a poor politician, but a good prophet, and that a prophet may be as essential to responsibility in politics as a politician or a philosopher?

Chapter 21

LIMITS OF AMERICAN INTERNATIONALISM:
1941–45

John M. Blum

During the Second World War the representatives of the American people persisted in two assumptions that had characterized national thinking for many years. They believed, as had the Founding Fathers and their successors, in the special virtue of the American experiment and those participating in it. To the particular goodness they saw in their own country and culture they contrasted the supposed corruption of the Old World. In that view the United States and American institutions at once represented and exerted an exemplary force for improving the condition of mankind. They believed, too, though with exceptions and qualifications, of course, in the possibility of mechanistic solutions for major political and economic problems. Just as many New Dealers in 1933 had supposed that the economy, after they primed the pump, would automatically function again at a high level of employment and productivity, so in 1944 many of them, and of their opponents, too, supposed that, after they had created the appropriate machinery, it would automatically and peacefully resolve future international conflicts. Those assumptions, along with circumstances that made the prospect of abandoning them unpleasant, persuaded the nation during the war to circumscribe its commitments, rhetorically so generous, to postwar internationalism.

American congressmen expressed their sense of special virtue, as they had in 1918, partly in their definition of the Second World War as a war against imperialism—imperialism in which the United States took no part. Attributing the guilt for imperialism to other nations, Americans reserved for themselves the mission of eradicating imperialism everywhere. The Second World War, if not a war against imperialism, was at least a war against aggression, but the United States had come rather late to the support of the early victims of Germany, Italy, and Japan. Further, the imperialistic ventures of the western European nations allied with the United States had ordinarily, whatever their faults, some qualities of intended benevolence that were totally foreign to Nazism. Charles Robertson, a North Dakota Republican, speaking in the House of Representatives on behalf of lend-lease, recognized that difference. "The German Chancellor," he said, "has permitted more far-reaching crimes against the free peoples of Europe in the last twelve months than was done by the British Government over a period of a thousand years."[1] Still, for Robertson and for many others, including the President, the liquidation of British, French, Dutch, and Belgian imperialism constituted part of American wartime purpose. They expected that the imperial powers would liberate their empires and sustain the new independence of subject peoples.

That expectation assumed a special stridency with respect to Great Britain, partly because of lingering American Anglophobia, partly because the British received far more American aid than did others whom the Nazis attacked. Those who opposed assistance of that kind to any recipient on any terms found the British a preferred target for their censures. Congressman Vito Marcantonio, a sometime Republican of East Harlem New York turned member of the American Labor Party, spoke for the Marxist left. "By turning over bombers to England," he said, "can anyone assure us that those bombers will not be used in massacring the Indian tribes . . . seeking . . . freedom from British exploitations."[2] A similar note was struck by Republican isolationists who opposed American involvement in the war and the expenditure of American money to supply England with military equipment. Those isolationists spoke again and again of the 400 million Indians in bondage, of the merciless British oppression of India, and of British subjugation of other peoples, including Boers, Africans, and not least the Irish. Just two days

---

[1] *Congressional Record*, 77 Cong., 1 Sess., 579. My discussions of imperialism and of internationalism in this essay benefited from two unpublished manuscripts of students who were enrolled in a graduate seminar at Yale University, respectively, F. G. Morain, "Congress and British Imperialism: 1941" and D. W. Crofts, "Congress and Internationalism: 1945."

[2] *Cong. Rec., op. cit.*, 560.

before Pearl Harbor, Republican John Robinson of Kentucky said, "If the President can have his way, our ships and our men will be fighting . . . to save the British Empire."[3] In that effort a virtuous America, he implied, had no proper part.

Others, less reluctant to assist Great Britain, nevertheless warned against British acquisitiveness. Over the long wash of history, they believed, British commercial shrewdness had regularly victimized the innocent Yankee. The wolves of Lombard Street might again dupe decent American businessmen. Whatever the courage of the British resistance to the Nazis, London, in this view, had contrived the system of imperial preference in order to cut Americans out of their legitimate share of world trade. Everett Dirksen of Illinois, then in the dawn of his unceasing grandiloquence, argued that "if the lend-lease bill is enacted into law, the President should insist that Great Britain secure some of her agricultural . . . commodities from this country. Great Britain has been buying her wheat, flour, cotton and meats from Canada, Argentina, Australia, and other colonies."[4] If Dirksen attached an unusual meaning to the conception of colonies, he also evoked a familiar suggestion of British conspiracy against the good folk of the American farm belt.

Other Republicans—Hamilton Fish of New York for one, Karl Mundt of South Dakota for another—proposed that in return for lend-lease the British surrender to the United States their possessions in the Caribbean. In that way, apparently, virtue would have its palpable reward and the Monroe Doctrine, which Americans rarely interpreted as imperialistic, would carry the Stars and Stripes and the blessings of freedom to the Caribbean people. Happily, Roosevelt and those around him, who knew better, realized that a legacy of the Caribbean from England would include liabilities, social and economic, with which the United States could well dispense.

Congressmen eager to aid Great Britain nevertheless shared the prevalent sense of special American virtue. Senator Claude Pepper of Florida, a vigorous liberal and internationalist, wanted, as he put it, to see the Indian people "have the freedom which every other people of the world should enjoy when this struggle

[3] *Ibid.*, 9463.
[4] *Ibid.*, 1766.

is . . . over."[5] It was, after all, the kind of freedom Roosevelt and Churchill seemed to have promised the entire world in the Atlantic Charter, and to which Roosevelt referred so eloquently in his Four Freedoms address in January 1941.

II

Americans at that time understood the implications of freedom of religion and freedom of dissent. They were, as it developed, less perceptive about the idea of freedom from want, which implied an obligation on the part of wealthy nations to assist those less privileged in the development of economies that could sustain their populations above the subsistence level. Similarly, freedom from fear, as the President explained, referred particularly to the fear of aggression and subjugation, which could be expunged only if strong nations accepted a collective obligation to keep the peace. The President's rhetoric ran ahead of the obligations that Americans were yet prepared to assume. It exceeded the willingness of Americans to apply the virtues they attributed to themselves in concrete policies directed to the economic rehabilitation of other nations and to the execution of enormous and unprecedented military responsibilities. National sentiment focused instead upon the creation of the United Nations, which was frequently believed to be both the major repository and the visible culmination of American internationalism.

That sentiment pervaded the war years. Among the American people, in the White House, in the Senate, there were obvious feelings of error and guilt about the rejection of the League of Nations in 1919. Roosevelt strove self-consciously to avoid the errors that he believed Wilson had made, errors that, in his view, had prevented the ratification of the Versailles Treaty. From first to last the President cultivated both the Congress and bipartisanship in the planning of the United Nations and other postwar international organizations. Delegations to the important conferences on those issues invariably included leading congressional Republicans as well as Democrats. Two of the main participants were Senator Tom Connally, the Texas Democrat who was Chairman of the Senate Foreign Relations Com-

[5] *Ibid.,* 8293.

mittee, and his fellow committee member, a former isolationist, Republican Arthur Vandenberg of Michigan. Connally, addressing the Senate during the debate on the United Nations Charter, referred to the "splendid . . . harmony within the United States delegation," while Vandenberg reported that during the conferences there had not been the "faintest hint of partisanship." As Connally also said: "Many representatives of foreign nations are still doubtful as to what the vote on the Charter will be here in the Senate. They remember 1919. They know how the League of Nations was slaughtered here on the floor. Can you not still see the blood?"[6] Neither he nor his colleagues nor their constituents wanted to miss their second chance. There was, he said, practical unanimity among the American people in support of the United Nations. So, too, was there practical unanimity in the Senate, which voted 89 to 2 to approve the charter.

Yet that very unanimity revealed an ominous blandness, a soft consensus rather than a hard commitment. That incisive critic of American foreign policy, then and later, Senator William Fulbright of Arkansas, exposed the inherent ambiguity in the vote. "Practically no measure of real importance," he said, "has ever been accepted with such docility. . . . Can it be that the Senators do not recognize that, if we are accepting this charter in good faith, it means a complete departure from our traditional policy in international relations?"[7] Fulbright welcomed the prospect of that departure but feared the docility that denied it. The Senate did not seem wholly to know what it had done. Vandenberg, for one, while advocating the United Nations because he believed it would provide "mechanisms for constant and friendly consultations" among nations, also believed that the United States retained "every basic attribute of its sovereignty" and that "the use of force" was not consistent with "the genius of this great experiment."[8] In that dominant view, the great experiment resolved itself, apparently, into a debating society with an undefined, mechanistic utility. Out of that interpretation of the United Nations there had emerged the ingredients of the Senate's consensus. Yet only Fulbright and Pepper questioned

[6] *Congressional Record,* 79 Cong., 1 Sess., 7958–59.

[7] *Ibid.,* 7962–64.

[8] *Ibid.,* 7956–60.

the easy and comforting belief that somehow approval of the charter and participation in debate would assure collective security. In itself, they knew, the charter guaranteed neither comfort nor peace. Fulbright especially recognized the need for deep and continuing American involvement in the affairs of troubled peoples, and understood that assertive national sovereignty had impeded the resolution of international problems. He hoped the United Nations would provide a balance to national sovereignty, "for the lack of which," as he put it, "we and the world have narrowly missed domination by . . . ruthless forces."[9]

That hope elicited the scorn of Robert Taft, the spokesman of the Republican right wing, and his colleague, Styles Bridges, the darling of the China lobby. They saw the United Nations as useful merely for settling arguments between small states, as a sheriff, pure and clean-shaven, on the payroll of the major powers, not even as a mechanism for the adjustment of major disputes, merely as a convenience for preventing nuisances like border controversies among Latin Americans. Their affirmative votes for the charter, even more than Vandenberg's, vitiated the meaning that Connally had attributed to unanimity. Fulbright's dismay at the Senate's docility provided the accurate interpretation of the real intentions of that body and of a considerable fraction, probably a considerable majority, of its constituents.

III

The Senate's characteristic preoccupation with its own grandeur, along with strong senatorial instincts for parsimony in overseas expenditures, conditioned the development of American policy for the relief and rehabilitation of war-torn areas of Europe. In 1943 the Department of State began work on the construction of UNRRA, the United Nations Relief and Rehabilitation Administration. Under interrogation by Vandenberg, Secretary Hull admitted at the time that he did not plan to submit the UNRRA agreement to the Senate for its approval. He proposed instead to pursue it as an executive agreement among heads of state, though of course the Congress would have to appropriate all funds for relief. Vandenberg immediately expressed, as did some

[9] New York *Times,* July 23, 1945.

of his colleagues, a deep concern for the preservation, if not the enlargement, of traditional Senatorial prerogatives. Hull got the point. He moved forward in the construction of UNRRA, as Vandenberg later put it, "with total Congressional consultation." Further, he incorporated the UNRRA agreement in the resolution sent to the Congress authorizing funds for the agency. By virtue then of approving the expenditures, Congress approved the agreement itself, though a few Republicans, including Robert Taft, would have preferred a formal treaty requiring a two-thirds vote in the Senate, a vote they might have been able to prevent.

Others rejected the whole idea of international relief and rehabilitation. Jessie Sumner, a Republican of Illinois, hostile to UNRRA, grieved by public expenditures to assist areas overrun by Nazis, called instead "for a tremendous drive for voluntary contributions, to be distributed by the Red Cross and the Quakers and other such organizations." She viewed the problem of international relief rather as Herbert Clark Hoover had in 1931 viewed the problem of domestic relief. Neither understood the size and severity of the issue; neither understood the need for mobilizing resources in relatively rich regions for distribution in impoverished areas. Revealing the bipartisan quality of political myopia, Senator Guy Gillette, an Iowa Democrat, opposed appropriating funds "for an organization which we did not create, an organization in which we would have . . . only one vote, an organization . . . with power to determine and change . . . its policies under which the money is to be expended and over which we would have no control except the negative control over appropriations." Perhaps Gillette wanted a majority vote for the United States within UNRRA. Perhaps he believed UNRRA incapable under any circumstances of calculating its budgetary needs. Apparently he did not realize that the necessity for relief and rehabilitation would grow with the ongoing reconquest of the continent of Europe. But probably Gillette, like those of similar mind, was distressed primarily at the thought of committing the United States to participation in a world organization whose function would involve continuing expenditure abroad, largely of American money. His internationalism, such as it was, like Jessie Sumner's, stopped in the bargain basement. Other congressmen approved generous overseas spending so long as their constituents shared the benefits. With its ordinary altruism, the western and southern farm bloc amended the UNRRA agreement so as to earmark $50 million for the purchase of American agricultural products, particularly raw wool and cotton. Here, too, American internationalism revealed its special fiber.[10]

IV

In the end the United States subscribed handsomely to UNRRA, but the issues raised during the debate indicated that enthusiasm for world organization tended to flag when appropriations had to confirm sentiment. That characteristic also attended continual discussions of lend-lease. The 1941 authorizing act for lend-lease demanded semi-annual appropriations thereafter, so that every six months Congress could review lend-lease policies and confine or enlarge lend-lease activity. It was during debates over lend-lease appropriations that congressmen had regularly condemned British rule in India and sometimes attacked the British system of imperial preference. Congressional attitudes hardened biases already strong within the executive departments. The Treasury, eager to make the dollar the dominant currency in the postwar world, also—in large degree out of deference for congressional sensitivities—strove throughout the war to keep British gold and dollar balances to a maximum of about a billion dollars, a figure the President endorsed, but a figure far too low for the postwar health of the United Kindom's economy.

Throughout the war Secretary of State Hull cultivated his obsession with free trade, for him the single most important postwar objective of American policy. In this respect Hull was the ultimate mechanist. He believed, apparently, that the removal of all barriers to international trade would permit the world economy to function like a perfect clock. In one sense, his obsession allied him, inadvertently and uncomprehendingly to be sure, with the point of view of Senator Gillette, for if free trade were the basis of a postwar international economy, then the United States, the one major power to survive the war with its economy intact, would reap the great gains in markets and profits. Rather than mechanism, the postwar economy would

[10] On UNRRA, including relevant quotations used here, see Roland Young, *Congressional Politics in the Second World War* (New York, 1956), pp. 184–87.

demand a vigorous and imaginative application of human intelligence to guide the equitable recovery and ultimate prosperity of all nations. The process would entail, initially at least, American sacrifices rather than American boons. Not surprisingly, the State Department's emphasis on free trade exactly suited much of American business, which was zealous to break into channels of distribution and trade in the Near and Middle East that Great Britain commanded. That issue also intruded upon and complicated wartime lend-lease discussions. Here again the vision of Shylocks on Lombard Street outwitting an innocent Uncle Sam provided comforting support for a nationalistic course. So, too, suspicions of Russian political designs explained the State Department's successful resistance to a Treasury proposal for a major postwar credit for the Soviet Union.

By 1945 Congress was weary of lend-lease and its cost, and frightened that the executive might use the program for postwar purposes. In that mood, Congress amended the lend-lease appropriation act so as to forbid expenditures for postwar relief, rehabilitation, or reconstruction. That phrase attacked in part the President's intermittent intention of extending lend-lease to Great Britain during Phase III of the war, the period after the surrender of Japan, in which the British economy would still need American assistance. It had been receiving that aid for so long that to withdraw it all at once would lead, in the palpable absence of British resources, to severe shortages of various civilian goods, particularly tobacco, meat, and wheat. Undeterred, Congress indulged itself in an economy wave in May and June 1945. By that time, Roosevelt had died, and President Truman and the Department of State broke promises made by Roosevelt and Henry Morgenthau in January to provide the United Kingdom during Phase II, the period of the war after the surrender of Germany but before the surrender of Japan, with both military equipment, especially airplanes, and civilian commodities, especially tobacco. In June 1945 Congress agreed to lend-lease appropriations only after Truman and his spokesmen rendered renewed assurances that lend-lease would not be used directly or indirectly as an aid to postwar rehabilitation, and that lend-lease would be discontinued within a month of the end of the Japanese war.

It was then supposed that the end of that war lay six to

twelve months away; in fact, it was only six weeks away. Yet without regard to the consequences of precipitant action, Truman in August abruptly terminated lend-lease in various orders, which he later said he deeply regretted, but which at the time he may simply have misunderstood. The United States first canceled all sailings of ships bearing lend-lease cargoes to Britain. Then, before promised discussions with the British government could commence, Truman on August 21, without qualification, announced the end of lend-lease.

The British, the major recipients of lend-lease and in 1945 the strongest potential friends for the future, recognized the generosity of the lend-lease program as it had operated for four years. Both the British press and the British government commented on the indispensability of the American contribution to the war effort and to the survival of a democratic Europe. Yet Winston Churchill, to whom Roosevelt had given the assurances that Truman destroyed, called the American decision about lend-lease "rough and harsh." Clement Attlee, who had just become leader in the House of Commons, regretted the abandonment of lend-lease without consultation. His statement carried an overtone of legitimate anxiety about the degree to which the United States would now go it alone in other matters vital to the interests of Great Britain and other allies.

In contrast, there were few Americans, in office or out, who believed that rehabilitation was part of the cost of war, few who believed that the principle of equality of sacrifice—so much discussed during the war—applied to rebuilding the societies that the war had devastated. Vandenberg and Connally, those tartars of the Senate, both insisted on confining lend-lease to the period of military operations. Congress vigorously endorsed Truman's policy. When Churchill made his critical remark, Senator Robert Wagner, neither an isolationist nor a conservative, said that he could not understand it, and Sol Bloom, the internationalist Democratic Chairman of the House Foreign Relations Committee, found the British response unreasonable. The British Embassy in Washington had a different, more trenchant view. "The dollar sign," the embassy cabled London, "is back in the Anglo-American equation." There for a time it remained.[11]

---

[11] On the issue of lend-lease, including the quotations used here, see H. Duncan Hall, *North American Supply* (London, 1955), pp. 455–62.

V

The dollar sign had already marked the agreements signed at Bretton Woods establishing the International Monetary Fund and the International Bank for Reconstruction and Development. The preliminary negotiations for those agreements proceeded largely between the United States and Great Britain. Initially each nation submitted plans designed in considerable measure to advance its own interests. In the succeeding, long process of compromise and accommodation, the American proposals benefited the United States in proportion to its greater financial and economic resources. In the consequences, the Fund, as the American planners had intended, was designed primarily to prevent the kind of competitive devaluations that had harassed international monetary relations during the interbellum years, rather than as a kind of international reserve bank, which the British planners had contemplated. That outcome tended further to aggrandize the already dominant role of the dollar among world currencies, precisely as the American Treasury and Congress had expected it would. Further, the United States, the major contributor to the resources of the Fund, demanded and obtained a major voice in the weighted voting procedure established to govern Fund policies. So, too, American proposals, American resources, and American influence dominated the plan for the International Bank.

That dominance, in the case of both agencies, subordinated the prospect of bilateral Anglo-American arrangements to the prospect of multilateral cooperation in the shaping of postwar economic affairs, but the internationalism associated with this multilateral emphasis was more superficial than real. American negotiators at Bretton Woods looked forward to American leadership in the Fund and Bank, to a consequent diminution of the British voice and share in world trade, and to the continuing position, achieved during the war, of New York as the capital city of world finance. The technical aspects of American monetary diplomacy, which both proceeded from and confirmed those political objectives, seemed to the British needlessly to constrict the operations of the Fund, but any more flexible or less nationalistic scheme would probably have exceeded the tolerance of congressional opinion, as the American Treasury argued. Further, the United States had a broader vision of the potential role of the International Bank than did any other economically developed country.

The difficulty lay not so much with some special American nationalism—all the nations represented at Bretton Woods consistently cultivated their own self-interest and prestige, the Soviet Union, France, and China perhaps most noisily. Rather, the trouble arose from a general failure of vision, a general failure to foresee the severity of postwar monetary problems, a general failure to recognize the huge size of the task that the Bank or some alternative source of capital would face in financing the development of the Southern Hemisphere. Like other Western peoples, Americans, while talking about a brave, new economic world, had yet to shake off the dust of the old one.

The right wing in the Senate remained dustiest, as always. "The United States," Senator Taft asserted during the debate on the Bretton Woods pacts, "should involve itself in no long-range program."[12] The Fund would merely pour American money down a rat hole; arrangements within the Fund to provide assistance for debtor nations from creditor nations struck Taft as "childishly absurd." His attitude, widespread among Republican congressmen, among small businessmen, and within the American Bankers Association, had constrained the President and his agents during the negotiations of the agreements. Now, with senatorial approval of those agreements at issue, the executive branch promised more than either Fund or Bank could achieve. Ratification, the Treasury and State Departments suggested, would guarantee, more or less automatically, stabilization of currency values, an end to all exchange controls, and a quick enhancement of American commerce—even, according to the Secretary of the Treasury in one speech in Detroit, a standing export market for over a million American automobiles each year. Manifestly the dollar sign affected both the terms and the image of the Bretton Woods agreements. Yet the Senate approved them by a vote of 53 to 23, a majority much smaller than that for the United Nations charter. The debate and vote on Bretton Woods, like the debates and votes of UNRRA and lend-lease, afforded a

---

[12] On Bretton Woods, see my forthcoming *Years of War: From the Morgenthau Diaries* III, Chs. V, IX.

rough measure of American resolution. In each instance the internationalism of the Congress receded, though by and large it still prevailed, in the face of predictably unavoidable costs.

VI

More important, Americans still drew back from the prospect of committing troops for an extended period to the occupation of enemy territories or the stabilization of Europe or Asia. Sensitive as he always was to public opinion, Roosevelt presumed that the pressure to bring the boys home would, within a few years of the fighting, overcome any contrary policy, whatever its basis in need. The premise of a quick American evacuation of Europe underlay the President's planning for the occupation and reconstruction of Germany, moved him on occasion to view the possibilities of postwar Russian friendship through necessarily rosy lenses, and in a measure constrained him from the kind of long-range planning for the peace, which in any case he found incompatible.

Indeed by August 1945 the federal government had begun to redefine national defense policy, though only temporarily, according to prewar assumptions of an impregnable "fortress America." Though the Japanese attack at Pearl Harbor had demonstrated forever the inadequacy of the oceans as a basis for protection, the development of the atomic bomb seemed for a time to promise an alternative barrier. At Hyde Park in 1943 Roosevelt had promised Churchill full exchange with Great Britain of atomic information, but the President's scientific and military advisers continually frustrated the fulfillment of that pledge, of which Truman appeared to be oblivious. Some of the scientists, Vannevar Bush for one, feared that a bilateral Anglo-American agreement about atomic energy would push Russia into a dangerous arms race. On that account they proposed a multilateral policy that would concentrate on the use of atomic power for peaceful purposes. But many of them also argued that the British were interested only in the postwar commercial possibilities of atomic energy and that the United States had no obligation to inform or assist a potential competitor in that field. Increasingly the case for multilateralism became a cover for a preference for unilateralism, for retaining for as long as possible an American atomic monopoly. Proponents of the case for that monopoly spoke now of the special virtue of Americans, of their particular trustworthiness as custodians of the bomb, now of the special needs of American defense. That point especially appealed to General Groves, the chief of the Manhattan Project, which had produced the new weapons, and to other professional soldiers.[13]

To the dismay of many of the scientists, Truman initially endorsed a measure designed to perpetuate postwar military management of atomic energy. By autumn 1945 the President had reversed his position and given his support to the McMahon Bill, ultimately enacted, to establish a civilian-dominated Atomic Energy Commission. He also championed the Baruch plan for United Nations control of atomic arms, a plan the Russians defeated. But full interchange of information with Great Britain never materialized, and the tolerances of President and Congress for a multinational approach to atomic energy remained small during the Second World War. Ultimately, after the hot war and at the start of the cold, it was the Soviet Union, not the United States, that blocked a sane solution to the problem through the United Nations. Initially, during the war and at the time it ended, American hesitations about releasing the country's hold—perforce transient—over atomic weapons, like American hesitations about committing troops to Europe and Asia, marked a significant limit to American internationalism.

VII

That limit was, of course, itself transient. The United States, during the decade after the German and Japanese surrenders, proceeded far beyond its apparent tolerances of 1945. The Truman Doctrine, the Marshall Plan, the creation of NATO, the Korean War, the inception of Point Four—all these policies demonstrated that the experience of the war had at the least brought the country by 1945 to a stage from which, in part

[13] On atomic questions, see Richard G. Hewlett and Oscar E. Anderson, Jr., *The New World* (University Park, Pennsylvania, 1962).

because of the unanticipated issues of the next ten years, Americans would move on to a relatively unreserved internationalism. But wartime policy, wartime debates, wartime opinion had not carried the United States that far when a new world dawned at Hiroshima.

American culture during the war could, after all, no more break completely with its past than could any other culture. The Congress, however much it molded public opinion by the very fact of making policies, which then prevailed and thus drew support, also in large degree responded to public opinion. The polls of the war years revealed a strong, positive correlation between the beliefs and expectations of the voters and the decisions and divisions in Washington. Sentiment for the United Nations was almost unanimous in the countryside as in the Capitol; it was also as vague as Fulbright suspected. The American people were not eager to pay heavy taxes for the rehabilitation of Europe; most of them did not know what the Bretton Woods agreements stipulated; relatively few of them in 1945 wanted to maintain American forces abroad or to share atomic secrets. From a nation so recently isolationist, from a people so tired of the succession of depression and war, from a culture so long so sure of its special virtue and of its special, exemplary mission, little more could have been expected.

What was remarkable, in retrospect, was the breadth rather than the narrowness of the limits on American internationalism. No other major power in 1945 had a broader policy; many were less altruistic. No other people was less concerned than were the American people with building a new world first of all at home. The limits on American internationalism were neither historically accidental, nor comparatively burdensome, nor absolutely rigid. But limits there distinctly were, limits that only the demands of the cold war and the courageous responses of the Truman administration were later to remove, limits that sentimentality and self-righteousness tended in 1945 to obscure. Their earnest wish for general goodness and perpetual peace had persuaded Americans by 1945 to reach for those goals; they were then still not ready also to stretch.

Chapter 22

POLITICAL POWER AND ACADEMIC RESPONSIBILITY: REFLECTIONS ON FRIEDRICH MEINECKE'S *DREI GENERATIONEN DEUTSCHER GELEHRTENPOLITIK*

Felix Gilbert

Forty-five years ago, when the scholar to whom this *Festschrift* is dedicated was a student at the University of Berlin, his teacher, Friedrich Meinecke, published an essay entitled *Drei Generationen deutscher Gelehrtenpolitik*.[1] The word *Gelehrtenpolitik* is almost untranslatable. It means much more than "the political role of German scholars." The term implies that the political activities of the German professors grew out of a common spirit peculiar to the German academic classes, that this approach was different from the political approach of any other group or class in German society and constituted a uniquely German phenomenon. The manner in which the German professor looked upon politics and acted in politics is the theme of Meinecke's essay.

The origin of this essay was, as Meinecke himself explained, accidental. Meinecke found on his desk simultaneously the political writings of Friedrich Theodor Vischer, one of the first German philosophers of art; of Gustav Schmoller, the head of the historical school of economics; and of Max Weber. These three books stimulated Meinecke to reflect on the role of the academic in German politics.

Meinecke distinguished, within a general trend from idealism to empiricism and realism, three stages in the development of the political attitude of the German professor. In the first period

[1] The article was first printed in the *Historische Zeitschrift*, Vol. CXXV (1922); I shall quote from the reprint of this article in Friedrich Meinecke, *Staat und Persönlichkeit* (Berlin, 1933), pp. 136–64.

philosophers dominated the academic scene and established the basic notions of a free and nationally united political life. In the second period, historians had a preponderant role fusing idealism with historical experience in the synthesis of classical liberalism. The third period brought economists into the foreground, men who could deal as experts with the new social and economic problems of the German national state. Meinecke admitted that the three authors whose political writings he was reviewing hardly fitted this scheme of a three-stage development. He treated Vischer as representative of an idealistic approach to politics, although Vischer's scholarly activity and intellectual influence actually belonged to the period in which historians were the leaders of German academic life. Max Weber was younger than Schmoller, and their views differed widely, but because both were economists Meinecke believed that both could be regarded as representatives of what he defined to be the third stage in the development of the political outlook of the German academic class. Meinecke was not worried about the discrepancy between the scheme he had set upon and the position of the scholars whose works he analyzed: he was interested in demonstrating the continuity and coherence in the political outlook of the German professor rather than in emphasizing changes and differences. Moreover, the subject was very close to his heart. His ideas were formed even before the appearance of Vischer's, Schmoller's, and Weber's books provided him with an opportunity to present his thoughts in print. The reasons for Meinecke's concern with this problem are obvious; the essay was written in the early years of the Weimar Republic, and Meinecke wondered whether the German professors would be able to make their voices heard in the changed circumstances of a parliamentary democracy. Meinecke's answer to this question was that the political change that had taken place need not imply a change in the political activity of the German professors. They could continue in the same role they had played before. Their task was "to weaken the impact of the destructive class struggle and to overcome it through social reforms and the creation of ethical, humane and national values connected with these reforms."[2] These are high claims, and they contrast sharply with

[2] *Ibid.*, p. 138: ". . . den zerrüttenden Klassenkampf zu dämpfen und durch soziale Reformen und dadurch neu geschaffene ethische, menschliche und nationale Werte innerlich zu überwinden."

the actual failure of the German academic class in the politics of the following decades. This gap between expectancy and performance casts doubt on the validity of Meinecke's ideas about the position of the academic in German political life; a reconsideration of his article might help to define more clearly the political role of the German professor in the last century.

I

When Meinecke's article is read today, the outstanding fact about it is that during the decade between its publication and the seizure of power by Hitler, Meinecke's fundamental assumption, the possibility of an intellectual outlook above and beyond the political and economic interests of single parties and groups, was subjected to a fundamental criticism. This was the result of the growing importance of sociology. If before 1918 Marx's sociology or the sociology of knowledge had been the concern of perceptive outsiders in the academic world, these issues became of central importance in philosophical and social studies after the revolution. Karl Mannheim has correctly observed: "German sociology is the product of one of the greatest social dissolutions and reorganizations, accompanied by the highest form of self-consciousness and self-criticism."[3]

In Germany, the twenties were the decade of the influence of Karl Mannheim and Carl Schmitt. If, according to Meinecke, the main theme of German professorial politics ought to be a reconciliation of the various social groups and forces within and through the state, Schmitt and Mannheim emphasized the opposite: politics as a field of action demanded decision and exclusion, not compromise and conciliation.

Carl Schmitt gave striking expression to this view with his formula that the constituent factor of politics was the establishment of a friend-foe relationship. He expanded this theory into a systematic attack against prevailing political concepts in his essay on *"Legalität und Legitimität."*[4] Written in 1932, it presented the case for an authoritarian regime against the defenders of

[3] Karl Mannheim, *Essays on Sociology and Social Psychology* (Paul Kecskemet, ed., New York, 1953), p. 210.

[4] Now reprinted in Carl Schmitt, *Verfassungsrechtliche Aufsätze* (Berlin, 1958), pp. 263–350.

parliamentary democracy. Schmitt argued against the identification of democracy with parliamentarism. According to Schmitt, a democracy is based on the assumption that its actions correspond to the will of the people, to the *volonté générale*. There is no reason to consider the legal framework established by a parliament as particularly sacrosanct and legitimate. If parliament can create laws by a 51 per cent majority, the will of 49 per cent of the people is disregarded. Thus, according to Schmitt a government appointed from above that achieves approval of its measures by plebiscite is equally legitimate. We need not be detained by the details of Schmitt's tortuous and artificial argument for the democratic legitimacy of a plebiscitarian dictatorship; the assumptions that underlie his arguments are what concern us. Schmitt rejects the notion that parties or individuals, by becoming members of a government, are able to raise themselves above a partial view and represent the interests of all groups of society. For Schmitt, the possession of power by one group implies that policy is conducted in the interest of this group and that other groups are excluded and their interests disregarded. A government is legitimate if it has enough force to organize efficient common action. The energy with which Schmitt subjected all conventional political concepts to ruthless criticism had an intellectual fascination even for those who did not agree with him—at least as long as he seemed to be a free agent and had not revealed his commitment to the aims of the German reactionaries.

Schmitt's concept of politics can be regarded as close to Marxist ideas on the nature of politics, though Schmitt cut off the utopian final aim of a socialist society in which everyone would be free and secure and receive his due. Schmitt's rejection of utopian thought served to increase the appeal of his writings rather than to diminish it. He seemed to build on the criticism of utopian thought that the sociology of knowledge had developed.

In the Germany of the twenties the magic name on this subject was Karl Mannheim.[5] Mannheim's work reached deeply into the sphere of political thought and action through his demonstration that, in the most literal sense, liberals and conservatives spoke different languages. For instance, the liberal would speak of the need for "making things" while the conservative would want to

[5] The following is based on the first edition of Karl Mannheim, *Ideologie und Utopie* (Bonn, 1929); in his later years, Mannheim modified his views.

"let things grow." This use of different terms derived from contrasting assumptions about the forces determining the political process, and they in turn were shaped by the diverging interests of the social classes to which the individuals belonged. Because of the lack of a common conceptual framework, an understanding among different classes was not possible. They all had their distinct ideologies but no common ideas. Each class had its image of an ideal future, and these wishes and desires were reflected in several different utopias. The lack of a generally valid utopia made cooperation and action for a common future impossible. Mannheim was interested in the relevance of his analysis for the feasibility of political science rather than in its consequences for practical politics. He maintained that, because nobody could transcend the limits of his own ideological framework, the suitable places for political studies were party schools; they could help to clarify the party member's own political assumptions. Political science at the universities had the task of studying the various political ideologies, with the purpose not of synthesizing them, but of testing their validity by relating them to social trends. Nevertheless, the attention the political scientist must give to social trends ought not to seduce him into believing that he could prophesy. Future developments, Mannheim emphasized, are a question of will.

Although nobody would claim that Schmitt's or Mannheim's views were generally accepted, they were representative in the sense that the problems and issues with which they dealt in their writings dominated the academic political thinking of the period. By emphasizing will and decision rather than intellect, the differences among social forces rather than a common national tradition, they undermined the presuppositions of the possibility of a common and valid outlook in the approach to politics. And Meinecke's thesis of the role of the academic class in German politics had been based on this assumption. In contrast to what Meinecke had hoped and expected, the professors were no longer recognized as the intellectual guides of government policy.

II

It is easy, of course, to state with the wisdom of hindsight that Meinecke misjudged the situation when he suggested that the development he had analyzed must not end in 1918 but might continue. Nevertheless, natural as errors in projecting future developments are, they raise the question of whether the past was presented correctly. We know more than Meinecke did, not only because we are aware of what happened in Germany after the publication of his article but also because much new material has been published on the political professors of the nineteenth century whose thought he was analyzing. Particularly Vischer, whom Meinecke treated as representative of the first stage of German academic politics, has been intensively studied.[6]

Meinecke saw in Vischer an example of a gradual change in the attitude of the German academic politician—the development from idealism to realism. Vischer was an adherent of German national unity; he stated that "for him, the greatness, power and honor of the nation stood above everything else,"[7] and after 1866 he was willing to take a positive attitude to Bismarck's Reich, sacrificing his republican and great-German convictions. But how important was the idea of German power and unity for Vischer? He came from Württemberg, and this was the only region where he felt at home and for which he cared. For a number of years he was Professor in Zürich, and he regarded these years as exile. When a professorship in Munich was offered to him, he was deterred by the idea of moving into an alien country. It is true that Vischer felt oppressed by the strict supervision under which Tübingen, Würtemberg's university, was kept by the King and the Minister of Education; his real clashes with authority, however, occurred because of his fight for the emancipation of science and scholarship from bondage to theological concepts. This was the great issue of his life. It is difficult to find any concern with social issues in Vischer's correspondence, and in the later years of his life political interests fade. Vischer appears remote from the concerns of later generations of German political professors. The motive that led Vischer to embrace national unity was not the desire to obtain a better life for all members

---

[6] See Fritz Schlawe, *Friedrich Theodor Vischer* (Stuttgart, 1959), with bibliography on p. 393; but see also *Briefwechsel zwischen Strauss und Vischer*, A. Rapp, ed., 2 vols. (Stuttgart, 1953); my statements about Vischer's political interests and personality are chiefly based on this correspondence between Vischer and Strauss.

[7] *"Grösse, Macht und Ehre der Nation ging mir über alles,"* quoted by Meinecke, *op. cit.*, p. 142.

of the nation or to make Germany a respected power in the society of states. Vischer expected that transfer of sovereignty from the single state to a national government would weaken the intellectual pressure exerted by the local authorities. Living in a larger community would make it possible for the intellectual to live as a "free man."

Personal problems and needs determined to a large extent Vischer's political aims and ideas. Meinecke described Vischer as combining in his splendid personality enjoyment of the life of the senses and spiritual strength, naïveté and reflection, bluntness and sensitivity, moral seriousness and quick wit.[8] Vischer may have had all these qualities but certainly not in harmonious balance. His letters give the impression of a restless and tormented person, never content with what he has, proud of standing alone but also anxious for praise and in need of friendship, unhappy in his relations with the other sex. These personal features deserve attention because similar characteristics can be found in other German intellectuals of this time and generation. David Friedrich Strauss, Vischer's compatriot and closest friend, had a similarly troubled life, full of disappointments in his relations with other human beings and particularly women. The fight for intellectual freedom against the pressure of theology and political authority was also complicated by personal instability in the cases of Kinkel and Herwegh. Their circles overlap with those of the Russian "Romantic Exiles" grouped around Herzen.[9] Indeed, in their utopian way of thinking and their anti-conventional behavior these German professors had much in common with the Russian political writers of this period.

The intellectual and personal attitude of these Russian liberals— their lack of realism, wavering between politics, literature, and aesthetics, their partisan vehemence, their libertinism—have been regarded as characteristic of the thinking and behavior of an intelligentsia. Might not the application of this concept also help to

[8] Meinecke, *op cit.*, p. 139: ". . . *sinnenfreudig und geisteskräftig, frisch naiv und seiner Naivität reflektierend bewusst, derb im Zupacken und feinfühlig bis in die Fingerspitzen, bald mit aufbrausendem Zorne, bald mit übermütigem Witze, immer dabei mit sittlichem Ernste . . .*"

[9] E. H. Carr, *The Romantic Exiles* (London, 1933); for the entanglements between the Herzens and the Herweghs, see particularly Chapters 3 and 4.

explain features of the thought and life of the German political professors of this period?

The role of an intelligentsia in the life of the nations of Europe and of the world has been great. We usually find the phenomenon that is called intelligentsia in a society that, at least intellectually, is not self-sufficient but dependent on influences from outside; the formation of an intelligentsia is preconditioned by the existence of a cultural slope. Members of an intelligentsia are intellectuals who come from undeveloped or underdeveloped countries and through study at foreign universities or through reading of books have absorbed the ideas and notions of a more progressive society. They become anxious to transform their own nation according to the pattern of the more advanced society. If they are inclined to action, they may become revolutionaries, although few have led a successful revolution. But the activities of most of these men remain purely literary. They are convinced of the need for political change but frustrated in the execution of their ideas by reactionary governments. They are not drawn into the activities of their society but remain outside. Because they cannot test the practicability of their ideas, their writings remain speculative and abstract. Intellectual disputes among them grow out of all proportion, and unhappiness about their lack of political fulfillment is reflected in the restlessness and instability of their personal lives.

Although originally the term intelligentsia—a Western word with a Russian ending—was used to describe what was regarded as a peculiarly Russian phenomenon, other nations of Eastern Europe were no less backward than Russia was in comparison to Western Europe; they also had their intelligentsia. The case of Germany is somewhat special.[10] Certainly Germany in the first half of the nineteenth century was more developed than Russia. It was in the middle of Europe, not only geographically but also politically and economically. But Germany was less advanced than England and France. The political and intellectual pressure the conservative or reactionary German governments exerted forced the advocates of change into the situation of impotent outsiders. The intellectual history of the various European

[10] For the problems of Germany's relations to the West, see Hajo Holborn, *"Der deutsche Idealismus in sozialgeschichtlicher Beleuchtung,"* *Historische Zeitschrift,* Vol. 174 (1952), pp. 362 *et seq.*

nations in the nineteenth century is usually conceived of as an autonomous development and treated in isolation; this view underlies the scheme of a development from idealism to realism in Germany. But can this formula really comprehend the great variety of intellectual movements and disputes in Germany in the first half of the nineteenth century—young Hegelians and *Junges Deutschland,* political poets, writers of social novels, historians, radical philosophers, theological disputes and aesthetic discussions? The one thing they had in common was that they all framed their concrete political demands in wide-ranging idealistic speculations; in order to explain this common feature a sociological approach might be the most appropriate one. Because the method, the concern, and, in some cases, the behavior of these German scholars and writers were very similar to the attitudes prevailing among the intellectuals of other, less advanced countries, it would appear that a good case can be made out for stating that the ideas of the German intellectuals of this generation and the form in which they were presented were shaped by a situation in which the intellectuals were out of step with the society in which they lived —a situation in which intellectuals became an intelligentsia.

III

By suggesting that the idealistic and philosophical approach of the German academic to political and social issues was conditioned by his alienation from the society in which he lived, we have widened the intellectual gap between the first and the second half of the nineteenth century, between what Meinecke called the various generations of German political professors.

It is indeed true that the academics who flourished in the times of the empire played a significant role in the political life of common political values. Meinecke treats Schmoller and Max Weber as representatives of this generation. Both were extremely powerful figures in their time. But it seems strange to place them together. Schmoller was a typical German *Geheimrat;* as Meinecke explained, he placed all his political and social hopes on the preservation of an intellectual aristocracy composed of civil servants, professors, and clergy. Max Weber was a fiery fighter for individual ethical responsibility against conformist acceptance of conventional values. In contrast to the conservative and authoritarian Schmoller he emerged as a protagonist of democracy. Nevertheless, the basic political attitudes of Schmoller and Max Weber are not as different as they might appear.[11] Max Weber's demand for constitutional changes in Germany arose from his contempt for the person of William II; a system that gave power to such an unstable personality could not survive in the modern world. An efficient political leadership was particularly needed because Weber believed that a great struggle was coming and that such a struggle was necessary to assure Germany's position as a world power. Max Weber had no strong belief in individual rights and democratic values, but he advocated a transition to democracy in Germany because the democratic process would improve the selection of political leadership. Schmoller was less skeptical about the qualities of the German ruling group than Weber. He believed that it could provide the needed energetic leadership. But he shared Weber's views about the historical constellation in which Germany found herself. Schmoller also thought it necessary that Germany embark on world politics; he was an enthusiastic advocate of German naval policy.

The thinking of Schmoller, Max Weber, and German political professors in general was dominated by the notion of world power, which is in some measure an irrational concept.[12] It contains a Darwinian element. Politics is viewed as a struggle of nations in which only the strongest nation survives. The state must be organized toward the development of a maximum of power. Entanglement in world politics requires a far-seeing and ruthless leadership. The institutions of society, the life of the people, must be fitted to the purposes of power politics. In this conceptual framework the academic scholar, the professor, had both a particular and a general task. He served the ruling élite as an expert, and he postulated loyalty to the existing system by ex-

[11] On Max Weber's political views, see Wolfgang Mommsen, *Max Weber und die deutsche Politik* (Tübingen, 1959); see also Mommsen's brief summary of his views in *Max Weber und die Soziologie Heute* (*Verhandlungen des fünfzehnter Deutschen Soziologentages*) (Tübingen, 1964), pp. 130–38. The criticisms which have been raised against Mommsen's interpretation seem to me unconvincing.

[12] A striking example of the all-pervasiveness of this notion is the "liberal" Lujo Brentano, see James J. Sheehan, *The Career of Lujo Brentano* (Chicago, 1966), pp. 179–82; there, on pp. 215–17, a very useful bibliography on the academic community under the Empire.

plaining and proclaiming the excellence of the political order in which the nation lived. Certainly there were differences and shadings in the political attitudes of German professors in the period of the empire. But the number of real outsiders was small. In general there was consensus. The professor was the defender of the ruling group.

Some reasons for this attitude were institutional. The German professor was a civil servant, and although in the period of the empire the governmental nature of his office did not involve concrete or detailed prescriptions of what the professor ought to say or think, it involved a tacit agreement as to what he ought not to do.

But the defense and idealization of Imperial Germany by the academic world had deeper roots. In the course of the nineteenth century German intellectuals twice suffered bitter defeats: first in the Revolution of 1848 and then in the struggle over the budget in Prussia. Moreover, the realization of their supreme aim, national unification, was not their work; it was effected by their conservative adversary, Bismarck, and the structure of the Reich, its strongly dynastic form and Prussian character, did not correspond to the notions the liberals and intellectuals had nourished. What attitude should the intellectuals assume toward the Bismarckian Reich?[13] Acceptance meant confession of defeat; rejection implied recognition of a final alienation from one's people.[14] The German political academics solved this dilemma by refusing to acknowledge the wide gap that existed between the aims of the past and the reality of the present; instead, they clothed the empire, its genesis and its institutions, in an idealistic

---

[13] For a discussion of this problem in a broad political context, see Leonard Krieger, *The German Idea of Freedom* (Boston, 1957), pp. 398 *et seq.*

[14] *"Politische Stellung und politischen Einfluss habe ich nie gehabt und nie erstrebt; aber in meinem innersten Wesen, und ich meine, mit dem Besten was in mir ist, bin ich stets ein animal politicum gewesen und wünschte ein Bürger zu sein. Das ist nicht möglich in unserer Nation, bei der der Einzelne, auch der Beste, über den Dienst im Gliede und den politischen Fetischismus nicht hinauskommt . . . ,"* from Theodor Mommsen's last will. These words were written in 1899. A political professor who rejected Bismarck's work immediately was Gervinus. For an interesting discussion of this problem, full of new material, see Karl-Georg Faber, *"Realpolitik als Ideologie,"* *Historische Zeitschrift,* Vol. CCIII (1966), pp. 1–45.

garb. In German intellectual history the development from idealism to realism was constructed as a logically necessary progress.[15]
An example, from a special field, is the *"Bismarckerei"* of the
historians who transformed this consummate craftsman of the
political game into a supra-dimensional figure drawing his strength
from the entire spectrum of German intellectual life.

This alliance with the existing order was a dangerous development for the maintenance of scholarly integrity. The professor has
two legitimate political roles: he can serve as an expert in the
particular field of his scholarly researches; and he can make himself heard as a social critic because critique in the sense of an
examination of the appropriateness of methods to aims is involved in all scholarly work. But since the scholar is a human
being whose beliefs and convictions are formed by personal experiences and social conditions he begins to tread on dangerous
ground when he becomes the ideological defender of an existing
order and proclaims positive values *ex cathedra*.[16] The overwhelming majority of German professors in the imperial era did
just this. It assured them some influence among the policy-
making administrators and constitutes the essential element of
what Meinecke called *deutsche Gelehrtenpolitik*. Because in imperial Germany the academics had been the ideological defenders of the existing regime, the younger generation became
receptive to the views of those who questioned the general validity

[15] "Ein grosser Sieg ist eine grosse Gefahr. Die menschliche Natur
erträgt ihn schwerer als eine Niederlage; ja es scheint selbst leichter zu
sein, einen solchen Sieg zu erringen als ihn so zu ertragen, dass daraus
keine schwerere Niederlage entsteht. Von allen schlimmen Folgen aber,
die der letzte mit Frankreich geführte Krieg hinter sich drein zieht, ist
vielleicht die schlimmste ein weitverbreiteter, ja allgemeiner Irrthum:
der Irrthum der öffentlichen Meinung und aller öffentlich Meinenden,
dass auch die deutsche Kultur in jenem Kampfe gesiegt habe und deshalb
jetzt mit den Kränzen geschmückt werden müsse, die so ausserordentlichen
Begebnissen und Erfolgen gemäss seien. Dieser Wahn ist höchst verder-
blich: nicht etwa weil er ein Wahn ist—denn es giebt die heilsamsten
und segensreichsten Irrthümer—sondern weil er im Stande ist, unseren
Sieg in eine völlige Niederlage zu verwandeln: in die Niederlage, ja
Exstirpation des deutschen Geistes zu Gunsten des 'deutschen Reiches'."
Friedrich Nietzsche, *Unzeitgemässe Betrachtungen, Erstes Stück: David
Strauss* (Leipzig, 1873), p. 1–2.

[16] The reader will know that this is a summarization and reformulation
of views, expressed by Max Weber in *"Wissenschaft als Beruf."* For
a broad descriptive statement on the role of intellectuals in society,
see Edward Shils, "The Intellectuals and the Powers," *Comparative Studies
in Society and History*, Vol. I (1958–59), particularly pp. 7–11.

of any ideology when the First World War had revealed the faults and weaknesses of the highly praised imperial system. One need hardly add that, of course, many were only too happy to crawl back to the customary role of propagandists of those in power when democracy was overthrown in 1933.

IV

How does Meinecke's own political activity fit into the picture he gave of the political role of the German professor? In many respects Meinecke seems to be a characteristic example of the phenomenon of *deutsche Gelehrtenpolitik*.[17] Meinecke's relations to the high officials of the empire, to Chancellor Bethmann and Foreign Secretary Kühlmann, show him clearly in the double role of adviser and ideological defender of the official policy. His *Weltbürgertum und Nationalstaat* provided the most serious and also most effective treatment of the relevance of the idealistic tradition to the new Reich. And he intimated that he had an understanding of the entire course of the *Gelehrtenpolitik* because his family, his upbringing and training had brought him in contact with all the generations that his essay distinguished. The essay has elements of a self-portrait.

But the fact remains that the author of the *Weltbürgertum* wrote also the *Idee der Staatsräson* with its assumption of an unbridgeable dualism between spiritual values and political causality, and that in the years of Nazism he wrote the *Historismus,* withdrawing from the world of politics into the realm of ideas. Despite Meinecke's deep involvement in the fate of the German national state, politics was never the only god for him; the world of the spirit was also autonomous. As much as Meinecke enjoyed occupying himself with the great figures of the period of German idealism, he was also distant from them, perhaps more distant than he himself was aware: the basis of his idealism was religious and not philosophical. Thus he could state with justification: "Alongside the positive attitude to the state which I have advocated, a certain amount of independence from the state

[17] For the following see particularly Friedrich Meinecke, *Erlebtes 1862–1919* (Stuttgart, 1964), and *Ausgewählter Briefwechsel* (*Werke, Band VI*) (Stuttgart, 1962).

has always remained alive in me, and now is awake in me more strongly than ever."[18] This letter was written in 1947; it shows that Meinecke recognized that he had undergone a development away from his early belief in the supreme value of the state. For this reason Meinecke's essay on the *Drei Generationen deutscher Gelehrtenpolitik* might be considered as having also biographical interest. In this essay Meinecke expressed his commitment to the world in which he had lived. But in making this world an object of analysis and study he indicated that he recognized its limits and to this extent, at least, was moving away from it.

[18] *"Neben und unter aller Staatsbejahung, wie ich sie vertreten habe, ist in mir immer ein Stück Independenz vom Statte lebendig geblieben und wacht nun heute Starker Auf." Ausgewählter Briefwechsel*, p. 271.

Chapter 23

THE CONDITIONS OF REVOLUTIONARY POWER*

Otto Kirchheimer

Revolutions articulate the fundamental issues of a society or polity by converting relationships into events. The study of revolutions, correspondingly, affords the hermeneutical advantage of spreading the intricate simultaneity of a diffused struggle out into a succession of discrete steps. The ambiguities of power that characterize the democratic era are among the fundamental issues that may well be clarified by their crystallization in revolutionary situations. Two crucial modern problems in particular seem susceptible to such an approach. First, the ambivalent relationship between the social bases and the political agents of power in a democratic system—the relationship that makes political parties at once the trustees and rulers of the social groups they claim to represent—can be exposed in the form of the sequential connections between the social conditions and the political achievements of popular revolutions. Second, the equally ambivalent relationship between the negative liberal and the positive democratic attitudes toward political power in the modern period can be exposed in the form of an analytical comparison between the pre-eminently liberal revolutions of the nineteenth century and the pre-eminently democratic revolutions of the twentieth.

Hence I want to try, for several revolutionary regimes of the nineteenth and twentieth centuries, to connect their course with what, for want of a better name, I shall call "confining conditions" —the particular social and intellectual conditions present at the

* Otto Kirchheimer died before he could undertake his planned revision of this paper, originally prepared for the 1965 meeting of the American Political Science Association and published in *The American Political Science Review*, LIX (1965), pp. 964–74. With the kind permission of Mrs. Anne Kirchheimer we have taken the liberty of adding a new introductory paragraph and amending what appears here as the second paragraph.—The Editors.

births of these regimes. Therefore I consider the nature of the confining conditions, chiefly those of social structure; the nature of the new regime; and the nature of the methods available to it, as well as those it adopts to overcome the confining conditions.

In discussing political action, we often ask the question: did the man or the group have to act the way he, or they, did? What other options were open, *e.g.,* to Stalin in the late 1920s? Not being satisfied with the answer that, given the character of Stalin, the eventual course of action was really to be expected all along, we might profitably shift the question to a different level. To what extent do the circumstances attendant upon the rise of a new regime determine its subsequent actions? The late Franz Neumann raised such questions in regard to the course of the National Socialist regime. His *Behemoth* was an impressive attempt to show how the confining conditions under which the regime worked—especially the fact that it came to power with the help of leaders of German heavy industry—not only switched the track for the National Socialists, but explained many of their patterns of actions long after their regime was firmly established.

Yet Neumann's account of the German state organization and its supersession by the movement-type party already foreshadows the problems which increasingly preoccupied his thoughts (although only in fragmentary publications) in his later years. To what extent can a revolutionary power structure move away from the specific constellation of forces which presided over its origin, and move off in a different direction of its own?

I

Neumann had little difficulty with the negative test. Whoever fails to put his hands on the switch—either because of a lack of the social prerequisites (France in 1848) or because of a lack of will power (Germany in 1918)—cannot deflect the current into new circuits. Neither the leaders of the incipient French labor and Socialist movement of 1848, nor the leaders of the numerically strong but unimaginative organizations of the German Socialists in 1918, ever tried to put their hands on the switches. Crowded from the center of power, they soon could not even hold to the position of initiating incremental changes. Even the modest role of setting into motion long-range changes, with all due anticipatory consideration of other power-holders' reactions, escapes the group which fails to make a political breakthrough. Such a group becomes an object, rather than a subject, of the political process.

The capacity to compress thoroughgoing or revolutionary change—as distinct from incremental change—into a minimum of time, according to the new power-holders' own timetable, is the test of revolutionary victory. What are the possible dimensions, and what are the limits, of such capacity for change? In his later publications, and on the basis of Soviet experience, Neumann held that political power could make itself supreme and thereby make itself the font of economic power.[1]

II

But what does this supremacy amount to? Let us first look at Hitler's Germany and Stalin's Russia. By the 1930s Germany had become a highly industrialized country. Yet its style of inter-group relations, in spite of formal constitutional change, still reflected the mood and conditions of a bygone era. Perhaps scaling down the politically and economically expensive position of Eastern agrarian elements might have eliminated enough of the anachronism to allow the restructuring of class relations on a more modern, cooperative basis.

Instead of opting for that sort of program, Germany started a course of imperialist conquests in the heart of Europe, with the new political élite lording it over both the domestic scene and the subject countries. This course entailed extraordinary risks, which only a revolutionary group, able to ride roughshod over all opposition, would take.

To put it another way, the industrialists were a specialized functional élite falling in with the deliberate option of a revolutionary political group. Whatever the apparent short-term risks and the factors of long-range instability in this choice, the conquest of Europe, western and eastern, represented one way of producing an entirely new realignment of internal forces, superseding the need

[1] See esp. Ch. 1, "Approaches to the study of political power," and Ch. 10, "Economics and Politics in the 20th century," in Franz Neumann, *The Democratic and the Authoritarian State* (Glencoe, 1957).

to rearrange internal group relations in a manner more common in Western Europe.

Inter-group relations had changed as a consequence of the economic crisis and were certainly overripe for restructuring. The degree of their restructuring was an open question, but not its direction. That restructuring had to take into account the loss of power suffered by the labor groups as a consequence of the economic crisis and of their own continuing fratricidal cleavages.

The brutal imperialism on a neo-populist basis, with its efficient mixture of revolutionary political organization and industrial-society elements, had its roots in the ideological and material conditions of German society. But this imperialism was at most the contingent, not the necessary outcome. Within the context of an advanced industrial society, an authoritarian-bureaucratic regime that might have tried to overcome the political disequilibrium with the support or incorporation of some sections of a crisis-inflated mass movement, was as much a possibility as the total seizure of power by a revolutionary mass movement itself. In fact, when the Nazis took over power, they operated for some months in a manner intended to leave the population in the dark as to whether their practices would correspond to or amalgamate with the bureaucratic-authoritarian solution. This tactic facilitated the undisturbed take-over of power by the mass movement.[2] Between the conditioning factors of its inception and the reality of the Third Reich, were the intervening visions, the organizing genius and the perseverance of the revolutionary political group.

Let us turn to the case of the Soviet Union. In order to obtain a measure of initial acceptance, the leaders of the Petrograd Revolution had to put their stamp of approval on the seizure of the gentry's land by the peasantry. However, this policy aggravated the age-old difficulties which had beset the Russian polity and which Stolypin's dissolution of the *Obshina* had only started to tackle: the need of accelerating transformation to an industrial society by simultaneously shifting population to the cities and modernizing agricultural methods. Stalin's forced collectivization was an answer to the difficulties caused by the lower rate of industrial growth and reagrarianization of the country in the 1920s,

---

[2] The various expectations during the transition period in 1933 can now be followed in Bracher-Sauer-Schulz, *Die Nationalsozialistische Machtergreifung* (Westdeutscher Verlag, Köln Opladen, 1960).

which coincided with the considerable rural exodus to the cities.[3] Having at his disposal a strong enough administrative apparatus to reverse the process of Kulakization under the NEP and to collectivize agriculture, Stalin had a range of choices in regard to the methods of collectivization. If he wanted to industrialize rapidly, however, he probably had little choice about the principle of collectivization. Left alone, the peasants would have dictated both the pace and the direction of industrialization by consuming more and delivering less food to the rest of the country.

What matters in this context is the interrelation between socio-economic conditioning and the discretionary element left to the decision of the regime. The setting up of larger agricultural units and the shifting of agricultural surplus population to industrial life were bound to take place under almost any regime. The revolutionary approval of land seizure by the peasantry, plus the conditions of the NEP period, had aggravated the regime's difficulties by creating an important new proprietary interest at a time when the regime was unable to offer enough industrial goods to entice the peasants to part voluntarily with their produce. Yet, at the same time, a coercive apparatus was at hand to collectivize the land, and collect food surpluses. The general problem of the relations between the agricultural sector and the industrial sectors of a modernizing society was given, irrespective of whether the country was to be governed by an autocracy, a bourgeois democracy, or the Communist Party. What the supremacy of a revolutionary group entailed was a much wider choice of means and strategies to carry out the transformation. The "whole-hog Stalin"[4] was not necessary, and Stalin's methods were counter-

[3] Alexander Gerschenkron, *Economic Backwardness in Historical Perspective* (Harvard University Press, 1962), pp. 119–51.

[4] Alex Nove, *Economic Rationality in Soviet Politics* (New York, 1964), p. 32. *Cf.* A. Erlich, *The Soviet Industrialisation Debate 1924–1928* (Harvard University Press, 1960): "A policy of moderate tempos would strengthen the position of the upper strata of the villages and would make the adroit balancing between them and the unruly radicals of the cities a necessity which could be adopted only as a temporary expedient. Had such a course been pursued over a long period of time the regime would have stood to lose not only from its possible failures but also from its successes. The alternative to such retreats and maneuvers leading to the gradual erosion of the dictatorial system was clearly a massive counterattack which would have broken once and for all the peasants' power over the basic decisions of economic policy. A high speed industrialisation with a strong emphasis on the capital goods sector

productive, if measured by the yardstick of what more gradual, part-cooperative collectivization could have obtained in both good will and direct production results. Yet given the need for accelerating the transformation as a condition for survival of the revolutionary group, the internal leadership struggle resulted in the decision that the gain in time would outweigh the costs of forced collectivization. Zigzagging in the course of the great industrialization debate, Stalin used changes in his own position to eliminate actual and potential rivals, and then used his ensuing supremacy over the dominant political group to enforce the most ruthless of the available options. But the need for industrialization created fundamental claims on any regime, as it had even on the Tsarist regime.

The social and economic frame of the particular society, then, lays down a conditioning perimeter within which the original choice has to be made and solutions have to be sought. Hitler, for example, could not—as some of his loyal adherents had dreamt—do for the German retailers and craftsmen what he could afford to do for the German peasant: he could not convert small shops into hereditary entailed estates, protected against hopeless competitive odds.[5] The very progress of accelerated rearmament and the preparations for foreign conquest necessitated the most efficient industrial production units, leaving the small independent with the option of becoming a dependent factory hand. In realigning his norms and expectations with those of the new power-holders, the doomed independent could at least adopt as his

---

which Stalin now favored provided the logical line for such a counter-attack" (p. 174).

"The overhang of agricultural excess population permitted the manning of equipment which was physically usable with the surplus peasants of yesterday, which could be removed from the countryside without a notable detriment to agricultural output and be employed at a real wage barely exceeding their wretchedly lower consumption levels of the earlier status" (p. 184).

[5] Gurland, Kirchheimer, Neumann, *The Fate of Small Business in Nazi Germany,* 78th Cong., 1st sess., *Hearings,* Sen. Special Committee to Study Problems of American Small Business, Comm. Print No. 14 (1943), p. 152.

The story and some figures can be found in Arthur Schweitzer, *Big Business in the Third Reich* (Bloomington, Ind., 1964), Chs. 4 and 5.

own the choice of the regime, perilous and adventurous though it might be. In this way the very exercise of the regime's option might change the social preconditions of his existence, releasing new psychic energies before the regime's long-term options bore visible results. Thus the socio-economic perimeter itself might seem expandable. Was it?

What we might call "expansion of the perimeter" is the alteration of the social structure or economic basis of society or—more slowly, but still visibly, by the processes of modern communications and education—the alteration of intellectual habits by the new masters of the polity. For the new rulers by then have arrived at a stage, which may come very quickly after a revolution, when they are working out the details of their options. They have arrested the acceleration of chaos, as in Soviet Russia, or mastered their new tasks of propaganda and control, as in Nazi Germany. In these cases the rulers were not crushed by what might be called "societal due dates."

Among these societal "due dates," one repeats itself so often as to become a major confining condition: foreign intervention in national revolutions. Usually we would think of confining conditions as factors embedded in the social structure out of which revolutions originate. But the shrinking of the world, both physically and intellectually, the attendant and anticipated impact of revolutionary upheaval on other countries, and the power increments expected from successful intervention, or the power losses feared from the emergence of a new recruit to revolutionary causes—all these have caused a succession of foreign interventions.

Even with the present-day technique of fighting or forestalling revolution by stage-managing counter-insurgency, foreign intervention often carries its own antidote. It encourages the revolutionary forces to telescope changes into shorter periods and facilitates popular acceptance of those changes; it makes for a degree of unification and acceptance of a new national symbolism otherwise hard to obtain. But the possibility of overcoming this confining condition is aleatory; success or failure may depend on policy shifts in the intervening country, over which the influence of the revolutionary élite is far more limited than it is on domestic conditions.

In the face of all these difficulties, the political group may lose its momentum, return to the incremental pattern, or even cave in completely. Too many checks may have been drawn at the same time against the new regime's limited bank account, and the regime's very weakness may have accelerated the simultaneous presentation of demands. Yet, on the other hand, its interdependent supply of physical force and capital of community confidence may just allow it to scrape through, keeping some commanding positions fairly intact. In this latter case, we want to analyze what happens to the initial conditioning perimeter: have the original confining conditions been changed by a decisive breakthrough? Has the new political system really become supreme and able to develop systematic patterns of its own? If so, we then measure revolutionary change by the new system's ability to extricate itself from the confining conditions of the previous period. The old data may still be present, though absorbed in a new context and thereby deprived of their confining nature.

The leaders of the USSR have achieved such a breakthrough, transforming Russia into a major industrial system. While they still experience difficulties with agrarian organization, and these in turn delay the fulfillment of urgent consumer expectations, such problems can scarcely endanger the subsistence level. Most of the confining conditions have been removed, at whatever cost to those who lived through—or died during—the long decades it took to accomplish that feat.

The German National Socialist experience remained abortive, but no conclusions as to the impossibility of overcoming the initial confining conditions can be drawn from the collapse due to external defeat in a two-front war. Certainly the wholesale program of conquest of Eastern Europe would have allowed a more drastic restructuring of internal group relations in Germany than would a more limited program of hegemony over Western Europe. The existence of a large industrial working class with a tradition of self-organization (even if momentarily without any organization), and of a bureaucratic and officer group only superficially and conditionally loyal to the regime, made the program of maximal conquest of Eastern Europe more attractive to the new rulers than the more restricted take-over of Western Europe. For such a conquest might have led to the pulverizing of existing German social relations for the benefit of the Nazi rulers. A vast imperial apparatus with Germans from all walks of life lording it over the indigenous Eastern Europeans, while German industry expanded into vast new territories, might have accomplished an efficient restructuring of German society. Such an apparatus would have constituted a major guarantee against renewed efforts of surviving splinters of former social and political élites to make come-back attempts—which actually were made at every new turn in the fortunes of the regime as long as its conquests were not consolidated.

In both the Russian case and the German case, the experiment was part of a unique conjunction of circumstances: the disorganization and breakdown of an economic and political system in Russia, and the incapacity and disorganization, although not quite the breakdown, in Germany, and the simultaneous activity and availability for power of a revolutionary group. In Germany the revolutionary group actively promoted the breakdown; in Russia it exploited a pre-existent one. The breakdown thus had the effect of releasing revolutionary energies; it was in a certain sense a counterconfiguration of the confining conditions, and made action possible toward overcoming it. In the one case the group was more opportunistic; in the other more doctrinaire; but, at any rate, both were acting outside the frame of the traditional conceptual apparatus of politicians. They made only short-range compromises, which they revoked as soon as the slightest margin of safety allowed them to do so. In both cases we might ask how the action of the revolutionary group related to the sum-total of confining conditions.

Due to the intervening external conditions, the German case does not carry much probative value either way. As to the USSR, the argument that the major outcome—conversion into an indus-trial society—would have taken place in any event does not upset our conclusion. The fact is that a "premature" industrial revolution, compressing various stages of social development into an extremely limited time span determined by its political élite —moreover, with primitive accumulation by the state and not private owners, and with national sovereignty exalted in the proc-ess—did take place. This is highly relevant to our original ques-tion: here a revolutionary regime did move beyond the confining conditions under which it arose.

III

To illuminate another facet of the problem, I want to discuss the conditions of collaboration of various political forces under a revolutionary regime. Where lies the well-spring of common action? To what extent does the variation in composition and orientation of such forces determine the confines of their actions from the very outset?

I have in mind here the well known episode of the relations between Robespierre and the Committee of Public Safety toward the Paris *sans-culottes* from autumn 1793 to early summer 1794. One might describe the situation after the autumn days of 1793 as an uneasy coalition between the committee and the Paris *sans-culottes,* ideologically represented and sometimes led by Hébert and Chaumette.[6] Neither group could have acted effectively without the other. Their presence served as a means for Robespierre to keep his hold over the Convention, as much as the Committee served as a means for the *sans-culottes* to push their political and economic demands. The common ground which provided both their dynamics and their larger justification was the unconditional pursuit of the revolutionary war. There was at best a partial meeting of minds and never a complete convergence on social and economic goals. In order to carry on the war and to avoid spiralling inflation, price and wage controls were indicated. Yet—apart from military procurement—farmers and

[6] For literature on the episode see the general discussion in Georges Lefebvre, *La Révolution francaise,* 3d ed. (Paris, 1963), pp. 354–430, and most interesting in this context his remarks on pp. 407–9; two more specialized works by Daniel Guérin, *La Lutte des classes sous la Première République, Bourgeois et "bras nus"* (*1793–1797*), 2 vols. (Paris, 1946), and Albert Soboul, *Les Sans-culottes Parisiens en l'an II, Mouvement Populaire et Gouvernement Révolutionnaire, 2 Juin, 1793—9 Thermidor an II* (Paris, 1958), esp. pp. 427–33, 503–4, 1025–35. Guérin draws explicitly conclusions as to the class content of the struggle between Robespierre and the *sans-culottes.* Soboul analyzes a wealth of hitherto unknown documents, among them papers of district assemblies and district clubs. His conclusions from the assembled material, though more shaded, are in line with those of Guérin as to the *sans-culottes*-Revolutionary Government relation. For the social composition of the *sans-culottes* see also G. Rudé, *The Crowd in the French Revolution* (London, 1959), pp. 178–84.

merchants were frequently able to circumvent price controls. The Paris city administration, on the other hand, was lukewarm in enforcing wage controls. Such contradictions were partly solved by the trial and guillotining of Hébert and Chaumette. Although their execution was followed in *jeu de bascule* fashion within two weeks by the execution of Danton and Desmoulins, the victory of Fleurus in June 1794 lifted, to some extent, the radical mortgage on Robespierre and allowed the dismantling of price controls. The result was to do away with the often uncontrollable district clubs, and to restrict the more egalitarian policies, in an attempt at securing a steady flow of bread at the official price to the urban population. The payoff came on the 9th of Thermidor when the National Guard did not come out for Robespierre, but went home; and when the district assemblies meeting that evening were split wide open between loyalty to the Convention or to the more radical politics of the *sans-culottes*.

But is this the only, or a sufficient, reason for the turn of events? First, a seemingly more accidental fact: on the decisive afternoon, when the National Guard was assembled on the *Place de Grève* with all its equipment, there was no leader resolute enough to make them march against the Convention. What about the less obvious links in the chain of causation? There was the matter of sheer physical fatigue of the Paris *militants,* who had been in the thick of the political struggle for the previous five years; and the fact that many of the younger ones had departed for the war fronts. There was the phenomenon which we now call the circulation of élites: the most vigorous and the most intelligent of them had meanwhile taken government jobs in the central administration and war machine, and had formed new and different bonds of allegiance. This brings us nearer to another, more Protean constellation: *sans-culottes* are a political, not a social, category. Their major ties were common political sympathies: hatred of the aristocracy and support of the new regime and the military program. This motley crew of unemployed, journeymen, artisans, shopkeepers, lawyers, teachers, government employees, and even a sprinkling of merchants, could scarcely have a unified *social* outlook. Some of them being independent producers and middlemen, and others being wage earners, they would scarcely see eye-to-eye on economic issues. They remained parcels of various occupational groups. They could join the revolu-

tionary battle all the more easily because their social and occupational distinctions had not always jelled into class-consciousness.
They remained accessible to a variety of sometimes contradictory
appeals, guiding their behavior in speech and action.

Suppose that Robespierre had saved his neck on the 9th of
Thermidor due to a fresh intervention of the National Guard.
Could this coalition of the national revolutionary government and
its advanced urban clientele have lasted? While trying to find its
way through a bedlam of conflicting interests, the Committee of
Public Safety was ideologically committed to uphold the sanctity
of private property—with exceptions necessitated by the conduct
of the war. Moreover, its policy toward the disposal of the agricultural properties of the *émigré* nobles and the church bears little
evidence of a sustained interest in the cause of the small peasant
and the landless farmhand. How would it have related itself in
the long run to the interests not only of the merchants but of the
upper echelons of the peasants? Even if we disregard the discordant interests among the *sans-culottes*—bound to come out more
sharply after the most urgent war pressures had receded—could
the Robespierre-*sans-culotte* combination have long outlasted the
immediate danger period of the war?

The year 1793 marks the definitive entry of the urban masses
upon the French political scene. But, given the forces present at
that particular historical juncture, the 1793–94 episode is a great
precursor of problems yet to come. Whenever they were in a
position to make their own political contribution in the decades
ahead, the peasants would make short shrift of "prematurely"
radical political ideas.

If we except exceedingly short periods in 1848 and 1871, and
abortive movements remaining below the most provisional governmental level, the people at large did not move into the center
of political decision. It is for this reason that the coalition of the
Committee of Public Safety and the *sans-culottes* of 1793–94 still
retains such a paradigmatic interest. For here we must raise the
question, to what extent the possibility existed—which became so
important in the Chinese and Russian revolutions of the twentieth
century—of jumping stages of societal development and compressing two revolutions into one? To what extent could the 1793–
94 combination have possessed the organizational cohesion, the
unity of purpose, and the technical means to overcome its con-

fining conditions—*i.e.,* its being surrounded by a sea of peasantry
and torn by the discordances between two constituent elements,
the bourgeois-governmental wing and the popular Paris-street
wing? The attitude of the governmental wing toward economic
and social policy issues shows how alien the conscious reshaping
of society by governmental fiat remained to them. They tried to
keep the backdoor through which such measures entered—wartime necessity and the pressure of their Paris allies—as well
guarded as they could under the circumstances of the day. The
breakup of the combination and Robespierre's subsequent defeat without serious intervention by his erstwhile radical associates highlight the lack of cohesive social consciousness needed
to take the revolution beyond its pristine bourgeois phase.

The heterogeneous nature of the short-lived coalition of the
1793–94 period of the Revolution was in itself the chief confining condition of that Revolution. The Paris *avant-garde,* with
all its revolutionary fervor, was anything but unified and anything
but uniformly proletarian (however we define "proletarian" in
pre-industrial Paris). The National government, temporary coalition partner of the revolutionary Paris Commune, was riven by
personal quarrels and conflicts among the various organs of government. Beyond that, and even more fundamental, the revolutionary government was unwilling to injure the interests of
merchants and agricultural property owners beyond what the
conduct of the war in its most desperate phase seemed to make
necessary. Organizational centralization, the "maximum" for food
prices, and the unfulfilled promise of the famous "Ventôse decrees": these were adopted to win the war, not to establish a
social millennium or create the cadres to maintain the revolutionary regime.

IV

So far my attention has been directed toward the capacity of
revolutionary groups to transcend the confining conditions which
surrounded their coming to power. I now want to move on to a
discussion of some facets of what Charles Beard called the "Second
American Revolution," the Civil War. Must I first justify inclusion
of the Civil War in this survey of relations of revolutionary out-

comes to pre-existent social structures? The Civil War, one might assert, was not started by a revolutionary group intent on chang- ing the social structure of society; it only settled a limited argu- ment over permissible forms of national property relations. And yet, the way the conflict was settled indicates an obvious connec- tion between the structure of southern *ante-bellum* society and the final outcome of the conflict. Should we say that the solution —which gave the Negro only the outward trappings of freedom— indicated the absence of such a revolutionary group, and let it go at that? The case is not improved if we amend this statement to read that no revolutionary group was in undisputed control of the state machinery, not even during the reconstruction period. For saying this much is enough to make us realize that, even in the nineteenth century, revolution and civil war, if not cohabiting in permanent fashion as they do in the twentieth, kept close enough quarters to justify simultaneous discussion. What I am looking for here is a key to the peculiar mixture between recessive elements— the reprise of parcels of the *ante-bellum* structure—and super- vening changes in southern society which marked the history of the conflict, of reunion and reaction.

Let me at the outset lay down some theses, mostly borrowed— with his kind permission—from an as-yet-unpublished manuscript of Barrington Moore concerning those features of the original conflict which might have had some bearing on the *post-bellum* development.[7]

(1) The two distinct forms of social organization—emergent eastern business society and southern slave-holding agrarian so- ciety—contained certain elements favoring coexistence.

(2) The political marriage of convenience between eastern iron and western grain, between higher tariffs and more land for the present and future farmers of the West, spared the eastern industrialists the need to search for accommodation with the south- ern planters.

(3) The outbreak of the war was facilitated by the absence of strong ties between the two sections, East and South, rather than by a head-on collision on economic issues.

(4) The weakness of the federal enforcement apparatus, tied

---

[7] It goes without saying that the conclusions I draw from Moore's analysis are entirely my own. (The reference is presumably to *Social Origins of Dictatorship and Democracy,* Beacon, 1966—The Eds.)

to the uncertainty of the eventual orientation of the territories, loomed large in the causal chain leading to the war.

By the 1850s the East had become a manufacturing center, with both East and West becoming less dependent on the South and more complementary to each other. All the same, until the 1860s cotton had remained second in eastern manufacturing and the East continued to provide financial, transportation, and marketing services for the South. Eastern business and western farmers showed little animosity toward the "peculiar institution" of their southern trading partners. Eastern factory hands, fearing the competition of freed slaves, were lukewarm on the slave issue. While the South experienced some shortage in available new slave labor, its production system had not become unworkable from the viewpoint of either discipline or profit.[8] Points of conflict between the South and East seemed negotiable, with eastern tariff demands possibly to be compromised against southern wishes for consideration in the settlement of virgin western lands. Such considerations, however, have to be seen against some barriers hard to overcome. In the days before the gigantic public expenditures possible under endlessly expandable defense labels, the East could do little for the South except to buy its cotton, and such trade could not be expanded at will. The resumption of the slave trade remained a nonnegotiable proposition; to that extent a moral issue was of direct political importance. England remained the most important customer of the South, a fact which nourished the expectation of a viable independent South. In the East, labor trouble which would make the industrial community run for aid to the southern planter was not yet on the horizon, leaving the moderates only narrow scope in their search for viable compromises.

In the presence of such weak links between the regions, strictly political factors, the impact of the battle over enforcement procedures for legislative compromises, loomed large. In a society with a simple authority structure, official powers rest largely on the willingness of the respective political clienteles to abide by

[8] Conrad and Meyer, "The Economics of Slavery in the Ante Bellum South," in *The Economics of Slavery and Other Econometric Studies* (Chicago, 1964). What is argued in such accounts is the question of profitability of slavery then and there, rather than long term development prospects, which form the basis of Eugene D. Genovese's *The Political Economy of Slavery* (New York, 1965). See esp. p. 204.

the terms of the agreements their political representatives reached. The clienteles' unwillingness to do so, coupled with great weakness and irresoluteness of the central authority, spelled uncertainty of expectations and diminished the individual's reliance on official procedures to a vanishing point. In such a situation, legislative compromises predicated on semi-automatic enforceability—the Fugitive Slave Act—or, like the Kansas-Nebraska Act, needing the services of an impartial state power able and willing to see things through, must falter in implementation. But somehow the notion of the state power ordering the relations of its citizens by active intervention was something rather alien to the thinking of the West in the nineteenth century. (We shall come back to this point a little later.) It certainly found little room in the minds of the pre-Civil War generation looking on the respective presidents, judges and governors with their marshals and troops either as useful auxiliaries or as foes.[9]

The war thus appears as the product of uncertainty as to how to delineate authoritatively the various claims—especially over the status of slavery in the territories—of two societies resting on different social orders: an emergent democratic business society and an agricultural economy grounded on slave labor. The postwar peace could have had one of two meanings: it could have meant a change in the sum total of southern property relations, destroying the planter aristocracy by the use of northern military power and handing over agricultural property titles to the former slaves. Yet, "Lincoln's war" had not been conducted for that purpose.[10] Nor did eastern business society, balanced on the one hand by labor's capacity to move west and on the other by the inexhaustible replenishment of its labor force from Europe, have such wide-ranging intentions, which would have endangered the basis of all private property relations. Consequently, after the 1866–68 intermezzo, orchestrated by the radical congressional reconstructionists, the narrower peace goals gained acendancy: only the property titles in slaves and in southern war bonds re-

[9] Allan Nevins, *Ordeal of the Nation*, vol. 2 (New York, 1941), Ch. 2.
[10] J. G. Randall and D. Donald, *The Civil War and Reconstruction*, 2d ed. (Boston, 1961), Ch. 22. Kenneth M. Stampp, *The Era of Reconstruction* (New York, 1965), p. 44: "Indeed it may be said that if it was Lincoln's destiny to go down in history as the Great Emancipator, rarely has a man embraced his destiny with greater reluctance than he."

mained cancelled. The "Thermidor" of 1877 was the inevitable conclusion from the carpetbaggers' and the Negroes' inability to keep themselves going without the aid of the federal government, and from that government's unwillingness to go on supporting them. But it brought out in full all those recessive traits which had their origin in the *ante-bellum* southern society. It transformed the southern Negro from a sheltered slave into a formally free but unprotected sharecropper. In the same breath it deprived him of the possibility of exercising his political rights as an entrance wedge for full participation in the American society. "Henceforth," as Vann Woodward says, "the nation as a nation will have nothing to do with him."[11]

If the Negro's transfer from his slave to his sharecropper status —including his right to exchange his existence as a southern bondsman for that of an eastern or western unskilled factory hand or a migratory worker—had been the only difference in the social structure as a consequence of the war, we might well conclude that in this particular instance the recessive traits, mirroring the conditioning perimeter, the existence of a slaveholding aristocracy, did indeed prevail. But this is only part of the story.

The fact is that the second American Revolution did take place, and many of its effects did penetrate into the South. To what extent the second revolution as a whole was causally linked to the Civil War, to what extent the war even accelerated the progress of industrial society, is problematic[12]; assertions of causal relation have a *post-hoc-ergo-propter-hoc* sound. And the system of enlarged corporate property protection, which came into constitutional interpretation by courtesy of the Fourteenth Amendment, would no doubt have found its way into court practice by some other route. The same may be true of the southern impact on congressional voting patterns, which would probably have established themselves anyhow whenever sufficiently important interests needed an alliance with the South. But the opening up of the South to the influx of eastern industry, accompanied as it was by an enlargement and shift of the social basis of the predominant group through the impoverishment of the planters and the rise of a mercantile southern middle class, is a feature directly resulting

[11] C. Vann Woodward, *Reunion and Reaction*, 2d ed. (New York, Anchor, 1956), p. 232.

[12] Thomas C. Cochran, "Did the Civil War Retard Industrialization?" in *The Inner Revolution* (Harper Torchbooks, 1964), pp. 39–54.

from the outcome of the Civil War. Opening the South bridged the separation between the two formerly distinct types of society and so worked toward establishing in the South a modified sub-type of American business society. In this sub-type, narrowed down since the Civil War to a limited district with no chance of enlargement, the Negro remains a disadvantaged sub-species of the least fortunate segment of the population.

The American case is most intriguing because here we have the juxtaposition of recessive conditions going back to the *antebellum* social structure and the general pattern of change taking place within American society in the second half of the nineteenth century. While the victory of the business society was a universal phenomenon, its particular democratic garb found an inhospitable territory in the South. Surviving in the transfigured form necessitated by the advance of the business society, the confining conditions, from which the war had arisen, left their imprint on southern society. The writ of the federal government and, much more firmly, the writ of business society ran across the whole country. But in the South, these writs were always modified by the survivals of the old caste structure; the political form of southern society remained ambiguously pre-democratic.

<h1 style="text-align:center">V</h1>

What separates the "Second Revolution" of mid-nineteenth-century America from the pronouncedly political revolutions of the twentieth century is the subsidiary part that state power played in the transformation of nineteenth-century society. In this respect there is a certain concordance between theory and practice. Nineteenth-century ideologists did not think of state power as something to be mobilized at will for the purpose of changing societal relations. Whatever the differences among Hegel's disciples, to this extent his panlogistic state concept had been drastically revised. His conservative disciple, Lorenz von Stein, built his doctrine on the juxtaposition of state and society. The fight for liberty and equality and the determination of the individual's position were to take place within society, with the state coming in only as a regulatory afterthought.[13] Stein's state amounted to a mixture of the

[13] Lorenz von Stein, *Geschichte der Sozialen Bewegung in Frankreich von 1789 bis auf unsere Tage,* Vol. I, *Der Begriff der Gesellschaft,* ed. Dr. Gottfried Salomon (Muenchen, 1921).

Rechtsstaat principle—in itself a guarantee of regularity of proceedings rather than of active intervention—and his dreams of a social monarchy which would both assure the integrity of society and even out the inequalities emerging from society's struggle.[14]

Marx was more interested in discovering the laws governing the development of society. The reciprocal relations between state and society, which had fascinated his contemporary Stein, had few mysteries for him. He had little doubt about the place of law, state, and intellectual structures and assigned them their roots firmly in the material conditions of society. Interference with the modalities of the social process was rather in the nature of becoming conscious of its inexorable course, at best with a proletarian advance guard as a midwife, but at any rate with no need for an independent directing force.

Against the background of his French experience, Tocqueville took to analyzing the partly chaotic, partly creative political scene of the United States in the early 1830s. Could the political authorities attempt to direct the societal process—that is to say, would individuals acting singly or jointly accept such decisions? He left little doubt that, given the state of mind of the American community, the banding together of freely acting individuals for self-appointed tasks—whatever the degree of administrative efficiency of such a procedure—was the only politically feasible way to make meaningful decisions.[15]

The acceptance of a number of amendments, civil rights and enforcement statutes was one of the ways to mark the official victory of the Civil War. But once the battle over enactment was won the documents turned into a series of political propositions; they had to be absorbed and in this process were modified and even turned around by the various authoritative interpreters active in the constitutional system. Nineteenth-century America felt no need for a central organ in charge of transforming a battlefield victory into a system of political legitimacy of universal validity.

[14] Lorenz von Stein, *Verwaltungslehre*, 2d ed. (1869), Vol. I, p. 82 *et seq.*

[15] *De la Démocratie en Amerique*, 14th ed. (Paris, 1864), Vol. I, p. 149.

VI

Let us now look at the much more traditional western and central European society of the mid-nineteenth century, the era of the Chartists and the repeal of the Corn Laws, Prussian pseudo-constitutionalism and the administrative system of Napoleon III. With all due consideration for differences in upbringing and societal outlook of their respective political élites—including for the European a somewhat greater distance between governing classes and the business community—the European ways of approaching political problems remained as circumscribed as those of their American counterparts. English conservatives might have a somewhat greater sense of urgency about what might be done for the submerged classes than their liberal brethren; the latter might be more confident in their ability to uphold what we now call civil liberties in the face of threatening lower-class agitation. Bismarck could make a show of demonstrating how a polity might be run, even if the bourgeoisie refrained from giving it budgetary support. But his was a conservative machine running it, scarcely given to innovation beyond the field of military techniques and bounties for promising business men. The differences appear to us today as nuances rather than qualitative distinctions. Neither was bent on pushing sudden social or political change, or remodeling the minds of men and the institutions of the country. Even the men of the Paris Commune, the most radical of the century's children ever to have acceded to government office, made few and cautious moves in the field of social policy.

The problem of diverse expectations based on the operation of free societal forces and the limited trust in the workings of the state machinery bring us nearer an explanation of why the Second American Revolution was accompanied by two seemingly discordant results. This revolution was carried out by independent social components of the polity, supported by, but not dependent on, the political machinery of the day. It succeeded well in transforming most of America; yet it allowed the political transformation of the South via the emancipation of the Negro to fizzle out for nearly a century. It is one thing to watch the destruction of property titles as an inevitable consequence of defeat in a rebellion. It is something entirely different to destroy them as part of a concerted plan to reorganize society by state fiat. Such a measure, though proposed, went beyond the horizon of the radical political leaders who thought in terms of advantageous political combinations rather than consciously engineered social revolutions.[16]

With the First World War as a watershed, we are able to see the decisive differences between nineteenth- and twentieth-century revolutions. Masses had been brought together in the nineteenth century by political organizations on a semi-permanent basis; their minds had been exercised by expectations of economic benefits, social innovation, or patriotic or religious exaltation. But only the First World War showed how the public authorities, first with the joyous and later on the increasingly reluctant cooperation of the population, could mobilize huge masses of men and technical forces of hitherto unknown destructiveness and link them in huge organizations for official national goals.

While the official apparatus was everywhere quickly dismantled after the war, the experience was not lost on a new crop of political organizers. If such great results could be reached for the traditional goal of acting on the power structure of other societies, why not use similar methods on the domestic structure? The official state apparatus with its limited vistas, its simultaneous mixture of tradition-bound procedure and immersion in the particular interests of one group or another, with its hesitant and uneasy role of arbitration, was neither intellectually nor technically equipped for such a task. It is the merger of political movement and official state organization, the simultaneous unfolding of the mechanisms of change and the purveying of new loyalties, which mark the differences between the revolutionary dynamics of the twentieth and the largely uncontrolled social and economic revolution of the nineteenth century. The nineteenth-century government concentrated the energies of its much more slender and haphazard apparatus on emergency periods.

The revolution of the twentieth century obliterates the distinction between emergency and normalcy. Movement plus state can or-

---

[16] Stampp, *op. cit.*, note 10 above, p. 130: "In addition confiscation was an attack on property rights—so much so that it is really more surprising that some of the middle class radicals favored it, than that most did not."

ganize the masses because: (a) the technical and intellectual equipment is now at hand to direct them toward major societal programs rather than simply liberating their energies from the bonds of tradition; (b) they have the means at hand to control people's livelihood by means of job assignments and graduated rewards unvailable under the largely agricultural and artisanal structure of the 1790s and still unavailable to the small enterprise and commission-merchant-type economy of the 1850s and 1860s; (c) they have fallen heir to endlessly and technically refined propaganda devices substituting for the uncertain leader-mass relations of the previous periods; and (d) they faced state organizations shaken up by war dislocation and economic crisis. Under these conditions Soviet Russia could carry through simultaneously the job of an economic and a political, a bourgeois and a post-bourgeois revolution in spite of the exceedingly narrow basis of its political élite. On the other hand, the premature revolutionary combination of 1793–94 not only dissolved quickly, but left its most advanced sector, the *sans-culottes,* with only the melancholy choice between desperate rioting—Germinal 1795—or falling back into a pre-organized stage of utter helplessness and agony.

Do I suggest that confining conditions had their place only in nineteenth-century society, where people looked for autonomous development tendencies in society and when the state was restricted to merely secondary functions? Does that mean that the political and technical innovations of the twentieth-century have created a capacity for unlimited political change?

The antithesis between state and society is itself not as meaningful as it appeared to theorists of the nineteenth century.[17] If we substitute government for state, as we do as a matter of course in an Anglo-American climate, we perceive that we are looking into the same mirror, only from different angles. The technical equipment at the disposal of the present generation introduces social change as a normal expectation with only the composition of the group in charge of the change a matter of controversy. Yet the government's new equipment may only allow it to catch up with the pressing problems raised by the sheer multiplication of numbers. In this context we recall Marx's famous dictum that society does

[17] The dubiousness of the state-society dichotomy is illuminated in Horst Ehmke, " 'Staat' und 'Gesellschaft' als Verfassungstheoretisches Problem," in *Staatsverfassung und Kirchenordnung, Festgabe fuer Rudolf Smend* (Tübingen, 1962).

not raise more problems than it can solve at any given moment.

There is also the fact that those who are making major political decisions are not working from a *tabula rasa,* merely projecting the most technically feasible solutions. The starting point for their projections, more likely than not, is their own personal experience in their own society, whether in conformism or revolt. Without pushing confining conditions into the area of psychoanalytical interpretations in vogue a decade ago,[18] let us nevertheless look for a moment at the life experiences of the top leaders of the German National Socialist Party, the difficulties these leaders had in finding places in or accommodation with the German society of the 1920s. These difficulties help explain the twofold direction of their thrust. The leaders had to smash the leadership of the pre-existing mass organizations to take power. But they also had a deep-seated desire—beyond rational considerations for the safeguarding of their future—to eradicate the very elements of the independent leadership cadres in the upper strata with which they had had to find accommodation during their initial period. These earlier leaders had committed the unforgiveable sin: they had been the ruling élite while their successors were still wandering in the dark.

In making this remark, however, do I enlarge the concept of confining conditions much too much? Do I elevate the shadow of the previous regime to the dignity of a confining condition, rather than restricting this concept, as in the case of the USSR, to those specific conditions whose elimination proved to be a *conditio sine qua non* for the survival of the revolutionary regime?

The wall between shadow and substance may, however, be thin, as the German case has amply shown. And shadows become substance when they affect people's minds. Thus shadows also belong to those pre-existent, given, and traditional circumstances from which human beings, according to the immortal introductory section of the 18th Brumaire, produce their own history. In this sense every revolution is both phenomenon and epiphenomenon; it is both concentrated reaction to yesterday's reality and a mere construct to live by until history turns another page and delivers us from the necessity of breathing yesterday's air, that air both fragrant and pestilential.

[18] Nathan Leites, *A Study of Bolshevism* (Glencoe, 1953).

Chapter 24

THE RESPONSIBILITY OF SCIENCE*

Herbert Marcuse

The proposition I want to put forth is the following: science (i.e., the scientist) is responsible for the use society makes of science; the scientist is responsible for the social consequences of science. I will argue that this proposition does not depend for its validity on any moral norms outside and beyond science, or on any religious or humanitarian point of view. Rather, I suggest that this proposition is dictated by the internal structure and *telos* of science, and by the place and function of science in the social reality. These are not two different grounds, one germane to science and the other external to it (sociological or political). They are essentially interrelated and, in this interrelation, shape the direction of scientific progress (and regression!). Science today is in a position of power that almost immediately translates pure scientific achievements into political and military weapons of global use and effectiveness. The fact that the organization and control of whole populations, in peace as well as in war, have become, in a strict sense, a *scientific* control and organization (from the most ordinary technical household gadgets to the highly sophisticated methods in public-opinion formation, publicity, and propaganda) inexorably unites scientific research and experiment with the powers and plans of the economic, political, and military establishment. Consequently, there are not two worlds: the world of science and the world of politics (and its ethics), the realm of pure theory and the realm of impure practice—there is only one world in which science and politics and ethics, theory and practice are inherently linked.

At first glance it seems as if history contradicts this proposition, for the development of the modern world has seen the bifur-

* Revised text of a lecture delivered at the Lake Arrowhead Center of the University of California, Los Angeles (July 1966).

cation of the realms that were united throughout most of the Middle Ages. Moreover, this separation was a precondition for the liberation of science from superimposed norms and values, a precondition for technical advance, and for that continual conquest of nature and man we call scientific progress. However, this historical fact has been outdated and the separation that was once liberative and progressive is now destructive and repressive. Or, to put it in another way, whereas the idea of pure theory once had a progressive function, it now serves, against the intention of the scientist, the repressive powers that dominate society. How has this come about?

Science proceeds by its own method of discovery, experimentation, and verification, and according to the logic of its own conceptual development, regardless of the social use and consequences of its discoveries. The scientist's intention is pure; he is motivated by "pure" curiosity; he seeks knowledge for the sake of knowledge. But, his work, once published, enters the market, becomes merchandise to be evaluated by prospective buyers and sellers, and by virtue of this *social* quality, his work satisfies *social* needs. Further, through its relation to prevalent social needs, the work of the scientist acquires a *social value;* his work takes on the characteristics of the predominant social trends, and becomes progressive or regressive, constructive or destructive, liberating or repressive in terms of the protection and amelioration of human life. But, it is said, the scientist at work in his study or laboratory cannot foresee the social consequences of his work; he cannot know whether what he is doing will turn out to be a constructive or destructive factor in history. Moreover, since the application of his discoveries is left to the engineer or the technician, and the final decision is left to the politician (the government), the problem of the social consequences of his work is a matter outside his domain, and consequently he cannot be held morally responsible.

Even if we grant this argument, does it justify the moral neutrality and indifference of science? I suggest that it does not. The scientist remains responsible as a scientist because the social development and application of science determine, to a considerable extent, the further internal conceptual development of science. The theoretical development of science is thus bent in a specific political direction, and the notion of theoretical purity and moral neutrality is thereby invalidated. Two examples may help to illustrate this point. Commenting on the fact that federal outlays for science in colleges and universities now exceed $1.3 billion and constitute two-thirds of the total research expenditures of these institutions, Harrison Brown, Professor of Geochemistry at the California Institute of Technology, says,

> Since most of these grants are from government agencies that are "mission oriented," the research programs inevitably will be tailored to the needs of the agency rather than the scientific conception of what is important from a purely scientific point of view.[1]

Senator Fulbright makes the same point in more general terms:

> I suspect that when a university becomes very closely oriented to the current needs of government, it takes on some of the atmosphere of a place of business while losing that of a place of learning. The sciences, I suspect, are emphasized at the expense of the humanities and, within the humanities, the behavioral school of social science at the expense of the more traditional— and to my mind more humane—approaches. Generally, I would expect an interest in salable information pertaining to current problems to be emphasized at the expense of general ideas pertaining to the human condition.[2]

In other words, the alleged neutrality of science, its vaunted indifference to values, actually promote the power of external forces over the internal scientific development.

Defenders of scientific neutrality often point to the fact that science has a built-in mechanism for detecting error. Thus C. P. Snow writes:

> Science is a self-correcting system. That is, no fraud (or honest mistake) is going to stay undetected for long. There is no need for an extrinsic scientific criticism, because criticism is inherent in the process itself. So that all that a fraud can do is waste the time of the scientists who have to clear it up.[3]

The trouble is that it is not "fraud" that enters into the scientific process, but perfectly legitimate "scientific" tasks and goals. The

[1] New York *Times* (May 11, 1966).
[2] Senator Fulbright at the Santa Barbara Center's Conference "The University in America" (May 1966).
[3] "The Moral Un-Neutrality of Science," in: *Science* (January 27, 1961), p. 257.

scientist is given problems that are within his competence and interest *as a scientist:* scientific problems; it just so happens that they are also problems of destruction of life, of chemical and bacteriological warfare. But if the self-correcting mechanism of science does not deal with these problems, the emphasis on the self-critical nature of science loses much of its validity.

Its own "value-indifference" blinds science to what happens to human existence. Or, to formulate it differently, and a little less kindly, value-free science blindly promotes certain social political values and, without abandoning pure theory, science sanctions an established practice. The puritanism of science turns into impurity. And this dialectic has now led to a situation in which science (and not only applied science) collaborates in the construction of the most effective machinery of annihilation in history.

How is it that the separation of knowledge and values, which was at first progressive, is now regressive? What is the relationship between progress and destruction? In a sense, destruction itself is progressive and liberating, and modern science in its beginnings was destructive in this progressive sense. It was destructive of medieval dogmatism and superstition, it was destructive of the holy alliance between philosophy and irrational authority, it was destructive of the theological justification of inequality and exploitation. Modern science developed in conflict with the powers that opposed freedom of thought; today science finds itself in alliance with the powers that threaten human autonomy and frustrate the attempt to achieve a free and rational existence.

What are the possibilities of reversing this trend? One thing must be clear at the outset: there is no possibility of a reversal of scientific progress, no possibility of a return to the golden age of "qualitative" science. It is true, of course, that a change would be imaginable only as an event in the development of science itself, *but* such scientific development can be expected only as the result of a comprehensive social change. What is required is nothing less than a complete transvaluation of goals and needs, the transformation of repressive and aggressive policies and institutions. The transformation of science is imaginable only in a transformed environment; a new science would require a new climate wherein new experiments and projects would be suggested to the intellect by new social needs. In its most general sense this transformation would entail the withering away of the social needs for wasteful parasitarian production and products, for aggressive defense, for competition in status and conformity, and would require the corresponding liberation of the individual needs for peace, joy, and tranquillity. Instead of the further conquest of nature, the restoration of nature; instead of the moon, the earth; instead of the occupation of outer space, the creation of inner space; instead of the not-so-peaceful co-existence of affluence and poverty, the abolition of affluence until poverty has disappeared; instead of guns and butter in the overdeveloped nations, sufficient margarine for all nations. Evidently this would be the most radical global change one could imagine. What can the scientist do about it? Apparently nothing.

But here too we are confronted with an illusion, for the scientist is no longer the dissociated withdrawn researcher but has become the pillar of the established institutions and policies. To the degree to which the economy becomes a technological system, to that degree science becomes a decisive factor in the economic processes of society. Even physical labor becomes increasingly dependent on scientific (technological) foundations. At the same time, the gap between pure and applied science is narrowed; the most abstract and formal achievements in logic and mathematics are translatable into very concrete and material values (for instance, computers). Science literally feeds the economy. Inasmuch as science is part of the basis of society it becomes a material power, an economic and political force, and every individual scientist is an aliquot part of this power. To the degree to which the scientist depends on government and industry for the support of his research, to that degree also government and industry depend on the scientist. The individual scientist may indeed be powerless to stem the tide of "scientific" destruction, but he can refuse to lend his hand and his brain to the perfection of destruction, and he can speak out. To be sure, his refusal and his protest are only individual expressions, and they may result in the loss of the necessary support for a particular project. There is always this risk. But his refusal may set government and industry thinking, and it may encourage others to follow. If we are inclined to disparage this effort as "merely negative," we should recall that very often before the negative has been the first positive step.

Today there is no conflict between science and society (the established society); they propel each other in the established direction of progress, a direction that appears increasingly dangerous to humanity. But there is a conflict between modern science as it is practiced and the inner *telos* of science. Science itself is threatened by its own progress, threatened by its advance as an instrument of value-free power rather than as an instrument of knowledge and truth. Science like all critical thinking originated in the effort to protect and improve human life in its struggle with nature; the inner *telos* of science is nothing other than the protection and amelioration of human existence. This has been the rationale of science, and its abandonment is tantamount to the rupture between science and reason. Science may indeed continue to grow, in a technical sense, and as a technique, but it will have lost its *raison d'être*.

Science as a human effort remains the strongest weapon and the most effective instrument in the struggle for a free and rational existence. This effort extends beyond the study, beyond the laboratory, beyond the classroom, and aims for the creation of an environment social as well as natural, wherein existence can be freed from its union with death and destruction. Such liberation would not be an external goal or by-product of science, but rather the realization of science itself.

EPILOGUE

Leonard Krieger and Fritz Stern

It is an historical truism that no two situations are ever alike, and an historical value that this inevitable dissimilarity is a good thing. Our historical studies in the theory and exercise of power give no cause for dispute or exception; the local force of time, place, and individual invention was never more in evidence and there is no gainsaying the insight that a study of power affords into our self-creating species. When the labels "power" and "responsibility" are conceived simplistically and nominalistically to cover the instruments and ends of political authority respectively, then the instances in the exercise of power can be plotted, to use a spatial analogy, as separate points along the infinitely divisible line between the two termini.

But there are grounds, from a more realistic point of view, for rationalizing this manifold of historical instances into a typology of power. For the two sets of views on power and responsibility that entered as assumptions into the modern world of the sixteenth century have persisted as separate types and developed a finite number of combinations, inhabited by the appropriate instances. One type of power, the politicized version of the original ethical conception of power, postulates the necessity of an implicit, realizable end for power to exist at all. The concomitant type of political responsibility specifies the primary obligation of agents and patients alike to act for the preservation of power, which is a worthy object of obligation by virtue of its inherent ends. The second type of power, the moralized version of the original political conception of power, postulates the separate existence of power as a means distinct from ends, and predicates, by virtue of this detachment, the ethically invalid tendency of power to become its own end. The second type of political responsibility, correspondingly, specifies the primary obligation, incumbent particularly upon the agent of power, to direct the instruments of power exclusively toward an end that lies beyond their own preservation and extension.

But these early combinations are not mere abstractions. They were produced by definite historical situations and in response to actual problems. The first set of attitudes toward power and responsibility was relevant to the circumstances that sponsored the institutions of the sovereign state, the second to the circumstances that sponsored the individual and social limits upon them, and both concepts of power have persisted to the present, characterizing men in all those subsequent situations that put these fundamental institutions and values in question. Hence it is easy to recognize in the line that runs from Machiavelli through Richelieu and Louis XIV exemplars of the first type of view on power and responsibility and in the line that starts contrapuntally with Erasmus and picks up strongly at the end of the eighteenth century from Schiller through Burckhardt, Acton and the whole liberal tradition the exemplars of the second type.

Still, there are other attitudes toward the issue of power and responsibility that are not classifiable along either of these familiar lines. They may, of course, always be explained as idiosyncratic, but such an explanation is hardly satisfactory for attitudes that are both most interesting in themselves and most characteristic of recent history. They may be illuminated analytically if we understand that the types of power and of responsibility, like all vital historical creations, have careers of their own and undergo development that leads them away from their original associations. The apparent confusions and dilemmas attendant upon the recent history of power may be explained in terms of the changing relationships of power and responsibility to each other. When power as the capacity to realize political ends is combined with the responsibility to non-political ends that are categorically distinct from the mechanics of power, the result is the conflict of values and the dilemmas of power associated with the ideas of Max Weber, Otto Hintze, Friedrich Naumann, and Friedrich Meinecke and with the practice of Bethmann Hollweg and Neville Chamberlain. Homologously, when the attitude toward power as a mere amoral or immoral instrument is combined with the attitude of responsibility to this instrument because all essential ends are deemed ethically unrealizable and therefore politically irrelevant, the result is the self-alienating commitment to the abhorred machinery of a power for which there is recognized neither an immanent end nor the path to a transcendent end—a result equally visible in the compromises of the German socialists and the convulsive totalitarianism of the Russian Bolsheviks.

Typologies furnish the beginnings, not the conclusions, of explanation. The classification of attitudes toward power and its obligations in their changing combinations would be little more than an intellectual game if it did not indicate a logical relationship of the terms it correlates. The typology of attitudes characteristic of recent history introduces two kinds of fundamental insights into the nature or power in our society—one that makes explicit a relationship that was merely implicit in earlier periods and that pertains to the whole of the modern age, and the other that sets off the distinctive quality of our own era.

First, then, the hybrid notions of power that have troubled our immediate forebears and continue to torment us indicate this basic truth about our culture: far from the popular condemnation of power as a means that becomes an end in itself, an indictment that has no historical basis, the nature of power has always been dependent upon the quality of the ends to which the holders of power have applied it. This truth is transparent in a figure like Bethmann Hollweg, whose resigned endorsement of German expansion was a function of a future closed to his ideals, but it applies across the board, from a Schiller, whose end of disciplined freedom produced a notion of power at once necessary and alien to it, through the revolutionaries of 1848, whose individualistic ends produced an aversion to the instruments of power that precluded their seizure, to a Lenin, whose unrestrained exercise of a political power he theoretically despised was the function of a Marxist goal that was irrelevant to his Russian situation. And, although he has not appeared in these pages, Hitler's demoniacal use of power apparently without end is psychologically and historically unthinkable without reference to the lost order that his petty-bourgeois soul vainly and paradoxically sought to restore through total revolution. Totalitarian power, then, may be viewed as the infinite striving after goals that are deemed unrealizable now by power and unrealizable ever by means other than power.

If the determination of power by ends is our general principle, then totalitarian power can stand as a limiting case for three of its generally applicable corollaries. First, power is exercised responsibly when the action or inaction of the power holder is undertaken for the fulfillment of an end that is deemed possible in the sense that the action or inaction can fulfill it. Second, the most important criterion for identifying the kind of responsible power being exercised is the proportion of possibility, in the view of the power holder, between the ends that can be fulfilled through political power and the ends that can be fulfilled without it: when the greater weight is attributed to the first, the responsibility is *to* power as part of an end; when the greater weight is attributed to the second, the responsibility is *by* power as a means. Third, the key to the quantitative assessment of this proportionate possibility in any responsible act of power is the qualitative relationship that is posited between the ends that can be fulfilled through political power and those that can be fulfilled without it: an antithetical relationship indicates a responsibility to power as part of an end; a complementary relationship indicates a responsibility by power as a means.

The historical typology of power has something to tell us, finally, about our own age. The first two periods in the modern history of power are comprehensible enough. In the first of these periods political power was legitimated because men's purposes were given a political analog which was realizable through collective compulsion. In the second period political power was mistrusted because individuals and groups of individuals set for themselves purposes that were attainable without political power and that they deemed inherently antithetical to political power. The politics appropriate to this period required a division of powers and a responsibility of governments to representative bodies whose primary function was precisely the restraint of power. The distinction between the internal legal definition of juridical responsibility and the external institutional definition of political responsibility marked the difference between the first and the second periods in the history of power.

The third phase has obviously revalidated political power by virtue of the universal acknowledgment of its democratic base, but it has also retained from its immediate liberal past the final ends of individual freedom, social brotherhood, or national culture—ends essentially independent of but existentially tied to political power. As the experience of our own century has demonstrated all too clearly, the triumph of popular sovereignty has not had the anticipated simple effect of guaranteeing the use of power for the realization of the liberal, social, or cultural ends, and the analysis of power helps to indicate the character of the perversion. The destructiveness of a Schönerer, unbalanced by the discrepancy between the equality of his political appeal and his nationalized ideal of an aristocracy which no politics could restore, was, however distinctive in substance, paradigmatic of the frustration that has accompanied all open-ended claims made on behalf of modern democratic power. The frustration is rooted in a conflict of ends induced by the validation, under the democratic aegis, of collective political ends that attract power, and their expansibility, under the same aegis, into social and cultural final ends that resist power. This conflict of ends has been mutually destructive: in varying degrees it has attenuated the role of ends as such in the exercise of political power and has tended to make of democracy a mere means for the legitimation of a self-perpetuating bureaucratic or factional political power.

But if the totalitarian challenge is the extreme case of the general tendency to make the control rather than the direction of public life the primary function of power, the resistance to it manifests a countervailing tendency that may well transform the whole historical syndrome of power. Just as totalitarian tendencies abolish the distinction between political and non-political ends by the extension of political instruments into all areas of human life, so does the successful resistance to it manifest the increasing power that science and education bestow on men in the prosecution of their non-political ends. Totalitarianism thus conveyed the shock of recognition to what had been rising slowly to the consciousness of our age—that men's intellectual and social ends, and the activities they undertake to realize those ends, are not simple non-political values to be abetted by or defended from political power, but rather structures with powers of their own. The effect of this development upon the power relationships of our society is twofold. First it alienates the realm of politics from nonpolitical ends—since these ends are now equipped with their own powerful organs—and stresses the responsibility of insulated political power to the machine that can only dispense welfare and defense,

the limited collective ends that are left to politics. Second, it re-
defines power away from its familiar focus on the overt compulsion of politics and toward the diffusion of covert compulsion in
the form of economic means, social pressure, and intellectual
convention. The result has been to reproduce the pattern of contemporary political power in the non-political sphere: non-political
ends are reduced to the immanent status of what can be achieved
by the instruments of non-political power. The net effect of this
post-totalitarianism is to limit the scope of power by homogenizing
it, and thus to resolve the historical problem of the responsibility
of power by restricting political power to possible political ends
and by securing appropriate non-political instruments of power for
non-political ends.

But even if, in the long reaches of time to come, the post-
totalitarian recoil will prove to have initiated an age successive to
and distinctive from the totalitarian era, this time is not yet with
us. Total political power remains a contemporary fact, not merely
in the segregated form of Communist regimes, but in the pervasive form of intrusive mechanical devices, headed by the omnip-
otent Bomb, at the disposal of the several governments. In both
forms political totalitarianism, actual or potential, still confronts
the social and cultural interests that have developed their own
organizations against it. In the light of the historical tendencies
exhibited by the use and idea of power, it seems clear that with
this confrontation we approach the conclusion of the long process
that made of power the most ambiguous, the most dramatic, and
the most representative theme of our history. Its career, as we
have seen in this volume, has been composed by the various
tensile blends of the two fundamental meanings that power has had
for our culture—the human capacity to realize a totally satisfying
moral ideal and the political means to accomplish the limited
collective ends which condition that moral capacity. But now,
with the political means themselves total in effect and with the
totality of the moral ideal shredded into a pluralism of limited
non-political ends, the historical exchange of essential qualities
seems almost complete and in the current confrontation of the
political and non-political structures of power the two elemental
attitudes toward power stand out isolated and mutually opposed.

Bereft of their historically fruitful ambiguity, the tension of
means and ends within one world is giving way to the internal

stability of several worlds, each equipped with its own system of compatible means and ends. Should this unraveling persist, our alternatives will be either the holocaust which is the appropriate collective end of a total political means with no effective reference to any values beyond collective ends or the anarchy of human goals which makes every exercise of power an act not of morality but of diplomacy. Only if we can once more relate the individuality of our final purposes to the generality of what we can perform with our political means will we be able to resume our past and to guarantee the continuity of what we, as a species, have become.

INDEX

464   INDEX

II, 387–401; House of Representatives (see Congress, American);
Senate (see Congress, American)
Universities, nationalist agitation
in, 245
UNRRA, 392–94, 398
USSR (Soviet Union), 349, 395,
398, 399, 400, 418, 419, 420,
421, 422, 437. See also Bolshevism; Communist Party, Russian and Russia
Utopian, 405, 406, 408

Vandenberg, Arthur, 391, 392, 393,
396
Vaterlandspartei, 276, 281
Vendôme, Duc de, 121
Venice, 110, 195
Ventôse decrees, 428
Vermeil, Edmond, 146
Versailles, Treaty of, 252–53
Vinci, Leonardo da, 188
Violence, 3, 4, 10
Vischer, Friedrich Theodor, 402,
403, 407, 408
Viviani, René, 294, 297, 298
Volkswehr, 329–30, 332

Wagner, Richard, 235
Wagner, Robert, 396
Waldeck, Benedikt, 169
War, theory of just, 58–59
War of the Spanish succession, 119
Watt, D. C., quoted, 354, 362n
Weber, Max, 200, 206, 211, 214–
18, 219, 260–61, 282, 402, 403,
410, 411, 412, 446
Weimar Republic. See Germany
Wels, Otto, 330
Weltherrschaft, German, 272, 273
Weltpolitik, 203–4, 205, 208, 257
Westarp, Kuno Graf von, 293

Westphalia, Treaty of, 98
Wheeler-Bennett, John, quoted, 366
White, Howard, 254n
White, Maria, 254n
William, Crown Prince of Prussia,
258, 264
William, Landgrave of Hesse, 66,
80
William I, King of Prussia and
German Kaiser, 170, 174, 254
William II, German Emperor, 200,
203, 206–7, 254, 256, 258, 259,
260, 263, 274, 275, 276, 277,
280, 284, 297, 304–5, 320, 411
William III, 110
William of Occam, 22–23
William of Orange, 228
Wilson, General Sir Henry, 299
Wilson, Sir Horace, 357, 368
Wilson, Woodrow, 277, 293, 383,
390
Wohltat, Helmut, 368
Woodward, Vann, 432
Workers' Opposition, 348
World court, 383, 384
World Politics (power), 409, 410
World War I, 221, 222, 262–85,
315, 316, 318–19, 322, 323, 342,
370, 372, 375, 383, 436; con-
troversy about causes of, 250–51
World War II, 222, 370, 374, 386;
American internationalism dur-
ing, 387–401

Yale, University, xii

Zabern affair, 257
Zechlin, Egmont, 254
Zinoviev, 343, 345–46
Zionism, 235, 236
Zollverein, 148